Hans TenDam was born in The Hague in 1943. An independent consultant and researcher, he has worked for business, non-profit and government agencies in the Netherlands, the EEC, Turkey, New Zealand and Brazil. An organiser of the first World Congress on Past-Life Therapy, he trains psychotherapists in past-life therapy. He is also a board member of the International Association of Regression Research and Therapies in California, and on the advisory team of the International Board of Regression Therapy in New York. He has published a number of works on the occult, mysticism, Tarot, reincarnation and past-life therapy.

By the same author:

Deep Healing

EXPLORING REINCARNATION

*The Classic Guide to the Evidence
for Past-Life Experiences*

HANS TENDAM

With a foreword by
Colin Wilson

RIDER

LONDON • SYDNEY • AUCKLAND • JOHANNESBURG

3 5 7 9 10 8 6 4 2

First published in 1987 by Penguin Books Ltd

This revised and updated edition first published in 2003 by Rider Books,
an imprint of Ebury Press, Random House,
20 Vauxhall Bridge Road, London SW1V 2SA

Random House Australia (Pty) Limited
20 Alfred Street, Milsons Point, Sydney,
New South Wales 2061, Australia

Random House New Zealand Limited
18 Poland Road, Glenfield,
Auckland 10, New Zealand

Random House South Africa (Pty) Limited
Endulini, 5A Jubilee Road,
Parktown 2193, South Africa

The Random House Group Limited Reg. No. 954009

Papers used by Rider are natural, recyclable products made from
wood grown in sustainable forest

Typeset by SX Composing DTP, Rayleigh, Essex
Printed and bound by Bookmarque Ltd, Croydon, Surrey
A CIP catalogue record for this book is available from the British Library

ISBN 0-7126-6020-8

CONTENTS

FOREWORD
BY COLIN WILSON

Of all the subjects grouped together under the general heading 'the paranormal'
– telepathy, extra-sensory perception (ESP) precognition, and so on,
reincarnation seems by far the most dubious and preposterous, and the least
acceptable to people of common sense. This was certainly my own feeling when,
in the late 1960s, I was asked to write a book on 'the occult' by an American
publisher. To tell the truth, I was inclined to feel that the whole subject was
probably the outcome of fantasy and wishful thinking. That very quickly altered
as I settled down to the systematic study of paranormal phenomena, and realized
how many reliable witnesses have vouched for their reality. Andrew Lang
pointed out that people who have seen ghosts are not hysterics, but 'steady
unimaginative, unexcitable people with just the odd experience'. The
philosopher Leibniz was one of the many people who saw Joseph of Copertino
rise off the ground while praying and float around like a seagull, while scientists,
poets, and philosophers witnessed Daniel Dunglas Home performing similar
feats in the nineteenth century. The conclusion seemed unavoidable: human
beings possess 'powers' of which they are normally unaware, but which can be
released in certain unusual states of consciousness.

Such a definition of 'the paranormal' struck me as both rational and
comprehensive – a simple extension of our recognition that great artists, in
moments of inspiration, can produce works that have a touch of the
superhuman.

However, in due course – about three-quarters of the way through *The Occult*
– I found myself confronted with the problem of 'the realm of spirits' and life
after death. I had been interested in spiritualism as a child – my grandmother
was a member of a spiritist church – and had decided, at the age of 16 or so, that
it was gross superstition. Now, as I settled down to studying the evidence, I had
to admit that this view was an oversimplification, and that in just a few cases the
evidence for life after death is positively overwhelming. I felt vaguely
embarrassed to have to admit that some of the evidence was so powerful for it

was, in a sense, quite irrelevant to my central thesis about man's 'hidden powers'. After writing about the evidence for 'survival', I ended the chapter with a hasty postscript on the subject of reincarnation. This I found even more embarrassing, because it seemed to fly in the face of our common-sense belief that our personalities are, to a large extent, a product of our bodies and our genetic inheritance. At a fairly late stage of my research, I came upon Professor Ian Stevenson's book, *Twenty Cases Suggestive of Reincarnation* (1966), and was deeply impressed by it. Unless Stevenson was a liar, or distorted his information with total disregard for accuracy, then it certainly looked as if the evidence for reincarnation was as powerful as the evidence for telepathy or ESP. On the surface, some of the cases sound preposterous:

> *A boy named Ravi, born in 1951, later gave details of his murder in his previous existence; this may explain the continuation of memory (i.e. because being murdered must be a fairly memorable experience); as a child of 6 he was killed and beheaded by a relative (aided by an accomplice) who hoped to inherit the property of the child's father. Ravi actually had a scar on his neck resembling a long knife wound. A child named Jasbir claimed to be a man who had been given poisoned sweets, and had died as a result of a fall from a cart in which he had sustained a head injury.*

And so on, each case apparently more unbelievable than the last. Yet Stevenson's documentation is unexceptionable, being presented with an exactitude that makes it sound like a sociological thesis.

Since then I have come across a number of other cases that have seemed to me virtually beyond criticism. Yet although I have written subsequent books on fields of the paranormal that deeply interest me – poltergeists, psychometry, life after death – I have deliberately avoided the challenge of writing a full-length book on reincarnation – not only because the amount of research involved is so daunting, but because I am still unable to fit reincarnation into my general picture of the paranormal. This is why, when a friend in Amsterdam told me that a Dutch psychologist had written the most comprehensive book on reincarnation ever attempted, and that he possessed a chapter of the English translation, I eagerly demanded to see it. And when I had read it, I wrote to Hans TenDam and pressed him to get the remainder translated, so that I could try to find a British publisher. When he finally wrote to tell me that it had been accepted, I was as delighted as if it had been one of my own books.

This is, I think, *the* great definitive work on reincarnation; it is hard to imagine it ever being superseded. In recent years there been many impressive and balanced works on reincarnation -Ian Stevenson's vast *Cases of the Reincarnation Type*, (1975–83), Reyna's *Reincarnation and Science* (1975) and a number of remarkable studies of 'hypnotic regression', such as *Encounters with the Past* by Peter Moss and Joe Keeton (1979). These works are not open to the objection directed at earlier books, such as those of Joan Grant, which could be too easily dismissed as mere romantic fantasy or self-deception, but their authors might still be attacked on the grounds that they are obviously emotionally committed to their subject. In chapter 9 of the present work, Hans TenDam remarks wryly: 'The reader who does not believe in reincarnation, but has managed to get this far anyway, will be happy to observe that even my credulity has limits.' Yet it seems to me that the whole merit of the book is that it makes no appeals to credulity. It is obvious that TenDam does accept the reality of reincarnation – I know this from speaking with him – but he has written not as a believer, but as a detached observer who simply wishes to present the most comprehensive picture of a vast subject. Some readers may find his approach in the early chapters a little too cool and detached, but if they persist, they will find themselves richly rewarded. As far as it is possible to make reincarnation plausible, TenDam has done it. This book will join Myers' *Human Personality and its Survival of Death*, Tyrrell's *Personality of Man* and Mavromatis's *Hypnagogia* as classics of the paranormal.

Colin Wilson

PREFACE TO THE NEW EDITION: THE ORIGIN AND AIM OF THIS BOOK

This book tries to be scientific about an unscientific subject. It is not scientific in the sense of rigid experiments under laboratory conditions. In this field, we are rather in the naturalistic stage: collecting and classifying experiences. Insofar as research has been done, we will refer to it. Whatever the quality of the empirical evidence available, it is a better guide than metaphysical speculation or the intuitive insights of self-styled teachers. This book tries also to be scholarly: it refers as extensively as possible to the published literature and tries to be both open-minded and critical. Uncritical believers and uncritical unbelievers will both be disgusted by it. I have written it for the rest.

All hypotheses are allowed, but we can make assumptions explicit, and test for internal consistency and against empirical evidence. The more extensive the evidence, the more careful and methodically collected, the better.

This book collects ideas about reincarnation. It examines the basis of those ideas: assumptions, arguments, authorities, experiences, research and previous publications. It sieves ideas out: the incomprehensible, the internally contradictory, those contradicted by available evidence. As for those ideas that are based on experiences, what other explanations are possible for those experiences? Finally, this book considers the theoretical conclusions and the most acceptable and reasonable ideas.

Reincarnation has long been in the no-man's-land between religion and science. In old times, knowledge was the province of theology, philosophy or the intermediate Gnosticism. People thinking about the human condition could turn to these three forms of speculation. Religion offered insights through belief in a sacred tradition, philosophy through thinking carefully and through Gnosticism by 'sacred thinking': reasoning from a purified intuition.

In modern science, careful observation, investigation and experimentation support careful thinking. The expanding sciences used the dialectic tool of human reason to sharpen their methodology and to create the apparatus of mathematics to analyse and test the structure of phenomena. Science found many old concepts obsolete or irrelevant, or simply untestable. Many human questions – such as the meaning of life, to mention but one example – appeared to be impossible to examine scientifically. Such questions fell to religion and philosophy. In the nineteenth century, after much mutual irritation, this global division of territory did take place: the natural falling to science and the spiritual to religion and philosophy. On one side, subjects we consider scientifically; on the other, subjects we consider religiously or agnostically – meaning that we do not try to consider them. Somewhere in between is philosophy: trying to think straight in the absence of scientific data or even empirical evidence.

However, the territorial division was never complete, as the debates on abortion, euthanasia, genetic engineering and cloning show. Subjects running across this division arouse irritation and fear on both sides. They are by their nature controversial. Consequently, past-life memories can only be controversial.

The first subject disturbing both sides of the divide was *animal magnetism*, related to what we know now as hypnosis. At the time the matter was disposed of effectively. Thought to be a natural force resembling the newly discovered electricity, animal magnetism was assigned to the field of science and experimentation, since it was an ordinary natural process and no business of religion. Science then pigeonholed it as suggestion, thereby declaring it to be normal, therefore insignificant, and therefore illusory. This intellectual hat-trick has only recently and only partly given way to a more serious consideration of hypnotic phenomena.

Spiritualism was the second spoilsport. To scientific minds it suggested a return to the Middle Ages, while the religious were alarmed that the mysteries of life and death were suddenly the object of experimentation. An area subjected to such enormous pressure from two sides easily falls prey to confusion, thus contributing to its own downfall. All the same, spiritualism has come out of it better than magnetism. It begat *psychical research*, which begat a scientific discipline: parapsychology. Countless people continue to believe and to be active in it. In the aftermath of wars in particular, many living and many deceased desire to make contact. After the First World War especially, spiritualism enjoyed a revival.

After the Second World War, it was rather clairvoyance that enjoyed a revival: so many people missing, so many people displaced! Today, as channelling, it has made its comeback. 'Are we going to channel or are we doing past lives tonight? I have some vitamin B12 injections at home,' I was asked at the home of some Californian colleagues, sometime in the 1980s. We decided on channelling, as getting the B12 injections would take too much time. Also, hypnosis has lately gotten more recognition and scientific attention, some pseudo-scientific debunking aside. The original magnetism has never collapsed completely.

The explosive increase of *past-life recall* during the last three decades is a third wave. In a sense, reincarnation is a comeback of magnetism, for at first the important means of recalling past lives were magnetic and later hypnotic. In a way it also signals a comeback for spiritualism, as this book will show. Most people who try, easily get impressions from previous lives, often quite vivid and quite remarkable, and often with interesting results. Hypnotic regression has long been the main tool for recall, but it is rapidly being replaced by methods that avoid, or employ only weak, trance induction, sometimes enabling people to have vivid recall of past-life episodes within a few minutes. This makes reincarnation no longer a matter of belief in general (religion) or of belief in the revelations and insights of the enlightened or initiated (Gnosticism), but an area of human experience.

I quote and discuss experiences that seem to be past-life recollections. That is a field of experience just as any other. I accept that those experiences may be what they seem to be, but I try to consider them coolly. I have no trouble accepting such experiences, as I have witnessed them countless times and had them myself many times. That still doesn't mean that I take my own experiences or those of others as gospel. As with all human experience, we encounter fuzziness, contradiction, distortion, imagination and hasty interpretation. So we have to register those experiences, preferably in great numbers, and note similarities and differences. What patterns emerge? And how can they be explained most acceptably?

This book is a panorama, drawn as widely as possible, about whatever is published on the subject of reincarnation. It also presents my recapitulation and my judgment. I give references throughout, so that readers may go back to the sources and find out for themselves. I try to arrive at a coherent set of ideas that are confirmed by evidence, or at least are not refuted by the evidence. On the basis of the available material and some thinking, we can sieve out many speculations about reincarnation. Whether reincarnation exists or not, or only in a particular way, one thing that reading this book may show is that many ideas about reincarnation are wrong or even nonsensical.

My insights have developed the last decades. Generally, the confirmation of and support for the idea of reincarnation has grown strongly. On the critical side of the balance, however, there is also more to report, Today, I am of the opinion that imagination and identification are more common than I used to think. People even may have experiences that contain correct, verifiable historical details they absolutely didn't know before, and still the experience may be based on fantasy. It may be compared to a writer engrossed in writing a fantasy story, who may discover later that his fantasies contain historically correct details he never knew. The intuitive side of our mind has strange ways and strange powers.

In this new edition I review about a hundred books that I have found since the first edition. I have given more space to both the dubious refutations and the dubious confirmations of the subject. Believers and unbelievers are all the same: people who know don't need to find out. Is this book proving reincarnation? Proof is not a scientific concept at all. It belongs to logic and mathematics – and in the courtroom. Tested hypotheses become less likely or more likely. What seems to be true, later may appear to be true only partially or under particular conditions. Or we find out that it is true in a different sense. There is no such thing as complete and irrevocable truth. On the other hand there is such thing as complete and irrevocable falsehood or nonsense.

I am not fond of narrow-minded scientists who offer quack arguments whenever they know beforehand that a subject is nonsense. I am even less fond of narrow-minded religious people who consider evolution to be a wrong idea, because it contradicts the Bible. They do not understand the first thing about science and – probably worse – do not understand the first thing about religion. Weak souls and weak minds are drawn to religion, because it offers to soothe both mind and soul. Psychopaths are drawn to religion, because they can cloak their inhumanity in the more-than-humane. All that is natural and in the end positive, because such people (if you believe in more lifetimes) will be forced by their religion to think and to feel differently. However, when there are too many of them, they silence the decent and sensible believers. Wherever there is mental compulsion and mental terror, neither science nor religion prospers, only dangerous backwardness. The war against that will rage on for a long time to come.

*

To prevent this new edition from expanding too much, I had to cut a number of subjects. The present edition contains less about unimportant sources, though I could not always resist the temptation to expose patent nonsense. I have condensed into one the three chapters about connections between lifetimes. Though still satisfied with my own analysis, in therapeutic practice those ideas are not too important. I have shortened chapters on regression and therapy, as I have dealt with them in another book, *Deep Healing*.

Writing is a lonely business, only fit for the social misfit. I always wondered about the scores of names some writers include in their acknowledgements. I have no such acknowledgments to make. But I want to thank the readers who appreciated the previous edition and let me know that. It helps in the wee hours. One uncommon acknowledgement I do want to make. Every writer uses dictionaries and the like. For someone who is not a native speaker of English, one book appeared to be the best companion of all, *Webster's Collegiate Thesaurus*. Thank you, Merriam-Webster; thank you, unknown Mairé Weir Kay.

I hope this new edition is clearer and stronger; more complete, more topical, more readable.

Hans TenDam, Ommen, January 2003

NOTE ON TEXT REFERENCES

References in the text cite the author and first edition of each book in order to give a clear historical framework to the development of ideas about reincarnation. The page numbers, however, may refer to a later edition, the one mentioned in the bibliography. For example (Jinarajadasa 1915:12) refers to page 12 of the eighth printing in 1973 of Jinarajadasa's book, which was originally published in 1915.

Whenever case histories are given without a reference, they refer to cases from my own private practice.

One

IDEAS ABOUT REINCARNATION

Many people believe in reincarnation or find the idea acceptable. We usually associate the belief with Hindus and Buddhists. Reincarnation is thought to be a typically Eastern idea and almost everyone in India is supposed to believe in it. This knowledge is as common as it is inaccurate. Many city-dwellers in India are familiar with the idea, but most villagers have never heard of it. Moreover, ideas in India about reincarnation are highly contradictory. Many Indians believe in karma: behaviour in our past life determining our present life. Others believe our last thoughts determine our next life, or worse still that our present life depends on whether our family had the right people perform the right rituals for the right fees at our death.

Western believers in reincarnation, dramatising their minority position, usually assume that 99 percent of the people around them do not believe in reincarnation and consider it an Asian superstition (see, for example, Desjardins (1977: 22). Banerjee (1980) wants to convince Americans that reincarnation is not something oriental. He is overdoing it: 'reincarnation is truly a part of the American psyche and culture,' and 'reincarnation: a living American phenomenon.' Non-Americans can't see anything American in it. 'Mom and apple pie' are also more widespread than Americans may assume.

Also the situation in the West differs from what many imagine: belief in reincarnation is widespread. In a 1968 Gallup poll Catholics and Protestants from eight Western countries were questioned about religious matters including reincarnation (Head & Cranston 1977: 486). In the Netherlands 10 percent believed in reincarnation, 55 percent did not and 35 percent didn't know, giving the Netherlands the lowest number of believers. The next year the US and Canada were polled. The percentages of believers in reincarnation were together as follows:

| The Netherlands | 10% | Austria | 12% |
| Sweden | 12% | Greece | 22% |

Norway	14%	France	23%
England	18%	West Germany	25%
United States	20%	Canada	26%

Presumably religious people are more inclined to believe in reincarnation than others. But then again, reincarnation is not a part of the Christian faith. Many consider it to be in conflict with it. Ian Stevenson comments: 'Nearly everyone outside the range of orthodox Christianity, Judaism, Islam, and Science – the last being a secular religion for many persons – believes in reincarnation" (1987: 26).

The number of believers in reincarnation is more likely to have increased than decreased during the last 15 years, owing to the general tendency towards alternative spiritual ideas. A *Sunday Telegraph* poll in 1979 found 28 percent of British adults believing in reincarnation. *The Times* found 29 percent in 1980 (Fisher 1985). This means an increase of 10 percent in the ten years since 1969. According to Gallup & Proctor's *Adventures in Immortality* (1983: 176, 178) in 1982 67 percent of Americans believed in life after death, and 23 percent in reincarnation. Most of them were young and urban. The Gallup Youth Survey of 1985 revealed that 27 percent of American teenagers believe in reincarnation.

In 1978 an opinion poll by Rede Globo, a leading TV network in Brazil, found that 78 percent of Brazilians believe in reincarnation. They top the bill.

So, a great many people believe in reincarnation. Why do they? Most of them do because they've been brought up to believe in it. But in the final analysis, belief is based on experiences, reflections and arguments that convince people of its plausibility. Limiting myself here to the sources of belief in reincarnation in Western societies, I will peruse the literature published on the subject during the last 150 years, and find out what world-views and philosophies subscribe to belief in reincarnation. The next chapter deals with reincarnation's occurrence in other and older cultures. The third chapter describes the reincarnation philosophies of two important esoteric schools of thought.

What arguments are used to make reincarnation acceptable? A classic form of reasoning is to quote authorities. If so many great, important, intelligent and generally respected people believed in reincarnation, who are we bluntly to reject it? A variant is to demonstrate that all through history most people in most cultures did believe in reincarnation. As you are the exception in not believing, the burden of proof is on you. Pointing out the inherent reasonableness of reincarnation, referring to authorities and people throughout history believing in it, is a favourite argument in gnostic propaganda literature used to prepare the unconverted for the truth. All this is 'porch argumentation'. Those who already believe in theosophy or anthroposophy, or similar philosophies, can then be transported to the holy place where the argument is in theosophical, anthroposophical or other esoteric terms. The holy of holies is reserved for those who have been through the affirmative experiences themselves. In esoteric schools, therefore, only initiates or those disciples who are at least far advanced in inner training are able to view their own past lives or those of others. Then there are the rational arguments. These point out how people start their lives unequal and how unequal are their fates, which is difficult to reconcile with divine justice, or the idea that only one life determines our eternal bliss or damnation. Such arguments only affect the religious-minded. To convince materialists who think everything begins with conception and ends with death, other arguments, like those regarding child prodigies, are used. How come 4-year-olds are gifted pianists or read Latin or have other extra-ordinary gifts? An indirect form of rational argument is to point out irrational elements in alternative interpretations.

Diametrically opposed to the gnostic arguments are the empirical arguments. Many people think they have recollections of past lives and that such recollections exhibit patterns and regularities. Wambach's work (1978) is the best example of this.

SEVEN SOURCES OF MODERN BELIEF IN REINCARNATION

The translation of Sanskrit texts from the late eighteenth century led to the discovery in the West of classical Indian culture, the earliest source of belief in reincarnation in modern European countries. Sanskrit proved to be the oldest language in the Indo-European group, so ancient Indian culture provided the oldest retrospection into our own cultural past. Max Mueller translated and studied many ancient Indian texts, and did much to popularise them. Classical Hindu and Buddhist texts influenced thinkers such as Schopenhauer, who defined Europe as the continent dominated by the incredibly narrow idea that there was no such thing as reincarnation.

*

The second source of belief in reincarnation is the spiritist *Léon Rivail*. Rivail, a French educationalist, became convinced that mediums really communicated with the dead, and that some of the dead gave sensible answers to sensible questions. His well-known work, *The Spirits' Book* (1857), contains a number of questions and answers about reincarnation. Rivail published that book with the names he purportedly had in previous lifetimes. The medium Madame Japhet channelled the name Allan, and the medium Madame Roze the name Kardec. Celina Béquet, alias Japhet, developed her psychic gifts by being magnetised by one Roustan, who was himself convinced of reincarnation. Already fifteen years earlier, in 1839, a spiritist book proclaiming reincarnation had been published in France: *The heavenly doctrine of our Lord Jesus Christ, manifested by three angels*. According to Celina Béquet, she had received the doctrine of reincarnation since 1846 from the spirits of her grandfather, St Theresa and others. In 1856 she met Rivail, who collected her material in *Le Livre des Esprits*, without even mentioning her name, though three-quarters of the book was hers; the rest came from messages that one Madame Bodin had channelled in a different circle (Alexander Aksakow in *Psychische Studien*, 1898: 258ff). That's male prominence for you.

These ideas about reincarnation were strongly challenged. First of all, many people did not believe in such methods. Second, many who did, and themselves asked questions on the subject, received different answers from the dead. Spiritualist groups who accepted reincarnation received communications about reincarnation, and groups rejecting it received communications discounting reincarnation. The spirits communicating with A.T. Davis assured that our development after death is in the hereafter only and that the idea of reincarnation is an error. Critics of Kardec suspected that his mediums were strongly under his suggestive influence. Considering that Rivail obtained the contents of his work from others, this criticism doesn't fly. Anyway, whoever posed the questions, few of them are suggestive. Consulting mediums may be an interesting procedure; it can hardly be classed as serious research.

Kardec's book caused an international schism among spiritualists. The 'spiritists' did believe in reincarnation and the 'spiritualists' did not. Most of the English and American groups were converted to spiritualism, refuting reincarnation, while the Continentals (including the Brazilians), mainly influenced by Kardec, accepted reincarnation.

Nowadays, 'spiritism' indicates contacting spirits by ouija-board, table-dancing or turning glasses, or direct by trance-mediums; 'spiritualism' is a philosophy derived from spiritual and psychic phenomena. A few days before his death, Rivail said that differences between the North American spiritualism and the Roman spiritism were immaterial (*Revue Spirite*, April 1869: 105). Was he hedging? All this be as may, but Kardec's publication is the only book about reincarnation before 1911 that fits in well with modern empirical regression experiences.

The third source of belief in reincarnation was *theosophy*. Theosophy probably did more than Kardec's spiritism to extend views on reincarnation and make the concept acceptable because, at least in its heyday, it was more cosmopolitan and socially active and had greater cultural and intellectual prestige than spiritualism. Helena Blavatsky provided the founding publications, while Annie Besant and above all Leadbeater provided the elaborations. They will be discussed in chapter 3. Theosophy tied in with Indian philosophy, as the title of an early theosophical work, *Esoteric Buddhism* by Sinnett (1883), reveals. According to the theosophical leaders, the 'Masters' who inspired the movement lived in the Himalayas. Consequently, the rise of theosophy renewed interest in Indian culture and religion, even in India itself.

Theosophy is gnostic and esoteric, based on revelations received in a special mental state of mind. Such a state is reached after a persistent and profound discipline, resulting in crossing a threshold called initiation. After that we perceive truth directly. Technically, this means trusting and developing intuition. The theosophical and anthroposophical ideas are neither confirmed by spontaneous recall cases nor by regressions. They are in many respects even completely at odds with whatever experiences we have.

Meanwhile, in Paris the French baron *Albert de Rochas d'Aiglun* developed a fourth approach, based on research, which was to become the most important source of past life knowledge. Colonel de Rochas was for many years director of the military polytechnic school in Paris. He experimented on the side with magnetism and hypnosis. In 1898 he noticed that subjects put into trance were fully able to recall past experiences. He discovered he could even instruct them to go back to early childhood and birth. When he took his subjects even further back, they had experiences clearly coming from past lives (de Rochas 1911). His work aroused great interest among theosophists. Colonel Olcott, a founding member of the theosophical movement, visited de Rochas and was impressed with his experiments. Maurice Maeterlinck, a well-known theosophical writer, devoted space to de Rochas in his book about death. All the same, the theosophists did little with de Rochas' work, probably because he was no theosophist, did not speak on behalf of a school of initiates and was simply conducting experiments. Moreover, he discovered an intermission between lives of only years or decades, strongly contradicting the theosophical doctrine of intermissions of 1,600, 1,300 and 1,200 years.

De Rochas' work so much contradicted theosophical concepts that it never gained ground in theosophy. Even theosophists who were impressed with it kept a safe distance. Van Ginkel (1917), for instance, thought that regression would become a method for past life recall in the far future.

Esotericists, like theosophists, disapproved of the use of magnetic or hypnotic trance. People in such trances supposedly lost their ego and power of judgment, becoming passive and submissive, easily led by the hypnotist. After all, man has to become less dependent and more conscious. Although there is much to be said for these views, the criticism is not entirely warranted, particularly the idea that a hypnotist easily influences the content of a regression. It is usually difficult, if not impossible, to influence what people see or experience. Often a remigrant cannot answer simple questions about the time and area he lived in, even when the hypnotist and any others present are mentally shouting it to him. In regressions where consciousness becomes divided or elliptic (the present consciousness remaining intact as observer of the past life being relived), the remigrant later describes the sometimes great conflict between the two states of consciousness about some specific information, and the inability of the present consciousness to influence the part recalling a past life. Good examples are to be found in Moss and Keeton (1979).

Another esotericist, Gerard Encausse, writing his occult works under the name of Papus, in about 1920 published *La Réincarnation*, an amazingly abstract and rambling book, which mentions de Rochas only in a footnote at the end, saying his work is interesting.

Spiritualists and parapsychologists also refuted de Rochas' findings strongly and explained them by his personal dominance and suggestion (Van Holthe tot Echten 1921). However, de Rochas, even more than Kardec, is in excellent agreement with modern empirical literature.

The successors to de Rochas were John Bjorkhem in Sweden and the psychiatrist Alexander Cannon in England. Cannon had academic standing: nine European universities awarded him degrees. Cannon regressed almost 1,400 volunteers. He accepted reincarnation only slowly, but conceded at last that 'Freud has been outflanked by reincarnation.' Cannon's work stimulated Morey Bernstein (1956), whose famous case, Bridey Murphy, triggered modern interest in regression and regression therapy. Joe Fisher estimated that past-life therapy has since been responsible for healing hundreds of thousands of people (Whitton & Fisher 1986: 62). Meanwhile, the total number may be fivefold.

The fifth source of belief in reincarnation was *Edgar Cayce*, who operated midway between spiritualism and hypnotic regression. The fact that nowadays, in the USA and the other English-speaking countries, most spiritists and even large parts of the population believe in reincarnation is mainly due to Cayce. By means of self-hypnosis Cayce put himself into deep trance, in which he drew from an expanded consciousness. He was his own inspirator and guide, as it were. Many books contain samples from his readings about reincarnation, and about karma in particular. People seeking advice about their own problems or those of their children were also given information based on the experiences and lessons of past lives. Gina Cerminara has written a book about reincarnation and karma (1950), based on Cayce's readings.

Hundreds of his cases illustrate Cayce's concept of reincarnation. Individual cases could sometimes be checked, and his other statements about people were usually accurate, even if he had never met them. On the whole Cayce had great success advising people on health and career problems. This made him more convincing than the average sensitive. Cayce also answered questions about reincarnation in general.

The writings of people with *spontaneous recall of past lives* form a sixth source. Such books are not in themselves proof of reincarnation, although they may be rich in obscure historical facts confirmed later. The first book of this kind to become popular was *Winged Pharaoh* by Joan Grant (1937). Jean Overton Fuller (1993) for many years studied ancient Egyptian history and language to validate or invalidate that story. Critically and in a detailed way, she tests Joan Grant's statements against historical and archaeological evidence. Her booklet reads like a detective novel. Many details and names fit later reconstructions of the lives of pharaohs of the First Dynasty and many items could be confirmed by more recent material only. The main stumbling block remains Joan Grant's mention of horses. The historical record of the horse in Egypt starts only 1,500 years later.

Joan Grant has described other lives in highly readable books, giving vivid impressions of life in earlier times. The spiritualistic aspect of her often unintentionally therapeutic work, and her collaboration with Denys Kelsey, led also to past-life therapy (Kelsey & Grant 1967). Joan Grant says relatively little about the mechanism of reincarnation and karma, but she vividly describes conditions after death and the interaction between the living and discarnates.

Second Time Round, by Edward Ryall (1974), is one of the few recall books the more critical investigators in the field take seriously.

The rise in past-life regressions and in past-life readings has led to a spate of past-life autobiographies. Usually these past lives are well-known, and surprisingly many are contemporaries of Jesus in Palestine. The New Testament may have become the most rewritten book ever. On top of the score of alternative gospels, usually channelled, there is a score of life stories about that time, based on apparent past-life memories.

The seventh source is the rise of *past-life therapy*, a form of regression therapy in which people relive traumatic experiences from past lives to resolve present problems (among others, Netherton & Shiffrin 1978; TenDam 1989; Lucas 1993). Interestingly enough, Netherton's method enables people to recall past lives within a few minutes without hypnosis, relaxation or visualisation. If there is trance involved, it is rather the effect of the reliving a past life than the cause.

Chapter 2 below discusses Hinduism and Buddhism. Chapter 4 elaborates on the spiritist sources and Edgar Cayce. Chapter 6 reviews the literature on regression. Chapter 8 gives more examples of autobiographies of past lifetimes. Chapter 16 is about past-life therapy.

THE REINCARNATION HYPOTHESIS COMPARED WITH OTHER CONCEPTS

The idea that people have already lived before they are born and may live again after they die, is viewed here as a hypothesis, to see where it takes us. We start with a provisional analysis to find out how acceptable or fertile it would be as a working hypothesis. Let us compare the reincarnation hypothesis with alternative hypotheses about the link between body and soul and the question of life and death. What are the general hypotheses, and to what extent does human experience support or contradict them?

Table 1 compares nine general hypotheses about the relationship between soul and body.

Table 1 Soul—body hypotheses

Materialism	Mind is a by-product of the body
Psychic collectivism	Mind is a temporarily individualised vital energy
Psychic transfer	Mind goes from the dead to the newborn
Spiritualism:	
Creationism	New soul produced by God
Traducianism	Soul split off from parents' souls
Generationism	Soul produced by parents
Pre-existence	Previous existence in soul world
Reincarnation	Consecutive human incarnations
Metempsychosis	Both human and animal incarnations

The first hypothesis is *materialism*, including all views rejecting a soul independent of the body, rejecting life and consciousness separate from the physical organism. In materialism the mind is a by-product of the body. Thoughts, feelings, emotions, plans, consciousness develop together with the body and end at death. This idea gained ground during the last century, although the Epicureans had already formulated a similar concept and worked out its moral meaning and existential consequences. Christopher Bache (1990) distinguished materialism from naturalism, but for my purpose here the difference is immaterial (no pun intended).

I have chosen the term '*psychic collectivism*' to include all ideas about the mind as having substance, without being an entity in itself, only being a separate entity when in the (human) body. Many cultures assume that at death the soul leaves the body as a vapour or cloud of vitality that is absorbed by the earth, and so gives new vital energy to plants, animals and human beings. In this view the soul is vital energy temporarily individualised at birth, when it separates from the encompassing psychic field that then feeds it. At death this field reabsorbs the soul. Fechner offers a philosophical variant of this view (see Bibliography).

A modern example of psychic collectivism is the theory of a Dutchman living in France who knew so many details about places where he had never been that it embarrassed him. Because he did not want to believe in past lives, he explained this by the idea that interconnected traces of experiences insufficiently integrated with the rest of the soul disengage themselves after death and start to float in the atmosphere as shreds of mist. People with a similar psyche may pick up these shreds of mist and carry them with them as their own knowledge (Van Nes 1958: 111).

I have chosen '*psychic transfer*' as a generic label for concepts related to the Buddhist *anatta* doctrine, which postulates that at birth people receive the mental and psychic patterns and characteristics left by people who died earlier. After death the resultant psychic characteristics again return to a sort of general fund, to be reassigned to those about to be born. Roughly speaking, there are two variants: the psychic heritage is more or less arbitrary, or it is inherited from a specific person who lived previously, without the newborn being that person. Buddhist doctrine compares the succession of embodiments with a candle lighting another candle. One follows the other, but they are quite different. The interesting thing about this comparison is its flaw. After all, reincarnation implies some time between one candle going out and the other being lit. If there is continuity, there is some flame in between lives and thus probably identity.

Schopenhauer, deeply influenced by Buddhism, states that only the will (whose will? one's own?) reincarnates (Head & Cranston 1977: 294). I can't make sense of such ideas.

This doctrine also has its followers in our time. Ironically, some of them accuse Madame Blavatsky of propagating the, in their view, incorrect reincarnation hypothesis through carelessness and misunderstanding when Madame Blavatsky herself was actually a firm believer in psychic transfer (Blavatsky 1886). Theosophy, however, as the work of Annie Besant and especially Charles Leadbeater clearly shows (see Bibliography), gradually but rapidly came to accept the reincarnation concept proper.

Hazrat Inayat Khan, the founder of modern Sufism, came up with a theory combining pre-existence and psychic transfer. The soul's journey down to the earth where she is going to incarnate is long and tiring. Therefore, there are places to rest along the way. The deceased, on the way up, are also on a long and tiring journey and rest at the same rest stops. Descending souls hear the tales of the ascending souls and later they think these are their own memories of past lives. This seems to be taken from Plato. Chapter 11 below will expose the nonsense of 'long and tiring journeys' in the discarnate state. According to Rohit Mehta (1977), the reincarnating entity is a 'pyschic–spiritual composite', grown through lifetimes. As there is no compulsion, there is no continuing factor connecting one life with another. Each life is new and fresh, without a past and without a future. Just before that he states that the human individuality creates ever-new personalities to complete itself. I was one reader left feeling seasick with these apparent inconsistencies.

Psychic collectivism and psychic transfer are midway between the materialistic and spiritualistic points of view. The *spiritualistic approach* embraces all concepts that regard the mind as an entity with a separate existence after the body's death: the soul. Spiritualistic ideas may be classified according to their view of the soul's fate after the body dies or its state before and during birth. The latter is more interesting. Three spiritualistic hypotheses assume the creation of the soul at birth:

- *Creationism*, asserting that the soul is created by God (from what?) at birth.
- *Traducianism*, asserting that, during the physical conception of a child, parts of the parents' souls split off and join around the embryo to form a new soul.
- *Generationism*, asserting that human beings possess a special creative power somehow enabling them to create the new soul during a (fertile) sexual act.

Aristotle embraced creationism, Zeno traducianism. These ideas from classical philosophy recur in Christian theology.

If the soul is not created at conception or birth, it already existed before birth. This leads to the idea of *pre-existence*: the soul exists before birth in a soul-world. It incarnates in a body and after death returns to the original soul-world, possibly improved or deteriorated. Exceptionally, return to a body is possible. This idea was widely accepted in early Christianity. *Reincarnation* presumes human souls return many times to human bodies. The characteristic feature of *metempsychosis* or transmigration of souls is that human souls can enter animals — and even plants — as well.

We may separate these nine general hypotheses into those based on, or analogous to, human experience, and those that represent mental fabrications, unconnected with any experience. Materialism, postulating that human life begins at birth and ends at death, is in this respect a reasonable hypothesis. Many things in life begin and end, and having no contact with people who aren't yet born or who have died is one of life's most intense experiences. The psychic collectivism hypothesis, though more obscure, is also reasonable in this respect. Our world has many analogous phenomena, where a diffused substance (a solution, a vapour or a suspension) may temporarily have a more fixed form (in a vessel, or absorbed). Apart from this, the first two hypotheses vary considerably in their degree of acceptability. That things have a beginning and an end may be even more abstract, but the materialistic hypothesis is also supported by actual human experience Our ignorance of an unborn child, and the greater impact of losing a friend or family member through death are real experiences Materialism is thus more than an intellectual analogy, it corresponds to actual experience. Psychic collectivism is mere analogy.

To imagine psychic transfer, or creationism, traducianism and generationism, is impossible because they are not based on any experiences. The Buddhist *anatta*-doctrine can be explained as a reaction to the rigid and morbid karma and reincarnation doctrines of the Brahman religion prevalent at the time of Buddha. The other three hypotheses are mere fabrications of philosophers and theologians.

Experiences that bear directly upon the probability or improbability of the nine hypotheses about the body–soul relationship come in five broad categories:

- Near-death experiences: people who, resuscitated after being clinically dead for some time, recount their experience.

- Parapsychological research into out-of-body experiences and astral projection.

- Spiritualistic evidence: communication with the dead, usually through a medium, and not in the context of parapsychological research.

- Experiences preceding birth: people in regression who recall their birth, the prenatal time in the womb, and sometimes the preceding period.

- Past-life recall: spontaneous recall with or without a trigger, and recall induced by various regression techniques.

An impressively wide literature covers these five empirical areas, varying from the experiences of the illiterate inhabitants of isolated regions to scientific research at universities (half-isolated regions inhabited by the very literate). Each of these areas reveals such distinct patterns that any serious student will find it difficult to dismiss

Table 2 Soul–body hypotheses tested against various kinds of empirical evidence

	Near-death experiences	Psychic research	Spirit-ualism	Prenatal memories	Past-life memories
Materialism	–	–	–	–	–
Psychic collectivism	–	0	–	–	–
Psychic transfer	–	0	–	–	–
Soul originates at birth	0	0	–/0	–	–
Pre-existence	0	–/+	–/+	+	–
Reincarnation	0	–/+	+/–	0/+	+
Metempsychosis	0	–/+	–/+	0	–/+

–: contradicted   +: affirmed   0: indecisive

the available empirical material. Gnostic literature is excluded here. Even if the intellectual standard is high, it remains revelation without evidence, while experiences that contradict the adopted gnostic framework are usually ignored or made suspect.

From now on creationism, traducianism and generationism will be dealt with together. Table 2 is the result of the first testing of the seven points of view against these five kinds of experience.

All five types of experience contradict the materialistic hypothesis. Psychic collectivism and psychic transfer are also contradicted on the whole, although parapsychology gives no definite outcome. Obviously, prenatal experiences and past-life recall contradict the idea that the soul is created at birth. The other types of experience give no clear indication about this, although much spiritualistic material refers to a form of pre-existence. Naturally, near-death experiences say nothing about pre-existence, reincarnation and metem-psychosis.

The parapsychological material is scanty on this point, and the spiritualistic material has been contradictory. That believers are in the majority is hardly relevant here. Prenatal experiences give no information about metempsychosis, but they do support the possibility of pre-existence and reincarnation. Finally, past-life recall definitely affirms reincarnation but gives little support to metempsychosis.

*

In 1988 Maurice Albertson and Kenneth Freeman from Colorado State University published a sweeping and highly interesting analysis of the credibility of reincarnation ideas. They considered the sources of those ideas to be:

- near-death experiences
- spontaneous childhood memories
- the unborn child
- life before life
- past-life regression
- past-life therapy
- earthbound spirits
- out-of-body experiences
- channelled information
- world religions
- western philosophy.

The criteria they used to test the credibility of these sources were:

- Great care was taken in collecting, selecting, interpreting, analysing and using the data, preferably by controlled research design and techniques, or at least under clinical or experiential circumstances.
- For information obtained from people, the question was asked if the subject could have acquired the content of his memories from some other source to which he normally had been exposed.
- The basic pattern of results repeats itself almost universally.
- The number of supporting cases is large or very large: tens, hundreds, thousands, tens of thousands.
- Many other patterns could be imagined, but no other pattern emerged with many replications.

After testing the sources against these criteria, Albertson and Freemen rated the credibility of these sources on a scale from 1 to 10, from very low to very high credibility.

They tested 25 hypotheses against all the material they had collected from those nine sources. They then used a score combining the credibility of the source with the degree to which it confirmed or refuted each hypothesis. They could confirm 24 out of 25 hypotheses, though the strength of confirmation varied widely. Chapter 9 will summarise their conclusions.

PROVISIONAL CONCLUSIONS

Materialism is a strong hypothesis, though refuted by all special experiences in this area. If materialism is true, all those experiences in all those fields are fantasy. The next three hypotheses are mental constructs which, to the extent they are concrete enough to be refuted, are contradicted by the empirical evidence. The only hypotheses that may be considered acceptable in the light of existing empirical evidence are those postulating continuity of the human soul: pre-existence, reincarnation and metempsychosis, pre-existence having the weakest affirmation and reincarnation the strongest.

Prevailing opinion being largely materialistic (or, in the diluted version, agnostic: we shall never know what happens after death because nobody has ever come back) makes our task relatively easy. If the prevalent belief is not a positive doctrine but a denial, all that is required to refute it are a few convincing cases. If people believe there are no fish in a lake, only one fish has to be caught there to refute the hypothesis. However, refuting a hypothesis is quite different from changing people's minds. After all, somebody may have put the fish there.

For our further consideration we take only materialism and spiritualism (in its three varieties: pre-existence, reincarnation and metempsychosis) seriously. As past-life experiences form the most specific and convincing material in support of the reincarnation hypothesis, we shall limit ourselves to a review of this material.

Alexander Cannon has collected about 500 cases of spontaneous past-life recall (1936), Muller about 700 (1970) and Stevenson about 2,000 (see Bibliography). The cases Muller collected are the most interesting because many are complicated and involve remarkable phenomena hardly credible to non-spiritualists. Stevenson has published by far the best-researched cases. Up to now he has described extensive research into about 65 cases of spontaneous recall in children (Stevenson 1966, 1975, 1977, 1980, 1983). Then there are the hypnotists and therapists who induce and guide regression to past lives. These are often recorded. Alexander Cannon regressed almost 1,400 people, The Englishman Arnall Bloxham made about 400 recordings of the regressions of about 50 people; Bjorkhem, a Swede, documented about 600 regressions (though he explained them afterwards as produced by obsessing entities), and Helen Wambach tops the lot with her 5,000 regressions of 1,100 people.

Ideas like psychic collectivism or psychic transference, and ideas that the soul is created at conception or birth, are not confirmed by any experience and can be discarded as pure speculation. Compared to them the materialistic hypothesis is stronger by its inherent logic, and by the apparent complete absence of people before birth and after death. However, materialism can only be maintained by discarding all the categories of experiences mentioned above – near-death experiences, parapsychology and psychic phenomena, spiritist experiences, prenatal memories and past-life recall – as being the product of fraud and fantasy. Though, as chapter 9 will show, not everything is as it seems, the main reason to use materialism as an overall explanation is intellectual laziness, or rather bigotry. We have to develop an empirical view on the basis of collecting and analysing cases of spontaneous or induced recall. We have to compare reincarnation with materialism, pre-existence and metempsychosis. Before we do that in chapters 9, 12 and 15, we will collect ideas on the subject in chapter 2, 3 and 4, and experiences in chapters 5, 6 and 7. In chapter 9 we will be critical of overly critical disbelievers. In chapter 8 we will first be critical of uncritical believers.

FURTHER READING

This section mentions the better general works on reincarnation. Details are given in the Bibliography at the end of this book. Literature about reincarnation ideas from particular philosophies and schools is mentioned in the 'further reading' sections at the end of chapters 2 and 3. Spiritist writings, and books about regression and therapy can be found at the end of the pertinent chapters. Books about Edgar Cayce can be found at the end of chapter 4, by Stevenson at the end of chapter 5, etcetera.

The first general book on reincarnation that treated the subject broadly and with common sense was *The Problem of Rebirth: An enquiry into the basis of the reincarnation hypothesis* by Ralph Shirley (1924). A more limited introduction to the subject is *The Power of Karma* by Alexander Cannon (1936). Ed. Bertholet (1949) wrote *La Réincarnation*, an impressive encyclopaedic work. *Reincarnation Based on Facts* by Karl Muller (1970) gives the most interesting and the most systematic collection of cases.

David Graham's *The Practical Side of Reincarnation* (1976) is based on interviews with people involved with reincarnation and regression, giving interesting examples and observations. Banerjee (1980) presents an overview of what had been written and done in the USA until then. A good English overview is *Reincarnation: Ancient beliefs and modern evidence* by David Christie-Murray (1981). The book by Sylvia Cranston and Gary Williams, *Reincarnation: A new horizon in science, religion and society* (1984), is informative, but weakly structured, full of hardly relevant material and much overlap with an earlier book.

Other acceptable general introductions are *Reincarnation in the Twentieth Century* by Martin Ebon (1970), *Life Beyond Life* by Hans Holzer (1985) and *Reincarnation: The evidence* by Liz Hodgkinson (1989). *Life Cycles: Reincarnation and the web of life* (1990) by Christopher Bache, a teacher in the psychology of religion, is one of the best books written about the subject.

Two

HISTORICAL BELIEFS IN REINCARNATION

This chapter gives a condensed overview of what people around the world have believed or still believe about reincarnation. It may remove four common misunderstandings:

- The idea that reincarnation is an Indian doctrine.
- The idea that reincarnation is a fatalistic doctrine.
- The idea that reincarnation was originally a Christian doctrine that has been removed by Church Council.
- The idea that reincarnation is a clear-cut doctrine at all, instead of being subjected (like any other religious belief) to pedantic righteousness, incoherent associations, incredible prejudice, alarming narrow-mindedness and foundationless speculation.

The general assumption that reincarnation is a typically Indian idea is as persistent as it is wrong. Ideas about reincarnation are found in diverse cultures all over the world, as Ian Stevenson says (1987: 26): 'Nearly everyone outside the range of orthodox Christianity, Judaism, Islam, and Science – the last being a secular religion for many persons – believes in reincarnation.' Some anthropologists have speculated that the original reincarnation belief came from an earlier, higher culture since lost (Atlantis?) and has left traces all around the world. This view is difficult to verify and rather unlikely, considering the distribution pattern and the widely divergent character of local ideas. Belief in reincarnation rather seems to have arisen independently in separate cultures.

Stevenson estimated that about 1 in 1,000 children spontaneously remembers a past life. Only among the Druses did he find a frequency of 1 in 500. In another count, 1 in 450 children in northern India remembered a past life. Regions where people believe in reincarnation have more cases of young children who recollect past lives. The rejection of reincarnation suppresses expression, recognition and dissemination of such memories. The reverse is not true. A prevailing belief in reincarnation does not stimulate recollection. Most parents do not talk about such subjects with children of three or four, and when children come to them with such memories, parents usually find it troublesome rather than interesting. Also, where belief in reincarnation is common, children's memories are often at odds with prevailing religious doctrines.

The regions with cases of spontaneous memories of reincarnation in young children are clearly delineated. One region is in West Africa, roughly encompassing Nigeria, Senegal, Ghana and surrounding territories. Another region is the home of the Druses in southeast Turkey, Lebanon and northern Israel. A third region is south and southeast Asia, encompassing India, Sri Lanka, Burma, Thailand, Nepal, Tibet, and Vietnam. The fourth is Japan. The fifth region is an area in southeast Alaska. Finally, there is the general area of the Western world, where in Europe as well as in the United States the number of cases is strongly increasing. Presumably, the incidence of young children remembering previous lives may be around equal everywhere: about 1 in 500.

Reincarnation beliefs in the various regions and cultures diverge strongly. Some cultures believe that we are born immediately after death, others believe in an intermission. Some believe that we always return as human beings, some believe that we can become superhuman and then no longer need to return, and some believe that we can return as animals, either as punishment or as a natural change.

Many views gradually pass into psychic collectivism. Culturally, views on death relate to those on sleep, while views on the soul usually relate to those on dreaming. Many cultures think that the soul wanders about during sleep, after departing for example from the nostrils and mouth as a vapour. Upon death, the soul floats around. Its energy may be absorbed by the land, enter the vegetation that other people eat, and so end up in semen. Often, the soul is pictured as small and flying. During sleep it departs from the body, for example through the mouth, in the form of a manikin, a snake, a porcupine, a mouse, an insect, a butterfly or a bird. During the day the soul usually inhabits the head. Therefore headhunting, decapitating someone to take over the power of his soul, differs from cannibalism, eating flesh. After death the soul is sometimes associated with vultures. The soul wants to repossess the body via the vultures. Finally, there are less unpleasant ideas: the soul will be absorbed in trees and flowers. In primitive cultures, notions of reincarnation, metempsychosis and psychic collectivism mingle in diverse ways.

Reincarnation can be seen as an inescapable fate or as a triumph of our free will. The Hindus generally believe that karma from past lives determines everything in our present life. They do not believe that the returning soul chooses its parents and they do not express any wishes about a coming life. On the other hand, the Tlingits, an Eskimo tribe in Alaska, do believe in choice of parents and often have wishes about their next life. They may tell relatives how they may recognise them in their next life. For them, reincarnation is no fate but an act of free will.

Margaret Mead compared cultures that believe in reincarnation with cultures that don't. The Eskimos and Balinese, who believe in reincarnation, believe children have prophetic gifts. Early on, they teach their children to do complicated things and trust that they can perform them, because in truth they are adults. Even old people continue to learn, because they trust their efforts will not be wasted. In general, such cultures suffer less from the generation gap. On the other hand, a culture such as the Manus believes that children are merely products of their parents. After death even the strongest spirits decay slowly into mud and slime. People in such cultures are written off socially and psychologically after the age of forty.

So, belief in reincarnation doesn't need to foster indolence and fatalism. Quite the opposite. Usually people think of Indian culture as passive compared to the activity of Western culture with its Christian faith. Every faith, however, including Christianity, can reinforce activity as well as passivity. One's personal attitude and response to a belief are decisive, except when the faith in question is basically pessimistic, like that of the Manus. Within such a perspective, considerable strength of mind is needed to remain active and responsible.

PRIMITIVE CULTURES

Africa My main source for belief in reincarnation in black Africa is James Addison (1936). He has documented such beliefs in 95 black tribes:

- 47 tribes believe in metempsychosis, accepting the possibility of returning as animals
- 36 tribes believe in reincarnation proper
- 12 tribes believe both are possible.

The reincarnation ideas probably are older, and metempsychosis younger. The Zulus have elaborate notions of reincarnation as a gradual perfection of the individual until return is no longer necessary. They believe a secret tradition exists in all of Africa, originating from ancient Egypt and supported by teachers returning voluntarily.

The belief in reincarnation is strongest in West Africa, where reincarnation is seen as good. People do not desire release from the cycle of birth and death. To incarnate is fine and good for a soul. Childlessness is a pity and polygamy is good because people prefer to return to the same family. After a birth, the medicine man divines who the child was previously. Birth signs are studied, and the young child has to pick out objects belonging to the deceased from among other objects. Children receive such names as: Father-has-returned, Mother-has-returned, He-has-returned. Grandparents and ancestors are expected to return usually in the same family. In the south of Nigeria people believe the soul may return in several persons of different sex. Like many other tribes, the Yorubas let the witch-doctors divine who the child was so they can give it a proper name. During the name-giving ritual they welcome the child with the exclamation 'Thou art come!' Their notions about karma are rather vague and conflicting. Good people return as people or as good animals. Bad people become wild animals. Apart from this karmic view, they believe somebody's wishes may have considerable influence on his return.

In Zaire, the Bagongo and the Bassongo have children who remember past lives. These tribes teach that after death souls descend to the earth core and remain there for between two months and two years, depending on how homesick they are for the world above. When the soul returns, it enters a child shortly before birth. Often, a newborn baby bears marks indicating who it was in its preceding life. A painful pregnancy is seen as indication of a painful death in a preceding life. Among the Bahumbu in Zaire, twins and triplets are honoured as reborn chiefs and surrounded with ceremony.

The Elgayos of Kenya believe that the soul enters the body after birth during the name-giving ceremony, when the child receives the name of the returning family member. This notion is also found in Uganda.

An interesting case is that of a black African who contentedly and frequently consults his spirit guide. Asked who this guide is, he says that it is himself in his preceding lifetime. In modern past-life therapy it is common procedure to make this option available.

Asia Reincarnation beliefs in Asia are no matter of tribal cultures, but of religions such as Hinduism and Buddhism. The section on Eastern religions below will return to this. The Burmese assume that the recurrence of children who remember past lives is intended to remind people of the truth of reincarnation. Interestingly enough, they believe that individuals return, although the official Buddhist doctrine, *anatta*, teaches that although people assume characteristics of one or more previous personalities, they are not identical with any previous personality. The Balinese have a strong tradition of reincarnation. They believe people are reborn in the same family again and again. There are some reincarnation views among the Japanese, probably dating from before the advent of Buddhism.

Europe The Celts believed that, after a number of lives, they could attain the 'white heaven', where they would behold God. After death the soul rests a while. People who lived badly return as the kind of animal to whom their character corresponded. After purification, they too will ultimately arrive in the white heaven. Teachers who voluntarily return from the white heaven inspire the advance of civilisation until everybody will have attained the white heaven. According to some, this is an Atlantic tradition, presumably coming via Ireland. If so, these thoughts came from the pre-Celtic inhabitants, as the Celts derived from eastern, not western Europe.

Caesar explained the contempt for death of the Celtic warriors by their belief that their soul wouldn't die, but would return in an other body (Passian 1985).

The old Germanic tribes, according to Guido von List, believed in life after death. Their hereafter consisted of six spheres (divine houses) from which they could return, except from the lowest and from the highest. They held that people would reincarnate in the same family with the same name. Reincarnation beliefs of all kinds have been found among the Danes, the Norse, the Icelanders, the East Goths, the Lombardians, the Lets and the Saxons. The Saxons, for example, believed that a person first became a rose or a dove for a while before he could go on to divine places. The Finns and the Laps also had reincarnation beliefs. Christianised Germanic tribes believed in reincarnation probably till well into the seventh century (Passian 1985).

Modern Wicca adherents, who feel themselves to be the inheritors of ancient nature religions and witchcraft, have reincarnation beliefs that resemble what we find in regression practice (Graham 1976). Whether those beliefs are really ancient, or whether they are modern ones in an ancient guise, I can't judge.

The Americas The Tlingits, inhabiting southeastern Alaska and northwestern Canada, until recently had elaborate reincarnation views and practices. They looked for stigmata – body marks at birth indicating the newborn's identity. The returning soul can choose its future mother. Particular attention is paid to dreams of pregnant women about deceased relatives. After death the deceased go to different places, one of which is for those who died violently. There is some belief in metempsychosis. Neighbouring Indian and Eskimo tribes also believe in reincarnation. The western Inuit assume that there are five ascending stages after this life. Overlapping reincarnations have been found among the Inuit, in which someone was reborn before the preceding personality had died.

In Canada, seven Indian tribes believe in reincarnation. In the rest of North America belief in reincarnation was widespread in the east. Indian tribes with such ideas included the Iroquois, the Algonquians, the Creeks, the Dakotas, the Winnebagos, the Kiowas, the Hopis and the Mohohavis. The Chippewas believed that people could relive situations from past lives and even future lives in dreams. The Pueblos believed in the return of young children who had died. They buried the body of such a child underneath the parental home so that the soul could easily find its way back to the family. A common idea was that people of pure heart could remember past lives. Many Indian tribes saw the white pioneers as returned generations from the past.

In Mexico and Central America, Indian tribes such as the Mayas, the Caribs and the Peruvians believed in reincarnation. The Mexican Indians believed in a form of metempsychosis. Prominent persons would return as beautiful songbirds and higher animals, while persons of lower rank would return as weasels, beetles and other lowly species.

The Incas believed that a person could return to his body if it was correctly mummified. Belief in reincarnation existed among Brazilian Indian tribes such as the Chiriquas. The Brazilian Indians call reincarnation *lambazap*. According to some, slaves from West Africa may have introduced these reincarnation ideas. Belief in reincarnation is also found among the Patagonians.

Australia and Oceania Australian aboriginals believed in reincarnation. Later this belief was strongest among the central and northern tribes. After the confrontation with the Europeans, the belief spread among the aboriginals that they would return as white men. One native, who was being executed, exclaimed joyfully in his last moments: 'Very good! Me jump up white fellow!'

In the northern Pacific Ocean reincarnation beliefs exist on Okinawa. People there hold that the soul leaves the body 49 days after death. After a varying intermission, never longer than seven generations (about 200 years), the soul returns in a body with a face and appearance resembling the preceding incarnation. They do not believe that people return as animals. Some souls remain discarnate and welcome the recently deceased.

For the rest, belief in reincarnation is found among tribes on Borneo and Celebes, among the Papuans, the Amoris and Asmanens, and on Tahiti, Fiji, Solomon Islands, among the Marquesans, and in the southern region of New Caledonia.

EASTERN RELIGIONS

Hinduism Well-educated people and those from the higher castes are familiar with reincarnation and karma ideas such as *punarjanma* (rebirth), karma (the law) and *samsara* (the reincarnation cycle). In the rural areas reincarnation is not seen as karmic, but as dependent on rituals and influences from all kinds of gods and spirits. How you return does not depend on how you lived, but on whether your son has executed the proper burial rites (*anyeshti*) to guarantee a happy rebirth. The lower castes, particularly in the villages, hardly believe in reincarnation.

Indian belief in reincarnation is ancient, but not that ancient. The Vedas contain only a belief in the hereafter. The earliest references are in the Upanishads, teaching *samsara*, and so placing retribution no longer in the hereafter, but in next lifetimes. The great differences in life circumstances are explained by karma. We sprang from the Supreme Being and essentially remain identical with it. Many successive incarnations make us forgetful of our origin, confused and torpid. But gradually, through a long succession of incarnations, we begin to realise where we must return to. Then, each life becomes an endeavour to return. Remaining blinded by the fascinations of material life becomes a sin. We must disengage ourselves and become spiritual, attain *moksha* (see below), and so ultimately find our way back to Brahmā.

Another Hindu view is that the souls, the *jivas*, begin as the simplest life forms. Via the mineral, the vegetable and the animal stage they finally reach the human stage, and ultimately become angels, after many more incarnations. Each jiva, each soul, has in it *atman*, the eternal, divine essence. *Samsara*, the cycle of continually recurrent lives, leads more or less naturally to growth and ripening. When our soul, however, has attained human self-awareness, we can choose and become personally responsible, and our own efforts determine our karma. An opposing view sees our awareness and choice as illusions, and holds that the law of karma continues to operate mechanically.

At any rate, we must learn, more or less by ourselves, through experience or conscious choice, to find release from our imperfections. We must learn that our experiences may continue to attach us to the delusions of material life.

Souls may pursue four universal desires or goals:

- *Kama*, or lust. This is immersing oneself in the pursuit of pleasure and the avoidance of suffering. In this stage the major sin is anger.

- *Artha*, or material advancement. Here the major sin is avarice.

- *Dharma*, or moral and religious virtue and integrity; literally: to fulfil the moral and religious law.

- *Moksha*, or deliverance from physical limitations and from reincarnation.

Some see these four desires as having a natural order: when somebody has sufficiently gratified one desire he will strive for the gratification of the next, higher desire. Others see the transition to a higher desire as the result of a struggle to destroy the lower desires. These opposing views pertain particularly to the transition between the first three desires. The transition from *dharma* to *moksha* is almost always perceived as the result of religious study, asceticism and conscious contemplation.

The Brahmins taught that for release from the cycle of rebirth an unselfish life was not enough, and prescribed (and paid for) prayers and sacrifices by priests were necessary. Other superstitions accrued: bathing at prescribed places and times in the Ganges removes sins, and whoever dies in Benares does not need to return (Passian 1985). The rigorous views on reincarnation and karma are closely related to the caste system, especially through the interpretation of Karma set down in the Laws of Manu, which elaborates the punishments for human imperfections. When we sin bodily, we return as mineral or plant. When we speak sinfully, we return as a bird or animal, and when we have sinful thoughts only, we return as a low-ranking person. He who has lived badly seeks a bad womb: the womb of a dog, a swine or a pariah. Only those who have behaved themselves end up in a good womb. Only a Brahmin, carrier of the holy cord, can attain *moksha*. Thus, a person who doesn't belong to the highest caste can contemplate and live ascetically until his bones ache, and yet the best he can attain is being born as a Brahmin in his next life. A modified belief is that people not carrying the holy cord can attain *moksha* through even more intense asceticism and heavy penance. The lower castes have found a practical solution to those oppressive doctrines: they don't believe them.

In the sixth century BC two reform movements arose against the gross discrimination of the prevailing faith: Buddhism and Jainism. Outside India Buddhism is widespread, but inside India it has virtually disappeared. Jainism is limited to about two million people in India. They carry weight, for they enjoy a good reputation and many of them hold prominent positions.

Buddhism Buddhists speak of rebirth rather than reincarnation. Buddhism teaches that Buddha himself was able to remember his previous lives, and instructed those who wanted to remember. Hinduism and Buddhism both believe in the workings of karma, and in *samsara*: the virtually endless repetition of lives with an illusion of personal existence until *moksha*, the liberation from all this, is attained. Some Buddhists entertain the view that a person's last thoughts strongly influence his next life and, at least, largely determine his surroundings after death, as the *Tibetan Book of Death* teaches, for example.

The main difference from the Hindu views on reincarnation is the Buddhist doctrine of *anatta*, which holds that, although characteristics of the deceased are transmitted to the life of a new person, the personal entity itself is discontinued. Thus, the soul lacks a permanent self; there is no *atman*. Therefore the doctrine is called *an-atman* or *an-atta*. The usual analogy is the flame of one candle lighting another candle. There is continuity, but no identity. A modem variant is the analogy of a billiard ball knocking against another billiard ball and passing on its momentum, without the two balls being the same. The *anatta*-doctrine is related to the abolition of the caste system in Buddhism.

The *anatta*-doctrine is found particularly in Theravada Buddhism. As already mentioned, this doctrine is officially adhered to in Burma, while the lay people believe in reincarnation proper, recurrent cases of recollection nourishing this belief.

According to some Tibetan Buddhists, rebirth occurs immediately. A Tibetan specialty is the reincarnation of lamas, called *sprul-sku*. Here, the entity is preserved because the disintegration of the personality is counteracted. This requires will power and psychic strength. People with unfinished missions sometimes return in this way. Since the fifteenth century, the reincarnations of important lamas have been identified according to fixed oracle and divination procedures.

Probably the best available exposition of reincarnation views in Tibetan Buddhism is the book by Lati Rinbochay and Jeffrey Hopkins (1979). The foreword and the preface state clearly the basic beliefs. It is clear that karma is less important than the attitude just before death. Their lucid exposition in plain language reveals how much superstition and shallow psychology the Tibetan belief contains. When less virtuous people die, they start to lose warmth from the top of the body, while more virtuous persons start to lose warmth from the feet. If a wish is not granted, people get angry. Apparently nobody is ever just sad and disappointed. If you lost considerable warmth owing to an illness, you desire warmth and so you go to a hot hell. Why not to a warm heaven? Because you desired something. A poor unfortunate dying of cold in Bergen Belsen will end up in a hell, because he or she desired some warmth. Other Buddhist texts abound with the same narrow-minded and infantile horror stories as in other religions. If somebody is doing the wrong things, 'he will be born again and again, born either blind, dull-witted, dumb, or as an outcast, always living in misery, always a victim of abuse. He will become a hermaphrodite or a eunuch, or be born in lifelong slavery. He [may also] become a woman, a dog, a pig, an ass, a camel or a poisonous snake, and [thus] be unable to put the Buddha's teachings into practice' (Willson 1984: 15). I wonder what happens to a woman who is a victim of abuse, and therefore must be doing wrong things because she cannot put the Buddha's teaching into practice. Note that the list implies metempsychosis. Buddhist ideas are as diverse and inconsistent as in any other religion.

Clericalism in Tibet has also led to a ritualisation of views on reincarnation and karma. It is not the quality of the present life which determines the next life, but the fulfilment or neglect of prescribed rituals. Even accidentally forgetting, just once, to give one of the holy statues its bowl of water during the daily water offerings at the family chapel will result in poverty in the next life. When a parrot repeats the mantram '*Om Mane Padme Hum*', even without understanding its meaning, it will return as a higher form of life (Rato 1977: 9–12).

Vicky Mackenzie (1995) reports on the life of Lama Yeshe, his death in 1984 and the discovery of his rebirth as Osel Hita Torres in Spain in 1985. The book is credible and well-written, though many details betray that we are here in the area of religion and so of special feelings, special people and special events. Why would one return so quickly, be recognised and continue in the same vein? The answer given is: out of compassion with all living beings here. When a patient in a regression answers like this, we know what to look for: guilt feelings from lives of power, violence and suppression. Maybe lamas should regress to the lifetimes before they became lamas.

Mahayana Buddhism teaches the coming of the Bodhisattvas. Bodhisattvas are people who have attained Nirvana and so are not obliged to return into a body any more but do so anyway out of compassion for still-suffering humanity. The doctrine of the return of great teachers is found in many religions, for example among the Celts, as mentioned before. We will come across other examples. Some Buddhist doctrines elaborate this idea into a whole pantheon of existing and future Bodhisattvas who become Buddha one by one according to a fixed schedule. This turns the highest compassion into a vehicle of superhuman machinery rather than a human experience.

Jainism Like Buddhism and Hinduism, Jainism knows *samsara* and *moksha*. The main difference from the other two religions is the view that karma is solely dependent on actual consequences of acts, not on the moral intent. To cause somebody's death unintentionally produces the same karma as to murder him in cold blood or blind passion. So Jainists are very conscientious. They practise *ahimsa*, complete pacifism, strict vegetarianism and unremitting service. According to Jainism, before *moksha* is attained, the soul can only exist in a body. So, after death, it immediately attaches itself to the conception of a child and is reborn after nine months. When people recall past lives with an intermission longer than nine months, this is interpreted as a forgotten in-between life as in a child who died young.

Views on reincarnation in Confucianism, Taoism and Shintoism are rare. Buddhism introduced rebirth into China, where it became part of folk religion.

THE CLASSICAL CULTURES

Egypt and Babylon We have little historical evidence for a belief in reincarnation in Egypt. The Egyptians thought that long ago the gods had departed and sinful spirits had remained behind who had to do penance for their sins in human bodies. According to Herodotus, the Egyptians were the first to believe in an immortal soul. He thought that the Egyptians were the first to teach metempsychosis. After death the soul would traverse all kinds of land, sea and air animals before it would return in a human body. Probably Herodotus mistook Pythagorean thoughts for Egyptian (Passian 1985: 19). But the Egyptians did teach that the soul could return. This would be in the original body, if it had been properly mummified. An intact mummy guaranteed a future domicile and also prevented the need for lower incarnations during the interval.

We have no indications of Babylonian beliefs in reincarnation.

Greece The Greek views on reincarnation come from the Orphic mysteries, which, again according to Herodotus, originally came from Egypt. However, the Orphic idea of the wheel of birth and death, where the soul is periodically caught in a body and strives towards deliverance, is closer to the classical Indian philosophy than to Egyptian thinking. The Orphic doctrine held that people consist of a small divine element and a large, bad, Titan element. Humans must learn to eliminate the Titan element inside them. This entails many reincarnations from which, ultimately, deliverance is possible. Reward and punishment for a life come in the next human or animal incarnations. The Orphic mysteries inspired the Elysian mysteries, in turn influencing Pindar among others. Pindar saw our present life as reward or punishment for the intermission. Reincarnation would take place after eight years.

A second source of Greek views on reincarnation was the Pythagoreans. Like his teacher Pherekydes, Pythagoras taught reincarnation, following presumably the Phoenicians, the Chaldeans and the Egyptians. The ability to recall past lives was regarded as a gift from Hermes. Allegedly, Pythagoras recalled his past lives, and therefore was called Mnesarchides. His previous lifetimes were, among others, Aethalides and Euphorbus, who fought at Troy.

According to Ovid, Pythagoras taught that good animals may become humans, and bad humans may become animals. After many animal incarnations, we may return as a human. This differs from the usual metempsychotic supposition that animal and human incarnations may alternate.

Hierokles taught that a human could never reincarnate as an animal or plant, but always incarnated as a human. Empedocles, a pupil of Pythagoras, taught that humans were originally semi-gods who had sinned. During 30,000 seasons they had to wander through all kinds of male and female lifetimes.

Plato gave reincarnation thinking new impulses, though he did not elaborate on it. Plato's *Phaedo* alleges that Socrates, under Orphic and Pythagorean influence, taught reincarnation. The impurities of the soul are a heavy burden, so the soul again and again feels itself drawn towards the earth.' Sensuous people blemish their soul and so incarnate more quickly. Plato saw the human capacity to know the truth as evidence for pre-existence, a new argument in views on reincarnation.

Further, he pointed to the many cycles in nature. In *Meno* in particular, Plato accounts for knowledge without previous learning by past lives. *Phaedrus* may be interpreted as containing views on reincarnation and karmic laws. In *The Republic* Plato describes encounters between arriving and departing souls. The arriving souls see the diverse workings of the universal law. Based on these examples and their own previous experience, they choose their life with all the consequences 'before the throne of necessity'. Then, they receive a draught of forgetfulness and enter life. Each returning soul chooses its destiny in life; character decides choice, fate decides the sequence.

Aristotle only teaches reincarnation in his early work *Eudemus*. Later he abandons the idea of reincarnation. His writings about the soul only contain indications of a belief in pre-existence.

In the last century before Christ, classical belief in reincarnation is at its lowest ebb. Stoic and Epicurean views predominate. Cicero, converting from agnosticism to Platonism, re-embraces the belief in reincarnation. He sees life as a punishment for sins in past lives. Important people contribute to society because they unconsciously sense that they will return to it once more. The legendary Apollonius of Tyana learned the reincarnation doctrine from Iarchas in Kashmir. Allegedly, in a previous incarnation as first mate on an Egyptian ship he had refused to deliver the boat into the hands of pirates. Plutarch considers people as beings wandering from life to life. According to him there are higher spirits ('genii') who only incarnate when they have done something wrong, particularly when they have had a bad influence on incarnated people.

The Neoplatonists, especially of the Alexandrian school, again pick up the ideas of reincarnation and elaborate them. There has been an involution: because of pride and a false desire for independence, our souls have ended up in the difficult and evil world we inhabit now. Plotinus (204–270), the architect of a Neoplatonism that resembles Christian ideas, says: 'Souls have free choice. They pass through different existences. What we come across today is the result of what we did yesterday. This is the law of development, the only law that explains divine providence' (Passian 1985).

According to Plotinus, our physical world is the least divine, but it is a good place to learn. Carelessness and obduracy cause us to be lost and imprisoned in the sensual limitations of physical existence. We tend to pursue lower desires and to wield power. However, in doing so, we gain experience and develop talents we can only develop in physical existence. In the end, we return to our original state, but now with all the experience and knowledge we acquired while incarnated. Throughout all our lifetimes a part of our soul remains itself, untouched, divine. Our periodic sojourns in the material state make us well aware of the perfection of the spiritual state. Our experiences with evil make us value the good. Humans may incarnate as animals. Practising civil virtues (compare with *dharma*) and becoming humane (compare with *artha* and *dharma*) allows us to return as humans. Living sensually makes us return as animals. Irresponsibility makes us return as a domestic animal. Devotion to evil makes us return as a ferocious animal; devotion to lust or gluttony makes us return as sensuous or voracious animals. Abuse of the senses makes us return as plants. Specific characteristics, therefore, lead to incarnations as specific kinds of animals. People who devoted themselves too much to music, but otherwise lived purely, return as songbirds. Tyrants return as eagles, and those who speak frivolously of divine subjects return as soaring birds. This is true allegorical thinking, as in many metempsychotic views. Neoplatonists like Proclus of Syria, however, declared that humans always return as humans, and animals always as animals.

JUDAISM, CHRISTIANITY AND ISLAM

Judaism At first sight, Judaism has few indications of a belief in reincarnation, but strong indications, for example in the Old Testament, of a belief in pre-existence. Reincarnation may often be implied or presumed as a common idea. In the time of Jesus, the Sadducees were strictly materialists, the Essenes believed in pre-existence, and the Pharisees believed that people are either reborn or destroy themselves in the underworld. The Pharisaic notion of reincarnation existed up until the ninth century. Since the eighth century the Karaite Jews have believed in reincarnation.

According to some Jewish thinkers, the number of incarnations is usually limited to three. Philo Judaeus mixes Platonic and Stoic ideas. He says that souls in a mortal body pick up earthly inclinations such as eagerness to learn. God is necessary for human deliverance. The legendary Simon Magus saw Helen of Troy returned in Mary Magdalene. The Samaritans held the doctrine of Taheb, according to which Adam reincarnated as Seth, Noah, Abraham and Moses. But doctrines that great leaders and teachers may return do not imply that common people normally reincarnate. Present Jewry knows two reincarnation traditions: within the *sephardim* the Cabbula, within the *ashkenazim* Chassidism. Jewish thinking contains four different ideas about the continuity of the soul (Gershom 1992):

1 survival by offspring;
2 physical resurrection;
3 an immortal soul in heaven;
4 reincarnation.

These ideas do not exclude each other and many Jews believe in combinations. According to David Gershom (1992), the *Bahir*, a book that is ascribed to the wise Talmudic rabbi, Nechunja Ben Ha-Kana from the second century, uses the biblical concept of 'generations' to mean 'incarnations'. The Covenant on Mount Sinai of the Lord with all generations (read all incarnations) then takes on a whole different meaning. This interpretation of 'incarnations' for 'generations' can also be found in the *Zohar*, a better-known cabbalistic text from about one century after the *Bahir*.

The *Bahir* refers in several other passages to reincarnation, as in:

> *Why has one just man a good life and another just man a bad life? Because the (other) just man was evil before and is now being punished. Is someone then being punished for deeds from childhood? Did not rabbi Shimon say that the Highest Court does not mete out punishment before one is twenty years of age? Rabbi Rachunaj said: 'I do not speak about the present life, but about what one has been already, in a previous life.'*

These words resemble a question asked of Jesus in the Gospel of John: 'Rabbi, who did sin, this man or his parents, as he was born blind?' Jesus and rabbi Nechunja were almost contemporaries. Gershom wonders if they might have studied the same esoteric doctrines.

All Chassidic Jews believe in reincarnation. The Loebavitsch version of the Chassidic prayer book even contains an evening prayer that forgives 'everyone who annoyed or angered me in this incarnation or in another' (Gershom 1992). The Chassidim believe that people who died prematurely get a supplementary lifetime. Pious Jews may be reborn among the heathens to promote understanding for Jews and help Jews.

Christianity Various passages in the New Testament indicate pre-existence and some appear to indicate reincarnation. The best-known example is John the Baptist, who is regarded as the returned Elijah. Such passages are found especially in Mark, but also in Matthew, Luke and John. John 9: 1–3 and John 17: 24 are seen as indications of a belief in reincarnation. Early Christianity seems to have been divided on the subject. Many church fathers accepted at least pre-existence. Gnostics like Justin the Martyr accepted reincarnation, but did consider recall of past lives impossible. According to him, people who were too unworthy to receive Christ would return as wild animals.

Apparently, Origen considered the gnostic pro-reincarnation arguments sound and also pointed to the well-known example of Elijah and John. Further, he made pre-existence of the soul seem plausible. Later propagandists of reincarnation saw his expositions as pro-reincarnation arguments. Because the Council of Constantinople condemned Origen's doctrines in the year 553, some modern gnostics like Annie Besant regard this year as the date when the reincarnation doctrine was exorcised from Christian thought. This view is questionable, to say the least.

The Second Council of Constantinople in 553 tried to resolve the difficulties arising from the Council of Chalcedon in 451, especially with the question of whether Christ had one or two natures. The Council of Constantinople concurred with the imperial politics of Justinian, who was trying to gain control over the West, and so wanted to diminish the theological discord between East and West. He put pressure on the Council. On 5 May, 553,165 bishops gathered under the chairmanship of Eutychius, the patriarch of Constantinople. The then Pope, Virgil, opposed this and sought refuge in a church. In his absence, the Council condemned the double nature (one of Origen's doctrines) confirmed by the Council of Chalcedon. The Pope continued to resist until 8 December 553, but finally yielded and ratified the Council's resolution on 23 February 554. With this, the unity of the two natures in Christ became the church's official doctrine. A secondary subject of the Council was the ratification of earlier condemnations of a number of Origen's views. It is impossible to ascertain the views at stake, but the doctrine of pre-existence was probably among them. The Western church rejected the Second Council of Constantinople. In Africa the imperial troops forced acceptance. The bishops of northern Italy distanced themselves from Rome and refused to acknowledge the Pope's ratification. They found support in Spain and France. The whole Council became irrelevant because of the Islamic conquest of most Monophysitic provinces.

The proposition that the church abjured the doctrine of reincarnation in 553 is untenable:

- It remains unclear which of Origen's doctrines were at stake. Almost certainly, they were about pre-existence, not about reincarnation. Origen taught, for example, that the various circumstances in people's lives were the result of sins they had committed during their spiritual pre-existence. The existence of the body was a purification from the sins committed during pre-existence.
- The condemnation of Origen's opinions was only a secondary subject for discussion.
- The Council was about ratification of earlier condemnations.
- Large parts of the church rejected the Council.

The doctrine of reincarnation has played no significant role in the development of Christianity. According to Guirdham (1974), the Cathars' belief in reincarnation was one of the causes of the church's enmity. In the twentieth century, a number of Christian treatises argue that reincarnation does not contradict Christian beliefs. A recent contribution is by Jan-Erik Sigdell (2001). In contrast, many theologians judge reincarnation to be an assault on Christianity. One of the first books in this vein is by Rosenberg (1952), who considers reincarnation to be a false Asian doctrine. Rosenberg knows a lot about reincarnation in the Cabbala. The most balanced treatment of this subject is by Christopher Bache (1990).

Islam Islam does not contain explicit belief in reincarnation, though a few Muslim sects believe in it. Several passages in the Qur'an could be interpreted in this way, but they could as well refer to spiritual rebirth. Most Muslims who believe in reincarnation are among the Shi'ites in West Asia. They do not think that what we do in one life has any effect on what happens to us in another. Instead they believe that we pass through a succession of lives in different circumstances, in each of which lives we must strive our best for moral perfection. Whether we succeed or fail in one life has no effect on our condition in a later one. Ultimately, however, on the Day of Judgment, the books of our actions are examined, the accounts of good and bad deeds summed up, and, according to the reckoning, God assigns us to Heaven or Hell for eternity (Stevenson 1987: 35).

Some Muslims think that after death the human soul may pass into an animal or into another person, depending on its state. Because a human soul may end up in an animal after death, there is the widespread custom of buying captive birds to set them free because the souls of dead people could be in them – a practice that created the bird-catching business. For the same reason, the Boras in Hindustan are vegetarians.

The Druses, a sect that is not purely Islamic, assume an immediate rebirth. The Jainists believe that upon death the soul is immediately connected to the conception of a new child and is reborn nine months later. The Druses, however, believe that the soul immediately returns in a child being born. Because of this immediate transition, great importance is attached to the last thoughts of the dying person, since they could have a strong influence on the new beginning. Of course, all instances of past-life recall have intermission periods. The Druses, too, explain these by forgotten short lives in between. They assume they are a closed incarnation group, and always incarnate as Druses because they are a chosen people (heard this before?). The number of Druse souls is therefore stable. When many people die, by war, famine or pestilence, the same number are not immediately reborn. The Druses account for this by a waiting place, somewhere in China. Understandably, they do regard recall cases critically.

GNOSTIC, MYSTIC AND ESOTERIC MOVEMENTS

Christianity and Judaism, as well as Islam, have gnostic movements. Gnosticism contains elements from the doctrines of Zoroaster, transmitted in Mithraism and Manichaeism. According to Zoroaster, the immortal soul enters this world for a short period, to gain experience. The soul may have descended from higher spheres or may be working its way up from a lower sphere. Contrasting with Indian ideas of about 8,400,000 incarnations, Persian views of reincarnation assume a small number of lives since they consider advance and decline of the soul as self-reinforcing processes. Good behaviour in one life eases good behaviour in the next. Misbehaviour in one life eases misbehaviour in the next. In a few lifetimes we either do not need to come back, or we cannot any more. Such Christian groups as the Paulicians, the Priscillians, the Bogomiles and the Cathars had similar ideas. Another common source is the ancient Orphic mysteries, which became known as the Hermetic tradition in the Hellenic world through Pythagoras, especially among the Neoplatonists. This tradition indisputably included reincarnation. According to Iranaeus, reincarnation was the central idea of the first gnostics. He refers to Simon Magus and to the strong Zoroastrian traditions in Gnosticism. He expounds the gnostic views that we return to gain rich experience, to compensate for guilt and to purify and improve ourselves. According to Iranaeus, the gnostics also taught that people not attaining gnosis would return as animals. Two pretty conflicting views, though.

The Sufi Jalal-ud-din-Rumi taught the Indian doctrine that the human soul originally incarnates in minerals, and develops via plant, animal and human lives into an angel and upwards. The Ismaelites, a Sufi group, distinguished *tanasukh*, the normal reincarnation, *rijat*, the return of spiritual leaders, and *hukul* or *burut*, the systematic, periodic return of those who have attained perfection. They thought Krishna returned as Buddha, and later as Mohammed.

The esoteric Jewish doctrine of the Cabbala involves reincarnation. The earlier cabbalistic texts had allusions to reincarnation only understandable by initiates. In the fourteenth century the kabala became more explicit. At first, reincarnation was called in Hebrew *ha'taka* (transport) or *ibbur* (impregnation). The thirteenth century *Zohar* calls reincarnation *gilgul*, which has remained the standard Hebrew term to this day. Originally, *gilgul* and *ibbur* meant the same. At the end of the fourteenth century, *ibbur* began to denote the entrance of a soul into someone else's body, a benign kind of possession. An *ibbur* was usually done for a good purpose, and the visiting soul would stay for a limited time to accomplish a specific mission. A soul who had fulfilled all 613 commandments of the Tora except one, could be 'channelled' as *ibbur* to fulfil the last *mitswa*. After finishing this mission, the *ibbur* would return to the spiritual world. This differs from a *dibbuk*, an evil soul that invades someone else's body and has to be exorcised. *Gilgul* acquired the specific meaning of being reborn in a new body.

Cabbalists interpreted *gilgul* quite differently and did not agree who returns and how often. The *Bahir* writes that reincarnation can go on for a thousand generations, meaning a thousand incarnations. Rabbi Yitzchak Luria, the sixteenth-century mystic, believed most souls returned only three or four times. This is the old difference between the Indian and the Persian views on reincarnation.

How common was the Cabbala in the Middle Ages? That is difficult to determine as the Cabbala was in practice hardly distinguishable from orthodox Judaism. A cabbalist and a non-cabbalist could sing the same liturgy, but experience it completely differently. The Cabbala was accessible only to the most learned rabbis. The esoteric symbolism would incite the uninformed laymen to heresies and common people could try to use it for magic or conjuring the spirits. The rabbis believed only holy people should do that. Selection was severe and often students had to swear secrecy. Only after the invention of book printing was the Cabbala openly studied and practised.

The cabbalist writers clearly do believe in pre-existence. The soul chooses a body. If it lives well and purifies itself, it will be absorbed in God in the afterlife. For many, one life suffices. Others need two or three lifetimes. An interesting detail is that unpleasant habits like stinginess and pettiness lead to a next life as a woman. Probably such writers were impractical and unbusinesslike men, driving their wives crazy. Anyway, what would happen to stingy and petty women?

An important argument for cabbalists believing in reincarnation was the impossibility of fulfilling all 613 *mitzvoth*. According to Gershom Scholem, the idea of transmigration gradually expanded drastically from a punishment for some specific sins to a general rule for all souls of Israel, and later all humans, and, in its widest sense, all of Creation (Gershom 1992). At long last, all people will ascend, even women. Then the dark angels will get their turn to find their chastening and purification in this world.

The Cabbala has many examples of reincarnations of Jewish leaders. Cain reincarnated as Jethro, Abel as Moses, Japhet as Samson. Adam returned as David, and in the future will return as the Mesjicha, the Messiah.

MODERN WESTERN HISTORY

The idea of reincarnation returned to the West with the revival of Platonism and Neoplatonism, succeeding the medieval world-view dominated by Aristotle. In 1439 George Gemisthos Pletho from Mithra visited Cosimo de Medici in Florence. This resulted in the founding of what became known as the Platonic Academy. The revival of Platonism emanated from this academy, and with it came related Hermetic, Pythagorean and Cabbalistic ideas. Associated with this Platonic and Neoplatonist revival are names such as Nicholas of Cusa, Trithemius of Spondheim, Paracelsus, Cornelius Agrippa and the German humanist Reuchlin, who influenced Melanchthon.

In the Netherlands, the Neoplatonic Van Helmont argued in 1690 that reincarnation means maturation and gradual redemption, until we build up a spiritual body that liberates us from reincarnation and has us partake in the ascension of Christ. He adds pungent details, such as that perjurers will be reborn forty times as bastards. What becomes of perjuring bastards he doesn't tell, but undoubtedly it is extremely unpleasant.

In his monad doctrine, Giordano Bruno offered a personal and abstract view of reincarnation. A monad is a microcosmic element, proceeding through all forms of life in an infinite number of worlds in all but endless cycles. Some of these worlds are inhabited, some further developed than ours. The idea of reincarnation on other planets is brought up here for the first time. Bruno's ideas were later to influence Leibniz, who also regarded the soul as a microcosmic monad. Death is just a dramatic instance of sleep, leaving behind our heavier body. A portion of our personality remains. Reincarnation is more metamorphosis than transmigration. According to Leibniz, we retain identity throughout our incarnations.

The Enlightenment and its accompanying deism toy with many Greek, Roman, and Eastern ideas, probably to get away from prevailing religious dogmas. Benjamin Franklin believed that no human experience is lost and that, as he said, new editions will keep coming out, with small improvements on the previous ones. Frederick the Great of Prussia was convinced that our best part remains and returns. He suspected he would not return as a king, but was sure he would lead another active life – and hoped he would meet less ingratitude. Following Bruno, Kant toyed with the idea that reincarnation could take place on other planets, via the sun to ever further and colder planets. Johann Bode and Louis Figuier believed just the opposite: human souls begin on cold planets and evolve towards ever warmer ones.

During the German Enlightenment in particular, many prominent men, such as Lessing, Von Herder and Goethe believed in reincarnation. Goethe believed he had lived at least a thousand times before, and was likely to return another thousand times. He regarded death essentially as a recurrent purge. He characterised man as a dialogue between God and Nature, and said that on other planets a higher and more profound dialogue could undoubtedly take place. Goethe believed he had been married to Frau Von Stein in a previous life and was convinced he had lived as a Roman before the Emperor Hadrian.

Charles Fourier believed that reincarnation would continue until the end of this earth, and that we would then reincarnate all together on a new planet.

Arthur Schopenhauer believed that primarily the human will reincarnates. During the intermission the will sleeps. We need to forget our previous lives to start anew, clean and refreshed. Only Buddha had clear recollections of his past lives. Schopenhauer believed in the Buddhist view of karma. Furthermore, he was convinced that in future lives we will again meet people we know now. This is hard to reconcile with the idea that individuals do not reincarnate and that only the will continues (whatever that may mean).

There are many further names of believers, such as Swedenborg, William Blake, Schiller, Mazzini, Herman Melville, Leo Tolstoy, Paul Gauguin, Arthur Conan Doyle, Gustav Mahler, etc., etc.; then, a large number of Americans from the beginning of the nineteenth century. More recent figures are David Lloyd George, Henry Ford, Rudyard Kipling, Jean Sibelius (who believed that millions of years ago he had been incarnated in swans and wild geese) and General Patton. Books seeking to make reincarnation plausible like to quote such famous people.

PROVISIONAL OVERVIEW

There is no such thing as the belief in reincarnation. Ideas about reincarnation are extremely diverse and contradictory, their only common thread being the view that after death people can, or must or want to return as humans. What are the major differences? Some see reincarnation in terms of natural laws, others in terms of reward or punishment, others again in terms of development. Return may be punishment for neglecting ritual, church obligations and so on. Believing in reincarnation may lead to the same kind of fatalism as the belief that someone else has suffered for our (even as yet uncommitted) sins. Reincarnation theories, like Christian and other religious ideas, are susceptible to being used in spiritual intimidation and blackmail.

A second difference lies in the number of reincarnations: is it a few, some hundreds or the Indian number, 8,400,000? To what extent do past lives influence the present life, and what are the causes of such an influence? Then again, what can be said about intermission? Or is there immediate reincarnation? And, if so, is it at birth or during conception? People do speculate and fantasise a lot. Reincarnation is yet another fertile subject.

FURTHER READING

The most important and available source book is *Reincarnation: the Phoenix Fire Mystery* by Head and Cranston (1977), which is the main source for this chapter. Originally published in 1961, it is first-rate, extensive and with many exact quotes; the only possible objections are that it is less complete than it suggests, somewhat neglecting non-English sources, and that it overestimates the role of theosophy. Another excellent book, unfortunately hardly available, is *La Réincarnation* by Bertholet (1949). His discussion of Eastern and classical thought is especially extensive and careful. Bertholet also discusses modern approaches including Kardec, experimental literature such as de Rochas, and other spiritist and parapsychological works His personal views are apparent only in a sometimes overly serious treatment of relatively unimportant sources. However, the extent of his reading is impressive, his discussion is wide and thorough, and he had more access to French works than Head and Cranston. For the real student, his work is a must. Another good French book is *La Réincarnation des Ames selon les Traditions Orientales et Occidentales* by des Georges (1966).

Other works are of lesser quality or more limited scope. One of the first books in this area is by E.D. Walker (1888), mostly containing reincarnation thoughts by literary men – witness the broad collection of included poems. Eva Martin's book *The Ring of Return: An anthology of references to reincarnation and spiritual evolution: from prose and poetry of all ages* (1927) has been reprinted and is a valuable predecessor to *The Phoenix Fire Mystery*. Martin quotes widely from poetry and other literature, and in this respect is halfway between Walker, and Head and Cranston. Many more or less theosophical books contain historical chapters (Atkinson 1908; Van Ginkel 1917).

An informative and extensive survey of German literature is given by Emil Bock (1932). While Walker is a theosophist thinker, Bock is an anthroposophist convert: Germans seem to have a patent on reincarnation, and all writers herald Rudolf Steiner. Eckhart (1937) published a work about reincarnation beliefs among the ancient Germans. Buddhist ideas about reincarnation are discussed by Alexandra David-Neel (1961), who writes many interesting things especially about Tibet, and by de Silva (1968), and in the first part of the book by Francis Story (1975). A few interesting remarks about Tibet can be found in Rato Khyongla Nawang Losang (1977). Mullin (1986) is good complement to Lati Rinpochay and Jeffrey Hopkins, *Death, Intermediate State and Rebirth in Tibetan Buddhism* (1979). Rinpochay and Hopkins offer more about Buddhist theory and Mullin more about Buddhist practices.

An excellent source of information about ideas in primitive cultures about the soul–body relationship is *Vehicles of Consciousness* by Poortman (1978). The theosophical background of the author focuses his interest without diminishing his scholarship.

Among others, James Pryse (1909) asserts that the New Testament contains reincarnation. The arguments do not convince me, though I am not a theologian or a philologist. Other books that look at reincarnation from a Christian perspective are Hampton (1925), Wilson (1936), MacGregor (1978) and Miranda (1981). De Arteaga (1983) is a Christian who looks critically at regressions: when strictly supervised by a Christian the recall comes from the Holy Ghost, but usually it is demonically inspired. Further books are by Howe (1987), Sigdell (2001), Bowen (n.d.) and McDermit (n.d.). Especially recommended is Bache (1990) for his scholarship, his common sense and his broadmindedness.

Three

ESOTERICISTS ON
REINCARNATION

Many of us want to know for sure how things really are, to escape from doubt into true, deep knowledge. The idea that we can develop our mind to perceive the higher truths of life, we may call *gnosticism*. How can we develop such a gnostic mind? By consulting those who went that way before us. Esoteric knowledge is not publicly available or even understandable, and comes from people who have been enlightened or initiated or divinely inspired. Literature is gnostic if written by people who have gained access to an inner source of knowledge. A gnostic does not believe in swallowing somebody else's opinions (at best second-hand knowledge) but in gaining personal access to the source of immediate knowledge (first-hand knowledge). If we develop sufficiently our inner mind, we may arrive at the truth on our own. Technically speaking, this implies a profound development of our intuition, and a limitation of our intellect to elaborate what we have discovered intuitively. Gnostics value their inner insights above traditional revelations, but also above sensory evidence and common-sense reasoning.

What gnostics think is always similar to what other gnostics think, yet always different. Gnostics exhort us to use their concepts and recipes to acquire personal first-hand knowledge, and find out for ourselves what the gnostic master has already found out. As a result of this paradox, I view all gnostic literature as propaganda. It would seem that gnostics are led by higher intuition, not by observation and intellect. Theosophy and especially anthroposophy are gnostic, like the views of other self-professed esoteric writers (among many others, Lewis Spence and Max Heindel in America). They discourage research into past-life phenomena, developing instead reincarnation theories based on the insights and inner experiences acquired by approved mystics, occultists and initiates. These form the foundation for the continual reinterpretation of existing gnostic concepts and literature. Modern gnostics talk about the pituitary gland and the endocrine system, about electromagnetic force fields, frequencies or natural evolution, but they add a spiritual twist to them. Often they suggest that modern science only proves what they or their precursors have known all along.

The most important modern gnostic movement is the theosophy of Helena Blavatsky. Theosophy spawned a great number of other gnostic schools. Many called themselves theosophical, and many others worked under their own, often fancy names. One such school, probably the most serious, is Rudolf Steiner's anthroposophy, with its own doctrines of reincarnation and karma. The theosophical doctrine of karma and reincarnation has a broad cosmic perspective of simultaneous involution and evolution, with elaborated but abstract views on incarnation and excarnation. Theosophy demonstrates the inspiring but confused and rambling character of gnostic literature, although it compares favourably with most related products. This chapter elaborates theosophical and anthroposophical views, as they have been the most influential – and probably still are. Other esotericists are mentioned at the end more briefly.

THEOSOPHY

The theosophists criticised Allan Kardec for neglecting the true nature and character of the intermission between lives, and lacking a clear karma doctrine as well as an explanatory philosophy. Apparently, the theosophists regard their views on *devachan*, the state between lives, their karma doctrine and their general occult philosophy as essential. In the development of theosophy, its ideas about reincarnation changed gradually but sweepingly, and some ideas have remained vague and somewhat contradictory.

Blavatsky believed in *anatta*, rather than in reincarnation. In volume I of *Isis Unveiled* she writes that reincarnation in nature is the exception rather than the rule, applying to the aborted, the stillborn, idiots and to a Messiah. Rising from death after the soul has left the body is just as impossible as reincarnation, with the former exceptions. In volume II she writes that Plato, Anaxagoras, Pythagoras and the Eleatic schools of Greece, just as the Chaldean priests, taught transmigration only in the sense of the soul moving from one sphere to another after death (Passian 1985). In an interview about life after death Blavatsky says that with unbelieving materialists the personality is usually completely destroyed after death. This means as little for the soul as it means for a wood to lose one tree (*Reincarnation* 1987: 28), or as it means for a train traveller to have slept for part of the journey (1987: 35). She explains the fact that many people do not understand her (1987: 24) by: 'But such is the materialism of the age that the more we explain, the less people seem capable of understanding what we say.'

THE HIGHER AND LOWER SELF: INDIVIDUALITY AND PERSONALITY

Following classic Indian views, theosophists believe in rhythmic world manifestations, *manvantaras*, alternated with periods of cosmic sleep, *pralayas*. When a *manvantara* begins, the elementary individual spirits, called *monads* after Leibniz, awaken. They are willing to endure the trying exertions of the physical universe. They learn to become creators themselves in matter, ultimately to become co-creators of the next universe. Monads develop gradually. They start with many mineral lifetimes, and they gradually ascend, via plant and animal lives, to human lives. This development is an involution as well as an evolution. The monad begins as a spiritual being, far removed from its physical counterpart. As this physical counterpart gradually evolves into a vehicle of consciousness and into a human being, the monad gradually involves, to inhabit and to meld into the person with his physical body, and so, finally gains self-consciousness.

Each great *manvantara* consists of smaller cycles in which manifestation and rest periods alternate. At the beginning of smaller *manvantaras* planets come into being where the monads can take the next step in their evolution. Our present humankind went through less dense material conditions in its previous mineral, plant and animal stages of monadic evolution. The human body is prepared from the higher mammals. Before the monad descends for the first time in a human body, it incarnates a few times in one of the highest animals: an elephant, a monkey (a degenerate product from cross-breeding between humans and animals), a dog, a cat or a horse.

Once we have become human, we continue our development under our own responsibility. Ultimately, we will return to our spiritual origin, but now self-aware and with a fully evolved body. From where we are now, our further evolution is toilsome, with the ever-present risk of entanglement in matter or in our ego. Our personal will as incarnated human beings is both a seduction and a cardinal result of evolution.

The laws of reincarnation and karma hold for all evolving beings in an evolving universe. Reincarnation is also a *manvantara–pralaya* rhythm of physical and spiritual lives. At the present degree of material density these transitions imply real birth and death. We have five drives to rebirth:

- the attraction of the earth
- our attachment to material objects and physical conditions
- our karma
- our desire for external impressions to reinforce self-awareness
- our desire for self-expression in the material world (*trishna*).

The first two drives are material motives, and the last two egocentric motives. Attachment to material objects and physical conditions is psychological. Karma is a natural law.

In the theosophical vision the total number of lives is immense. On each planetary cycle we have many thousands of incarnations. According to Sinnett (1883: 61), we have had almost 800 incarnations so far on our planet, and we need many more to attain perfection in this world, becoming members of the universal brotherhood, helpers and teachers for the rest of humanity. Ultimately, we attain *nirvana* as a personal *pralaya*. But the golden thread of individuality remains, and afterwards we will progress further.

Compared to classic Hinduism, theosophy regards the wheel of rebirth less as continuous suffering from which to seek release, and more as planned development under our own responsibility, and so also subject to our capriciousness. But this capriciousness is a fact of evolution. The general plan entails opportunities to deviate from the plan.

Theosophy speaks of the higher self, the monad, going through all lifetimes; and of the lower self, the emanation or projection of the higher self that differs in each life. The lower self has a quasi-independent consciousness, connected with the body. The relationship between the higher self and the lower self is like that of an actor and the role he is playing. Initiation strengthens and secures the relationship.

The human microcosm has seven manifestations or bodies: *atma, budhhi, manas,* the mental body, the astral body, the etheric body and the physical body. The higher self, the real individuality, consists of *atma, budhhi* and *manas. Manas* is the real ego, in its manifestation also called the causal body. The personality, the lower self, is the astral soul, deceasing after each incarnation in the astral field of *kamaloka*. The mental, astral, etheric and physical bodies each contain indestructible elements, the 'permanent atoms'. These atoms and the aura register the experience of each life.

The theosophists locate the lower self in the mental, the astral, the etheric or the physical body. They mention astral–etheric or etheric–physical phenomena. *Budhhi* is the second vehicle of the microcosm, but the buddhic web permeates the etheric body, the sixth vehicle, and maintains all seven bodies. This is, at the least, a confusing use of words.

The earliest literature claims that each personality dissolves completely. Blavatsky was sure that we, the way we are here and now as living persons, will die and never return (1886). In the case of an unnatural death, such as an abortion, an early childhood death, an accident or a murder, or in the case of idiocy, rebirth may occur before the lower self has dissolved in *kamaloka*. The more we forget our original spiritual nature, the less is the connection between lower and higher self. Only initiates may retain their personalities.

FROM DEATH TO REBIRTH

From *buddhi*, the second vehicle, a web of life threads extends into the etheric body and reaches out into the physical body. At death these life threads withdraw and wrap themselves around a core in the heart into a flame of gold and purple. Then they go to the third cerebral cavity and, together with the permanent atom and the life flame, they depart through the top of the head. During this process, we experience a panoramic review of our sensory life, the life review of our whole life in the physical brain. The life panorama later repeats itself in our astral brain. The consciousness of our lower self remains attached to the physical brain. When our physical body decays, our common lower-self consciousness decays also. Recollection of past lives is therefore impossible.

The remaining part of the lower self ends up in *kamaloka*, the astral field surrounding and permeating the earth. There, we indulge all our desires, without the administration and detachment of conscience. After the energy of our desire has spent itself, the permanent atom withdraws further into the mental field. A particularly bad astral self does not dissolve and may attach itself to the astral body of an animal. The essences of the spent desires remain as astral elements, the *skandha*. They are the fruits of the past life and so the seeds for the next one. They are the carriers of karma. An alcoholic leaves a *skandha* behind made out of corresponding astral matter. In a next life, this *skandha* gives a tendency to the same vice. We do not necessarily become alcoholic, but we lean to it.

At the end of the *kamaloka* period we fall asleep and reawaken in *devachan*, the mental world of thoughts. This world also has no causes, only effects. Here, we indulge in thoughts. *Devachan* is a haven of rest, a world of self-created illusions. However, we may acquire new knowledge here, and thus — it seems — acquire new thoughts. We seem to meet other people, but they remain thought projections. Everyone lives alone among ideas. The wealth of thoughts we had during our lifetime decides how long we stay in *devachan*. If we lived thoughtlessly, instinctively, we return almost immediately after our vibrations in *kamaloka* end. If we have spent our thoughts, we discard our mental body and we arrive in *manas*, our real home, where we are conscious as the higher self in our causal body.

When we return to a new lifetime, a thin golden thread of buddhic matter with the permanent atoms attached to it appears out of the trinity of *atma, buddhi* and *manas*. The permanent atoms are animated one by one, attracting the *skandhas* left behind on the various planes. The thread branches out into the buddhic web of life, sustaining and inspiring all bodies.

How do the five drives for return influence the body and the life we return to? The pull of the earth is general and does not lead to a specific life. Attachment to material objects and conditions depends on the state of the permanent atoms and the *skandhas*. The desire for experience and self-expression in the material world is also not specific. Next to the condition of the permanent atoms and the *skandhas*, and the general workings of karma, theosophical literature mentions four other factors shaping a new life:

- what we can learn
- how we relate with other people who have been born or are going to be born
- what we ourselves want (the more we are advanced, the more freedom)
- special missions we have accepted.

The major influences on the physical body are the elemental and the etheric matrix. The four or seven 'Lords of Karma', also called the *lipika*, manage the reincarnation process. They are high cosmic administrators of karma, registering everything in the *akasha* record and allocating the karmic lots. They form the building elemental and the etheric double of each physical body. The elemental determines the quality mix of the attracted substances. He governs the growth of the body and floats around the mother. He departs at the latest during the seventh year. This elemental is a living being that serves human evolution, and so evolves itself. For the greater part, karma operates via the *skandhas* and, for the rest, via the building elemental and the etheric body. When our ego is well-developed, we may contact, through this elemental, the Lords of Karma to declare our willingness to take on extra karma.

Other influences are heredity and the thoughts and feelings of the mother during the pregnancy. Some people are interested in how their bodies develop, others hardly or not at all. The more evolved we are, the more we look alike in our different lifetimes. The Masters always have the same physical appearance. Common people do not choose their parents and hour of birth. For them, it is a natural process. The more advanced we are, the more exact are the choices we make.

How our talents and dispositions develop will depend strongly on our environment. We are not fully incarnated until the age of 21. Before that, our character is a continuation of our preceding character, but still easily influenced. The influence of educators is greater than we usually realise. Distinct characteristics, however, come from past lives. The moment of death is not always predetermined, is not always karmic and is difficult to foresee.

INTERMISSION AND CHANGE OF GENDER

The estimated intermissions between incarnations consistently shorten during the development of theosophy. In *Esoteric Buddhism*, Sinnett assumes a normal intermission of more than 8,000 years (1883: 143). As we are in the body only about 1.2 percent of the time, he considers *devachan* as being more important. This conflicts with the view that in *devachan* we merely elaborate and spend our thoughts and that the length of stay there depends on the wealth of thoughts during life. Soon, the given intermissions change to between 2,000 and 3,000 years. Later again, intermissions of 700 and 1,200 years are mentioned. People who incarnate in different sub-races require an intermission of 1,200 years, while those who incarnate in the same sub-race have an intermission of 700 years. The 700-year intermission entails a shorter, but more intensive stay in *devachan*. Later still, Leadbeater provides this elaborate classification (1910):

- 1,500 to 2,300 years: mature, advanced souls; initiates
- 700 to 1,200 years: those who are going along or nearing the path of initiation; of these, about 5 years in Kamaloka and up to 50 years on the Manas plane
- 600 to 1,000 years: upper class; 20 to 25 years in Kamaloka, short stay in Manas
- about 500 years: upper-middle class; 25 years in Kamaloka, no sojourn in Manas
- 200 to 300 years: lower-middle class; 40 years in Kamaloka
- 100 to 200 years: qualified workers; 40 years in Kamaloka
- 60 to 100 years: non-qualified labourers; 40 to 50 years in Kamaloka
- 40 to 60 years: good-for-nothings and drunks; only in Kamaloka
- about 5 years: the lowest class; only in the lower part of Kamaloka or earth-bound, vegetative.

Leadbeater seems to assume that soul stature and social status generally match. He also seems to imply that the higher classes have no good-for-nothings or drunks.

The richness of our cultural and spiritual life (determining how long we stay in *devachan*), the intensity of our emotional life (determining how long we stay in *kamaloka*) and the length and nature of our preceding life (for example, an early death, idiocy or an accident), cause deviations from these averages. In general, the less strength of mind we have, the more we have to learn, and the more experience we need.

Some theosophical writers claim that between three and seven incarnations in the same gender is the rule. Others write that seven male and seven female incarnations alternate. Alcyone (the entity of Krishnamurti) has four to eight consecutive incarnations in the same gender every time (Besant & Leadbeater 1924). Some people seem to change gender easily, and others with difficulty. After an early death, people often reincarnate in the same sub-race, and then usually change gender.

A strong attachment to particular families or peoples may result in a return to the same environment. Jews are supposed often to reincarnate as Jews because they regard themselves as the chosen people. The same could be true for the Druses, and for each other group that, for whatever reason, feels good about itself.

KARMA

Theosophists firmly believe that karma is the universal law of cause and effect. All of our behaviour both expresses our past, including past lives, and shapes our future, including future lives. Everything falls back on us, but because of *maya*, the illusion created by the delay between cause and effect, we fail to see what is happening to us as a result of what we did. The theosophical view of karma has three levels:

- as natural law of cause and effect, without providence or release
- as reward or punishment
- as guidance, compensation, evolution and healing.

When we act naturally, according to our nature and responding to the situation, our acts have purely natural consequences. This is the first kind of karma, free from reward and punishment and without guidance. Theosophical literature gives few illustrations of natural karmic effects. One example is that cruelty in one life leads to insanity in the next.

Most theosophical expositions of karma are about the moral, corrective workings of karma. In general, misdeeds are punished and victims recompensed. The relation between act and karmic consequence is according to natural law, but is pliable. We may be punished for misdeeds in up to seven future lives. A murderer is not necessarily murdered in his next life. More likely, he may have to save his past victims at the cost of his own life; or he dedicates his life to serving others. Simple retribution is an exception. The bad luck of a worthy person is the consequence of past evil deeds. The good luck of an unworthy person is the consequence of past good deeds.

An example of guidance and compensation is that undeserved accidents and disasters may be subtracted from our negative karma. When we have no negative karma to be compensated, we are miraculously rescued, or we will be compensated by positive karma or a reward in *devachan*.

Suffering from a disease is non-specific karma. Generally, 'small karma', karma from unimportant acts, is collected in a broad karmic mass before being released. Our karmic mass may be divided into *sanchita karma*, *prarabdha karma*, and *kryamana karma*. Sanchita karma is the general karmic mass from past lives. Only a part of this is 'ripe' or *prarabdha* karma, influencing our behaviour in this life. The karmic mass we create in this life is the *kryamana* karma that will be added to the *sanchita* karma after this life. However, a portion is settled directly in this life. This is 'small-change' karma. Good deeds for selfish reasons result in pleasant conditions. Truly altruistic deeds result in self-development.

Apparently, the cardinal fact of our evolution is gaining self-awareness and so free choice, and as a karmic result, we have become caught in matter and self-centeredness. This is mainly because of indulging in sex and so losing the 'third eye' of clairvoyance.

Each karma doctrine leads to the question of free will versus predestination. The theosophists answer that karma neither precludes free choice, nor help from others. Help is always possible, and free will is never absolutely arbitrary, but always a limited free choice. If everything were predestined, karma would be meaningless. To evolve, our acts have to have real consequences. Karma is the consequence of choices we made, plus compensation for undeserved disturbances in life. The more developed we are, the more subtly and precisely our karma works.

Karma may be a tool of self-liberation, especially after we understand how it works. We should not be freed *from* karma, but *by* karma. Once we start our spiritual development, we attain our goal in the seventh life after our first steps. We acquit the debt we accumulate during this process towards the initiates, by helping other people to progress. Only neglect of received insights creates guilt. We may get stuck on the way, but we still remain sensitive to once-acquired truths in following lives. Consequently, many people are sensitive to theosophical doctrines. The only causes of real retrogression are deliberate cruelty and black magic.

Finally, karma plays a role in larger groups of people such as cultures, or in institutions such as congregations.

PAST-LIFE RECALL

We have forgotten past lives, since the physical brain containing them has vanished and the astral brain of the lower personality decomposed. According to Sinnett (1883), general recollection of past lives will therefore be possible only in some faraway future. Van Ginkel (1917) expects that regression by hypnotic or magnetic trance will become the most important way to recollect past lives, but also only in the distant future. Luckily, every experience is registered not only in the physical brain and in the lower self, but also in the higher self, so that via *manas*, the causal body, past lives may be recalled.

Spiritual development that has made us aware of our higher self, and preferably initiation, is necessary to recall past lives. With buddhic powers, we can perceive the previous lives of others.

Leadbeater writes (1899) that recalling past lives in normal consciousness is preferable, because this allows taking notes. The surroundings hardly matter, provided the mind is calm, open and unprejudiced. The emerging pictures of past lives are like film images that can be speeded up, slowed down, or stopped to examine details. We can also relive our past, instead of remaining observers. Sometimes we recognise somebody in a recollection of a past life as a person we know now, but Leadbeater warns that intuitive identification is untrustworthy. It is better to take a person in a past life and look into the next incarnations, until we see the present incarnation. Masters are easy to recognise, since their aspect hardly changes.

The best-known theosophic publications about reincarnations of individual people are *Man: Whence, how and whither* and its sequel *The Lives of Alcyone*, mapping the incarnations of a large number of masters, famous people and prominent theosophists, later centred on the soul of Alcyone, recently recognised as Krishnamurti (Besant & Leadbeater 1913, 1924). Another work about the reincarnations of other theosophists later appeared in four volumes (Leadbeater 1941: 50).

—— ANTHROPOSOPHY ——

Gnostic thought systems typically spawn related philosophies in their more independent adherents. This happened also with theosophy. Many schools have derived from it, some almost identical, others almost unrecognisable. In Europe, the most influential movement to branch off from theosophy is the anthroposophy of Rudolf Steiner. The following is based on his books and lectures on reincarnation and karma.

THE EVOLUTION OF HUMANKIND

Out of Rudolf Steiner's extensive reflections on the development of humankind, I choose those directly related to his views on karma and reincarnation.

During the preceding incarnation of our earth, called the Old Moon, the present human souls were at the animal level. The then humans are now angels. At that earlier stage, a number of these souls, known as the Luciferic spirits, intensified and cultivated their ego consciousness, separated themselves more or less from the mainstream of evolution and fell behind. During our development on earth, in the time of Lemuria, these Luciferic spirits inspired the fall of man. As a result, we overly involuted, dislodging from the spiritual, falling into the material. During Lemuria, the moon separated itself from the earth (the sun had already separated itself from the earth in the preceding age of Hyperborea).

After the moon's separation, human self-awareness incarnated for the first time. With this began upright walking, which led to reincarnation in our sense. Walking freed our hands, and after that came speech and independent thinking. What somebody does with his hands is connected to his individual karma. What he says is connected to the national karma, and his thoughts are connected to the karma of mankind. We have an original fund of spiritual power that we gradually consume in the course of our incarnations.

We would reach a dead end at the end of this planetary cycle, but for Christ, who has broken through the Luciferic inspiration and opened up new possibilities. Without Golgotha, reincarnation would ultimately lead to mechanical people with empty souls.

Until the second post-Atlantic age, the ancient Persian age from 5067 to 2907 BC, people remembered their past lives. In the third age, the period from 2907 to 747 BC, encompassing the Egyptian, Babylonian and Chaldean cultures, past-life recall dwindled. Elsewhere, Steiner claims that knowledge of reincarnation was lost in the Kali-yuga, stretching from 3101 BC to AD 1899. At the time of Christ's appearance, belief in reincarnation was at an absolute low.

Past-life recall was lost when priests started to drink wine. The wedding feast at Cana alludes to this. Christ himself forbade the teaching of reincarnation. Since then, we have forgotten all about reincarnation to learn to concentrate on the present life alone.

Ideas about reincarnation began to come back during the eighteenth-century Enlightenment, in the work of Lessing among others, but now in a new, Christianised form. These Christian ideas relate the object to the development of humankind, while the earlier Buddhist idea related the subject to individual development. In his own lifetime, Steiner says, the desire to recall previous incarnations is growing. At the end of the twentieth century, Christ will become the new Lord of Karma and will join our individual karma to the karma of humankind. In the future, the karmic consequences of our acts will become ever more directly visible. Resistance to the idea of reincarnation will come particularly from the Anglo-American sub-race, although the mission of this race is precisely to give theories about reincarnation and karma a scientific base.

BETWEEN DEATH AND REBIRTH

After death, we feel we are growing out of our body and becoming one with the surrounding world. Then follows a panoramic review of our past life. This review takes as long as we are able to stay awake at one time during our life, a couple of days at most. After that our etheric body dies, so that all our thoughts disappear and only the corresponding emotions remain. An extract from our physical body remains identical in all incarnations. The extract from the etheric body, on the other hand, is different in each life. Then we arrive in the astral world (the Kamaloka of the theosophists). Again, we experience a panorama of our life, but this time backwards, and intensely emotional. The length of this review of life is as long as the time we slept during life, or about a third of the length of our life. During this review we experience as our own feelings how others experienced our acts. This imprints the urge to make up for wrong acts in our astral body.

This review takes place in the moon sphere with the help of moon beings who give our emotional experiences substance, in cooperation with the angels that link one life to the next. In the sphere of Venus we come under the influence of the archangels. Then, we go to the sphere of Mercury, where we come under the influence of the Archai. Finally, in the sun sphere, we meet the so-called second hierarchy: the Exusiai, the Dynamis and the Kyriotetes. Bad karma cannot get through the sun sphere to the Saturn sphere, where we are consecutively subjected to the influences of the Thrones, the Cherubim and the Seraphim. When we return, the energies that went through the sun domain form our predisposition to health, and the energies that did not go through the sun domain, related to procreation and the moon, form our predisposition to illness.

INTERMISSION AND CHANGE OF GENDER

Like the theosophical writers, Steiner begins with long intermission periods and finishes with shorter ones. He starts by saying that we reincarnate once in each zodiacal era, every 2,600 years. This seems to be a mistake. A so-called sidereal year is nearly 26,000 years long, or 2,160 years per star sign on the average. (He did use this proper length in his later calculations of the post-Atlantic ages.)

Later, Steiner says that we incarnate every 1,300 years, to have within each period of 2,600 years one male and one female incarnation. He explains his earlier statement by saying that male and female incarnations are so different that occultists regard such a couple as one incarnation. We tend to alternate between a female and a male lifetime. Up to three times in the same gender is still normal, and seven times in the same gender is the maximum.

According to Steiner, those who lived around 1900 had lived before between AD 300 and 900. Apparently, he takes a margin of about 300 years around this 1,300-year intermission. Five years later, around 1910, he says that the people living at that time have lived two, three or four times since Palestine, amounting to intermissions averaging 950, 700 or 500 years. Apparently, he then thought in terms of a 700-year interval with a margin of about 200 years, which was also the accepted idea in theosophical circles at that time. Finally, he claims reincarnation in the same culture or nation is rare, with the exception of the 'Central European community of nations'. Apparently, this community – undefined, but presumably equal to the German-speaking part of Europe – is something special.

KARMIC PATTERNS

During the first period of his discourses, Steiner's concepts were close to those of the theosophists, and he continued to use theosophical vocabulary. Most of his audience was theosophically oriented and he himself operated within the Theosophical Association. In the 1920s, towards the end of his life, he constructed a complete anthroposophical world-view of his own, where reincarnation and karma had their specific places. In between, roughly between 1912 and 1918, he came up with ideas about karma that seemed to bear little relation to his thoughts before and after – and to each other.

Steiner characterises karma as a moral, spiritual, cosmic order alongside the natural, physical order. Everything physically accidental is karmically determined, and everything karmically accidental is physically determined. Thus karma is the spiritual law of cause and effect pervading all inner and outward human acts. Knowledge and understanding of karma does not change it; at most it brings about a shift. Karma leaves free will intact. Free will functions in karmically determined situations. (Apparently, free will is a third principle next to karma and physical causality.) Like theosophy, anthroposophy emphasises that help is always possible. Explaining somebody's problems as karmic is no excuse not to help.

Another idea is that karma has to do specifically with the consequences of Luciferically inspired behaviour. Sometimes Steiner claims that karma is mainly valid for a person's acts during his life, and at other times that karma is purely spiritual, only active in the spiritual world in between lifetimes. Karma from the first half of our life plays out during the second half. A lively childhood leads to a spiritually rich old age. Reverence during childhood leads to beneficence in old age, noble wrath leads to loving mildness, and devotion to continued youthfulness. Egoism and forced development during childhood lead to early aging.

In 1912 Steiner began a number of discourses on karma as interaction between the microcosm and the macrocosm. By this time, he regards our judgments as the source of our karma. Our imaginative judgments are radiated out to the environment via our bones, our inspirational judgments via our muscles, and our intuitive judgments via our nerves. Everything wrong in our judgment is reflected back to us. That is our karma. Everything correct in these judgments is absorbed by the cosmos to build up the occult Jupiter, the next incarnation of our earth (GA 134: I).

Two years later he says that our muscles are crystallised karma, as they embody the spirit guiding us to our karmic place (GA 153: I). Apparently, karma functions mainly by getting us to certain places at certain times. This is an extremely limited view of karma. Besides, our muscles do not determine where we go, our nerves do. Later still, Steiner says that our acts register into the surrounding ether, acts that are read out as karma in the next life (*GA* 157: IV). Then he returns to the concept of karma as based on a spiritual radiation of human judgments continuing to operate after death (*GA* 181: V, VI).

Next to individual karma, there is national karma and the karma of humankind. A common fate may result from a common death in a disaster. In the absence of existing karma, it may create positive karma such as inciting a common undertaking. During important historical events individual karma and general karma interconnect.

There is continuity through lives – like talents saved. There is also involution: thoughts in one life lead to feelings in the next, feelings in one life lead to habits in the next, habits from one life lead to body characteristics, and bodily acts in one life lead to environment in the next. And there is oscillation between opposites: between male and female lifetimes, between being talented in one life and being awkward in the next (what about the continuity of talents?). Family members in one life may be friends in another life, and friends in one life may be relatives again in another life. During our childhood we meet mostly people we knew around middle age in our preceding life, and during middle age we meet people we knew during our youth in our preceding life. The last part of life has no specific karma or no karma at all. Serious past lifetimes shine through in the present. Superficial past lifetimes don't shine through. Such people laugh and grin a lot.

Steiner gives many examples of specific relations between lifetimes. Materialism and rejection of the spiritual lead to a dark intermission, and in the next life to egoistic thinking. Egotist mysticism leads to a rudderless inter-mission and to a defective intelligence in the next life. Deceit in one life leads to flippancy and indifference in the next. Thoughtlessness in one life leads to forgetfulness in the next, and forgetfulness in turn leads to nervousness. Morality without beauty develops the astral without the etheric and leads to weakness or idiocy in the next life. Thinking trivially and conventionally leads to greed and gluttony in the next life. Those who think slowly in one life, move slowly in the next life – and the other way round (*GA* 235: 159).

The clearest examples are those where the etheric conditions of one life (habits) induce physical properties in the next one. Mathematical ability in one life leads to good eyesight in the next; architectural ability in one life leads to good hearing in the next. Thoughtful people are thin in their next life, thoughtless people are fat in their next life. People who think often get a beautiful skin with soft lines in their next life, and those who do little thinking get a spotty skin with coarse lines. A dulled life results in a need to sleep a lot in the next life. People who are active and interested get a low, sharp, powerful forehead in their next life; they have strong bones and fast-growing, buoyant hair, and in general express strong spirits. Those who were indolent and uninterested show the opposite physical and psychological characteristics. People with sympathetic faces liked paintings in their preceding life. Dislike of paintings gives an unsympathetic face in the next life. People not interested in the stars get a flabby body in their next life. People without interest in music get asthma or lung diseases in their next life.

Specific diseases have specific karmic origins, if they are karmic at all. The industrial proletarian's hatred expresses itself in the next life as tuberculosis. A weak sense of self predisposes us in our next life to cholera, and an exaggerated sense of self predisposes us to malaria. People who are prone to emotional outbursts are predisposed to diphtheria in their next life. People who patiently suffer illness, pain and hardship, will be beautiful in their next life. A violent death gives the idealism needed to accomplish important aims in the next life. Infectious diseases lead to beautiful surroundings in a next life, and fatal illness to fortified internal organs. (Apparently, fatal infectious diseases give both.) A feeble-minded person who experiences hard-heartedness may become generous and benevolent in his next life. Someone who caused others pain will be melancholic in his next life. Facility with languages leads to freedom from prejudice in the next life.

Finally, those who think that subsequent lives are all nonsense will have nonsensical subsequent lives! (This explains much of what we see around us. And as far as the future is concerned, dear reader, thou art warned.)

PAST-LIFE RECALL

The results of our past lives permeate us when we sleep deep without dreams. We can also during the day become sensitive to the workings of karma in our life, though we cannot simply infer karmic causes and effects from factual acts and events. We can only discover karma with the higher levels of awareness that Steiner calls inspiration and intuition. We cannot recall concrete events from past lives, but only the corresponding feelings. Identifying karmic influences is possible, but requires subtle observation. Steiner calls this karma research. By paying attention to apparent coincidences that influence the course of our life, we learn to distinguish karmically predestined acts from free acts. It is important to see our fate as a spiritual reality in which our higher self is active. In the future we will start to see our past lives through our relation with Christ, which will provide us with the necessary confidence to evolve further. Meanwhile, special exercises can make us aware of karma. Steiner gives three kinds of exercises.

REINCARNATION AND KARMA IN SOCIETAL DEVELOPMENT

According to Steiner, belief in reincarnation and karma will stimulate new social developments and be a counterweight to an ever more complex society. Awareness of reincarnation and karma does not lead to escapism, but rather to acceptance of and love for our allotted position in life. Realising that we are building our own future strengthens our feeling of responsibility for the future of our society. Steiner recommends telling children about reincarnation and karma.

In his later work, Steiner identified previous lives of a number of historical figures, mainly thinkers from all ages, and prominent social, cultural and political figures from his own time. In the Middle Ages Lessing was a scholastic Dominican and in ancient Greece an initiate in the mysteries. Garibaldi was an Irish monk who founded a monastery in Alsace. Ernst Häckel was the monk Hildebrand, who became Pope Gregory VII. Nietzsche was an ascetic Franciscan. Many scientists, like Vischer, were Arabs. Francis Bacon was the reincarnated Harun al Rashid. Laplace was a scholar at the court of Mamun in Baghdad. Charles Darwin was the reincarnation of Tarik, the Moorish commander who entered Spain in the eighth century. Steiner gave many indications about past lives of prominent social, cultural or political figures of his own day. Opponents of Germany in the First World War are not shown in a particularly favourable light. Many of them had been – like many materialistic scientists – unchristian Arabs.

To find out how Steiner got all his insights into reincarnation and karma, read his karma exercises and the first volume of his series about esoteric reflections on karmic relations (*GA* 235). Rudolf Steiner is a gnostic *par excellence*, probably the most intellectual and impressive of the last centuries. The problems of gnosticism show nowhere as clearly as in his anthroposophy.

A gnostic invokes in us the desire to gain first-hand knowledge, pointing the way. Followers, however, have to start by believing in his revelations, hardly a gnostic attitude. The gnostic student is called to a temporary belief in order ultimately to arrive at his own insights on the basis of this. However, this personal insight may never conflict with the insights of his precursor who, after all, had first-hand knowledge of the truth. At the most, the next generation can elaborate and embroider. A gnostic also does not argue. He usually paints his intuitions abstractly, but full of feeling. Others have to absorb them with little rational judgment and discussion. This basic conflict and eternal paradox of gnosticism, its uneasy marriage between belief and exploration, leads irrevocably to continual separations, since there are always people who have personal interpretations and insights that 'enrich' or 'correct' those of their predecessors. The emancipation of gnostics is always painful, because it implies separation from their own spiritual mother or father. Most of them, then, emancipate themselves only halfway, continuing to believe in the value of what was before them, but reinterpreting it. The saddest part of such reinterpretations is their epistemological naivety: they are again presented as 'truth', because the gnostic intellect is embedded in vehement and liberating emotions.

Third-rate followers do not go for truth at all, but for emotional deliverance and intellectual comfort. They often see all of these separations and idio-syncrasies as so many different revelations of the same truth. And since all roads lead to Rome, remaining at home does as well.

Gnostic ideas, for example on reincarnation and karma, are an impressive collection of concepts full of atmosphere, but abstract, many of them incoherent or even contradictory. Chapter 14 below compares a number of theosophical and anthroposophical doctrines with the material to date on actual experiences. These remain the arbiter, also about utterances from masters, initiates, esotericists and their apostles.

——— OTHER ESOTERICISTS ———

Others than Rudolf Steiner objected to the line of Annie Besant and Charles Leadbeater. People like William Judge saw themselves as continuing the true line of Helena Blavatsky. His Universal Theosophy Fellowship has published on reincarnation (*Reincarnation* 1987). The eleven essays in this book are, in my opinion, a prime example of noble metaphysical rattling. The editor explains what it is all about: 'The founders of the modern Theosophical Movement, H.P. Blavatsky and W.Q. Judge, brought the sacred inheritance of humanity within the reach of intrepid seekers of wisdom in our time. With the dawn of the Aquarian Age there is a fresh concern with secular monasticism and a way of life based upon authentic use of ancient wisdom as noetic theurgy.' Got it?

Judge presumes that all matter, because it is subject to changes, is therefore reincarnating (p. 7): 'a constant change of form . . . is, broadly speaking, reincarnation'. I can hardly imagine a more serious error of thinking. And what about (p. 7): 'Thus what is now called human flesh is so much matter that one day was wholly mineral, later on vegetable, and now refined into human atoms.' What could possibly be human about atoms? And the air we breath or the salt we take? Have they passed on through the vegetable kingdom? And what happens to our 'refined human atoms' when we urinate? According to Judge, our body and physical life in general are equal to hell (p. 11). Robert Crosbie, the next essayist, tells us (p. 19): 'Every cell in our bodies has its birth, youth, manhood, decay and death, and its reincarnation.' Has he ever heard about the division of cells?

The Pathwork is based on the teachings of Eva Pierrakos, who channelled between 1958 and 1978 in New York. Her 'Guide' is one of the many discarnates who tell us about life. The way her lectures open shows what it is all about: a religious mood in which we accept the limits of our mind humbly and willingly and where that same mind is fed with intimations of higher truths. The content of the lectures is consistent. They do not conflict with what we know from other sources, but they express a limited vision: everything is planned, well-organised in every detail and arranged wisely and hierarchically. They are polished and systematised and without an inkling of the many other processes before birth and after death. For people with religious needs, coming from a rigid belief system and looking for a combination of personal development and home-coming they may be meaningful, but for practical researchers or therapists they are useless.

The transition between channelled information and esoteric information is gradual. Mediums like Edgar Cayce and Grace Loehr mainly gave individual readings. Eva Pierrakos mainly gave a philosophy. Some great system builders have been presented in this chapter. The next chapter will show that many mediums also transmitted general insights, usually answering specific questions. From the work of Cayce and the Loehr–Daniels readings others have published systematic summaries

Regression researchers and therapists may also feel the need for system building. Some, like Joel Whitton, find in sessions confirmation of their particular esoteric beliefs. Many others see their astrological insights confirmed. Before birth and after death enthusiastic therapists and experimenters often encounter wise guides and learn to communicate with them during sessions. All this puts their work in a higher, more spiritual perspective, probably because of an attitude that is more religious than scientific. This often results in curious reflections, like this one from Bruce Goldberg (1982: 39):

> We are aided in making these reincarnation decisions by our Masters and Guides. These highly evolved entities have completed their karmic cycles and their purpose is simply to help and advise us as to our next lives. They do not moralize or pass judgment. They simply counsel us and try to help as best they can. The individual soul always has free will to ignore their advice. Many of our decisions are poorly made for this very reason. These Masters and Guides also receive advice from even higher entities with higher vibrational rates in the seven higher planes. These much more advanced entities receive their advice from even more evolved sources, the ultimate authority being God or ALL THAT IS (as many parapsychologists refer to God). The final result is, of course, excellent guidance.

This reminds me of a group of facilitators who, for all their proficiency in communication and cooperation, failed to accomplish anything, and concluded that this was because they had no super-facilitator. The troubles in life sometimes! In practice, pupils may surpass their teachers. Nietzsche once exclaimed: 'To educate educators! But they first must educate themselves!' Goldberg's pyramid of super-counselling looks as though it gives a basis to human development, but it takes the ground from under our feet. In his view, freedom consists of being able to accept or refuse the wisdom of others. Moreover, he puts the cart before the horse: the ultimate result is fantastic counselling. And this unending absurdity has a name. Development in his view amounts to going to ever-higher teachers presiding over ever-higher kindergartens. The result of all our building efforts is ever-better scaffolding. To put up the scaffolding, we need even better scaffolding, which is put up with even better scaffolding, *ad infinitum*, *ad absurdum*. Life becomes mysterious when we are misty-eyed.

Goldberg seems to be an active and practical therapist. However, like many others, he yields to his desire for a cosmic, comprehensive perspective. Freud would label it an oceanic need.

Sometimes even past-life therapists can seem to be frustrated high priests and initiates with the irresistible urge to pour their wisdom into the uninitiated. I see such enthusiasts all over the world. Thorwald Dethlefsen, a German past-life counsellor, uses regressions as a springboard for metaphysics. His first book about reincarnation (1974) contains the protocols of some sessions and the next 90 pages explain the workings of the world and mankind. His second book contains a large number of protocols and sensible comments on them (1976). However, his third book leaves experience far behind with the ominous subtitle *Esoteric Psychology – the ultimate knowledge of the perfection of humanity* (1979). His book discusses the 'ultimate principles of reality' and provides such blinding insights as 'life is rhythm', or even (1979: 69):

Breathing is the basic human experience. We can study the laws of polarity in the light of breathing. They can be applied to the whole universe. For so below, so above. When we breathe in, then, without further ado and with absolute certainty, breathing out follows as the opposite pole.

I doubt whether Dethlefsen understands the physiology of breathing. Apparently he has never heard of respiratory problems. And why the universe should be studied in the light of respiration also remains unclear. Why not in the light of daily motions, or of Friday–afternoon traffic congestion?

Dethlefsen also provides sensible and pertinent psychological insights, undoubtedly partly because of his practical experience, but they vanish into the blue when he starts his cosmic bubble-blowing. Every now and then he becomes ostentatiously practical, as with his example of someone who crashes into a tree at 120 miles an hour and dies. According to him, the driver gained understanding of the principles of energy (120 mph) and resistance (tree) from this experience. This is clearly no example from a regression. People learn the most incredible life lessons, but I have never heard anything in a life review as abstract as this. Also, equating speed with energy warrants some pessimism about the author's knowledge of physics. His astrological reflections, too, appear to me to lack any knowledge of the empirical work in this area.

*

Helen Wambach asked her subjects, among other things, why they had been born in the twentieth century. One of them answered: 'I chose the twentieth century because of the historical transition from a religious to a scientific vision, and at the end of this period, a spiritual awakening' (Wambach 1979: 69). Others also reported a feeling of liberation after the shift from a religious to a scientific orientation. We should go forwards, not backwards. The scientific world-view may need to be drastically enriched and transformed, but rebirth differs from returning to the womb, as attentive readers of the New Testament should know. Science is not the be-all and end-all either, and science is more complex and uncertain than dogmatic scientists believe. Scientific procedure itself is subject to the shuffling and fumbling of analysis and the draughts of scepticism. But, fumbling, we come along; shuffling, we learn to walk; stumbling and picking ourselves up we emancipate ourselves.

FURTHER READING

Theosophical literature lacks systematic treatment of reincarnation and karma doctrines. *Isis Unveiled* (1877) and *The Secret Doctrine* (1888) by H. P. Blavatsky have brief references, to be found via the index. Sinnett (1883) devotes a few passages to it. An article by H.P. Blavatsky (1886) is concerned with the confusion surrounding the reincarnation concept, and many bits and pieces may be found in the profuse literature from that time. Virginia Hanson has collected them (1975a). The first book completely devoted to the subject is by E.D. Walker (1888): informative, but lacking empirical material. Then there are the two books by Anderson (1894), full of uninformative praise, but with impressive titles. From about 1895 Annie Besant published short essays on the subject (see Bibliography). The major writer on the subject is Leadbeater, although his discussions remain limited to short publications, and chapters and passages in other books.

Man. Whence, how and whither (1913) and *The Lives of Alcyone* of Besant and Leadbeater (1924), Leadbeater's *The Band of Servers* (1941) and his posthumous *The Soul's Growth Through Reincarnation* (1949–50) tell about the consecutive lives of important historical figures and important theosophists. The work by Arthur E. Powell (1925, 1926, 1927, 1928), who compiled the theosophical literature about the various bodies, is important and interesting. His chapters on karma and reincarnation are informative. Head and Cranston (1977) are informative about the 'theosophical renaissance'. In the early years of the twentieth century many booklets and brochures appeared, by Charles Johnston, Katherine Tingley, W.W. Atkinson, Snowden Ward, Irving Cooper, Jinarajadasa and Olive Stevenson Howell among others. The Dutchman Van Ginkel gave a thorough and extensive treatment (1917). Popular theosophical introductions are of low quality: Christmas Humphreys, Charles Hampton, Geoffrey Hodson, James Perkins, Gertrud Van Pelt and Leoline Wright. I didn't read Laurence Bendit (1965) and E.L. Gardner (1965). Relatively the best theosophical introduction to the subject is *Reincarnation Explored* by John Algeo (1987). Geddes MacGregor writes reasonably and informatively about reincarnation and Christianity from a theosophical perspective.

For anthroposophical literature, the Collected Works (*Gesamtausgabe*) of Rudolf Steiner are the main source. The 24 volumes dealing with reincarnation and karma are listed in the Bibliography. The most informative on the subject are volumes 17, 34 and 120, and the six-volume series, *Esoterische Betrachtungen karmischer Zusammenhänge* (*GA* 235–40), especially the first.

Other anthroposophical authors on this subject are Friedrich Rittelmeyer (1931), Emil Bock (1932), Gunther Wachsmuth (1933), Friedrich Husemann (1938), Eugen Kolisko (1940), Rudolf Frieling (1974), Willem Veltman (1974, 1993), Hugo Verbrugh (1980), Alan Howard (1980), Evelyn Capel (1980) and Van Schaik (1995). Veltman is especially informative and readable. Anthroposophical thoughts about the relationship between reincarnation and Christianity can be found in Archiati (1996) and Hans Stolp (1996). Thea Stanley Hughes (1976) gives an acceptable popular introduction to reincarnation with a subdued anthroposophical background.

Some authors writing out of Eastern traditions are not esotericists in the narrow sense of the word, but write purely from their own religious revelations, like Swami Abhedananda, Sri Aurobindo, Hazrat Inayat Khan, Sri Chinmoy, Swami Paramananda and Swami Prabhupada. Generally, in my opinion, these books are edifying, vague and contradict experience.

G. Encausse wrote *La Réincarnation* under his pen name Papus in 1925. Later writers that seem to tie into Western esoteric traditions are Manly Hall, Spencer Lewis and John VanAuken. Douglas Baker (1977), like Rudolf Steiner, explores the karmic origins of diseases. Maybe Baker knows about karma, but not about argumentation. His other books about reincarnation (1978, 1981) do not inspire confidence either. He scatters his incoherent and irrelevant quotations like his titles and memberships.

Two books from Thorwald Dethlefsen (1974 and 1979) I consider also to be esoteric expositions.

Mona Rolfe (1975) lectures in trance. Noticeably so. In connection with the dawning Age of Aquarius she explains the deeper meaning of the book of Genesis (1975: 31): 'No soul who has progressed beyond the Garden of Remembrance, that is, the seventh plane of the astral plane, can at any time be subject to the law of cause and effect.' If we advance enough, we are no longer subject to causality. 'If . . . then' – a clear example of causality. What plane do we need to reach to be no longer subject to faulty reasoning?

I find A.T. Mann (1995) to be even worse. His book contains historical nonsense: Harun al Rashid was an Arab philosopher; Johannes Stein was one of Steiner's teachers (he was a pupil); Rudolf Steiner copied ideas from Edgar Cayce – who worked when Steiner was dead and buried; the Renaissance, the Enlightenment and the Era of Colonialism were all 1500–1720 and the Reformation was 1720–1840.

More philosophical are the essays of Norman Gregor and Jeane Dixon. Irmgard Demetriades (1983) compares classical religions, modern mystics and occultists with the revelations of the Austrian mystic Jakob Lorber. Christine Hartley (1972) has written probably the most reasonable metaphysical book about reincarnation.

Four

PSYCHIC INFORMATION ABOUT PAST LIVES

Sensitive people may receive impressions of past lives, sometimes in trance. Some sensitives talk about the lives of others or about the subject of reincarnation in general. Recalling past lives can only partially be regarded as a paranormal ability. Many people can have such memories, usually after some trance-induction. Methods that do not induce trance, like those of Netherton, work with a trance self-induced by the patient, but this occurs spontaneously and also with people without evidence of previous paranormal gifts.

Intense involvement with the subject may also lead to psychic impressions. Past-life therapists may pick up images or sensations that are related to the unfolding story of a client. David Gershom was told by somebody that she died in her past life by being hurled with many others into a fire hole. Suddenly he smells burnt meat. He goes to the kitchen, where everything is OK. On the porch he doesn't smell anything, but in the house the smell returns. His allergic wife with her sensitive nose notices nothing. When he realises that this is a psychic impression, the smell disappears (1996).

I distinguish:

- psychic impressions: vague extra-sensory impressions during normal consciousness
- clear perception during shifted consciousness, as in dreams, trances and out-of-body experiences
- clairvoyance: clear extra-sensory perception during normal consciousness.

This chapter gives examples of people who sensed or perceived their own past lives or those of others: first, people with recollections of their own previous lives, then people who perceived previous lives of others, and finally discarnates who tell about reincarnation via mediums. Then we will look at general information about reincarnation from psychic sources: Allan Kardec, Helen

Roberts, Ruth Montgomery and Jane Roberts, Edgar Cayce and the Loehr–Daniels readings.

PAST-LIFE MEMORIES AND PSYCHIC ABILITIES

Any connection could shed light on the access to and the nature of the past-life memory. If the two are strongly connected, it might be difficult to refute clairvoyance and telepathy as explanations for apparent past-life memories. Do the memories of psychics differ from those of other people? Interestingly, people who are able to go into trance, or who are clairvoyant, and recollect past lives, are generally well able to distinguish between their own experiences and those of other people. So, identification (or, as Stevenson calls it, personation) does not happen automatically with impressions of past lives. Attributing clearly personal experiences to clairvoyance has no secure basis. Many psychics have little or no recollection of past lives, and possible recollections are often limited to scattered images or episodes. If recollections of past lives were based on psychic ability, many more psychics would have past-life recall.

I did a survey among people attending my lectures on reincarnation. The group was too small for general conclusions, but a number of relationships between psychic abilities and types of spontaneous past-life memories appeared to be fairly significant. Table 3.1 shows some results from this survey (TenDam 1980).

Table 3 Psychic abilities and types of spontaneous past-life memories

	Inspira-tion	Heal-ing	Clair-voyance	Tele-pathy	Predic-tion
Dreams	80%	98%	95%	90%	80%
General feeling	95%	99%	95%	–	–
Recognising people	98%	80%	–	–	
Memories without clear cause	98%	–	–	–	–
Recognising places	95%	–	–	–	–

In the survey group, people who professed paranormal ability did have more past-life memories. The greatest difference between the 'normal' and 'paranormal' people was that those with paranormal abilities had more memories in dreams. The paranormal abilities most strongly correlated to past-life memories were flashes of inspiration, healing hands (magnetism) and clairvoyance.

People with flashes of inspiration have more memories of past lives and more memories without immediate cause, and recognise places more often (in general, recollection of places is correlated to a greater number of memories). Healers and clairvoyants tend to recognise people. There was no correlation between predicting impressions and recollection of past lives, but there was an emphatic correlation between predictions and the number of memories of past lives. Prognostic abilities may not contribute to crossing the threshold to the past, but facilitate it considerably once the threshold has been crossed. A more straight-forward explanation, but just as surprising, would be that people with recollection of past lives get prognostic impressions more easily. Perception of the past in this case leads to easier perception of the future, but the reverse does not hold.

Even if recollection of past lives is possible without psychic abilities, the memory itself has to be parapsychological or rather paraphysiological, because such memories cannot be stored in the physical body. Esoteric or gnostic clairvoyants mention three sources of reincarnation memories: the personalities of the past lives; the continually reincarnating soul, also called the higher self; and a kind of general memory fund sometimes described as the memory of nature, or the *akasha* records, a database storing all experiences of all people who ever lived, or all experiences of each living being, or storing everything that ever happens. The last version is debatable, since it presupposes observation without observers or observation equipment, or some kind of recorder co-existing with the universe, registering everything without an observation point.

Experiments with the *mind mirror* show that therapeutic past-life regressions exhibit a brain-wave pattern similar to that of psychic activities: alpha and beta, together with delta. Chapter 7 will elaborate on this.

PEOPLE WITH PSYCHIC IMPRESSIONS OF THEIR OWN PAST LIVES

During a spiritual séance in 1869 the spirit of a living niece of one of the participants appears. She says that in her previous life, during the reign of Louis XIV, she had been a nun. A nobleman who tried to elope with a guest of the convent had knocked her down and she had died as a result. She gave more details and added that while she was asleep, she tended to hang around the old church of the convent in the form of her previous lifetime. She had also done this before she was reborn. To prove her identity, she wrote something down via the medium's hand, which only she and the participating uncle knew about. This convinced him, and he asked her during the séance if during the day, while she was awake, she was aware of her past life. She answered that in the daytime she only had the vague notion of a violent death and a dream episode. Later, when the uncle met his niece, he asked her if she ever dreamed she was being murdered. She answered negatively, but said she did have nightmares sometimes about a Roman Catholic priest who was fleeing from a church being chased by armed men. He dictated a few words to her, and her handwriting was practically the same as that produced during the séance. (Bertholet 1949: 561; Muller 1970: 172). Works on spiritualism contain other examples of spirits of living people appearing while the body sleeps, and taking on the identity of a past life.

Ivy Beaumont was a schoolteacher from Blackpool, who died in 1961. She developed her psychic powers around 1927. Guided by Frederic Wood, who wrote *This Egyptian Miracle* (1955) about her, she developed trances, automatic writing and clairvoyance. In a semi-trance an entity calling itself Nona appeared and produced more than 4,000 sentences in the Egyptian language of the eighteenth dynasty. Another medium reported in 1930 that Ivy Beaumont herself had lived during this time as Vola, who was well-acquainted with Nona. Later, Ivy got clear recollections herself. She remembered her youth in Syria, the capture and plunder of the city by Egyptian troops, her journey as a hostage to Egypt, the customs of the people there, a number of Egyptians, situations on the Nile, the Pharaoh's palace, where she lived for a while under the protection of

Queen Telita, her connection with the temple of Karnak and her duties as a priestess. She died in a sailing accident along with her royal patroness. In trance, she could sing Egyptian hymns and perform the old dances. During a session in which she operated as Vola she suddenly cried 'Stop that!' in Egyptian. When she came out of trance she complained her guide had tugged at her. Since control spirits never feel the physical discomforts of a medium, Vola and Ivy had to be one and the same.

Ivy also remembered a life in which she died during Nero's persecutions, a life in New England during the seventeenth century, and finally a life as a French girl of noble family who escaped to England during the Revolution. However, her Egyptian life was the clearest and most convincing. Her pronunciation of ancient Egyptian has been recorded (Wood 1955).

Initially, her recollections came out only during trance, but later also when awake, during normal consciousness. Apparently, some bridge was formed. This is one of the many examples of the past personality coming to life again. An impersonal *akasha* is out of the question.

Joan Grant is the best-known of those remembering past lives in trance. Her first book about a past life, *Winged Pharaoh* (1937), is generally known. As she recounts in her autobiography *Time Out of Mind* (1956), her memories first surfaced when she was doing psychometry of a scarab. In trance sessions she dictated sections, which were pieced together only later. Session transcripts beginning in the middle of a particular situation fitted exactly with session transcripts from a later date. Thus, in trance, she dictated portions, which were later put together in the right order to make a whole biography. This seems to imply that the book had been programmed, and was read out during trance. This makes the book excellent literature, but as an example of a past-life memory less convincing. People with recollections of past lives coming up only slowly and fragmentarily, interspersed with the reactions of the present person, are often more convincing in their imperfection. Other books by Joan Grant are less known, but well worth reading (see Bibliography).

Joan Grant was able to receive information about other people's past lives psychometrically, especially if there was a connection with a present problem (Grant 1956; Kelsey & Grant 1967). She attributes her psychic abilities to the training she received in past lives, such as in Egypt. This corresponds with data from regressions. People with psychic abilities go back to diverse and sometimes obscure forms of temple training in all kinds of periods and places.

Egypt is the most frequent, and the South America of the Mayas or Incas a good second.

An example of clairvoyant impressions from one's own past life is *The Boy Who Saw True*, the diary of a young English boy dating from 1885 to 1887. Later investigations have shown that the 'discoverer' and editor of the diary, Cyril Scott, was the diarist himself. The boy sees auras and discovers later that other people do not see them. He often gets psychic impressions of people or what is going to happen to them. He sees nature spirits and discarnate people, such as his deceased grandfather, and an impressive spirit with a gorgeous aura whom he initially identifies as Jesus. He senses that people who fall in love with each other somehow knew each other before. Later, he has a strange dream in which he sees himself in bygone times. (Compare my survey results!) Then his spiritual teacher, who has meanwhile explained that he is not Jesus, tells him these impressions are no dreams, but recollections of a past life. It confuses him when his deceased grandfather appears not to believe in reincarnation at all. His guide, however, tells him that people who have taken off their body may change their thoughts as little as those who have taken off their overcoat. He first gets memories of a life as an Indian, apparently receiving spiritual training. His present guide was also his teacher at that time. Later, memories of other lifetimes come up, mainly during his voyages abroad.

Oliver Fox experimented for many years with out-of-body experiences and published articles and a book about them. Once, when he was 42, he had a past-life experience. He had left his body, and decided to visit the ruins of some Tibetan temple. He concentrated and expected to feel the usual fast horizontal movement. Rather he felt to his horror the ground beneath him cave in, and fell through a tunnel for a long time. When he stopped and came to his senses, he saw vague, bright colours in which his situation slowly became visible. He was naked and chained to an X-shaped frame, while being tortured to death. Blood gushed from many wounds all over his body, and glowing irons had almost destroyed his eyes. The pain was more unbearable every second. He heard the voice of a man saying 'Thou art Theseus!' He answered that he wasn't Theseus, but Oliver Fox. At that moment the world imploded, and in the middle of blinding light, deafening noise and a raging storm he came back to his bed. He was certain he had relived the last moments of a previous life (Fox 1962: 105).

PSYCHIC INFORMATION ABOUT
PAST LIVES OF OTHERS

Friedrich Schwickert (1855–1930), a captain, asked about sightseeing opportunities in the port of Smyrna. He was advised to make a trip to Ephesus with a guide. On the way, everything became so familiar to him that he sent his guide back. Many years later, visiting the court of the Maharaja of Kapurtala, he was involved in a conversation with a Brahmin. The Brahmin brought him into another state of consciousness and he saw his previous life unreel in front of him like a movie. He was a cavalry commander who died in a battle at Ephesus (Muller 1970: 167).

Demeter Georgewitz-Wietzer (1873–1949) was an Austrian engineer who wrote books on parapsychological subjects under the pseudonym Surya. When he was 23, a clairvoyant in Vienna told him he saw him in a yellow-white Persian costume. Five years later, a Persian scholar with whom he corresponded told him that in his preceding life he had been a Turcoman Persian who was connected to his own order. Seventeen years later, a female psychic in Graz, knowing nothing of these experiences, told him that in his preceding life he had been a Persian mystic who studied white magic. One of his acquaintances, an Austrian military commander from the First World War with an interest and experience in parapsychology, told him during their last encounter that they had a good relationship because they had lived together before in Persia, where they had been interested in the same subjects as in this life (Muller 1970: 175).

Augustin Lesage (1876–1954), a French miner, became a psychic painter at 36, and produced more than 700 paintings thereafter. When he was 62, an English clairvoyant gave him a scarab and said that he would visit Egypt. Towards the end of that year, he painted a large canvas called 'Egyptian Harvest' and took it with him when he and his friend Alfred visited Egypt the following year. At the temple of Karnak he felt strongly that he knew the place. He visited the recently discovered grave of the Egyptian painter Mena, who had lived around 1500 BC. On the wall of the grave was a painting resembling his own. In the grave, he felt so happy that he could hardly leave. He received many impressions, but they were too vague for him to be sure whether he himself had been Mena. He told another friend he would try to find out after his death. Some time after his death, this friend received the following message via a medium: 'Tell Alfred it is true. I was Mena.' The medium had never met or heard of Lesage. Alfred was absent when the message came through (Muller 1970: 163; Victor 1980).

Arthur Guirdham, an English doctor, got involved with reincarnation after studying dreams and memory fragments of one of his patients. His study sensitised him; he started to receive impressions himself, and gradually learned to perceive discarnates and communicate with them. Sometimes they told him about his past lifetimes, but more often affirmed, clarified or corrected his own impressions and conclusions (Guirdham 1970, 1974). Later he could explore other past lives. In *The Lake and the Castle* (1976) he describes a life in around 1800, and lives in early medieval England and in Roman times. *The Island* (1980) describes a life in Greece, about 1250 BC. The stories seem trustworthy, though polished, especially the last one, and they remain partisan literature, always expounding and defending dualism, the philosophy Guirdham adheres to throughout his lives.

Clarice Toyne (1976) has a 'teacher from the beyond' telling her who was who in a previous life, to make reincarnation plausible for the general public. She then collects biographical information on both lives to highlight the parallels between them. Teilhard de Chardin was Blaise Pascal, Danny Kaye was Hans-Christian Andersen, Bernard Shaw was Voltaire, de Gaulle was Joseph II and '*Le Grand Condé*' (the most striking similarity). Victor Hugo and Charles Baudelaire are reincarnated among her acquaintances.

Hiroshi Motoyama gives spiritual consultations in which past lives often figure. In contrast with Western psychics, he often refers to the connections of individual karma with what he calls national karma. His advice remains limited to changing behaviour, praying and meditating (Motoyama 1992).

DISCARNATES ABOUT REINCARNATION

The contents of many books on spiritual subjects are channelled either in trance or fully conscious. Blavatsky apparently wrote *Isis Unveiled* (1877) and

The Secret Doctrine (1888) largely under inspiration. Alice Bailey also wrote her books in this way – according to her, inspired by 'the Tibetan', a theosophical Master.

Many discarnates eagerly convey their brainchildren to the incarnates. The mediumistic and spiritualistic literature abounds with spirits who, often adorned with the name of a deceased celebrity, cater to the needs of the living. In the Victorian age they brought edifying sermons and exalted poetry. Nowadays, many present themselves as messengers from other planets where everything is better, inciting us to stop warring, to be nice to each other and to develop higher consciousness. Their presentations conspicuously lack knowledge, practical sense, sound judgment and sometimes even good taste. In this way, frustrated souls may rather harmlessly satisfy themselves. They give many people beautiful feelings and keep them off the streets. It all becomes doubtful when they arouse or frighten people with prophecies. Discarnates who approach living people to pass on their messages are usually of limited interest and credibility. Swallowing their stuff is more stupid than buying goods at the door. Civil people do not intrude themselves upon others, certainly not when discarnate. They only contact people they know about subjects these people are personally interested in, without urging or suggesting that they publish their statements.

The Loehr–Daniels readings, themselves channelled, contain interesting observations on this (Quinn: 214–15):

> You know . . . the kind of personality who in a social gathering will take the stage and be the life of the party? Well, that can happen among these entities who are so very eager to contact Earth beings. Earth beings give them an opening through the Ouija board, and they're going to use that opening and bring through whatever can excite and hold the attention of their audience.
>
> . . . There are many on the other side who have made the transition from Earthliving and have some expanded insights into life that those in Earthliving do not have. They are eager to share that insight. But unfortunately, some of them are like children who might receive a diploma when they finish the sixth grade. Because these entities have received the diploma of transition, they conclude there is no more learning to be achieved. They are blind to the fact that there are junior high school years and senior high school years and college years and post-college years. There are Earth beings who come over on this side where the fact of having made the transition from Earth is, in a manner of speaking, their sixth grade diploma. They feel they are finished, that they have arrived, and that now they are authorities. For such ones the Ouija board and the pendulum and automatic writing

provide means to be the teachers, the authorities, they want to be. Perhaps even to speak with the degree of authority they wanted to have in Earthliving, but did not achieve.

There are too many spiritualist publications with communications from the dead about reincarnation to mention all of them. Many can be found in articles and spiritualist magazines, and many in books. Some people, like Arthur Ford, go on after death to communicate to their colleagues. Others manifest themselves to announce their coming rebirth. Karl Muller gives many examples of personal and general communications by the dead about reincarnation.

A spirit told Joachim Winckelman (1885–1956) that they had lived together in the eighteenth century. A group of spirits told him that reincarnation happens faster nowadays than in the past, because human souls can develop faster under the present circumstances. Also, many souls incarnate for the first time. Consequently, the world population is growing very fast.

Alex Sundien held trance sessions in Denmark from 1943 to 1955. His book about these contains paragraphs on reincarnation. The ghost of a murdered man says his death was a punishment because he himself had murdered people in a previous life. Many guides and helpers have developed to the point where they no longer need to reincarnate. Some souls remain in the lower spheres of the astral worlds after death and can only enter the higher spheres after a few more reincarnations. Sometimes homosexuality is caused by a recent change of sex. These statements all fit the general pattern.

ANNOUNCEMENTS OF REBIRTH

Rudolf Passian calls Baroness Adelma von Vay (1840–1925) from the Steiermark in Austria 'the Cayce of the 19th century'. Being a devout Roman Catholic, she had no idea of spiritism or reincarnation. One day she started to manifest automatic writing and a form of clairvoyance, 'seeing in a glass of water'. What she – often allegorically – saw, was usually explained by automatic writing. She became known beyond Europe for her diagnosis and advice. She was often sought out for help in illnesses doctors could not treat. In her books, Adelma von Vay mentions cases where past lives influenced or caused disease, especially epilepsy (Passian 1985). For example:

The two-year old daughter of a lady friend of the Baroness during teething suffered from cramps the doctors could not relieve. Her mother disliked the spiritism of her friend Adelma von Vay, but consulted her in her despair. Adelma's guides told her the girl was being bothered by a discarnate spirit, Raimund. Adelma contacted Raimund, who manifested himself as wild and badmouthed. At last he was made to realise how badly he was behaving and to let go of the child. The girl was restored and Raimund, who was told that he had to be reborn with the mother of the girl, promised to be a good brother to her. By letter, Adelma von Vay congratulated her friend over the coming birth of a son, though she hadn't said anything about a pregnancy and hadn't met her in two months. Her friend wrote back that her daughter was now completely restored and that she herself had just conceived. She wondered how Adelma knew. The friend indeed gave birth to a son. As a grown-up, he was very devoted to his sister.

A male relative of Baroness Von Vay died at 58. He had been a good person, but shallow and a bon vivant. Eight months after his decease he wrote by her hand that he would like to return to earth. 'They told me here that we have two choices: either remaining a spirit and developing in that way, or become a baby again. My children may still have Mass said for their poor father while I'm back in diapers!' He was greatly amused and said he knew a couple who had been married for ten years and were still childless. He would be born there and enjoyed the prospect. He gave the names and street of his prospective parents. A year later indeed a boy was born there.

During a séance in France in May 1924, the name is spelled of the deceased servant of the father of a participant. After a few difficult attempts, communication improves and the spirit says he is going to be born again in the family of some acquaintances of one of those present. He gives the name of these acquaintances, the place where they live and the composition of the family. He says he will be born again on the morning of 24 September 1924, and may be recognised by his ear. The deceased servant had had a right ear sticking out. The family in question was not informed. At 8 a.m. on the predicted day the doctor who had been present at the séance was told a boy had just been born in that family. When he visited the family three days later with his wife, the baby cried because of the visitors, but immediately calmed down with the doctor's wife. The mother remarked that it was as if he knew her. The baby had a bandage around its head because the right ear stuck out and had to be pressed back. (Muller 1970: 192)

During a spiritist séance in Venezuela in 1957, a spirit that had already communicated often, manifested itself with considerable difficulty. It said it was on the point of being born as a woman with a beautiful face but with a crippled leg. It dreaded the birth because it was going to be a difficult life. The mother, who at that moment was in the city hospital, had already been brought to the delivery room twice. Since the birth was difficult, the doctors were preparing for a Caesarean operation. The encouragement of the spiritist circle strengthened the spirit. After that, the group received a message from another spirit that the birth had taken place, without a Caesarean operation, with the exact time of birth. The group checked the data about the birth and found them correct, right down to the crippled leg. (Muller 1970: 190)

A Burmese woman whose husband was away on a long journey dreamt that a deceased friend asked to be reborn as her child; she did not like this and in the dream told him not to come. When her husband returned, he told her that he had dreamed of the same old friend and had told him in his dream that he would be welcome to be reborn in their family. In due course a child was born who later made statements suggesting that his father's acceptance had prevailed over his mother's attempted veto. (Stevenson 1987: 99)

OBSESSIONS AND REINCARNATION

An important field of spiritism related to reincarnation is that of obsessions. Adelma von Vay treated three cases of ill-willed obsessive spirits. One example:

A farmer had had epilepsy for eight years. Each attack started with a violent pain in the ring finger of his left hand. This pain radiated towards his heart and then he fainted. Adelma's guides told her that an unhappy spirit was causing this illness. The veins of the patient were weak, especially the vein to the finger in question. A female spirit, one Marie, used this weakness. Adelma was advised to magnetise the farmer daily and contact this Marie. Marie reported that she wanted to pull the man to her, as he was her husband who was reborn to frustrate her. She had been patient long enough. Marie, as the wife of this man, had been extremely jealous. Even after death she had tormented him with her jealousy. His guide had recommended him to be reborn to relieve himself from her.

Marie was admonished for a whole week, it being explained to her that jealousy has nothing to do with love and that she would surely lose her husband if she went on harassing him. How could he love his tormentor? One day, Marie said she understood that her husband in his present life knew nothing about her and that all she did was pointless, if only for this reason. To overcome her jealousy and temper, she had to accept rebirth as his child.

The attacks ceased and when the farmer departed, Adelma joked, 'If God gives you another child, I will be its godmother.' The farmer was 60 years old and already a grandfather. One year afterwards, a daughter was born to him. The child was sickly and died of dysentry after three months. A few days after the child had died, Marie wrote by Adelma's hand that rebirth had been painful for her. She would wait now for him and he would be pleased with her improvement.

The Brazilian spiritist hospitals receive patients who cannot be cured elsewhere. They diagnose about 80 percent of their cases as obsession: a discarnate nested disturbingly in somebody's aura or body. Often there is a karmic relationship. Brazilian doctors and mediums who have written about this include Bezerra de Menezes (1946) and Ignacio Ferreira (1955). According to Ferreira, who dealt with over 1,000 cases in twenty-five years, passive obsession is the most widespread. In passive obsession the obsessor does not mean to harm anybody, or may even want to protect somebody, and enters the victim's aura in ignorance, but is still disturbing. In his book he describes extensively eleven cases of obsession related to previous lives.

The spirit of a late doctor who paralysed an 11-year-old boy explained he was acting out of vengeance. After the cure, the obsessor let go, saying he wanted to develop himself further, and expected to be reborn in France. A captain had serious digestive problems and swollen veins and it looked as though he was going to have a stroke. It turned out that a male entity was obsessing him. He had known the captain and his wife in a previous life when he had been an opponent who had committed suicide because of them. Another man suffered epileptic attacks at night. The spirit of a negligent doctor who had done harm to his patients during his life turned out to be the cause of these. In his preceding life the patient had denounced the doctor, who subsequently committed suicide and had a bad time after his death. The obsessor said he himself had no idea how he had found the patient. (Muller 1970: 196)

A woman of 60 had been mentally disturbed for more than twelve years. She had been in various institutions. Every time, she got better, but when she returned home the problems began anew. A medium diagnosed obsession by the woman's brother-in-law, who had died thirteen years before. During his life they got along with difficulty, and after his death he had discovered why. In his preceding life he had been the son of a Russian nobleman. The woman, who had been his sister, had had him imprisoned so she could get their inheritance. He had sworn to avenge himself and wanted to imprison her, now in an institution. It was made clear to him that his vengeance was blocking his own well-being and further development. In an emotional scene, brother and sister forgave each other via the medium. From that moment on, the patient was cured and lived another twelve years in excellent mental health. (Muller 1970: 199)

ALLAN KARDEC

Allan Kardec collected answers from discarnates to many questions, channelled by mediums. According to Gabriel Delanne (1894: 7), Kardec did not believe in reincarnation until he began to study spiritualism. The following summary of what *The Spirits' Book* (Kardec 1857) says on reincarnation owes much to the compilation by Muller (1970: 35).

Human souls have been evolved from animal souls. Once souls reach the human stage, they do not return to animal bodies. The aim of reincarnation is to continue evolving, nursing one's ills, and redressing errors. Human souls differ greatly in their state of development. The discarnate soul is androgynous. The sex of incarnations changes. Many people have the same sex in a number of consecutive lives. The choice of sex depends strongly on the procured trials and learning experiences. There are no male–female twin souls. Souls are not halves of a higher entity.

Sometimes a person reincarnates almost immediately, but sometimes the interval may take thousands of years. This is partly a question of personal preference. During the intermission a soul may stay in spheres above its own level for some time. This stimulates its desire to develop further. Consecutive lives are often only weakly linked. Circumstances may differ greatly, and talents may remain dormant in a life, enabling other talents to develop better.

Human souls are in different stages of development. Many are on earth for the first time, but in individuals this is difficult to assess. People may incarnate in lower circumstances, even on a lower planet because this fits their development, or to fulfil missions. They retain their capacities, but their possibilities to express themselves are often limited. On every planet a childhood is necessary, although on some planets it is less cramped and clumsy than on others.

To get ahead a soul thinks about its past lives and listens to more advanced souls. This may improve its karma, but it has to test any progress on earth. The soul chooses its general fate and the trials it will be subjected to in its coming life. Not every specific occurrence is planned and determined beforehand. A soul senses the time for a new life drawing near. It can choose its body when it is permitted to do so. A soul that is going to prepare for a new incarnation may ask help from higher souls. If it descends from a good sphere, its friends will accompany it until its birth. When the pregnancy begins, a ribbon of ectoplasm links the soul to the foetus. This ribbon gradually shortens. Slowly, the soul feels itself getting more vague, and then loses its awareness, knowledge and memory.

Twins may have been friends in a previous life. Family ties often come out of friendships in past lives. Often, we know acquaintances, neighbours, people we work with from a past life, sometimes as family members. Mental similarity between children and parents is caused more by the sympathy between their souls than by heredity. A good or bad upbringing may make a big difference, especially for rather weak souls. A weak soul may ask for good parents. Parents cannot attract a good soul through their thoughts or prayers. An infant who died has had a life contributing little to its development. Sometimes such a short life completes a life cut off early just before, but usually it is the parents' karma. The soul of a mentally deficient person is undergoing punishment and is often aware of this.

Resemblances between incarnations, especially facial resemblance, are due to the ability of the soul to influence the growth of the body. Vague memories and insights from past lives may lead to inborn feelings and thoughts such as the notion of divine guidance, or of life after death. Someone's mentality may correspond from one life to the next, but can also develop through inner changes and be influenced by general and social circumstances.

Reincarnation, as presented in Kardec's book, is not compulsory, except perhaps for lazy or underdeveloped souls. We want to return because we want to develop.

EDGAR CAYCE

Edgar Cayce, who died in 1945, gave 14,236 trance readings. The transcripts total 49,135 pages and are kept in the Association for Research and Enlightenment library in Virginia Beach, Virginia. Most of these were physical health readings, and many are accredited as accurate and helpful. Around 2,500 are labelled 'life readings', of which several hundred give a past life related to the client's present life (*Psychography*: 35). Gina Cerminara wrote the first influential books about Cayce's insights into past lives and into reincarnation in general. Her books fit in with other experiences and with what we learn from regressions.

Maybe the first books about Cayce are based on the best readings. A later book by Mary Ann Woodward (1985) presents what I believe to be worthless readings

– vague rumblings and answers that repeat the questions. Just an example. The reading begins (1985: 122): 'As we find, in giving that as may be helpful for this particular body, many of the physical conditions as well as the mental attitudes must be taken in consideration – if the applications of that as we find might be helpful would be applied in that spirit of cooperative forces in bringing relief.' You understand? At the end of the session not one iota has been said. Fragments of concrete diagnosis and therapy are few and far between. Most of the session consists of sermons of a preacher about diseases that he doesn't understand and even less can treat. People are admonished to pray. That may help, but for such advice you don't need to go into trance. Woodward takes corkers and clinchers for pearls of wisdom to someone mutilated: 'Let the scars be removed from your own mental and spiritual self.' Wow! But which? And how? Even a gold digger with a track record like Cayce may dig mud as easily as gold.

John Van Auken's book (1984) is meant as a broad, popular introduction to Cayce's insights into reincarnation. Van Auken says that we do not ourselves reincarnate, but that our personalities are created fresh and anew each time. On the next page he says that the virtues and vices, the victories and defeats of former times, are our own. According to him, there is only one group of human souls, created before earth existed, and no other souls have ever been added (1984: 2). So we must have waited billions of years for our first incarnation. And the present size of humankind implies that we must have had immensely long intermissions between lives in ancient times. The very diverse regression experiences of first lives on earth – and experiences before that – refute all this completely. A few pages further, Van Auken writes (1984: 10):

> Ancient Egypt also presents us with technological power greater than that we possess today. Few modern engineers believe that pyramids can be constructed comparable to those in Giza. Even with our present high-technology we could not form or move those stones, or assemble them in a finished structure that would last four thousand years.

With all respect for the incredible performance of the ancient Egyptians, there has probably been no time in the last ten centuries that we couldn't do that. That we cannot do it today is hogwash.

Van Auken sketches the development through lifetimes of a client of Edgar Cayce, Barbara Murry. Cayce recognised her as his older sister Lela, who died when two years old. She was a soul who – like Cayce himself – was related to the soul of Jesus. One of her incarnations would have been in Egypt, where she was the first specimen of the white race. The whole story with its prequel reads as a noble unreal dream, loosely connected to theosophical ideas. I think this makes for a bumpy road for a critical reader.

> Ra Ta [the Egyptian lifetime of Cayce] anxiously watched as the newborn was being received from the womb, and as it was being cleaned and prepared for presentation. His eyes searched for the telltale signs of beastliness or celestialness and the true characteristics of a pure human form. Again and again he scanned every detail of her body. Nothing, absolutely nothing was distorted or contaminated. She was truly human.' (1984: 62)

There you go with your arm-pit hairs, your acne, your pimples, your flap ears, your false teeth and your flat feet: not truly human!

> Ra Ta and his companions had finally achieved the white body. The red had already been perfected, as well as the black, and the brown and the yellow were also near completion . . . Man was no longer a beast of the world, but a descendant from another world above, a beautiful descendant.' (1984: 63)

Is it just me, or does this smack of more than a hint of racism?

Jess Stearn (1989) summarised the readings about Cayce himself, his wife, his secretary and other acquaintances he knew from previous lives. Cayce's readings about past lives and their aftermath in this life may be eminently reasonable – his readings about Atlantis and ancient Egypt are eminently unreasonable. His explanation of physical handicaps as the consequence of moral shortcomings in lifetimes more than 10,000 year ago is very improbable from what we know from regression therapy. That information may be scientifically unproven is no issue, but when thoughts are illogical and also conflicting with everything we know, the story is different. How can humans 50,000 years ago be only thought forms (by the way, completely contradicting Van Auken's conclusions from Cayce's material) that gradually began to materialise, when we know for sure that humans and humanoids have been roaming this planet for several million years? Also, the later (?!) misery between men and dinosaurs is very unlikely – and that is phrasing it politely. If people had been contemporaries of the dinosaurs, that would have been scores of million years ago. Cayce also predicted that before the end of the twentieth century parts of Atlantis would rise again from the sea and that the American East Coast and West Coast would sink into the sea. Intuitive powers are wondrous indeed – Cayce himself is a shining example – but no matter how valid intuition is, it is not reliable.

The most interesting part of Stearn's book is the story of how he encountered Cayce's work and how he came to write his biography, *The Sleeping Prophet*. A good picture of what Cayce has said about reincarnation can be had from the books of Gina Cerminara.

THE LOEHR–DANIELS READINGS

After Edgar Cayce the most interesting source of life readings is one Dr John Christopher Daniels, channelled by Grace Wittenberger-Loehr between 1951 and 1979. Her work was continued by her husband Franklin Loehr till his death in 1988. Franklin Loehr was a minister, and the pious Christian vocabulary testifies to that. But the contents of the readings are concrete, interesting, reasonable, modest and sometimes funny. About 4,800 readings have been documented, 17 pages on average, about nine different people on average, totalling past-life information about 45,000 people. 'Dr John' also answers general questions about reincarnation. The pattern emerging from these readings fits into what is generally known, but contains many specific ideas.

In the course of the years, some readings were about people who were related to other people who had requested readings previously, sometimes years before. Professor Horton Amidon collected 163 of these cases (1985) and found only one contradiction. Probably the most important books about the Loehr–Daniels readings are *Karma, the Great Teacher* (1985) and *Destiny of the Soul* (1987) by Helen Roberts. I summarise.

The soul divides itself into a masculine and a feminine half that incarnate separately. Both halves have male and female lives. The masculine half has to learn to express itself in a female body, and the feminine half has to learn to express itself in a male body.

We have between 60 and 100 lives. Young souls are in their first ten to twelve lives, which are mainly about getting accustomed and starting up. The next 40 to 60 are 'karmic' lives that entail our major learning experiences. Then we become 'old souls', more involved in being of service to others and repaying, in a sense, through the development of others what we have received in previous lives. Karma then is less important, though we still tie up loose ends, complete unfinished business, process undigested emotions and make up for lessons missed (1985: 20).

Intermission periods between lives don't have fixed duration, but between seven and ten lives in a thousand years is common (1985: 6). Lives that ended in abortion or in early childhood don't count, as they have no real meaning for the soul (1985: 261).

Dr John refers to 'cycles of seven' and 'cycles of three' as the most common development patterns. Those numbers are rules of thumb. A long cycle may consist of six, eight or nine lives. A short cycle may take four lives and occasionally two. Non-cylical lives may be interspersed by long cycles. One or two female lives may be interspersed by a long series of male lives, and the other way round, to avoid the soul getting stuck in the emphasis of that cycle.

A common theme for a short cycle is the development of balance in some aspect of life. The first life may sway too much to an extreme, e.g. in power. The second life corrects this to the other extreme, e.g., powerlessness. An experienced soul may find balance in that second life, but often the response is overdone and a third life is needed to balance this quality (1985: 21). Sometimes a short cycle is for the purpose of learning a difficult lesson thoroughly (1985: 35).

Some lives are rest lives. A soul may rest and refresh itself on other planes after difficult earth lives, but it is fitting and right that relaxation takes place on the same plane as that on which the efforts and painful experiences occurred. After too many hard lives on earth, a soul may start to resist earth life (1985: 271).

Twin souls began their individual existence at the same time, coming from the same source (Quinn: 104). Cycle mates are compatible souls that during a cycle often incarnate together. Usually, cycle mates come from the same cosmic family, and often they are of the opposite sex. Souls of different cosmic families may also be compatible and be excellent cycle mates (1985: 42). Soul mates usually don't live at the same time. The discarnate one is often guiding the incarnate one. Or soul mates live in different regions without ever meeting. Their souls may meet in sleep, on other levels (Quinn: 104).

Man started as an earthly, animal being. He partook in all evolutionary processes from the simplest beginnings of life on earth. When human souls were ready to connect to a physical body, the most fitting animals were chosen. The soul stimulated the brain to further development. We are the result of the interaction of souls with the highest form of animal life on earth (1985: 145).

The relationship between soul and personality is more complex than that between actor and role:

It is a popular notion that the soul knows everything and that the answer to almost any personality problem is to relax into the soul and such. This is not true. Upon many occasions the person must lead the soul. (1985: 319).

The personality often must take the leadership from the soul and for the soul. When there is weakness in a soul, a person can by its own will, its own decisions and choices, decide and choose what it will do and what it will be. Thus the person can become the savior in these particular areas of weakness for its own soul. (1987: 107)

Also after death, the personality is not absorbed by the soul, but retains some independence, sometimes too much:

This soul was aghast at what happened. The personhood, that oriental despot, even after he died, could not be reached..Evil was reaching out toward him on the lower astral side — but he had been first reached by some who were good. His own mother was one who had reached him in consciousness when he was murdered and went over — he was rather quickly put permanently to sleep and did not have much of an afterlife . . . This incarnation had gotten away from it, but that did not relieve the soul of its responsibility. (1985: 63)

The particular problem of this soul was a certain anxiety which has developed primarily from the soul's possibly too great identification with its incarnate and excarnate personhoods. (1985: 235).

This soul, partly in the desire to protect its personhood but even more in a rather morbid curiosity as to just what was happening, was drawn into a rather close identification with the person, and so experienced the catastrophic events of the fires for three days and three horrible nights, and then death (1985: 365)

We may plan many lives, but we don't plan everything and we don't realise every plan. Sometimes the plan of life stops early, so a person has to design the rest of his or her life while going, possibly with some inspiration from guides or teachers (1985: 115). There may be unplanned accidents. Spirits may protect people with a mission, but this is rare (1985: 307). Even a planned marriage may not come about. We have to learn to deal with the unexpected. There are many insecurities on earth: accidents, disease, war, free will of the people involved, etcetera. Many events are meant to be, even destined to be, but few are so predestined that no change is possible. An intended marriage may be confounded in several ways and may be postponed to a next life or even cancelled completely (1985: 391). We must learn to deal with the unexpected.

There are many contingencies on earth: accidents, illnesses, war, arbitrary decisions of people, and so on. Many people see ill health as karmic, but that is only true in some cases (Quinn: 148). Though many events are meant to be, even predestined, they are rarely predestined to the extent that they cannot be changed. Dr John also says that what happens to us is not as decisive as what we do with it (1987: 94).

When a soul has collected negative emotions and fears, it may release them by creating a mentally unbalanced personality. Dr John calls such lives 'sewer lives' or 'drainage lives' (1985: 227). Few lifetimes have the resolution of karmic debts as their main aim – no more than 5 percent.

What happens to souls that continue to exploit bad energies instead of resolving or transmuting them? Reflections on this issue are collected in the second book by Helen Roberts (1987). The soul that opts definitely for the dark side and has become inhumane and lost its conscience, will be 'recycled'. She loses her individuality. Whatever is valuable is used elsewhere and the rest dissolves. Unbounded self-pity and persistent self-chosen stupidity are two common routes to extinction. Unbounded lust, unbounded self-centredness and cruelty attract evil influences that keep the soul dark and exploited. Guilt about mistakes can also lead to darkness and lead from bad to worse (1987: 203). Sometimes a soul gets another try and restarts its evolution (1987: 99). A soul can also pull back at the last moment and ask for another try (1987: 108).

What happens with souls who go on developing? The personality of each life remains. Our previous lives can feed and guide our present life, and souls can even develop in between lives, but the same personality never returns identically. The many different personalities may become too much to handle. The house fills up, the family is overcrowded. Then many past lifetimes integrate to form a kind of super-personality. Dr John call this stage 'cohesion' and the result a 'solity'. Cohesion is not a question of action, but of being. The solity is an entity that is less than the soul, but more than the separate personalities of separate lifetimes. One of the functions of a solity is for the soul to retain its individuality in fields of existence where time and space distances no longer help us to experience ourselves as separate beings. In this stage, reincarnation is no longer necessary. But if we reincarnate, our solity may act as the guide of the incarnated personality.

The post-human stages of development Dr John calls respectively 'Sons of God', Elohim, Mini-Creators and Co-Creators (1987: 251). Elohim are carrying responsibilities that are, so to speak, hundreds of times that of a human soul. By exception, Elohim may reincarnate. Examples are Moses, Elijah and, naturally, Jesus. A more recent example is Emerson (1987: 262). Mini-Creators learn to shape planetary systems from star collisions (1987: 266). They may also create souls, though they often lack the wisdom and power to do that well. Their souls stand more chance of being recycled. That is a pity, but as long as we go on procreating in the present numbers, it will stay this way (1987: 119).

RUTH MONTGOMERY
AND JANE ROBERTS

The American medium Arthur Ford received impressions of his own past lives and those of others. After his death Ruth Montgomery received messages from him through automatic writing (in this case, typing) about the conditions after death, about reincarnation in general, and about the reincarnations of some people in particular (Montgomery 1971). What Ford says about the conditions after death is consistent with many reports from others. But even after his death, Arthur Ford remains an enthusiast. Descriptions of the discarnate life are filled with impassioned deliberations and sermons. He and his companions describe their state as unity with God, as the most divine state imaginable. What does Ford have to say about reincarnation in his blessed state?

We prepare for a new incarnation by extensive consideration and assimilation of previous lives to select items for compensation, improvement, development, test or consolidation.

Once we know what we want, we look for suitable circumstances. Our sex is often the same as the one we had in our past few lives. Many of us have a preferred sex. Sometimes, sex alternates for educative purposes. When we can we may look for parents ourselves. In this choice, we consider the sex of an available embryo, as well as the opportunities offered by our prospective educators, and sometimes the learning experience involved in being born to particular parents. If there are several candidates for one embryo, the candidates are weighed one against the other, resulting almost automatically in the most suitable candidate, as in a kind of computer clearance.

Once our parents have been determined, we may hang about in their vicinity for a while to convince ourselves that this choice fits with our plans. We enter the foetus usually during birth, but sometimes shortly before or after. If we hesitate too long, the child may die. If somebody enters a defective body, he usually does this to work off some karma faster. This is especially true for congenital mental handicaps. Karma is also worked off through serious accidents during childhood. Usually, we unconsciously desired that opportunity. But not all accidents are foreseen, and they may be due to coincidences that are not karmic.

Ruth Montgomery, always the journalist, asks the deceased Ford about the further vicissitudes of the deceased famous. Abraham Lincoln is living in New Orleans and works together with universities and institutes to find a solution to the race problem. George Washington died as a soldier in Vietnam after leading a platoon on a dangerous mission and being taken prisoner. Rudolph Valentino is happily married and lives in Paris. Napoleon was an ordinary soldier in his next life, and then had two short lives in Portugal and Brazil.

What do we do with such tit-bits? They feed our curiosity without satisfying it, being more what we would expect from a gossip magazine than from someone living in unity with the divine.

Ford recounts that in Palestine he was once the father of Lazarus, Martha Maria, and a third sister, Ruth, a previous incarnation of Ruth Montgomery herself. A later book elaborately describes the fortunes of this Palestinian family (Montgomery 1974). According to the information on the spine, the book is non-fiction, so apparently it purports to be true.

It is difficult to say anything sensible about such stories. They are most convincing if the lives are not about, or in the direct vicinity of, a famous person, and if they give the reader the feeling of being in a bygone age. The books by Joan Grant and by Arthur Guirdham, and especially the book by Edward Ryall (1974), are good examples of this. About the events in Palestine, however, there are too many competing versions. At least the version by Montgomery's inspirators does not directly contradict the New Testament, although their additions abound in exalted feelings, appropriate to a noble and sentimental parson's vision of events.

A lot of what Montgomery writes (or Ford says) makes sense, but the distinction between careful reports and enthusiastic embellishments by the communicating discarnates remains fuzzy.

*

Jane Roberts published a number of books recording information that she received from a discarnate soul who calls himself Seth. Her books are probably the best-known publications of channelled spirit messages during the last few years. Seth is a gnostic spirit-philosopher who wants to tell us the real nature of the world and of mankind. His epistemology and metaphysics are elaborately explained in a scientific-sounding jargon. They are typically didactic expositions of somebody disseminating the truth, without any trace of dialectic. Vocabulary and exposition seem to embrace logic, but are incoherent and without critical discourse. Doubts are countered by assurance, not by argument.

Of himself, Seth says: 'In the first place I am a teacher, although I was never a scholar. Mainly, I am someone with a message: you create the world you know' (Roberts 1972). His basic message is more or less that our physical surroundings and our physical body originated from our own thoughts and are sustained by them. Apparently, he takes the physical universe for a part of his present discarnate environment. Thus, his philosophy is more or less Platonic. The physical world is only a semi-real reflection of the real mental world. Reminiscent of Christian Science, he summons us to believe in the reality of good, and not in the reality of evil. Experiences that seem to indicate the contrary are merely apparent. All edifying testimonial literature tends to herald coming redemption. Seth is no exception. Around the year 2075 (still safely far away) people get an intimate contact with their inner being, a being that will mediate between man and the world. I am not sure what this means, but it does not sound encouraging. He continues by heralding new prophets, and to top it all off, 'the third Christ personality', whatever that may be.

Seth also has some things to say about reincarnation. I will summarise his discourse, although it is complex and interwoven with his notion of reality and the human soul. In his philosophy, time is not linear, and so incarnations do not take place consecutively. According to him, our incarnations are plays acted next to each other simultaneously. The ostensible causal relationships between lives and the current concept of karma are therefore illusions from which we must free ourselves to become truly creative. To assume that plays can be acted in a world without time, without succession of events, is ridiculous, and it remains unclear how this tallies with the forecast that around 2075 we will all be in contact with our real selves.

FURTHER READING

Well-known mediumistic books including reincarnation start with Allan Kardec (1857). Spiritism has produced few important new books on reincarnation, though channeling, mediumship while remaining fully aware, has become a favourite source for many people who want to know something about their past lives. The major publication is Karl Muller's *Reincarnation, based on facts* (1970). Muller, who spoke nine languages, collected many and diverse past-life cases, especially spiritist ones.

Spiritist books I could not find are *The Soul of Nyria* by Rosa Caroline Praed (1914) and *The New Nuctemeron* by Marjorie Livingstone (1930). Other spiritist books on reincarnation have been written by Marcus Knight (1950), Harriet Boswell (1969) and Maria Penkala (1972).

The books by Joan Grant (1938–56) have been mentioned in the text, like those of Arthur Guirdham (1970–80). Ruth Montgomery wrote several on the subject, beginning with *A World Beyond* (1971). Also note the extraordinary claim on the blurb: 'The first eye-witness account of the hereafter.' Jane Roberts didn't limit herself to one book. Seth went on speaking. Speaking is silver.

Apart from biographies about Cayce, such as those by Sugrue (1942), Millard (1972) and Stearn, there is an *Edgar Cayce Series* of at least fifteen titles with excerpts from his readings, e.g., *Edgar Cayce on Atlantis* by Edgar Evans Cayce (1968). His son Hugh Lynn Cayce edited this series and wrote a book about his father's work (1964). Many books by other writers are about Cayce's readings. The first and best known is by Gina Cerminara (1950), who also wrote a second book on the subject (1967). Much of Edgar Cayce's work and Gina Cerminara's rendition of it, is mentioned in later chapters. Other books are by Noel Langley (1967), Mary Ann Woodward (1972) and I.C. Sharma (1975). Violet Shelley (1979) concludes in *Reincarnation Unnecessary* on the basis of Cayce's readings that reincarnation doesn't need to go on. I find the title to be quite misleading. Apparently Cayce had said in a few instances that somebody had not necessarily to return to earth.

Books about the Loehr–Daniels readings are by Noreen Quinn (n.d.) and Roy Smith (1975). Noreen Quinn says that Hugh Lynn Cayce and Gina Cerminara helped her in processing the material to avoid the mistakes they themselves had made. Helen Nethery Hussey wrote two booklets: *Karmic Justice for Women* (1981) and *Karmic Roots* (1981). The first booklet gives two unabridged Loehr–Daniels life readings as examples of karmic reactions to a life in which a man dominated and suppressed his wife. The second booklet is about a black person and a white person who exchanged colours in two different lifetimes. Helen Hussey later wrote with Sandra Sherrod a book on the readings (1983) and finally, as Helen Roberts, two larger works: *Karma, the Great Teacher*, a book about one hundred readings, and *Destiny of the Soul* (1987). The research of Amidon (1985) has been mentioned in the text of this chapter.

Five

YOUNG CHILDREN
WHO REMEMBER
PREVIOUS LIVES

Recollection is only the most explicit form in which past lives may leave traces. Someone sees the landscape of southern Spain in a film and is overwhelmed by an intense, inexplicable feeling of melancholy. Someone hears the name Julius Caesar for the first time and is filled with a sudden, unreasonable hatred. Such emotions without explanation in the present life may indicate a past life. Idiosyncrasies, phobias and monosymptomatic neuroses (consisting of one isolated symptom only) without traumatic experiences in this life can also be traces from past lives. The full list of traces includes:

- appearance (e.g. face and birth marks)
- behaviour (e.g. curious dressing or eating and drinking habits)
- abilities (e.g. child prodigies)
- intuition (assessing people or situations)
- preferences (for countries, styles, art forms, etc.)
- postulates (rigid attitudes to life)
- emotions
- recollections.

Among the capabilities that may come from past lives is the ability immediately to recognise and assess, usually subsumed under the vague label 'intuition'. Much in intuition may, if we go back far enough, be the result of earlier experiences, earlier learning and long practice (Shirley 1924: 32). Appearance and behaviour can contain traits of past lives. Usually, these remain implicit, but young children who remember previous lives may exhibit typical behaviour that ties in clearly with what they seem to remember. They may perform rituals for getting up, eating or greeting that are unknown or unusual in the area but are common elsewhere. A charming example is the little girl who slams her milk mug down on the table and wipes her mouth as if she had just put down a pint of beer with great satisfaction. When her parents reprimand her, she bursts into tears and says it is a tribute to her comrades who she does not want to forget. When the family inquires further, she makes remarks about a past life (Muller 1970: 60; Head & Cranston 1977: 396). The girl also looks markedly different from the rest of her family.

Peculiar, inexplicable preferences are halfway between more explicit and more implicit indications. They may be preferences for a particular food, a particular language or country, a particular architectural style, a particular kind of music, and so on. Walter Pater said: 'Taste is the memory of a culture once known.' Of course, peculiarities develop in this life, but many abilities, emotions preferences and idiosyncrasies contain traces of past lives. A strong indication of past lives is extraordinary ability in young children, the child prodigies who have exceptional musical, linguistic or mathematical talents, or such exotic talents a puppeteering (Fielding 1898: 336).

Karl Schlotterbeck subsumes all traces before recollection under the correct but vague label of 'patterns', and continues: 'but these patterns and impressions are only appetizers when we are looking for our past lives. We all wish for clearer memories in the form of sensory information' (1987: 13).

The first seven kinds of traces of past lives may all help to trigger recollection. Past-life therapy uses emotions and rigid attitudes to awaken recollection, to process and to release these emotions and beliefs. Exploration of past lives out of curiosity may use the other peculiarities as starting points.

Children who have just started to talk may speak about their preceding life. Almost all of them show other traces: birth signs, preferences, idiosyncrasies or remarkable skills. Child cases have been methodically investigated to see if they confirm reincarnation. Recent books are more practical: they suggest how parents may deal with these children, their memories and their feelings.

THE LIFE WORK OF IAN STEVENSON

Investigating child cases is expensive and time-consuming. Few people do it, and fewer do it well. The most well-known names in this field are Ian Stevenson

Hemendra Banerjee, Francis Story and Hernani Andrade. Ian Stevenson, from the Department of Parapsychology of the University of Virginia, is the international authority in the area of child case research. He has collected about 2,000 cases of apparent past-life recall. Of these he has examined about half extensively. He has reported his findings in books and numerous articles. In northern India he examined 105 cases, in Sri Lanka 80, and a few dozen in Turkey, Lebanon, Alaska, Thailand and Burma.

Banerjee worked in India from the 1950s, where he founded the Indian Institute of Parapsychology, and has been living in the United States since 1970. Banerjee seems to be an enthusiast who is not shy of publicity and works fast. His book *The Once and Future Life* (1979) carries as subtitle *An astonishing twenty-five-year study on reincarnation*. It does not even come close to Stevenson's work. Banerjee writes pearls such as: 'It is a scientific fact that a person cannot remember that which he or she has not previously learned' (Banerjee 1979: 17). His concept of reincarnation is definitely religious and not empirical (1979: 24). Story worked with Stevenson in India, and Andrade worked in Brazil, also cooperating with Stevenson.

Research into child cases may be compared with legal investigation. It is important to get as many precise and independent testimonies as possible. If a child has never been near the place where the past person lived, and has not met any people from there, it is possible to test and experiment on the spot.

Stevenson takes careful account of all alternative explanations of apparent recollection. He has done solid study of the psychology of recollection and testimony and of the methods to evaluate eyewitness reports. The introduction to his third book (1975) gives a particularly valuable overview of this area. His opponents are less informed. Daniel Cohen (1975) makes sixteen insinuating remarks in eight pages about a particular case, then explains this case as 'wishful thinking' on Stevenson's part, and ends by claiming Stevenson's other cases are less convincing. This is reminiscent of the trivial explanation of paranormal phenomena by 'suggestion', the favourite explanation of laymen in the area of the paranormal and, worse, in the area of suggestion. But if we know that something is nonsense, we do not need to treat it seriously; we just explain it by something ordinary, which at the same time is not real: suggestion.

Of the many cases Stevenson examined, I will use three examples from his series *Cases of the Reincarnation Type* (1975–83). I am paraphrasing them here as illustrations, leaving out the facts, circumstances and research methods that make up the evidence.

Laxmi Narain, the 17-year-old son of a rich landowner and tax official, lived in the city of Pilibhit in Uttar Pradesh. His father died and left him a considerable fortune. He was a rather spoilt child who, at the time of his father's death, had not even finished primary school, and spent his money freely on food, drink, clothes and women. He was also generous, so he ultimately spent all of his fortune. After a few weeks of the high life, he would regularly withdraw into his house and devote his time to religious thought. After one or two weeks he would have had enough of this and then the dolce vita would begin again. This continued in a repetitive cycle. Like so many spoilt children, he was hot-tempered. Once when he saw a visitor leaving the house of his favorite prostitute, he shot and killed him. He went into hiding and was able, probably by using bribes, to avoid a court case. After this, he moved to another town, where he died within a year, probably at the age of 32. That was in December 1918.

In 1921 a boy called Bishen Chand was born in Bareilly, also in Uttar Pradesh. When he was only 10 months old, he spoke the word 'pilivit'. When he began to talk, he talked about his life as Laxmi Narain. The following elements of his recollections were written down before Bishen Chand was accompanied to Pilibhit to check his story:

Laxmi Narain lived in Mohalla in Pilibhit. His father was a rich landowner of the Kayastha caste. His uncle was Har Narain. His school was near the river. He learned Urdu, Hindi and English. His English teacher in the sixth grade was fat and had a beard. When his father died there was a large crowd at the funeral.

His house had two floors with separate entrances for men and women. His uncle Har Prusad had a green house. He used to have kite races with his neighbour Sunder Lal, who had a house with a green fence. He had a short, dark servant, Maikua, of the Kahar caste who was a good cook. He won a lawsuit against some family members. He shot a man who had just left the house of Padma, his favourite prostitute and mistress. He was drunk at the time. After the murder, he hid in his garden, where his mother sent him food. Later, he got some work in Shahjahanpur, where he died at the age of twenty.

Almost all of this proved to be correct. The only incorrect statements were the age of his death, the neighbourhood in Pilibhit, and Har Narain not being the name of his uncle, but of his father. However, there was somebody in Pilibhit whom everybody called Uncle Har Narain. This could explain the confusion. In Pilibhit, Bishen Chand recognised his house and the house of his neighbour, Sunder Lal. In his house he recognised the room where he had hidden some money. The money was actually found in this room, although not in exactly the place he indicated. He recognised the place where there had formerly been a staircase. He recognised a trader's house and the place of a former watchmaker's shop. Most of the recollections began to fade after he turned 7. Emotions related to the previous life *were especially feelings for people from that life. He was attached to his previous mother. He refused gifts from some other previous relatives. 'Then you wanted my blood, now you want to placate me with money.' Apparently, he was referring to the family quarrel and the ensuing lawsuit.*

With difficulty, he accepted the needy circumstances under which he was now growing up. For example, it irritated him that his father did not buy him silk clothes. As a child, he had the same hot-tempered character as Laxmi Narain had apparently had. He was extraordinarily proud of the story of how he had shot his rival. When he was about 17 his violent tendencies disappeared. He remained hot-tempered until he was middle-aged, although he was more and more repentant after his moods. When he was 23 years old, he met his previous mistress once again, who was now about 50. He embraced her and fainted with emotion. In the evening, he visited her with a bottle of wine (although he was now teetotal) and, in vain, tried to convince her to resume their past relationship. He was bitter that his old house had fallen into disrepair, and scoffed at the news that some merchant had received marks of honour.

As for preferences, he liked meat and fish from childhood, and adored alcohol, although he grew up in a family of vegetarian teetotallers. As a boy of 4 or 5 he used to sneak sips of the medicinal brandy. His preference for meat and fish remained until his middle age. His tendency to drink vanished. When he was an adult, he accepted that he could not indulge his desire for expensive clothes. As a child, he was already interested in music, and this remained, just as with Laxmi Narain. As a child he liked to fly kites, but his present father repressed this tendency. As a 6-year-old boy, he advised his father to get a mistress. Growing up, his sexual preoccupations vanished. Bishen Chand married and led a quiet life in this respect. As for abilities, his knowledge of Urdu was notable, as was his ability to play the tabla, a musical instrument. He mastered both, without ever having been taught, and without example in his direct surroundings. When he was 8 he stopped playing the tabla.

Between the ages of 3 and 7 his behaviour was distinctly different from that of his family. Every day would witness some comparison with his past life. He was contemptuous of the poverty in the house. 'Even my servant would not eat this.' He took off his clothes and demanded silk garments.

We do not know if Laxmi Narain and Bishen Chand looked alike; presumably, there was no notable resemblance. Interestingly, an eye trouble Bishen Chand had as a child was cured by a medicine Laxmi Narain's mother sent him, with the information that this medicine had helped her son. (Stevenson 1975: 176)

Another example is Lalitha Abeyawardena, born in August 1962 near Colombo in Sri Lanka (Stevenson 1977: 117). When she was 2½ years old she began to talk, and almost immediately told of her past life. She said she had been a teacher in Mirigama (about 60 kilometres to the north). Her husband was a teacher as well. She gave the name of the school, described the way there from her house, and described the shops. She named a few family members and said she had died of an intestinal disease in a hospital. She was emotional and cried often when she talked about her past life, being worried about the children she had left behind. However, she did not want to return and see her husband again.

The teacher was called Nilanthie and was born in 1914. She married in 1939 and died in 1953. She married an assistant teacher who was teaching at the school where her father later became a principal. After a few years of marriage, her husband became interested in other women and perhaps started to drink. He fell in love with someone else and wanted a divorce, and therefore accused his wife of adultery. She denied this and he tried to choke her and threatened her with a knife. In spite of the problems, she remained with her three children. Finally, she did decide to leave. Her husband brought her to her oldest brother. According to her brother, her husband had beaten her and, although she was sick and had a fever, forced her to bathe outside in cold water. Three days later she died of 'non-specific enteritis', perhaps typhus.

Lalitha's recollection of her life as Nilanthie includes about sixty statements. Besides her own name, she remembered the names of her husband and her sons. She knew where her brothers and sisters lived and remembered such incidents as her younger brother biting her finger when she fed him, and much later visiting her on his motorbike. She listed the classes and the schools in which she had taught, gave information about her direct surroundings and the shops there, and gave the names of a few people and a few villages in the area. Further, she was able to talk about her husband's infidelity, the beatings he gave her, the circumstances leading to her death, and her age at that time. She recognised a number of people from her past, but not all. When she was 5 and went to school, her recollection had largely faded.

Sometimes Lalitha was aware that time had passed; sometimes she spoke in the present and begged for her youngest daughter who was perhaps crying from hunger. When she spoke about her past life she made an almost adult impression. Apparently her emotions were still strong, for she cried a lot. Her hate and fear towards her past husband were strong. She was afraid of sickness in others and in herself. She felt sympathy for her past brothers. Like Nilanthie, Lalitha was pious and interested in religion. She was interested in books and often played teacher. She liked the kukulala (a yam-like root) and loved flowers. She was strongly against drinking and had little interest in housekeeping. Nilanthie had a husband who drank and a helper who did her housekeeping while she was teaching. A difference was that Lalitha did not like beef, although Nilanthie ate it. She was 18 months old when she sat in the lotus position, and 2 when she began to sing religious gathas. At that age she *also took a pencil and immediately held it correctly. She picked flowers for temples and she was fond of bringing offerings in the Buddhist manner. Opinions differed about the physical resemblance of the two women. Lalitha had birthmarks but they were unrelated to her life as Nilanthie. (Stevenson 1977: 117)*

The third example is Necati Çaylak who was born in 1963 in Karaali near Antakya in Turkey (Stevenson 1980: 229). When he was about 3 he recounted that he had died in a car accident on the bridge near the highway (5 kilometres further on), and named the people who had been in the car with him. Later, when he saw the bridge for the first time, he started to cry and described the accident again. He said the car had not turned over, but had 'climbed up' against the railing. He said he had lost a shoe during the accident. He did not want to cross the bridge.

After that, he began to talk about his previous life. He was called Abdülkerim and had a wife and four children. When he was 3, he named the village where he had lived and almost all the people he could remember. There had been an accident on the bridge about a month before he was born. The widow of Abdülkerim Haddoroglu from Bedirge, the man who had died in this accident in February 1963, visited Necati in the fall of 1966. Necati recognised her and, less clearly, her three escorts.

Abdülkerim Haddoroglu was born in 1934 and lived in Bedirge, another village near Antakya, almost all his life. He had a taxi for a few months, but could not drive. Otherwise, he was a farmer all his life. He married and had three children. When he died, his wife was expecting a fourth. He was 29 years old at the time. The accident happened shortly after Ramadan, when Abdülkerim and his friends had drunk raki. They asked someone to drive them back in a minibus because they themselves had had too many drinks. Blinded by the lights of an oncoming truck, the vehicle drove into a sidewall of the bridge. Abdülkerim died at once and did indeed lose a shoe. The other passengers and the driver were wounded.

Necati remembered many details about this previous life and death correctly: the names of his wife, his children, his father, his mother, and his sister, and the village his wife came from. The information about the accident was correct: the place, the minibus and the fact they came from Antakya after having drunk at a religious festival.

Other details were incorrect: his father's last name, that he had been the driver and that the car had 'climbed up' the wall. He mixed up the names of the passengers, partly with those of other persons involved, such as the owner of the car. He recognised his wife, some relatives and acquaintances. However, the accounts of these meetings were unclear and inconsistent in some places.

His fear of the bridge, remaining until he was 10, corresponds with other children's *fears of the cause or location of their past death. He was afraid of cars until he was 7, when he became interested in them. When he was 10 he wanted to become a chauffeur. Even as a child he liked raki.*

He was the most intelligent child in the family and had a tendency to give his older brothers advice. He suffered from headaches until he was 10. His recollections remained virtually unchanged, including the errors. (Stevenson 1980: 299)

CHILDREN IN THE WEST WHO REMEMBER PAST LIVES

The oldest and also strangest case I know is from 1878: the 'Watseka Wonder' in the United States. A 14-year-old girl, Lurancy Vennum, suffers seizures, regains consciousness and says she is Mary Roff, a girl who died 17 years before. Richard Webb is among those who tell the story (1974: 146).

More cases are scattered throughout psychic research and parapsychology journals and in the regular press. The first real collection was by Peter and Mary Harrison (1983). They describe 26 cases of children in England. They don't say for how long – or how briefly – they had to search for them. The very diverse cases are described without scientific pretence, but carefully reported. In some cases the preceding life could be identified. They have examples of return within the same family and even to the same parents. These cases fit the general pattern as described by Stevenson. The example of the English boy remembering how he died as the pilot of a German bomber parallels similar cases Stevenson encountered in Thailand.

Some unaffected remarks about the interlife are interesting: 'Some of the sick people got fruit to make them better after they died' . . . He was taught that all he had to do, was to think of the flower, stage by stage, and the flower would appear . . . and the colour of the flower would correspond to the colour willed by him.' Apparently there is education in how to deal with psychoplastic reality. Chapter 10 returns to this. Stephen Ramsay: 'I wakened up sometimes and went to sleep again.' Simon Brown: 'After a long time I woke up and my dog was with me.' One boy remembers being a ghost in a cemetery for a long time.

In the Netherlands, Joanne Klink collected statements from young children about their birth and about previous lives (1990). Her aim was to get Christians thinking. If her books don't do that, what will? She gives children a voice by taking them seriously. Much of what is sacred to children is being ignored or rejected or criticised because it doesn't fit parental materialism or dogmatism.

In Brazil, Hernani Andrade has been the main researcher in this field. Brazilian past-life therapists still encounter such cases nowadays. One example is the medical doctor Edison Flávio Martins (1999). A black maid tells a 2-year-old white girl that she is so pretty and so light. The girls becomes angry, as she isn't white, she is black! When she is 10, she tells her parents that as an infant she was always surprised about her father. How could her husband be her father? Later she recalls a journey on a slave ship where she carried his child and he was beaten to death by a slave driver. Now she understands why she hates her aunt, her father's sister. She continues to feel so close to blacks and admires them so much that her later husband becomes jealous of them.

STATISTICS ABOUT CHILD CASES

Between 25 and 75 percent of the past lives that children remember can be identified and verified, usually because the deceased personality's family is still alive. Karl Muller found in child cases intermissions between death in the preceding life and birth in the new life of usually less than twelve years. Stevenson found intermissions between one and four years. Bache (1990) confirms short intermissions in cases of young children remembering their preceding life. Intermissions of more than 12 years are rare. The median of intermissions in the Lebanon was 6 months, among the Alevis in Turkey 9 months, in Sri Lanka 18 months, and among the Tlingits in Alaska 48 months. Of 616 cases in 10 different cultures, the median intermission was 15 months. In the East intermissions are shorter on the average than in the West.

Stevenson found in 46 percent of cases in India that the preceding personality had had a violent death. In Sri Lanka this was 42 percent, and correlated strongly with unidentified past lives. Maybe this is because of the greater distances between places of death and places of rebirth in Sri Lanka. Other countries have similar percentages.

One of the most interesting, and potentially most important, of the recurrent features is the high incidence of violent death among the previous personalities of the cases. We found that among 725 cases from six different cultures, 61 percent of the subjects remembered previous lives that ended in violent death. This incidence far exceeds the incidence of violent death in the general populations of the countries where these cases occurred. But we need to ask whether it might arise from biases in the reporting of cases to us. Violent deaths attract more attention than natural ones, and our informants may have remembered longer and better the cases in which violent deaths figured than those in which the previous life recalled had ended naturally.

We were able to study indirectly the influence that violent death might have on the reporting of cases through a comparison of two series of cases in India. The cases of the first series were collected unsystematically over a period of about twenty years. Entry into this series depended on the casual, unforced memories of informants who for one reason or another notified one of my associates or me about a case. There were 193 cases in this series. The 19 cases in the second, much smaller, series were detected during the systematic survey in the Agra District. Informants were selected randomly and asked to search their memories for any case of the reincarnation type they could remember. In the larger, unsystematically collected series, the incidence of violent death in the previous life was 49 percent; in the smaller series it was only 35 percent. The difference suggests that some of the high incidence of violent death in our series may be due to informants' remembering cases with violent death more than they remember those with natural death; however, an incidence of 35 percent violent deaths still far exceeds that in the general population of India, which (for the comparable period) was less than 7 percent.

The high incidence of violent death in these cases seems therefore to be a natural feature, not an artifact of reporting. It seems likely that one or more circumstances of violent deaths make them more memorable than natural ones. This is further suggested by another of our results. We have found that in solved cases with violent deaths 94 percent of the subjects mentioned the manner of death, whereas when the death had occurred naturally only 52 percent of the subjects mentioned it.

Returning . . . to the group of cases as a whole — solved and unsolved ones — 72 percent of the subjects remembered the previous personality's manner of dying, but only 63 percent remembered his name. Among solved cases 94 percent of the subjects remembered the mode of death when it was violent, but only 52 percent remembered it when it was natural. Among solved cases 76 percent of the subjects remembered the previous personality's name. It appears, therefore, that if reincarnation occurs and a person dies violently and reincarnates with only a few memories of the previous life, the violent death is more likely to figure among those memories than the person's name. This development repeated in numerous cases might partly account for the much higher incidence of remembered violent death among unsolved compared with solved cases.' (Stevenson 1987: 163)

In Sri Lanka, the median of the age of death was 28, while the median life expectancy there was 32 years. Shorter lifetimes can be expected when almost half of the cases died violently. The common belief that people who die violently return faster, seems to be confirmed. Of the cases in the northwest of the United States – where statistics are most reliable – cases of violent death had a significantly shorter intermission than cases of natural death. For India the same holds true (Stevenson 1987: 137).

> *Sometimes the children act as if they have been snatched without warning from the body of an adult and thrust into that of a helpless child. When Celal Kapan, a subject in Turkey, began to speak, almost his first words were: 'What am I doing here? I was at the port.' When he could say more, he described details in the life of a dockworker who had fallen asleep in the hold of a ship that was being loaded. Unfortunately, a crane operator who did not know he was there, allowed a heavy oil drum to drop on him, killing him instantly. From the evidence of the case, one might say that this sleeping man regained consciousness in the body of a two-year-old child. These cases remind me of the case of a woman who had a stroke and became unconscious while playing bridge. When she regained consciousness several days later, her first words were: 'What's trumps?' (Stevenson 1987: 105)*

When do children begin talking about their preceding life? In India – 235 cases – the average was 38 months. In five other cultures, children start at the same age; in 79 American cases the average age was also 38 months (Stevenson 1987: 103). Children go on talking about their preceding lifetime till somewhat less than 7½ years if the preceding life is identified, and just under 6 when the preceding life is not identified. A child recalling a preceding life has no more than about three years to talk about it. When their stories cannot be confirmed, family members lose interest earlier and do not encourage the child to talk about it (Stevenson 1987: 106). According to Surya, the Indians explain this by the soul incarnating completely around the seventh year, when the 'veil of Maya' descends and memories of the spiritual realm – and previous lives – disappear. De Rochas also seems to have found that what he calls the fluidic body melds with the physical body at about seven years (Passian 1985: 7). Hans Holzer states that the memories usually fade at school age, but that sometimes the memories return at the age of 17 or 18, even more intensely and in more detail (Holzer 1985: 56). Stevenson thinks it likely that at around six years an overabundance of verbal information starts to suppress memory images. School especially would drive out past-life memories (1987: 107). Some children retain their memories while growing up, and for a few the recollections increase.

Sometimes, when a child can finally tell someone about its memories, it then forgets everything. Ron Hubbard reports such a case of a 5-year-old girl. Or forgetting sets in after visiting the previous family (Stevenson 1987: 106). Maybe in such cases a dammed-up flood is released and spends itself. One of the most decisive conditions for remembering a preceding life is unfinished business. Telling or visiting then gives closure. This resembles the disappearance of nightmares and other complaints after a successful regression.

Memories differ in kind. Some children remember loose fragments, sometimes incidents like the death experience, while others recall longer stretches or even their whole life. Stevenson found that recollection of past lives differed greatly in precision and detail, similar to normal recollection. Particularly problematic are precise dating, the chronology of the occurrences and the particular circumstances of events. Memory of the names of previous personalities differs strongly, presumably because of different use of names in different cultures. Children in India, Burma and Thailand often remember what they were called in their preceding life, but children in Sri Lanka and North America don't. The Sinhalese in Sri Lanka hardly use given names. They call each other rather by title or family relationship (Stevenson 1987: 108). Just as with ordinary recollection, remembering or forgetting depends less on the time that has elapsed than on the intensity of the original experience and of the experiences since.

Children exhibit many similarities with their preceding life: in habits, behaviour, idiosyncrasies and preferences. Interestingly, Stevenson found that Asiatic children remembering a preceding life as a European or American complained more often about the tropical heat than others did (Talbot 1987: 42). So there is more than just recollection, there is also continuity in emotions and attitudes and habits. Some exhibit glossolalia, speaking a foreign language without learning it, others exhibit what Stevenson calls glossophobia, resistance to learning the language of the present lifetime. The preceding language is still in the way.

Some children talk detachedly about their past life, but most remain strongly involved with the people and events of their past life. Some cry when they talk about their preceding lifetime, others still hate their murderer. If their present brothers or sisters tease them by telling them that a previous spouse or friend or child has become ill or died, they burst into tears (Stevenson 1987: 105).

Stigmas, birthmarks that refer to a preceding life, often a previous death, occur in different regions in different frequencies, between 5 percent and 50 percent of cases. Stevenson expected, probably because of his theosophical background, to encounter clear indications of karmic connections, in the form of any type of reward or punishment, retribution or compensation. Surprisingly, he found indications of karma in only 4 cases out of 106, and these indications were weak. In his work reincarnation looks like a very probable hypothesis, and karma, at least in the case of children, like a very improbable one.

Karl Muller found that in child cases 9 percent returned in the same family (Muller 1970). Ian Stevenson found this in 5 to 10 percent of his cases. The East and the West hardly differ in this respect. Rebirth may happen as nephew, niece, grandchild, brother, sister, or even as one's own child. Initially, Stevenson found fewer such cases in northern India. Closer inspection found that rebirths in the same family or even the same household were usually kept private. In Sri Lanka only 3 out of 80 cases were in the same family. Perhaps this is related to the usually larger distances between reincarnations in Sri Lanka.

Among the Tlingits, people always reincarnate within the same family. In about 75 percent of cases they were related to the mother. This fits with their matrilineal society: a Tlingit has the status of his mother and belongs to the group his mother belongs to. When people return in the same family among the patrilineal Igbo in Nigeria, the reverse is true: they were usually related to the father's family. Stevenson often received family trees from Nigeria that did not contain women. In 43 cases of return to the same family among the Igbos 32, or 74 percent were related to the father and only 11, or 26 percent, to the mother's family. In Burma women have almost equal status to men, and among the Burmese return to the same family evens out between the father's side and the mother's side (Stevenson 1987: 170).

Among the Alevis, the Tlingits and in Burma more mothers have announcing dreams about the child to be born, who the child is and how it can be recognised. An announcing dream will be easier to recall if the dreamer recognises the person in the dream. In Sri Lanka hardly anybody returns in the same family and there are hardly any announcing dreams. The cases in India support this idea: announcing dreams are only mentioned in cases of return to the same family (Stevenson 1987: 170).

Turkish cases usually reincarnate in a neighbouring village. In Sri Lanka reincarnation is farther from the place of death, often between 75 to 150 km (Stevenson 1966: 171). When the place of the previous death is far from the place of the previous life, the place of death appears to be more decisive for the place of return. In Thailand one child remembered being an American pilot who died there, and another remembered being a Japanese pilot shot down there.

Young children remembering their preceding lifetime, have often died incompletely, kept hanging about and returned fast (see chapter 10).

Many children recalled what after their death happened to family members or friends and acquaintances. Apparently, the deceased stayed near the place where they lived and died and as a discarnate still perceived the living. Some say they did this (Stevenson 1987: 109).

In Sri Lanka few recalled the time between lives. In Thailand and Burma more children recalled the intermission. Thailand and Burma also had more cases of metempsychosis, recollections of being an animal. Sri Lanka had only one case: someone who remembered being a hare between two human lives. Chapter 12 will return to remembering animal lifetimes.

In his cases Muller found that 6 percent of the boys recalled a female previous life, while 16 percent of the girls recalled a male previous life. Stevenson found change of gender to be the largest geographic difference. It varies from 50 percent among the Kutchin (Athabaskan) from the northwest of Canada to complete absence in the Lebanon, Turkey and among the tribes of southeast Alaska and British Columbia. Other countries fall in between: 3 percent in India, 9 percent in Sri Lanka, 13 percent in Thailand, 15 percent in the United States and 28 percent in Burma. In almost all cultures with change of gender, three times as many girls remember a preceding life as men compared to boys remembering a preceding life as women (Stevenson 1987: 173).

In which respects do regions with many children's cases differ from other regions? First by belief in reincarnation. Further by the following (Stevenson 1987: 166–7):

- They think more about the dead. They consider them to be still present, active and able to influence thoughts, feelings and events. They can help us and we can help them.

- They think more about the living. Family ties especially are stronger and more honoured.

- They know many more causes than people in the West. They do not believe in chance. Things like illnesses happen because someone or something wants it to happen – out of good-will or ill-will – or because it is bound to happen.
- They believe more in telepathy and the paranormal. They believe that dreams can be meaningful and that we can meet the deceased in our dreams.
- They attach less importance to words; they have more room for images.
- They have a different sense of time: Western people can be irritated by the lack of punctuality of Asiatics and Africans, but they often see our obsession with clocks as pitiable subservience.
- They have less to do – or at least less the feeling they should be engaged all the time. So they have more time for reflection and this may ease the emergence of memories.

However, in such non-Western cultures, children cannot always talk freely about their recollections. In India, many cases are kept hidden or even suppressed. In a series of researched cases in India, 27 percent of the mothers and 23 percent of the fathers had stopped their children, sometimes with corporal punishment, from talking about their past life. And these were only the cases in which the suppression failed (Stevenson 1987: 119).

Of the 1,095 cases researched by Stevenson, 62 percent were boys and 38 percent were girls. There was a similar imbalance in the gender of the preceding lifetimes: 66 percent men and 34 percent women. This was true in almost all cultures. A partial explanation might be that parents are more apt to suppress recollection in girls because girls are supposed to be inconspicuous, at least till they are married. Remembering a past life may decrease their marital chances. Stevenson came across at least one example (1987: 219).

Sometimes there is more than one case within one family. In one such family, the father was so fed up with his children telling about their preceding lives that he forcefully, but in vain, prohibited his youngest child from talking about his previous lifetime.

FURTHER READING

As will have become clear, Ian Stevenson is the authority on the subject of children's cases (Stevenson 1966, 1975, 1977, 1980, 1983, 1987). His research methods, his general reflections and conclusions can be found in his general introduction and the introduction of Indian cases (1975), the introduction of his cases in Sri Lanka (1977), the Lebanon and Turkey (1980) and his general discussion at the end of that book. His *Children Who Remember Previous Lives. A Question of Reincarnation* from 1987 summarises and analyses all his conclusions. One of the few truly excellent books on reincarnation, it is in a class by itself.

The case of Shanti Devi is a classic (Gupta *et al.* 1936). Francis Story, who collaborated with Ian Stevenson, reports a number of cases in his book of 1975. His previous publication of 1959 has been included in this book.

Travel books and books about foreign cultures may contain cases of children who remember past lives, e.g. the books of Hall Fielding on Burma (1898) and Lafcadio Hearn about Japan (1897). Margot Klausner gives examples from the Druses (1975).

Peter and Mary Harrison (1983) published the first collection of children's cases in England. Carol Bowman's work is a breakthrough (1997, 2001). She collected children's cases in the United States. She writes about what it means for parents and close family members to have a child talking about his or her previous life. Her second book deals with children who remember having been a deceased family member, sometimes the same child returning to the same mother. With the modern-day wonders of television, telephone and above all the Internet, new cases are emerging in ever-growing numbers. Bowman gives parents practical suggestions on how to deal with such children.

Six

PAST-LIFE RECALL
OF ADULTS

Napoleon sometimes proclaimed that he had been Charlemagne (Head & Cranston 1977: 286). Such a statement means little, even if he himself believed it. It is an association with an obvious historical example, possibly intensified to identification.

The claim of Charles Emerson, the brother of Ralph Waldo Emerson, that he remembered having been with the Greeks before Troy is less obviously meaningless, since his role there differed strongly from his life as Emerson (Head & Cranston 1977: 315). Still, everybody with a classical education knows the *Iliad*. He too may have identified with an appealing historical example. Association is even less obvious when Thoreau remembered walking in the misty past with Hawthorne along the Scamander in Asia. He also remembered a life 1,800 years before in Judea – where he had never heard of Christ – and a life as a shepherd in Assyria (Head & Cranston 1977: 317). Such statements do not convince without further confirmation, although there is hardly compensation or identification with historical events.

The French writer Gustave Flaubert said he had always lived. He remembered the Pharaohs and had clear impressions of all kinds of eras, occupations and circumstances (Head & Cranston 1977: 333). His recollection apparently remained within known history. Rainer Maria Rilke was convinced he had been in Moscow in a past lifetime (Head & Cranston 1977: 371). Such ideas often arise from a strong feeling of recognition when we visit an unknown place for the first time.

This chapter discusses six different types of recollection:

- recognition of places at first sight
- recognition of people at first sight
- recollection in dreams

- recollection triggered by objects, pictures, or books

- recollection triggered by similar situations

- recollection cropping up in exceptional physical or emotional circumstances, after accidents or during illness.

As this list indicates, recollection of past lives, just like common recollection, is often triggered by association. It occurs independently of previous belief in reincarnation. Out of the 127 cases cited by Lenz (1979), 119 had no previous belief in reincarnation, 5 had no previous opinion, and only 3 already believed in reincarnation.

I did a small survey among people attending lectures about reincarnation on the content and circumstances of apparent recollection of past lives. I received the following answers in the following numbers:

No memory at all	44
General feeling of having lived before	30
Feeling of recognising people	30
Dream fragments	27
Feeling of recognising places	24
Recollection without clear trigger	21
Recollection when relaxing or visualising	15
Recollection in the presence of a psychic	12
Recollection during illness, accidents, loss of consciousness, etc.	0

The survey was only limited and the sample had an over-representation of sensitives. Those who had become acquainted with the subject via personal contacts knew more about the subject and were more convinced of it. Oddly enough, they also had more memories of their own. Perhaps people with past-life recall have a stronger preference for personal contacts, compared with reading literature or attending lectures. People with psychic gifts were less oriented to existing doctrines in their ideas. Anthroposophically oriented people had learned more via personal contacts and less via lectures than those theosophically oriented, but they had less personal recollection.

RECOGNITION OF PLACES
AT FIRST SIGHT

Guilfoyle asked people if they ever had the feeling they had been at some place before when they were visiting it for the first time. About 35 percent never had, 50 percent had one or two times, and 15 percent more times. Six percent had had intense experiences apparently from beyond the present life (Muller 1970: 109).

> On his first visit to Genoa, Hermann Grundei had the powerful feeling he already knew the old part of the city. On later visits to Italy he had similar impressions in Verona, Bologna and Florence, but not in Venice, Naples or Palermo. He slowly recollected a life in the fourteenth or fifteenth century as a monk who performed diplomatic missions for clerical authorities. He recollected clearly his appearance, his name and his death. On his other voyages he had a similar experience in Constantinople. (Muller 1970: 111)

> Seabrook tells the story of a young Lebanese who comes to a village during a long voyage and recognizes the place. He remembers his name and gives proofs of his identity. He is able to point out his house and remembers that he had hidden some money. Following his instructions, the money is found. The previous person died shortly before he was born. The village people acknowledge him as the reincarnated villager. (Muller 1970: 110)

Recognition of places at first sight is strongly related to the *déjà-vu* experience. Believers in reincarnation assume that apparent *déjà-vu* experiences with people or places is probably recollections of past lives. This may be unjustified in most cases. *Déjà-vu* does not necessarily refer to past lives. There is, after all, also *jamais vu*: when a familiar situation suddenly becomes strange and new. Similar, but stronger mental short-circuits are depersonalisation (no longer feeling oneself as a person, and derealisation (no longer sensing the environment as real, but rather as if it were artificial, like cardboard).

It seems to me that we can explain a *déjà-vu* experience only as a recollection from a past life when it has more pointers, like knowing objects, houses or locations yet unseen. Pseudo-recall cannot be precluded in cases of well-known historical or tourist places. Important indications for real recollection are clear and specific emotions and feeling, or seeing oneself as someone else. Experiences containing discoveries are certainly more than *déjà-vu*.

A man recognises a landscape and remembers that a presently overgrown cliff had an inscription on it. He goes to the cliff and discovers a mutilated and worn inscription behind the overgrowth.

A famous example is the honeymooning Hungarian couple. The woman recognises the landscape during a riverboat trip, and insists on going ashore to visit a castle. In the castle she stops at a wall and remembers being murdered behind it. The wall is knocked down and a sealed-off space appears, containing two skeletons. (Cannon 1936: 34)

Alexander Cannon gives an example of an apparently false memory:

A woman is travelling for the first time through Minnesota with her daughter. During a stop at a station she is surprised that the place is completely familiar to her. She recognizes a farm as the place where she once lived. As the stop is long enough to take a walk, she visits the farm with her daughter, and the layout and furnishings of the house are exactly as she had described them to her daughter. She recounted this incident to her friends. One of them investigated the matter and discovered that the farm had been built when the woman in question was already adult. At the time of her birth there were as yet no buildings in the area. (Cannon 1936: 32)

Clearly this is no past-life memory. Identification with someone else can only have been through telepathy with someone who had been living in the house. *Déjà-vu* seems to be out of the question because the woman could describe the layout and the furnishings even though she had not been there. Fantasy and pseudo-memory are also out of the question. A psychodrama is impossible because nothing personal or problematic is going on. A strong form of psychometric clairvoyance could be possible, and the hypothesis of a collective memory cannot be ruled out. However, these last interpretations fail to explain why she felt she had lived in the house.

The most likely explanation is a combination of *déjà-vu*, imagination and (self-) deception. The woman may have had a *déjà-vu* experience, a feeling that she recognised the place. She looks for an explanation and imagines she has been there before. During the visit to the farm (perhaps still in a *déjà-vu* mood) she has new feelings of recognition and tells her daughter it is exactly how she remembers it. Afterwards she says she had already told her daughter beforehand (imagination or self-deception). Perhaps to pass the time during the wait at the station, she elaborates her experience and makes it more impressive, first for herself and later for others.

This is the most likely explanation because it contains the fewest paranormal presuppositions and because alternative explanations are less likely. If there had been telepathic contact with a present or former inhabitant of the farm, then the inhabitants rather than the furnishings of the house would have been familiar. The hypothesis of a collective memory and psychometric clairvoyance are less plausible because of identification: she feels she has lived there herself. If this woman showed earlier signs of having telepathic or psychometric abilities then these explanations become more likely.

Out-of-body experiences at night – visiting some place in a dream – may sometimes account for recognition of places. There are examples of people recognising an existing house from dreams, while the inhabitants had thought the house was haunted, and now seeing the visiting person in real life, they recognise him as the ghost (Shirley 1924: 79). This may also explain the previous example.

In my survey, recognition of places was correlated with flashes of inspiration.

RECOGNITION OF PEOPLE AT FIRST SIGHT

Recognising people at first sight is common. Many times it may be *déjà-vu* rather than a past-life memory. Faces may seem familiar to us because we associate them with faces we already know; or somebody's acts, or words, seem immediately familiar to us, producing a feeling of recollection. A feeling of immediate intimacy, sympathy or antipathy is not sufficient reason to assume a past life. Love at first sight, if real, certainly comes from a relationship in a previous life. Strong feelings of recognition may be the starting point for regressions to past lives (Sutphen 1976). About one-third of Lenz's cases were induced by meeting someone, although the recollection seldom came at first sight. The usual first response was one of uncommon familiarity.

In my survey, healing hands, and to a lesser extent clairvoyance, were correlated with recognising other people.

Lanfranco Davito, an Italian policeman, is on duty when a stranger comes towards him in the street. Suddenly, he remembers this man clubbing him to death during a tribal quarrel, and he goes white with fear. Later, other recollections of this primitive life come up. (Muller 1970: 119)

The most interesting cases are meetings with mutual recognition.

During a walk in 1930, Gerda Walter, a German parapsychologist, was introduced by a friend to a retired captain. Immediately, she had the feeling she had met him before, although this seemed improbable. She wondered if it could have been in a previous life, and at once saw a clear image. She was a man riding on a horse through a gloomy forest without paths, surrounded by tree trunks and knowing that somewhere behind him lay a burning or besieged castle or large house. She felt it was a matter of life and death. Then she saw that a farmer or a charcoal-burner who was walking to the left of him, led his horse. She immediately sensed that this was the captain to whom she had just been introduced. A little later, the captain told her that she might think it strange and not worth mentioning, but that he felt that in a past life he had rendered her a great service. How, he did not know, but he had had this feeling from the first moment he saw her. (Muller 1970: 118)

Strong feelings of recognition can be the starting-point for past-life regressions. Dick Sutphen gives several examples (Sutphen 1976). In my survey, healers especially and to a lesser extent psychics often seemed to recognise others.

In the First World War, a teacher of elocution, H.G. Scheffler from Reutlingen, had lived through the battlefield and came to doubt all his previous beliefs. After the war he studied philosophy and read Kant, then Schopenhauer and so interested himself in Buddhism. He read about the doctrine of reincarnation, which seemed very logical to him. As he liked to have proof, he started to practise yoga. After years of discipline, he received during meditation, the most impressive experience ever.

He saw a gardener in the park of a castle. On the carriage drive he saw the butler running towards him. From far he yelled 'Hey Dudley!' When the gardener turned around, so Scheffler could see his face, he recognised himself. Suddenly he knew it to be 1587. The castle stood northwest of Edinburgh. The butler, with whom he was good friends, told him that Mary Stuart had been executed and that he was afraid the baron would be imprisoned. Then the scene faded.

Years later, in the autumn of 1926, Scheffler was in Berlin on a stormy and rainy afternoon on his way to the station. The street was deserted. The rain lashed his face and there was no taxi in sight. Just before crossing the next side street, he felt inexplicably fidgety. On the corner, he bumped into a gentleman. Both muttered an excuse and Scheffler was sure he knew this man. They both continued on their way and Scheffler looked over his shoulder. The stranger had stopped and turned around. They walked back to each other. Scheffler introduced himself and said: 'Excuse me, but I feel we know each other. I just don't know how.' The other introduced himself as Dr Thomas and said he didn't recognise Scheffler, but before he had entered the last street, he had suddenly felt something important was about to happen. When he bumped into Scheffler, he felt that this was it.

Scheffler invited Dr Thomas to enter a bar. Their first common interest appeared to be philosophy. Dr Thomas, an art historian, had involved himself in non-European views on the world and had become convinced he had lived several times before. In meditation he had glimpsed past lives. The lifetime he knew most about was in Scotland during the time of Mary Stuart. He had been the butler of a Scottish baron near Edinburgh and had been as solitary as in his present life. He had only one friend there, the manager of the park. Scheffler asked him if he remembered the name of that friend. 'Yes, James Dudley.' (Passian 1985)

Max Heindel tells the story of one Roberts who grew up in London, where his father had a brewery. He fell in love with a servant girl and married her against his father's wishes. They emigrated to Australia and started a small farm in the wilderness. He built a hut, next to a brook. A daughter was born there. When she was two years old, Roberts had left the hut to cut wood. An armed man identified himself as a detective and arrested him for a bank robbery that had taken place on the night Roberts had left London. Roberts was transported to England. After many months, his innocence was proven. Only then was his worry about his wife and daughter taken seriously. An expedition to the hut found their skeletons. Meanwhile, Roberts's father had died. Though he had Roberts cut out of his will, his brother shared the inheritance with him and Roberts left for the United States.

Fifteen years later, he was walking in Santa Barbara, when a little girl came running up to him, put her arms around his knees and called him 'daddy'. Roberts suspected a scam, but the mother excused herself profusely and tried to pull her daughter away. The child held on and maintained he was her father.

This so impressed Roberts that, after a few days, he visited the girl and her mother. Immediately the child ran to him and called him her daddy. The girl said that she had lived with him and another mummy in a small house next to a brook. She was forbidden to walk on the plank across the water. No other houses were in sight. One day, her father had left and had not returned. When they ran out of food, her mother lay down and became very silent. 'Then I also died, but I didn't die, I came here.' (Passian 1985)

RECOLLECTION IN DREAMS

Roger Woolger writes that a conversation about regressions may suffice to trigger a dream about a past life (Woolger 1988). The literature contains few cases of dreams that were clearly about past lives. We remember dreams usually only vaguely, and they are not evidential enough to warrant telling them in writing. Karl Muller gives three examples that were confirmed later.

> *A woman had had a recurrent dream since she was 5 years old. She met a boy, and suddenly they would find themselves in an old house on a flat hilltop. She could see the house in detail. They were playing in a corridor at the top of the stairs. She ran away from her friend and fell through the staircase to the stone floor below. While falling, she saw the black-and-white tiled floor rushing towards her, and everything went blank. Usually, she had this dream when about to take an important decision in her life. As an adult, she was once asked to visit the troubled inhabitants of a haunted house. To her astonishment, the house appeared to be the house of her dreams. She was told that a few centuries before, a boy and a girl had fallen to their deaths while playing. When she saw two miniatures, she exclaimed 'My father and my mother!' These were indeed the parents of the two children. (Shirley 1924: 65; Muller 1970: 95)*

Lenz had 19 cases, or 15 percent of his survey, who had memories in dreams, often about several lifetimes. He noted the following differences from common dreams (Lenz 1979: 32):

- unusual sensations
- awareness during the dream of seeing scenes from past lives
- uncommon vividness, so that details can be described even years later
- a subsequent change of attitude towards death and dying.

The first three differences are true for all vivid or lucid dreams. The fourth is typical for all kinds of past-life memories.

> *Erlo van Waveren was a Dutchman who established himself in New York as a Jungian therapist. From 1945 onwards, he had dreams about past lives and in 1966 he did a more or less spontaneous Gestalt therapy on himself, in which he integrated several past lives. In the six past lifetimes he experienced as subpersonalities, he had been a historically known bishop four times. Still, his experiences seem real enough. Hampered by a thick layer of Christian and Jungian mystifications, a true integration process seems to happen. He was with his experiences, as he calls it himself 'in deep isolation' then, and later also among psychoanalysts. (Van Waveren 1978: 23).*

A lonely precursor of past-life therapy and so worth reading.

Holzer states that recurrent dreams are inevitably connected with some sort of reincarnation memory (Holzer 1986: 26). This seems a rather sweeping statement, but could well be true. He states also that the difference between a truly personal memory and one telepathically received is that the dreamer in dreams of the first type feels or sees himself in the scene, while in receiving memories of others he only watches from the outside. Recurrent dreams are excellent starting-points for regressions. Schlotterbeck states the same, but adds that, as in any therapy, dreams just before the start of regression therapy may also be significant. Completing the dream during a session is often a powerful tool, and may release past-life memories. He gives some examples (Schlotterbeck 1987: 23). My experiences confirm this. In my survey, paranormally gifted people dreamt more about previous lives than others.

A very unusual story is *The Search for Omm Sety* (1989). Dorothy Eady, an Englishwoman, was not just convinced she had lived in Egypt, but was also visited during the nights by her pharaoh-lover from the past. A rare example of an incredible story that is still credible. As an example of a past-life memory, it is too irregular.

A girl is sentenced to death and commits suicide because a prince falls in love with her. The prince is cursed and locked into a prison-like interlife before he is allowed (!) to meet his previous love again. 'I will never forget the terrible look in the eyes . . . You can only say that the eyes had the look of somebody in hell who had suddenly found a way out' (1989: 23). For me, this is no love story, but a story of narrow-mindedness and abuse of mental power. It seems an extreme example of rotten priestcraft. After her first experiences, Eady went to Egypt and lived there the rest of her life. She became a valued collaborator of archaeologists.

RECOLLECTION TRIGGERED BY OBJECTS, PICTURES OR BOOKS

When Giuseppe Costa was a child, a small picture of Constantinople and the Bosporus triggered vague memories of ships and battles, with strong emotions. As a boy of 10, he visited Venice for the first time and recognized it. The following night he dreamt he was

30 years old, and commanding some medieval ships. The flags impressed him particularly. The dream was extensive and chronological. Later he recognized other places, but he only started to believe in a previous life after an out-of-body experience. After visiting the castle of Verres, he identified himself as Ibleto di Challant who lived in the fourteenth century (Costa 1923; Brazzini 1952: 120; Muller 1970: 87).

Francis Lefebvre daydreamed about the sea as a boy. When he was 36 he visited museums in Portugal. Seeing a big drum and a ship's bell, and later a golden object, triggered memories of the life of Vasco da Gama, the Portuguese discoverer. His wife found that a portrait of da Gama looked just like her husband when he was angry. This is one of the few documented examples of recollection of a famous past personality. Lefebvre concedes that his conviction is difficult to prove (Lefebvre 1959: 3–11; Muller 1970: 90).

Joan Grant's memories started when she psychometrically read a scarab that was apparently hers in a previous life (Grant 1956). Lenz had 9 cases out of 127 who claimed that memories occurred when hearing a piece of music, seeing a painting, or coming into contact with some object (Lenz 1979: 29).

Graham tells the story of an American doctor who attends a lecture about an almost forgotten British doctor of the nineteenth century. Suddenly he feels a shock shooting through his spine upwards; sits upright ands realises the lecture is about himself; he recognises many names mentioned. Later he visits England and has many experiences that confirm this insight. (1976: 32)

Yonassan Gershom talked with people about their past-life memories as Jewish victims of the Nazis (1992). When he wrote his book he had already collected 1,500 cases. Talking about them helps to process the experiences, though Gershom is no therapist. His book shows that we can process traumas and repercussions of past lives in daily life, outside explicit therapy. It boils down to dreaming about it, reading about the time and the circumstances, discovering and understanding connections with the present life, and expression in drawing, painting, talking and writing. This process takes more time and is precarious, but often truly cathartic. Gershom later collected stories of people who wrote to him after they had read his first book (1996). All but one told him they had died in their twenties, their teens or as young children (1996: 125).

One woman starts to feel sick, gets a blanket from her host and has an asthma attack because the blanket reminds her of a concentration camp blanket. She is hospitalised and during the night dreams she is a teenage boy during the Holocaust. The words 'You can't go home any more' remain with her all day. Later the doctor tells her she had been close to death. But she felt that coming home was much more important than staying alive. 'Dying is easy. But never coming home again!' (1996: 51)

RECOLLECTION TRIGGERED BY SIMILAR SITUATIONS

Berlin 1943, Sunday: there are bombing raids. As on every Sunday, Hermann Grundei checks the books he keeps in an old safe in a dark corridor. Slowly, he gets the feeling that he has lived exactly the same way before. His impressions become stronger, until he sees clearly the end of his preceding life. He sees himself checking his books during a holiday, drawing them out of an old safe in a dark corner. His inspection shows he is bankrupt, embezzled by his bookkeeper. He shoots himself through his right temple.

Grundei thought the incident occurred between 1870 and 1885, probably when he was living in a small seaport and doing something with ships and timber. In 1952 he began to write to seaports and got confirmation of this history from one of them, with the information that the son of the man in question was still alive. In 1956 he visited that son. They both felt as if they were family members meeting after a long time. They looked alike and they spoke alike. People assumed they were brothers. In an old school picture he recognised his two sons, but not his two daughters (Muller 1970: 122).

Interestingly enough, Grundei happened to be born 35 days before his preceding identity shot himself. Such a 'negative intermission' is rare, but more documented instances are known. Chapter 14 returns to this subject.

RECOLLECTION UNDER EXTRAORDINARY CIRCUMSTANCES

An English technician was still under anaesthetic after an operation, when he began to explain in refined French that he was a French nobleman, describing his life shortly before the Revolution and his death by guillotine. His re-experience contained touch and smell. When the technician came round, he remembered everything as a dream. He could still feel a ring on his finger, but he could no longer speak French. (Muller 1970: 126)

Hermann Medingen, a German racing car driver, had a serious accident in 1924. After a brief, terrible pain, he was outside his body. He saw various past lives, as a man and as a woman, as if he were looking in different mirrors. (Muller 1970: 127)

Charles Lindbergh slept, during his flight over the ocean, for some time with his eyes open. Being dissociated, he felt simultaneously in the past, the present and the future. He saw people, heard voices, and felt ancient relationships and friendships he seemed to know from past lives. (Lindbergh 1953; Head & Cranston 1977: 390)

Georg Neidhart, a German coppersmith, lost his wife and child as a young man. After weeks of despair he began to see images and scenes from old times. Later, he had virtually complete recollection of this life and was able to localise and identify it. (Neidhart 1959; Muller 1970: 100)

Other experiences may come up under controlled trance, as in yoga or meditation. In 13 percent of Lenz's cases prayer or meditation triggered recollection. He notes that these people appear to accept their memories more readily than the other cases.

ADULT RECOLLECTIONS: A SUMMARY

With adult recollections we need to rule out *déjà-vu*, pseudo-memory and imagination. The value of fragmentary recollection is difficult to determine, unless there are verifiable details. The first test is to screen for clarity and concreteness, just as with any normal recollection. A second test is whether the different elements of the recollection are mutually consistent, and consistent with other recollections. A third test is to compare the contents of our memory with objective, historical facts.

The examples from Hans Holzer indicate that historical testing alone is not enough. Some of his best-researched examples, including one he calls 'the perfect case for reincarnation' (Holzer 1985: 60), are clearly not reincarnations, but obsessions, or rather spirit attachments. Under hypnosis the former personalities state explicitly that they entered only later, during the life of the subject.

Recollection is usually triggered by association: places returned to, people met, objects recognised and similarities in situations. Recollection also comes up in gradual or acute dissociation: under narcosis, after deep despair, through lack of sleep, in the wake of an accident, in dreams. Furthermore, there can be association with something psychological. The latter can be seen in regressions in which the induction does not indicate the place where the remigrant will land. Often, the emerging life is significant now. A good example of this is Glaskin's first regressions (Glaskin 1974: 21, 207).

A number of visions start like an out-of-body experience, not unlike the experiences of the clinically dead that Moody and others describe. According to Lenz, this is the common pattern (Lenz 1979: 47), but this is not confirmed by any other source. He states that 29 out of his 127 cases had some form of tunnel experience (like out-of-body experiences) when returning, also a highly unusual finding.

Often memories start to come more easily after the first recollection, and they tend to be less visionary, more like common recollections. 'The rest I have just come to know. It was as if I had amnesia, and after my past-life visions I just started to remember things I had forgotten' (Lenz 1979: 41).

FURTHER READING

There are no comprehensive books on past-life recall of adults to match those about children's cases. Most cases are dispersed through the literature on the subject. Karl Muller (1970) has a chapter on past-life recall in adults. The most comprehensive publication is by Frederick Lenz (1979). Hans Holzer (1985) is interesting about cases of spontaneous recall.

The best-known example of lasting recall is the book by Edward Ryall (1974), because of its completeness and its credibility. Other references are given in the text of this chapter.

Seven

REGRESSION: INDUCED MEMORIES OF PAST LIVES

If we have past lives, almost all of us have forgotten them. We have already forgotten much of our present life. We practically all have amnesia regarding the period before our birth, our birth and the first years of our life. Our first memories may begin at about the end of the third year, sometimes a bit earlier and often later. We may believe in past lives and still not remember them – and some remember them, but don't believe in them.

The way to recall past lives is the same as to recall lost memories of this life. This way is called age regression. Full regression, originally a hypnotic state, brings back memories, but more intense, more like reliving than remembering. Everything that has happened since may be almost forgotten; we experience the situation just as it happened at the time. Techniques of reliving and regression can bring back repressed and lost memories and also give access to the first, never-remembered part of our life. This shows that we all seem to have a complete and uninterrupted memory of everything we have consciously and unconsciously experienced. There is a tape we can play back to any significant moment of our life. In deep regression, some people may describe what happened around them during surgery they have undergone, though they were out cold during the operation. People who go into reliving or regression do so out of curiosity, as part of psychotherapy or as subjects in an experiment. To avoid talking about patients, clients or subjects, I will usually call them *remigrants*.

Over 25 years ago, Joseph de Louise said (Graham 1976: 106):

> Maybe only two out of ten people can actually have a regression experience to a past life with the techniques we've got now. It is my feeling that as we go into the next twenty or thirty years, there are going to be breakthroughs in different techniques to enable us to go into past lives, to go into that memory bank or that soul bank or that universal bank and bring this information out.

He was right. After a few years, Wambach got 90 percent of her subjects to relive an apparent past life. Today, it is almost common to visit a past-life therapist. Books tell us how we can guide people at home into past lives or how we access our own without help. Understandably, many of those ways are unreliable. The next chapter is about uncritical explorations by 'believers'.

Colavida in Spain probably discovered age regression in 1887. Six years later, Albert de Rochas rediscovered the technique when experimenting with magnetism and hypnosis in Paris. Soon, past lives appeared in de Rochas' work. He is the great pioneer in this area. His book *Les Vies Successives* (1911) is the first book on this subject and still worth reading. Albert de Rochas found that if he took people further and further back they could experience their birth and that he could even go back to the time before they had been born. Surprisingly, if they returned further and were asked about the first concrete experience coming up, a death from a preceding life emerged more often than the time in the womb. As mentioned earlier, spiritualists, gnostics and esotericists criticised de Rochas, because his results conflicted with the gnostic and esoteric teachings and because he induced trance. Gnostics, like the theosophists, saw this as an atavistic and questionable method, because it circumvented the subject's self-awareness. They objected that subjects were so open to suggestion during trance that their ostensible memories of past lives were merely responses to de Rochas' dominant and suggestive presence. However, the results of de Rochas' experiments are in excellent agreement with later research, such as Stevenson's.

Regression techniques lay dormant until the publication of *The Search for Bridey Murphy* (Bernstein 1956). The story about this book is a book in itself. It had merciless reviews and was widely refuted by public opinion. Meanwhile, the refutations were refuted in turn. Obviously, Bernstein's book was the victim of the no-man's-land between the church and science (Cerminara 1967). A scientist (Ducasse 1960) weighed all the evidence for and against and concluded the facts to be incontrovertible. He then went on to explain these by the generous hypothesis of super-ESP (super-extra-sensory perception), a hypothesis that can never be disproved and is therefore as useless as it is impartial.

Bernstein's work was inspired not by Albert de Rochas, but by Alexander Cannon and possibly by Ron Hubbard, the founder of *dianetics* and *scientology*. Hubbard developed non-hypnotic regression techniques expressly intended to further mental health. Hubbard's influence has been mainly indirect since his techniques are applied within a rigid organisational framework, protected by church status, copyrights and strict membership discipline. However, former members of his movement have done much work.

All the same, Bernstein's book did arouse a great deal of interest in regression. *The Three Lives of Naomi Henry* (Blythe 1956) was the British answer to *The Search for Bridey Murphy*. The *Daily Express*, which sponsored the experiment, quit right away when the remigrant entered an afterdeath experience and fell silent. The sessions were brought out on gramophone records. In Cornwall, Arnall Bloxham used hypnosis to regress people to past lives. He taped the sessions and published *Who was Ann Ockenden?* (1958) about the past-life sessions of a prolific subject. A BBC television programme later examined a number of these regressions containing historically verifiable material (Iverson 1976).

The most important modern publications are reports of regressions and the subjects' experiences during such sessions (Moss & Keeton 1979). Sometimes the records are supplemented with historical verification of data from the sessions (Underwood & Wilder 1975; Dethlefsen 1977; Williston & Johnstone 1983).

The work of Helen Wambach is the most important breakthrough, if only because of its sheer volume. She successfully regressed about 1,000 subjects to five different lives each, producing summaries of about 5,000 regressions, which she analysed statistically (Wambach 1978). She also regressed people to the period before birth. Around 750 people had such experiences, which she also classified statistically (Wambach 1979).

Helen Wambach initially found that 70 percent of her participants relived past lives, and this percentage increased to 90 after she improved her methods. In a random sample of the remaining 10 percent, about half could relive past lives under individual supervision. The remaining 5 percent were resistant to every form of relaxation or abandonment. They remained stressed and neurotically alert. Wambach suspects that this tension is related either to fear of death or of losing control (Wambach 1978).

Edith Fiore describes a case that seems to support this explanation. A remigrant could not or would not relax. When relaxation finally did occur, the barrier appeared to be caused by a traumatic death experience in the preceding life, as a patient bleeding to death during a lobotomy in a psychiatric hospital (Fiore 1978).

Morris Netherton discovered that remigrants sometimes seem to block because they enter a situation where secrecy is necessary or extorted. Such a block can be simply removed by asking, 'Does something have to remain a secret?'

RELIVING AND REGRESSION

We may experience the past in different ways and with different degrees of intensity. I distinguish five levels in order of increasing access to the past and decreasing access to the present. Table 4 below gives an overview of these levels, which I will discuss in order. *Past Lives, Future Lives: Accounts of regressions and progressions through hypnosis* by Bruce Goldberg distinguishes the same levels of recall as I do. What I call reliving and regression, he calls pseudo-revivification and revivification (Goldberg 1982: 58). *Soul Search: Spiritual growth through knowledge of past lifetimes*, also distinguishes five regression levels (Williston & Johnstone 1983: 53). I call these five levels:

Levels	Division of Consciousness		Contents of consciousness of the past
	Present	Past	
Memory			Information
			+
Recollection			Sensory impressions
			+
Reliving			Feelings and thoughts
			+
Regression			Forgetting everything since
			+
Identification			Transporting present into past

On the first level of *memory* we remain aware of the present surroundings. You know where you are now; you know your own history. You know you are only bringing back information about something that has already passed. If you think about it or if somebody asks you about it, you can bring back information about the past; for example, where you lived when you were in the sixth form of elementary school and the name of your teacher. To do this, you do not need to re-experience anything from that time. Facts such as names, dates and addresses can come up without any image. On the level of memory you are only engaged with facts that come up, sometimes accompanied by fleeting impressions of how it used to be, but these impressions remain vague, in the background. The experience, the awareness remains in the present.

The second level is *recollection*. Here, the past comes back in the form of images and other sensory impressions. You can recall what the street where you lived looked like. You recall the face of a friend at school and how you fell down on the way home from school and how your grazed knee hurt. In recollections, images of happenings that impressed you are embedded in a background of vague images blending into each other. You may remember what you heard, what you felt, what you smelled and tasted, although this is more difficult for most people than visual recollection. You can practise recollecting as concretely and completely as possible. Someone else can help you with this by means of direct questions and open suggestions to get your recollections detailed and clear. An open suggestion is, for example: 'You can hear the hum of voices in your classroom again,' or: 'You smell that distasteful cabbage again that has been put on the table.'

A recollection may be so complete that you not only hear the noises again, but also smell the scents and taste how it was to eat spinach as a child or your first ice-cream with whipped cream, and even the feelings and thoughts that you had come up again. This is *reliving*. Besides sensory recollections, our feelings, our thoughts, our mood from that time come up as well. You feel how you felt; you think what you thought then. This creates a curious split consciousness. You remain who you are now, but at the same time you experience yourself as a 10-year-old boy or a 12-year-old girl. (You may also experience such an 'elliptic consciousness' with two focal points if you stare intensely into the mirror or at an old photograph of yourself.) In reliving, your consciousness is divided between the present and the past.

With real *regression* not only do we experience the past again, but also everything that has happened between then and now is pushed into the background and is virtually inaccessible to your consciousness. Reliving still has an uninterrupted connection between the two focal points of consciousness. With real regression, this connection is gone. Regression to the age of 12 means that you live again, feel and think again as this 12-year-old and that you have lost everything you experienced since then. If your awareness of the present remains intact, then you experience this as if disconnected: it has no influence at all on the awareness of the past. If you are supervised during a hypnotic regression, you may hear yourself answer from your past awareness without your present personality being able to intervene. The temporary loss of memory of everything since applies only to that part of your consciousness that is in regression. Usually the present awareness continues to exist alongside it.

Someone is brought back to an incarnation in the second half of the last century in England and is asked the name of the queen. The illiterate slum girl cannot answer this question, although the present personality tries, almost gnashing its teeth, to intervene and say it was Victoria. But it cannot intervene. Everybody present knows the answer and mentally screams it at the person, but to no avail. Such phenomena prove sufficiently the invalidity of the lay argument that someone in trance is open to suggestion and reacts telepathically to those present, especially to the hypnotist. Such things can be accomplished by hypnosis with some people, but only if paranormal abilities are already present, if the trance is deep enough and if special instructions are given.

Without hypnosis, access to the present personality remains and questions can be posed in turn to the present and the past personality. Clumsy guidance sometimes gets the past and the present personality mixed up during the regression. Emotional or intellectual blocks may result in interventions from the present personality. Sometimes the present personality answers when, for whatever reason, the past personality cannot answer. In light levels of trance, the difference is often unclear, especially for the amateur therapist.

Sometimes the therapist questions alternately the past and the present consciousness. That alternation will have the regression sliding back into reliving. Sometimes the interaction between the two viewpoints is funny: when the past life was in the other gender or had very different opinions. In one session, a young woman relives a male Neanderthal lifetime. He dies in a rock fall. Asked for his last thought, the remigrant calls with a heavy voice 'Ugh!' immediately followed by a girlish voice 'oh, sorry!'

Regression may deepen into *identification*. In identification any awareness of a separate present vanishes. During regression you will hardly realise that you are lying talking on a bed, you forget pretty much the situation of the moment, you react from the past. With identification you include the present, as far as you are aware of it, in the situation then. You will place the interviewing counsellor in the situation from the past life you are reliving.

This begins with irritation about the stupid questions about things everybody knows (see, for example, Moss & Keeton 1979: 34–5, where a fine example of split consciousness is also given). Feeling suspicious about questions on things that ought to remain a secret may lead to an argument with the interviewer (Dethlefsen 1976: 225; Fiore 1978: 11). Goldberg gives good examples of the identification stage (Goldberg 1982: 76, 77, 103).

The regressions of Nyria (Praed 1914) are a nice example of the identification stage. Nyria is a Roman slave girl who is constantly afraid she will betray the Christians or her mistress with her indiscreet disclosures to the hypnotist. She keeps asking who the hypnotist is and why she meets her in the most unlikely places? Doesn't she have any slaves of her own, that she needs to ask Nyria so many questions? And if she came in a sedan, then what has happened to the sedan? And shouldn't she go and get the sedan for her? (Shirley 1924: 37). In Nyria's case, the sessions connected with each other exactly (Shirley 1924: 40), just as with Joan Grant, though in Joan Grant's *Winged Pharaoh* (1937) the sessions came out in non-chronological order and had to be slotted together afterwards

At the level of identification it is possible to create new experiences belonging to a particular lifetime. For example, we take someone back to his eleventh year and bring up a topic he had never heard of at that age. When he comes out of this state, that conversation seems to him to have taken place when he was 11, unless hypnotic instruction erases it again.

Besides the five levels of awareness of the past, the past may manifest itself in the present body in different levels of intensity. Reliving may produce strong somatics, especially when reliving intense emotional or bodily experiences, like the last birth and the last death before that. Our breath may become laboured or we assume a foetal position. In reliving experiences of dying in past lives, difficult breathing, temperature changes and so on are common. Or we are reliving a thrashing and red streaks appear on our back or our face, even without hypnosis, as Netherton's work shows (1978: 79). Or our facial expression changes completely, like another face coming through. Richard Webb says this is the same as the 'transfiguration', formerly known from deep-trance mediums. He witnessed it with Arthur Ford (Webb 1974: 82).

Xenoglossy is speaking foreign languages we cannot normally speak. It occurs in less than 0.01 percent of cases (Wambach 1986). According to Netherton, it can also be attained with his method without using any hypnosis (1978: 79). Dethlefsen expects that this ability can be developed methodically. If true, this would have great implications for foreign language education and linguistic research. Interestingly, selective repression is possible. For example, a hypnotist may instruct the remigrant that he will understand the language spoken to him and will answer in this language. This also prevents impasses in regressions to infancy.

> *A 17-year-old French girl is brought back in her life year by year and in her fifth year speaks in Gascon and can no longer speak French when asked to do so. An Englishwoman is brought back to a past life and does not react to any instructions. A Swedish woman, who is present by chance, asks her something in Swedish and immediately she answers in fluent Swedish, although she cannot speak Swedish in this life. (Moss & Keeton 1979: 169)*

HYPNOSIS AND TRANCE
IN REGRESSIONS

So far hypnosis has been the most common method of bringing back memories of past lives in people without spontaneous recollection. A related, but apparently obsolete method is the magnetic induction of trance. Methods working with only a light trance, without classic hypnosis, have spread fast and wide. Merely finding the right triggers may give access to the memory of past lives. A beginning regression seems to induce its own trance.

Techniques of hypnotic trance induction are outside the scope of this book. For real regression a rather deep trance is needed, for reliving a shallower one. The trance needed to gain access to the past-life memory differs from the trance needed to keep the regression or reliving experience going. We may remember a seemingly insignificant detail and become absorbed by the unfolding story. The converse also happens: we may need an extensive induction for a deep trance the first time, but the next session is easier, although this time it may be only reliving. The same may happen when reading books. We may get absorbed in a story and become enthralled. Or it may cost us a great effort of concentration to start reading a book and understand it, but it keeps getting easier, until we easily pick it up again after an interruption.

We may compare a *barrier* to regression with aversion to reading, because we cannot read well or we think reading is something for sissies. Running up against a *block* is like a difficult or unpleasant part we come across in a book or a letter. Our first reaction is to withdraw and we can only return by setting ourselves to it. To overcome a barrier, the trance needs to be either deeper or less deep, for the matter to be digested either more intensely or more at a distance. Blocks have to be removed by dealing with them, not by circumventing them.

In later sessions a shallower trance is often sufficient, unless new emotional material crops up. Lighter trances bring reliving rather than regression or even only recollection. This has the advantage that we stay alert, but the disadvantage that the experience becomes thin and that our imagination, which is activated during a regression, may easily add elements.

During trance, we hardly notice background noise. Our sense of time alters. Usually, we underestimate the duration of the session afterwards. The deeper the trance, the greater the difference between the estimated and real duration. After a deep trance of two-and-a-half hours, we may feel we have been busy for twenty minutes. A decrease by a factor of three is common even after a light trance. After a one-and-a-half-hour regression we think we have been working for half an hour. The reverse may happen too. Bruce Goldberg reports a subjective lengthening of time, instead of the more common shortening. After twenty minutes, some people feel as if they have been away for more than an hour (Goldberg 1982: 7).

Depth of hypnotic trance can be estimated according to the hypnotic symptoms during trance. In this way Le Cron and Bordeaux designed a 50-point scale, as follows:

- preparation stages   1–5
- light hypnotic stages   6–20
- middle hypnotic stages   22–30
- deep hypnotic stages   31–49
- complete trance   50

With conventional hypnotic techniques, about 50 percent of people would reach medium trance and 20 percent deep trance. Le Cron and Bordeaux place age regression at level 42, about halfway into the deep stage. In hypnosis, age regression means real regression, not just recall or reliving. During hypnotic regression the voice and the posture change, corresponding to the previous age or to the previous personality.

Trance and trance depth can be more objectively determined by monitoring psychosomatic changes. First, during trance the muscles relax. This can be measured by the decrease in electrical activity of the muscles, especially of the muscles of the forehead, because these indicate mental strain or relaxation. Some people who want to learn to relax or to meditate apply myo-feedback using a machine translating muscular tension in sound. Usually, the machine emits a low hum when our muscles are relaxed and a high pitch when we become tense.

A similar, older machine is the E-meter, or emotion meter, which measures the electric resistance of the skin. Supposedly, deeper trance leads, through changes in the sympathetic nerve system, to less perspiration and so to higher skin resistance. The term E-meter comes from the use of this skin-resistance meter to trace emotional tension. Saying an emotionally laden word in the presence of a subject decreases his skin resistance immediately, before any conscious response. The skin resistance meter connected to registration equipment, then called a polygraph, is used as a lie detector. This application is controversial, because it is politically sensitive and because it does not measure lies, but the emotion accompanying lies. People who feel guilty and afraid may react out of fear that they will not be believed and more hardened characters do not necessarily feel any emotion. Applying the polygraph properly requires proper training.

Next to decreased muscle tension and decreased sweat secretion, there is a third physiological change, the altered pattern of brain waves as determined by an electro-encephalogram (EEG). This shows the dominant rhythm of electrical brain activity. For example, in a deep sleep we have a slow dominant rhythm of 2 to 4 waves per second (delta rhythm). The dream state has about 8 waves per second (theta rhythm). Someone who is awake and alert, especially when strongly involved or concentrated on something, will have a dominant rhythm of more than 15 waves per second (beta rhythm). If people relax without becoming sleepy, a rhythm of about 12 waves per second results (alpha rhythm). The levels of brain activity are shown in Table 4. There are individual differences and the correspondence with mind states may be less stringent than this overview suggests.

Table 4 typical brain rhythms and levels of awareness

Beta rhythm	24/sec	alert
Alpha rhythm	12/sec	daydreaming, *reverie*
Theta rhythm	6/sec	dreaming
Delta rhythm	3/sec	sleeping
Deep delta rhythm	1.5/sec	cataleptic sleep, hibernation, coma, exteriorisation

These frequencies are typical values. In fact they are frequency ranges. Beta is from about 18 to almost 40, alpha from 10 to 16, theta from 5 to 8 waves per second. When we are alert, we have beta rhythm, of the left brain and often of the right brain as well. In other mental states the brain wave pattern is for left and right to be about equal. Visualisation is typically in alpha. Evoking emotions starts in low alpha. In theta we contact our subconscious.

The induction of a shift of consciousness usually begins with relaxation, producing alpha waves. The remigrant becomes calm, clear and balanced. In classic hypnosis this occurs through verbal instructions and suggestions, but it can be achieved more directly with sensory stimuli. The simplest way to enter deeper levels is to deepen the relaxation. When the subject is connected to an electro-encephalograph, it will show the brain rhythm slowing down.

When the therapist just wants to determine whether the remigrant is sufficiently relaxed, the myo-feedback meter, indicating muscle relaxation, gives the most direct information. If he wants to keep track of the depth of trance during the session, then the more sensitive E-meter is useful. EEG-data are probably the most reliable, but the use of electrodes on the head may be inconvenient and some subjects have unpleasant feelings about it.

In classical meditation, alpha rhythm is dominant and there is a smaller peak in theta. In modern types of meditation, rather weak beta waves over the whole range are added, without suppressing alpha and theta. In experiments with telepathy, psychometry or telekinesis, subjects show strong beta, strong alpha and strong delta. The alpha waves are concentrated in a small range, the delta waves are strongest at the lowest frequencies (deep delta – 1 or 2/sec) and the pattern of beta depends on the nature of the experiment (telepathy, psychometry, telekinesis). Winafred Lucas has researched all this with Maxwell Cade's *mind mirror*, which measures the distribution of brain waves on all frequencies, separately for the left and the right brain (Lucas 1989).

There are four common objections to hypnosis. The first objection is that the hypnotic trance is psychologically or physically damaging. All indications are to the contrary. Hypnosis often eases or solves psychosomatic complaints, even without any particular suggestion in this direction.

Secondly, some people are afraid of losing consciousness and control and perhaps 'never returning'. This fear is comparable to fear of out-of-body experiences and is even more unfounded. A deep hypnotic trance that is not properly terminated just passes into a deep sleep and subjects wake up when they have rested (Although this may be a long time for someone who lacked sleep.) What may remain, however, is a hypnotic tie with the hypnotist (as some hypnotists create and reinforce), which is not sufficiently undone at the end of the session. Then people may remain fuzzy, in some cases even for a few weeks. Since it is difficult to ascertain to what extent a bond with the voice or the person of the hypnotist has been created, it is good practise to give an instruction at the end of the session that dissolves any tie that may have developed.

So the third objection is real: a hypnotist may take advantage of us. A hypnotist can give us no instructions or post-hypnotic suggestions contrary to our beliefs and values. But a smart and patient hypnotist can mislead us in deep trance. No one can suggest that we should jump out of a window on the fifth floor, but one can suggest that the window is a door to a beautiful garden.

A fourth worry is that frequent hypnosis weakens the will. With normal hypnosis this is out of the question. Only when people want to be hypnotised because of a morbid desire to abandon themselves and surrender to someone else, and if the hypnotist encourages this with powerful post-hypnotic suggestions, may personal independence be weakened.

Mistrust of hypnosis is usually comes from watching stage hypnosis or of reading or hearing scary stories. In stage hypnosis, people are bound to the hypnotist by explicit instructions. The hypnotist narrows the consciousness towards complete dependence. During stage hypnosis, people do things they would or could never do using their common sense. In part, the success of stage hypnosis is based on ridicule. The subjects of stage hypnotists are always selected as being easy to hypnotise and they are willing to be manipulated in front of an audience. Since in stage hypnosis these two aspects coincide, they are confused. Being easily hypnotised has nothing to do with lack of willpower. Being easy to hypnotise is more related to the ability to immerse ourselves in something. Good book readers and good music listeners can usually be hypnotised well, as well as those who meditate well. This does not mean they will respond to crude suggestions or will trust someone who wants them to do odd things. A remigrant may be hypnotised deeply without any inclination to follow other instructions than those related to the regression.

During deep trance the remigrant remains linked to the present through the hypnotist's voice. When no special relation has been evoked and the hypnotist suggests things the remigrant does not experience or does not want to experience, he just blocks and if he is further pressed, he simply returns, in spite of any instruction. During a hypnosis without instructions for dependence, suggestions to see things not there don't work and we cannot be forced to experience things we don't want or to say things we don't want.

Hypnosis is a psychosomatic shift in consciousness, not a loss of will. In itself, hypnotic trance is not harmful but healing. For the rest, everything depends on the competence and the trustworthiness of the hypnotist. For this reason, be guided by someone you trust.

RELIVING AND REGRESSION INDUCED BY MAGNETISM

A magnetist makes *passes*, that is, he moves or brushes his hands past the body. He may also hold his hands still or hold one still and make passes with the other. Or he may touch the body with one or both hands. Often he supports the activity of his hands with his eyes and with mental concentration.

The first to write about magnetism was Paracelsus. Later, Mesmer, who introduced the term 'animal magnetism', worked with it and induced hypnosis mostly with passes. The third important figure in the field of magnetism is Karl von Reichenbach, a well-known scientist who did pioneer research into the nature of these phenomena (Von Reichenbach 1849). Eventually it was Albert de Rochas who used magnetism to induce age regression (de Rochas 1911).

De Rochas placed his subject on a chair, held his right hand on the subject's forehead and made passes along the length of the body, with his left hand. The more passes he made, the further the subject regressed. When he wanted to bring the subject back to the present, he made horizontal movements with both hands in front of the subject, starting from the body's vertical middle line. If he continued these passes, the subject crossed the present and went into the future.

The magnetic trance is related to the hypnotic trance. A hypnotic trance of a mediumistic subject we can probably direct to a magnetic trance. Hypnosis uses the mental doors of perception and imagination; magnetism uses the energetic doors of the body. Therefore, hypnosis is probably a broader and more flexible method than magnetism. An indication for this could be that the scales to measure the depth of a trance, such as those of Le Cron and Bordeaux, differ for individual persons. Apparently the depth of the magnetic trance can be measured more uniformly by its symptoms.

De Rochas distinguished five levels of magnetic trance. The first level is that of *lethargy*. Our limbs become heavy and limp, perception of the surroundings diminishes, memory weakens, suggestibility and skin sensitivity increase.

The second level of magnetic trance is *somnambulism*, so called because of its similarity to sleepwalking. Suggestibility is much higher and skin sensitivity strongly lowered. When a needle is stuck in our skin, we don't feel anything. This is the state of (real) performing fakirs, who after the show pin a large medal on a large safety pin through their naked skin.

The third level is *rapport*, in which we take over the sensations of the magnetist. When we are pricked in our arm, we feel nothing, but when the magnetist is pricked in the arm, we call 'ouch' and a red mark appears on the corresponding spot on our arm. Our memory is inaccessible, we are no longer suggestible, we see auras and the felt skin is about 2 inches outside the real skin.

At the fourth level, of *sympathy*, we identify with the magnetist and can perceive and express the magnetist's thoughts and feelings and the perception of auras has vanished again.

Finally, in *exteriorisation* the centre of our perception can be moved around at will, including to places where we have never been.

The symptoms of the first two levels of magnetisation are almost the same as those in medium and deep hypnosis, but the symptoms of the other levels can only be induced in very deep hypnosis and only with some people. Presumably, fewer people can be brought into trance through magnetism than through hypnosis. Sympathy, the fourth level of magnetic trance, corresponds to the natural relation between a mother and her unborn child.

The magnetic trance creates an intimate relation with the magnetist. That does not need to happen in applications of magnetism in healing, as in Reiki. Although the magnetist transfers psychosomatic energy to the magnetised subject, this does not have to result in blurred identity.

De Rochas avoided any transference of his own thoughts and ideas to his mediums. 'To support the somnambulic memory', he sometimes pressed his thumb to the root of the nose of the subject.

An 18-year old girl reports during a regression, that she is married to a Breton fisherman. When her husband dies in a shipwreck, she kills herself by jumping into the sea from a cliff. When she relives her act of despair, her breath halts and she makes movements as if she is involuntarily swallowing water and shouts incoherently. To spare her further suffering, de

Rochas instructs her several times to go ahead in time. Now she says that drowning is horrible. She is now in the 'grey', neither happy, nor unhappy. She did not find her deceased husband.

Most subjects said they were in a grey state between lifetimes. They saw their still living family and friends, but were not seen by them. People who were killed, stayed longer near their physical body. People who died naturally, usually witness their own funeral and hear what is being said.

When people had lived very badly, they found themselves in the 'dark', where they were attacked by evil influences and suffered remorse. They experienced rebirth as a liberation.

One Josephine returns to her earliest childhood. When she relives being five, she can write a few words only, plays with a doll and behaves like an infant. Further back, she can't talk and shows by her bodily position that she is in the womb. After being taken back even further, a male personality appears. He is disinclined to talk and says gruffly that he sees nothing as he is in the dark. He is suspicious and wants to know why he is being interrogated. At long last, de Rochas wins his confidence. The man says he is Jean-Claude Bourdon, born in 1812 in Champvent and only goes to school in wintertime. He served with the artillery in Besançon. He had to serve seven years, but after four years he was relieved from his duty, because his father had died. He cannot recall the names of his officers, but the mischief he did together with his companions and his adventures with girls he does remember.

In his native village, his fiancé Jeanette waits for him. He has no intention of marrying her. When de Rochas reminds him that he makes the girl unhappy, he retorts: 'So what? She will neither be the first, nor the last!' He remains a bachelor, takes care of himself and dies after a long illness at the age of 70. De Rochas asks him if he has a priest coming. 'Do you believe in the stupid things he says? When you die, it is over!' And Bourdon curses. He dies and feels he stays connected to his body for a rather long time. He witnesses his funeral while he drifts over the coffin and hears how people say that it is good that he died. In church, the priest walks around the coffin, blessing it and so creates a wall of light, preventing evil spirits from attacking the deceased. They also shy away from the holy water, 'because when they touch it, they will dissolve'. The prayers of the priest do calm Bourdon, but only for a while. After being buried, he stays near his decaying body and feels disgusted by it. De Rochas asks if he sees vermin. 'Of course, as they haven't salted me!'

Jean-Claude remains in the darkness, which is very unpleasant to him, but which doesn't make him suffer. He is only plagued by thirst at times, as he was a real soak. He realises that death is different from what he expected. If he had known this, he wouldn't have made fun of the priest.

At last, rays of light pierce the darkness. He feels he has to start a new life, this time as a woman. Women suffer more than men and he wants to redeem the wrongs he did to girls and women. He approaches the woman who will be his mother. He is around her till the birth begins and he gradually enters the body of the baby. Till his seventh year he sees a mist around his body in which he sees many things.

In a later session, de Rochas goes back even further. Before Jean-Claude appears an old woman, called Philomene Charpigny, born in 1702. After her marriage in 1732, her name was Carteron and she had children who died young. Before the lifetime of Philomene, Josephine was a girl who died young. And again before that, she was a violent man. Because of this, he suffered much in 'the dark'; this repeated itself after the death of the little girl, as she had had no time to atone for his crimes.

De Rochas had some of his subjects go back ten lifetimes. However often the experiments were repeated, the descriptions and even the different handwritings remained identical. When they relived the period of the pregnancy, the subject assumed a foetal position: arms pressed to the body, fists before the eyes, till the fifth month. This happened any time a new life began (Passian 1985: 36–8).

Magnetic trance induction seems to be employed rarely nowadays, as hypnotic and imaginative methods have replaced it. Some hypnotists reinforce induction with magnetic passes or with pseudo-magnetic passes accompanied by appropriate verbal suggestions. Some therapists start with Reiki. Practitioners like Marcia Moore effectively mix hypnosis, visualisation and magnetic passes (Moore 1978: 46).

PAST-LIFE RECALL INDUCED BY IMAGINATION OR FOCUSING

Instead of inducing a trance first, the therapist may start on the level of recall, continue at reliving and eventually reach real regression. Visual images substitute for and trigger initial memories, facilitating the transition to a past life. This is the method of visualisation or imagination. Many therapists use relaxation with some hypnotic and imaginative induction.

The first step in imagination, just as with hypnosis, is physical and mental relaxation. Then, the therapist has the remigrant focus his attention on his bodily sensations. He focuses attention on the muscles to relax them more, on breathing and on heartbeat and pulse. This immersion in one's body draws attention away from the environment, helps one to relax and stimulates the imaginative powers.

The next step is to let the remigrant imagine a typical environment: a garden, a valley, a mountain, a large meadow of flowers, a beach; standing in a cave entrance, cruising down a river, floating in air, etc. The transition to a past life is then pictured by walking down a path or a staircase, ascending a staircase, going through a tunnel, crossing a river, crossing a bridge or going through a mist. A professional, careful and elaborate procedure is the Christos experiment described by Glaskin (1974).

On this level of inner imagining, people may express personal problems in an intense and meaningful dream. The experience is real, in that they not only visualise the problem, but also may solve it within the same story. This is the technique of the *waking dream* (*rève éveillé*), an inner psychodrama that is accompanied and guided by a therapist. Waking dreams can be elaborated by Gestalt techniques like normal dreams, but more effectively.

The psychodramatic waking dream is enacted in more or less symbolic images. For example, you see a gentleman on the box of an old farm cart stuck in the mud. When you come closer, the face of the gentleman becomes that of your father. This image shows how you see your father or how you believe he feels. The therapist may ask you, for example, how you feel, seeing your father in this way. He may ask you to speak to the gentleman or to go and help him and to see what happens. So the story may unfurl as a fantasy with an intense psychological reality.

However, when someone wants to relive a past life and gets stuck on the imaginative level, the expectation of a historical experience may result in a psychodramatic tale enacted in apparently historical scenery. This scenery will only contain material from normal memory. How do we know the difference between real past-life recall, a psychodramatic waking dream and just fantasies? What can we do to increase the probability of past-life recall? First of all, we continually ask for emotions. With a fantasy story, emotions remain weak or absent. In a psychodrama real emotions as well as blocks come up quickly because a waking dream confronts psychological imperfections rather than trivia. Apparently the subconscious uses the opportunity to bring up unfinished business.

A second option is to ask for body sensations. Often, after being anchored into the bodily feeling, things come up that surprise the remigrant. Strong indications for real recall are seeing new things, having uncommon experiences, like tasting unknown food and especially to feel oneself in the body of the opposite sex: a woman experiencing an erection, a man giving birth to a child. It is also possible, though time-consuming, to check historical details.

For many remigrants such experiences – going against their own preferences and expectations and giving answers contrary to their opinions – are the most convincing. They are vivid illustrations of 'elliptic consciousness', one field of consciousness with two centres.

An advantage of a fairly deep hypnotic trance over a light, imaginatively induced trance is the possibility of checking whether historical details are coming from the remigrant's ordinary memory. With a sufficiently deep trance, deceit can be virtually ruled out. We may ask the remigrant directly if he got any information from books or otherwise and may elicit answers by finger signals. Also, rewinding and forwarding within a life and between lives is more accurate under hypnosis. Another advantage of hypnotic trance is that artificial instructions to retrieve information, such as counting to three or snapping one's fingers, are stronger and more secure.

Netherton uses 'postulates', ingrained programmes, vows, promises, ingrown attitudes, verbally fixed in the mind and sometimes repressed, as triggers for past-life recall. When we describe our problems or fears, these postulates come up as repetitive statements. The point is to pick out these ritual formulas, preferably giving them an expressive character. For example: 'I have to get out of this!' or 'Nobody likes me,' or 'I don't need anybody.'

Repeating or having us repeat these key sentences a few times, elicits their suppressed emotional charge and focuses us. Directly following this, we are asked to picture ourselves in a situation in which this sentence is literally true or actually spoken, with all its corresponding emotions. For example: 'You are now going to go back to a situation in which you experienced all this for the first time. While I count to five you will go to that situation. On the count of five you will be there. You feel cold and fear. You are in a great hurry. It is dark. You have to get out of this! One, two, three, four, five. What is the first thing you see or feel, the first impression that comes to mind?'

Here, the experience comes directly from the emotion evoked and crystallises around the repeated key sentence. Almost always we arrive in a specific and emotional experience, often in a past life. When we have sufficiently worked through this experience, the therapist may repeat the procedure with the same key sentence. Usually, a new situation appears, until the postulate complex has lost its charge. If we return to an already relived situation, we had apparently digested that situation insufficiently.

OTHER ENTRIES TO PAST LIVES

An older method somewhat similar to Netherton's is Ron Hubbard's *dianetics* (Hubbard 1950), later re-christened as *scientology*. Hubbard developed his own methodology and terminology. He used the E-meter and a stringent procedure to track down and work out mental and emotional problems. This procedure almost invariably leads to past lives. People who spent some time in scientology contributed much to the development of regression therapy. Scientology itself is a strictly organised movement requiring committed, even closed-minded participants and discouraging noncommittal interest. The set-up is businesslike, to say the least. Hubbard's books are interesting, but, judging by my own experience, if you order them from his organisation, you have to add to the purchase price years of being plagued with brochures and personal invitations.

Another alternative method, probably rare, is the use of drugs, such as marihuana, LSD, psychedelic mushrooms or psychedelic tea. The disadvantage of drugs is that resulting experiences can be given little guidance. Another great disadvantage is the probability of dependence and addiction. Some people disapprove of hypnosis but have no objections to taking drugs. The argument is that under hypnosis you are dependent on the hypnotist and on drugs you are dependent on nobody (except your dealer). In my opinion, self-hypnosis and hypnosis by a trustworthy hypnotist are wholesome and drugs are definitely unhealthy. The only one to do methodical research into past-life memory access by drugs is Stanislav Grof, at the Esalen Institute.

Gnostic and esoteric circles object to magnetism and hypnosis as well as to drugs. They normally propose their own prolonged meditation exercises as the only sure and true way. The anthroposophical karma exercises are an example. All such exercises assume that memories of past lives are only accessible for the most serious and devoted students, who have to immerse themselves for months or years with abstract deep feelings and abstract high thoughts, with superficial results.

My own survey indicated that people who had come into contact with the subject of reincarnation via a spiritual movement were on average less sensitive and had fewer memories of their own. At any rate, spiritual philosophies that instill tidbits of abstract reincarnation wisdom, but question and discourage personal experience are of little value.

Chapter 4 gave examples of psychic entries to past lives: by mediumistic trance, incidentally by psychometrics and by clairvoyance. Entry by magnetic passes also borders on the paranormal. Ranking the various methods of entry according to the increasing psychic sensitivity required from the remigrant or the therapist gives the following list:

- by a mental, emotional or somatic bridge: a symptom that is already trance-like and only needs focusing
- by imagination
- by hypnotism
- by magnetism
- by psychic trance
- by clairvoyance – usually somebody else's.

THE PAST-LIFE MEMORY

The evidence from reliving and regression sessions indicates that the memory storing the experiences of our past lives neither ages nor fades. Memories lose none of their brilliance. Many writers, for example Kelsey and Grant (1967), have pointed out that clarity does not fade with time. Focus, intensity and completeness remain intact. Apparently, our soul registers every experience, conscious as well as unconscious. It stores all our sensory impressions, all our feelings and thoughts, all our half-conscious and subconscious reactions.

The capacity of this memory seems practically unlimited. In computer terms, it is RAM (Random Access Memory): it is directly accessible at each point. We do not need to unwind a chronological tape till we are where we want or need to be. Its storage is continuous, precisely dated and localised, since we can identify the time and place of every event. In addition, our memory is structured around associations, as is apparent from, for example, trauma chains. It resembles bookkeeping by double entry: a chronological, continuous registration with random access and a continuous assimilation and structuring, which results in associative patterns, similar to our ordinary memory. We can access immediately any desired moment, using as the entry point a problem, a preference, a location relating to anything. Similar to computer-aided design, we can recall situations from various spatial positions, angles and perspectives. We can identify with our previous self, but also from the outside or through the eyes of others present. We can separate ourselves from our past self and look at situations from a distance for example from above. We can relive a situation and observe our own reaction and those of others, even if we overlooked them then. Such transformations are particularly important in reliving disorganised, confusing or tense situations.

Reliving and regression are the same for our present life, with the same possibilities and difficulties. Here, too, we can seek out subconscious registers, we can place ourselves outside of ourselves or put ourselves in the position of others using complete and unfading memory. Various psychotherapies have discovered this, including Transactional Analysis and therapies that use reliving the birth and prenatal conditions.

We seem to reach past lives via this general, non-physical memory. The remembrances of long-ago lifetimes may remain as clear as those of recent lives. By trance, a shift in consciousness, we can access this memory. An even more direct route is via emotions and postulates that carry their own trance. A third entry to this memory is through restimulation: a strong similarity, a strong association between our present life situation and one from a past life.

In exploratory regressions undertaken out of curiosity, eventful situations come up sooner than humdrum ones, and eventful lives sooner than humdrum lives. Emotionally charged situations emerge more easily, the charge depending on the original intensity and the subsequent lack of assimilation usually because of negative emotions. In conditions of light trance without specific instructions, traumatic death experiences are often the first events to come up.

Psychics mainly pick up situations from past lives relating to the present life situation. The same is true for situations that come up in methods like the Christos experiment, which do not explicitly induce trance, but go fairly deep and which through their procedures avoid overwhelming experiences. Sometimes the door to the memory of past lives is difficult to find, but it is rarely barred and then only by ourselves. In the absence of neurotic inhibition or psychotic delusions, the right key usually gives entry.

Specific entry barriers are when the therapy situation or the trance condition themselves evoke associations with traumatic experiences, especially death experiences, or when the first experience to emerge is loaded with secrecy

Morris Netherton talks about 'shut-off commands'. When such shut-off commands operate about relaxation, memory or trance, they block access until special interventions identify and remove them. Sometimes they may have blocked relaxation in general, so removing them is more important than remembering past lives.

DO-IT-YOURSELF METHODS

Some books teach how to guide others to experience past lifetimes. Other books teach how to discover or relive our own past lifetimes. The classic manual for the amateur who is no therapist and who isn't interested in becoming one, is that by Bryan Jamieson (1976). Jamieson has the remigrants imagining that they switch off their body, part by part. Then they visualise on elevator that takes them to another liftime. He writes dry, business-like prose and clearly knows what he is talking about. Why should we be interested in past lifetimes? He answers that memory loss is sad (1976: 4):

> Some lose the ability to remember for short periods of time, others suffer a total loss of memory. These severe cases of amnesia are truly sad, as these people find a large part of their lives has ceased to be a part of their conscious present – perhaps everything from the past. These unfortunate people are left with a hopeless wondering for the rest of their lives, forced to begin life anew without foundation or root. In a less tragic way, I feel many of us are rootless because we too are unable to remember – who we were, what we did with our lives and what lessons we learned in the many lives that preceded this one. We too must begin anew. We, however, now have the option to remember, thanks to this and other methods of regression.

His remigrants needed on average eight minutes to reach the right trance level. More than half did not believe at all in reincarnation before their regression. After a two-hour session one of them believes he has been occupied for about fifteen minutes (1976: 14). There are some nice examples of elliptic consciousness (1976: 12):

> 'He kept asking me if I would like to move on, but I figured I might as well hang in there, I was too socked to care. All I wanted to do was hang on, hoping that the storm would end. About that time everybody on board started getting sick, too. I knew I was going to have to clean it all up, so I decided to accept Bryan's offer and move on.'

The regressions did change the remigrants. After one lifetime as poor as a church mouse in the nineteenth century, a remigrant says (1976: 14): 'I'll say one thing for being regressed: it really makes you think. Things aren't so bad nowadays. As a matter of fact, in comparison, they're damn good – we don't know what poor is.' After the regression, remigrants took themselves less seriously, were more tolerant and more responsible and enjoyed themselves more. Though no therapy was tried, several shed problems: phobias, negative self-images, prejudice.

As might be expected, Jamieson's remigrants often touch on violent deaths. He suggests never breaking off the experience, but letting the remigrant describe what he sees and feels while still around the body. Otherwise, he may feel physical discomfort or pain for about an hour.

Jamieson has no bad experiences with people who had one or two drinks before the session – he even advises this – but warns explicitly against people who used LSD. People who smoke marihuana once in a while give no problems in regressions. He adds that he knows that alcohol is taboo in spiritual circles, but that – in moderation – it relaxes people, which eases the session. Arthur Ingalls writes the opposite: 'I have found that if a person has had alcohol or drugs within a day or two of the session the subject is not able to visualize and report' (*Psychography*: 125). Believers are bad observers – and unbelievers as well.

When remigrants run into a problem during the session, Jamieson has them contact the higher self, or whatever they may call it. He himself speaks about the Source. When we have contacted that, we visualise and recall data like names, places and dates more easily. The remigrant poses the question, waits a few moments and the answer emerges spontaneously in words or images. Apparently, Jamieson unfreezes the intuition. Intuition, by the way, is wonderful and much more often yields hits than sceptics can imagine, but it is not infallible and may produce the greatest nonsense just as elegantly as the highest truths. According to Jamieson, posing the question takes longer than getting the answer. Interestingly, this goes more easily after the remigrant has relived a death experience.

When people see clouds or feel themselves floating or drifting, they are in alpha. If they see flashes, clear colours or geometric symbols, he asks them to go to a higher level. If that doesn't work, we might as well stop.

Following instructions to move into the next situation, after some moments remigrants sigh. The sigh indicates that they have arrived and that we can give the next suggestion or question. During a death experience, a heavy sigh means that they have left the body. If their breath becomes laboured, Jamieson suggests that they experience the situation from the outside, like an observer – or he moves them to a calmer situation.

Jamieson assures us that remigrants can only relive their own past lifetimes. Generally, this is true, but there are more exceptions than Jamieson assumes.

People who want to experiment with all this will find some manuals listed at the end of this chapter. The practical suggestions in this chapter may be helpful for a beginning practitioner, but it is much better to have watched an experienced practitioner at work. People may enter into very emotional and very confusing or even threatening experiences, and practitioners without a psychotherapeutic background usually don't know how to handle this. Even some experienced practitioners have unwise ways of dealing with such situations. Most therapists, especially those with a professional psychological background, are rightly doubtful about laymen guiding regressions.

Florence McClain writes (1989):

> All you need, is this book, time and a friend who can read . . . During a period of almost twenty years, I have never encountered in over 2000 regressions a situation that led to a traumatic experience . . . Very rarely, you will come across a traumatic situation in a regression experience .

She recommends safety measures: avoid negative words and expressions; emphasise that the regression is only an exercise in remembering; and close with positive statements. Still, few practitioners would agree with her. Roger Woolger (1987: 13):

> Any psychological work that goes to the deeper levels of the unconscious mind is likely to bring up powerful emotions, disturbing memories and fantasy material. Such often overwhelming psychic contents may seem to the uninitiated and even to experts to belong to the realm of classical madness. Past life exploration can be like taking the lid off Pandora's box; it can unleash potent forces over which we may have little control. For this reason, it is my firm belief that guiding regressions and research into past lives should only be undertaken by those fully trained in psychotherapy. This is not a parlor game, simple as the procedures may seem when first witnessed.
>
> At the same time, there is powerful learning to be had from this extraordinary process. It is no exaggeration to say there are among my clients those whose whole life orientation has been changed by only one or two pastlife sessions.

RESEARCH

Thelma Freedman has collected and commented on the research in this area (2000). Kampman and Hirvenoja (1978 – in Freedman 2000) investigated whether people with apparent memories of past lives differed from those without. They did psychological tests on students who were asked under hypnosis to go back to a time before their birth. Kampman and Hirvenoja considered past lives as 'hypnotically induced secondary personalities' and guided their subjects accordingly. So they found much fantasy material. Their general conclusion was: 'producing multiple personalities in healthy subjects in deep trance is a healthy, progressive procedure, dealing with unconscious knowledge in a creative way,' and they found a positive correlation between mental health and the production of such secondary personalities. They don't say how they measured mental health or how many subjects they studied (Freedman 2000: 28).

In a study with volunteers from the general public, James reported (1993 – also in Freedman 2000) that 81 of his 104 volunteers experienced past lifetimes. None was engaged in therapy or had a psychiatric background. James found that subjects who went deeper into trance were more likely to experience past lives and had more detailed experiences. In 1995, James published the findings of another study. He wanted to discover whether people experiencing past lives had similar backgrounds or ideas. James analysed 78 variables and found few or none correlated with age, gender, education, religion or the expectation of having a past-life experience. Because 98 percent believed in reincarnation (that's what you get if you ask volunteers), he could not test the effect of belief (Freedman 2000: 16). From other publications we know this effect to be weak.

A different line of research is measuring brain activity during regressions. In the 1970s, Bryan Jamieson had his sessions monitored by Kirk Peffer. No significant difference was found from the normal waking state: frequencies from 1.5 Hertz to over 40 Hertz, often with high alpha. Some remigrants stayed in beta all the time, while others varied during the session. No remigrant was hypnotised and none fell asleep. Though induction and guidance remained the same, no two remigrants had a similar brain wave pattern. Jamieson wondered if the technology was too primitive (Jamieson 1976: 6).

Probably he was right, because in the 1980s, Winafred Lucas found other and clearer results. Lucas used the *mind mirror*, with both client and therapist. She reported in the *Proceedings of the Second International Conference on Paranormal Research*, reprinted in the *Journal of Regression Therapy* (1989). Past-life therapists show a combination of very fast beta, with very slow delta. Some of them have smaller intermediary peaks in alpha and theta. Remigrants show strong alpha and strong delta with average to strong beta and fluctuating peaks of theta. It seems delta relates to a state of telepathy, also called the radar state. Remigrants see much (alpha) and feel much (theta) that comes up from their personal unconscious (theta) or even from normally inaccessible layers (delta); simultaneously they digest and process these experiences (beta). Therapists are consciously and intensely involved (beta) and simultaneously tuned in to the patients (delta); some therapists engage themselves in the images (alpha) and emotions (theta) of the story. A regression is a complete and complex experience!

Therapist patterns especially, but also patient patterns, showed beta peaks. Therapist beta was often sharp, not soft or rounded, which would have suggested a more calm and peaceful type of guidance. As most patients showed strong beta, beta seems necessary for the conscious understanding and digestion that is taking place during the session (Lucas 1989: 65).

Apparently, the idea that deep trance blocks beta is wrong. Peter Morrison, from the Anna Wise Institute, used to see decrease of beta as characteristic of the altered state of meditation, and at first was confused by this aggressive beta, but at the end of the research admitted that peaks of beta seemed characteristic of regression work.

Almost all patients and most therapists developed symmetrical alpha (left and right brain about equal), often beginning as extensive high alpha and slowly including lower frequencies. Symmetrical alpha is characteristic of meditation. Alpha seems to have two functions: reliving emotional situations and a state of imagining. While unconscious contents are emerging (theta and possibly delta) in images of slow alpha, it ascends through high alpha to beta-consciousness. Theta appeared together with alpha in most patients and in those therapists that joined their patients in an altered state. Theta is considered to suggest contact with the personal unconscious.

Alpha and theta in the therapist and the patient are not necessary for a successful regression. Several therapists and one patient showed minimal alpha and theta. The presence of delta in patients was strongly confirmed. Delta also showed in the pattern of therapists, but less so. The delta of experienced therapists was stronger than that of the two inexperienced therapists (Lucas 1989: 66).

There was one exception to the general pattern: two patients who were experts in meditation. During the induction they immediately entered the general meditation state – extensive symmetrical alpha plus symmetrical theta – and stayed there. Beta disappeared and delta didn't emerge. Skin resistance increased and remained stable, even during experiences that could be considered emotional. Although they described apparent previous lives, they could change details and even main themes when it was suggested they do so, something that was lacking in all other regressions. These two patients appeared to be hardly involved in their stories and at closure there was little result or understanding. So the mind mirror possibly can distinguish between real regressions and lively imagination.

People who meditate consider beta as interference, but beta seems necessary for personal transformation. The strong presence of beta in guiding regression work is understandable, because of the conscious effort to manage the process. The presence of beta in the patients suggests that consciousness is needed to digest the material. Beta peaks, especially together with strong alpha and theta and including delta, produced a pattern so far only witnessed in paranormal experiments.

Possibly, memories are stored in a mental field and recalled by some radar mechanism in the delta state. Material retrieved in this way, usually (but not always) emerges in the personal unconscious (theta) and then produces emotional images (alpha). From there it is taken up in beta to be recognised and processed. Maybe the delta of the therapist eases retrieval of memories from past lives and deepens understanding of the meaning. Or delta enables the therapist to enter, at least partially, into the experience of the patient and so helps to improve questioning, guidance and support. Winafred Lucas concludes (1989: 71):

> The ease with which delta is obtained by an increasing number of people is a recent phenomenon. If there is a mind field, it is becoming rapidly more available. No longer is it limited to the elite in the Mystery Schools, nor is it necessary for a skilled Yoga meditator to work for years to retrieve a past lifetime, as was true in the 1920s, as documented by Paul Brunton (1937) when he reported that remembering former embodiments required years of concentrated meditation using a technique of going backward in memory. We do not know how many people currently can retrieve past lives, but they are increasing in number. The Mind Mirror demonstrates how far we have come in being able to make beta and delta waves at the same time. Perhaps this is an earmark of the evolution of consciousness.

FURTHER READING

The oldest book with records of reliving and regressions is by de Rochas (1911), who worked with magnetism. Another classic is Bjørkhem's book (1942) probably published only in Swedish. References to it can be found in Muller (1910) and Passian (1905). Then there is Bridey Murphy's well-known story (Bernstein 1956). Arnall Bloxham published a number of his sessions (1958). Some of Hubbard's experiences and those of his pupils since 1950 were published in *Have You Lived Before This Life?* (1958). Recent records or parts of records were published by Gerald Glaskin (1974), Peter Underwood and Leonard Wilder (1975), Dick Sutphen (1976, 1978), Thorwald Dethlefsen (1977), and Peter Moss and Joe Keeton (1979). Williston and Johnstone (1983) give good examples of regressions and historical confirmation, though they are overly enthusiastic in places.

Jeffrey Iverson (1976) and Helen Wambach (1978) present summaries. Short case descriptions can be found in Joan Grant and Denys Kelsey (1967), Karl Muller (1970) and David Christie-Murray (1981). Morris Netherton (1978) and Edith Fiore (1978) give examples from therapies.

Guides on how to induce regressions contain mainly visualisations. Colin Bennett gave early practical hints (1953) and later J.H. Brennan (1971). Gerald Glaskin describes a procedure he calls the Christos experiment (1974). Bryan Jamieson (1976) is methodical and very practical. Florence McClain also describes a careful procedure (1986[a]).

Rudolf Steiner's karma exercises are from 1924 (*GA* 236). Other do-it-yourself books are from the 1980s. Bettye Binder, a past-life therapist, wrote a small manual on how to discriminate with personal impressions between memories and fantasies; how to deal better with emotions like anger, guilt, reproach and remorse; and in general how to live better (1985). Michael Talbot (1987) wrote a reasonable manual. Maya Pilkington and the Diagram Group (1988) produced an incredible razzmatazz of interesting tidbits, and what read to me like awkward summaries, random loose ends and strange illustrations. Much better are the books by Gloria Chadwick (1988) and by the old hand Brennan (1989).

Eight

NEW AGE EXPLORATIONS OF PREVIOUS LIVES

For people who know only intellect, the discovery of intuition is a revelation. Without collecting data, interpreting and analysing and judging it, the right answer comes in a flash. Brain waves may untangle knots and open new avenues. Automatic (or, rather, spontaneous) writing unlocks treasures, divination produces wondrous results, psychics hit the nail on the head in an incredible fashion. Intuition can be pure gold.

Now, gold is tricky business. When gold diggers are prospecting in a river, they can make three mistakes:

- Assuming there is no gold, while there is.
- Assuming there is gold, while there isn't.
- Assuming that all is gold that glitters.

Intuition indeed finds gold, but we need the sieves of our intellect. Even if the oracle gives five hits in a row, the sixth answer may be nonsense. Even if somebody channels our deceased aunt and grandpa without a shadow of a doubt, the third entity showing up may be fantasy or a projection of our hope or fear or a cheat or a busybody or just noise. Gold is seductive. We become addicted to deep knowledge pouring in just as easily as to big money pouring in.

This chapter deals with unfounded beliefs. About many things we can't be sure whether they are true or not; they may at best be plausible. But about many other things we may be sure that they are wrong: because they are obscure, inconsistent or conflicting with plain facts or the experiences of many. Most people who live by their own or someone else's intuition realise that not every random brain wave is true and significant. Usually they resolve this by getting themselves into the right mood, the right state of mind. In a spiritual and sincere mood, they believe, false or twisted information won't come up. Unfortunately, this is a cardinal error. Read the oldest known protocols of mediumistic sessions with spirits (Casaubon 1659). The Holy Trinity is evoked, Jesus and Mary and the Saints, and what manifests are the usual, imposing, keep-them-on-a-string kind of elevated spirits with their mouth-watering promises and prophecies of wonderful things just around the corner. Meanwhile they instigate the sitters to change partners. For spiritual reasons, of course. The only thing missing in those early sittings is references to higher planets in more advanced star systems.

Exalted grumbling in trance or while channelling, exalted twiddling by automatic writing, is all founded on misunderstanding the possibilities and impossibilities of intuition. Intuition brings gold, but also mire. The better we tune in to the spiritual, the more exalted the mire. By opening ourselves up, we simply access an infinite source of knowledge. This doesn't necessarily give us wisdom, but may give us an addiction to foreign energies. The other side contains not only stray entities and earth-bound spirits, but multitudes of frustrated would-be priests and other busybodies.

Warnings abound. What we draw from the mental or spiritual spheres depends on what we bring to them, especially when we start exploring as a hobby. Christopher Bache says it awkwardly, but truly (1990: 120): 'We must use our present ego-consciousness to explore what might be called the deep psyche. When we do this, we find that the deep psyche organises itself differently depending on how ego-consciousness is focused as it approaches it.'

NEW AGE:
UNLEASHING THE INTUITION

The New Age opened the sluices of the intuition. Though the intellect was not discarded, it played second fiddle. The great benefit of the New Age is that many subjects that were explained away and expelled have again become topics of conversation and study. The great harm of the New Age is that unfounded disbelief is exchanged for unfounded belief and superstition.

When did the New Age begin to explore reincarnation? Right at the start, in the early 1960s. Past-life regressions and *life readings* by psychics who tell you who you have been in your previous lives were already fairly common then. Marcia Moore, who also engaged in yoga and astrology, is a central figure in these years. Her husband, Howard Alltounian, an anaesthetist, experimented with the use of ketamine to ease access to previous lives. Supposedly, it worked better than hypnosis and would give livelier experiences (Graham 1976: 162–3). Moore, like many others, preferred visualisations to classical hypnosis. Jess Stearn is one of the first to write about her and the subject (from 1965 on).

Many visualised using more or less traditional occult ideas. For example, Christine Hartley (1972), who collaborated with Dion Fortune. The first half of her book is a mixture of philosophical essays and edifying sermons, while the second half contains more personal experiences. This is a classic example of the strength and weakness of visualising by people interested in the occult. There is much about Egypt, the destruction of Atlantis and being near famous historical people, including a daughter of Akhenaten and an Esclarmonde the Foix. Interspersed in all this there are also credible stories.

Egypt and Atlantis return *ad nauseam* in the New Age literature, later joined by Indian cultures like the Mayas and Incas. Another item that becomes a craze is consulting the Higher Self. Then you go straight for true knowledge and wisdom. This results in much that is valuable, even essential, but above all a lot of edification, beauty and mist. Noreen Quinn comments: 'Many people, coming into a rudimentary understanding of reincarnation, feel the soul is all-knowing and that if they could only find a way to let that soul wisdom pour through, the personality would have it made. "'T'aint necessarily so", say the Grace Loehr Life Readings. The soul, too, must learn, must grow' (Quinn: 145).

Later, the torch of the New Age was taken over by people like Ruth Montgomery and Dick Sutphen. Next to Shirley MacLaine, Sutphen was the main popularist of reincarnation and past-life therapy till Brian Weiss came along. Sutphen is the prototype of the side of New Age that tries to remain in touch with common sense. His *Past-Life Therapy in Action* (1983) is a good example of his approach: fast dialogues bringing people to instant enlightenment and five more extensive regressions. It contains a lot of overstatement and simplification and too much Sutphen. Altogether, it is no-nonsense and, though irritating, also instructive. Other typical New Age themes that can be found in Sutphen include consulting discarnate guides, ingathering (collecting people who know each other from previous lives) and recognising yourself in historical figures.

In *We're Here: An investigation into gay reincarnation* (1999) Lynn Kear gives an overview of what has been written about reincarnation and homosexuality and publishes interviews with gays and lesbians about their ideas on or experiences with past lives. Many of the interviewees have more common sense and are more to the point than most writers on reincarnation. This is the bright side of the New Age: normal, sensible people who can now deal with a subject that has been suppressed for so long.

UNBOUNDED VISUALISATIONS

Meanwhile many people discovered that relaxing and visualising create a light trance in which memories of past lives may emerge. If that is done soberly, carefully and methodically, as in the Christos experiment (Glaskin 1974, 1978, 1979) or as Jamieson (1976) works, the harvest is extraordinarily interesting. But when the standard of work is low, careless enthusiasts join the fray. Many past-life visualisations are ungrounded. Winafred Lucas found in her mind-mirror research a fundamental difference between the relaxed, hardly charged style of visualisation of people who often meditated (mainly alpha and some theta brain waves) and therapy sessions dealing with charged material from apparent previous lifetimes (beta and delta brain waves mainly). Thelma Freedman confirms the difference (Freedman 2000: 30):

> I found the fluent, low-affect style of Lucas' meditators characteristic of the subjects in the directed fantasy condition and the slower, more affect-laden, difficult-to-change style characteristic of the same subjects in the past life report condition. Anecdotally, I once worked with an insightful client who had practised transcendental meditation for some years and who compared the two states of meditation and hypnosis as being side-by-side but distinctly different from each other. She said she could slide from one to the other at will, but that there was very little overlap between the two states.

Noreen Quinn rightly compares recovering material from the subconscious with solving a puzzle. What emerges is one thing, how we place it quite another (Quinn: 213):

> You look into the subconscious and you find a piece of something — now just where does that piece fit in the puzzle of the subconscious? Does it fit into the area of past lives? Does it fit into the area of fantasies of the personality of this life? Does it fit into the area of

fantasies of past personalities? For surely, you must recognize that if present-life personalities can fantasise, can imagine things happening, past-personality lives have also been able to fantasise, to imagine. Therefore, what one comes upon when one releases the conscious and lets the subconscious run loose may be a fragmentary truth, but one must know where that fragmentary truth fits. Does it fit into the area of past lives? Does it fit into the area of fantasy? Does it fit into the area of psychic communication? If so, does it fit into the area of psychic communication from wise, loving, understanding guides and teachers or does it fit into the area of psychic communications with mischievous spirits who enjoy messing up other people's lives?

More publications based on the Loehr–Daniels readings emphasise the importance of staying grounded. An overly spiritual lady gets the following advice in a reading (Roberts 1987: 69):

Establish herself in a positive way within society. Make a practical success of this life. That is really a higher spiritual development for her than some mystical, meditative approach or some strange explosion of consciousness, which really is not of great lasting value or very deep spiritual value.

Or about someone who tried to heal tuberculosis by Christian Science (Smith 162):

Sometimes it is necessary for a soul to learn that an earth body, made up of physical elements responds well to physical care and that an earth body is subject to conditions inherent in earth-living. This is an experience often given to one who has centered its attention and learning on its, you might say, metaphysical attributes and has a tendency toward pride in its manipulation of spiritual laws.

I have nothing against easy past-life recall. Why make it difficult if it can be easy? But often people deal too easily and lightheartedly with the contents. If it was heavy, rewrite it. If necessary, erase it. What truly happened is of no importance; what counts is that we feel good here and now. We are entitled to that, aren't we?

Typical of the New Age is what William James called the 'once-born': people who find the spiritual not after traversing valleys of shadows, but who avoid valleys or even deny that valleys exist. They go straight for the light. They want to feel better and better, become more and more aware, entering a state of unbroken bliss, if possible. This positivism leads in therapy to avoiding negative experiences or touching them only lightly. Some therapists simply erase painful episodes and even painful past lives hypnotically. Something positive may be fantasised instead. We have to avoid bad feelings by all means. If something painful or evil still emerges, we have to forgive — even without understanding who did what and why and what this says about us. Forgiveness is liberating without the need to understand, without looking in the mirror and without being confronted with the not-so-nice forms of anger within ourselves: envy, resentment, jealousy, bitterness, revenge, hate, blood lust. Patients cover up the dark sides, especially their own dark side. They refuse to face the truth because of shame, guilt, humiliation and dismay or simply because they have been spoilt. Therapists evoke as soon as possible the Higher Self or guides and masters.

All this is less than trustworthy. When we want to walk a glacier trail and our guide evokes first the patron saints, then a couple of deceased guides and finally prays extensively to the Lord himself, our confidence in the guide will not be increased. The soul that confronts — and overcomes — distress, becomes deeper. The soul that avoids or denies distress, becomes shallower.

FAMOUS PAST LIVES AND INGATHERING

Believing that you were once a famous historical or even legendary person has been common since people in the West started to believe in reincarnation, during the Romantic period. Goethe heard of an Italian town where a circle of people remembered having been Mary Magdalene and the apostles. Rudolf Steiner recalled sitting in a bar in Budapest with reincarnations of Emperor Joseph II, Frederick the Great, Madame de Pompadour, Seneca, the Duke of Reichstadt, Marie-Antoinette and Wenzel Kaunitz (Steiner 1924: 145–6).

After the publication of *Winged Pharaoh* past lives in Egypt became popular. One of the 'followers' of Joan Grant was Elisabeth Haich, who wrote *Initiation* (1965)) about her life as an Egyptian initiate. I have no reason to doubt her Egyptian life or her special gifts, but her initiation is more interesting for psychoanalysts than for past-life researchers.

W. Weden (1978) at least limited himself to the lifetime of a simple priest in Egypt. Grace Cooke's memories of a lifetime in South America and a lifetime in Egypt have been republished in *The Illumined Ones* (1966). This resembles the books of Joan Grant, but is more romanticised. It could be real recall, but is extremely polished and elevated. Ada Stewart wrote *Falcon: The autobiography of His Grace James the IV, King of Scots* (1970). About the truth of the matter I cannot judge, but it is well-written and the preface seems credible.

According to Noreen Quinn (p. 212), when we prepare a new life, we may use a prototype: taking somebody else's lifetime as a model. The example may inspire us, but we also may identify too much with it. When we later start to dig in our subconscious, indiscriminately and unmethodically, we may think we are dealing with our own previous lifetime. Rudolf Steiner launches an idea that goes even further: according to him, when incarnating we can get the copy of the astral body or the etheric body of a prominent personality implanted. He calls this 'spiritual economy'. It may later lead to incorrect identifications. If this far-fetched idea were true, it seems to me very unhealthy.

Barbara Lynne Devlin, a friend of Marcia Moore, wrote *I am Mary Shelley* (1977). This is a book about *ingathering*: the circle around Lord Byron and Percy Bysshe and Mary Shelley discover themselves and each other by regressions, channelling and guides. Mary Wollstonecraft Shelley was the writer of *Frankenstein*. Barbara Devlin traces back the theme of the monster of Frankenstein to an experience in Atlantis. All have had other lifetimes with, among others, Jesus and Robin Hood. The stories are detailed and interspersed with encounters and happenings in this lifetime. The book is a good illustration of how 'research' is being done in the New Age.

In *Earthly Purpose: The incredible true story of a group reincarnation* (1990) Dick Sutphen talks about his life and those of many others in Mexican Teotihuacán, AD 580. This is much more than simple channelling. Sutphen has guided numerous group regressions to this specific time and sold tapes with instructions to go back and check if you have been there too. People are stimulated to write down and elaborate their experiences. Sutphen adds to this collected regression material historical sources, readings of Edgar Cayce, remarks of Velikovsky and publications of Ruth Montgomery. He himself holds Higher-Self sessions, does automatic writing and requests dreams. His wife does automatic writing of her own and channels Dick's guides. On top of it all they use their thinking minds. They develop theories from what they read and test these against channelled information. Meanwhile we are served portions of Dick's love life. This ingathering is grand: 25,000 souls have planned to return each 700 years. Sutphen helps them to recall their origin and their commitments. The guides talk remarkably like advanced New Age people and use classical occult frameworks (1990: 76).

Janet Cunningham's *A Tribe Returned* (1994) is one of the more credible *ingathering* books, because it is also tied up with therapy. Members of a small Red Indian tribe that were slaughtered together now remember and start to recognise each other in this lifetime.

Mary Montaño (1995) lived before as Franz Xavier Sussmayer, a younger colleague of Wolfgang Amadeus Mozart, who, according to the writer, returned as the American piano player William Kapell (1922–53). The story switches between scenes from her life now and her life as Sussmayer, mainly from the last years of Mozart's life. Interspersed are scenes from Kapell's life, which she witnessed from the beyond. Her sources are regressions, meditations, guides and psychics. Apparently all these sources fit together. As psychics sense what people carry around, that is no independent source. Nor is meditation when you already have all kinds of ideas. But is it all true? Could be. My main doubt is that the story and the dialogues are too modern, too sentimental. If this is just a modern filter, the filter is thick and consistent. About the connection between Sussmayer and Montaño I have no opinion, but that Mozart should have returned as again a musician, again dying early, is not very much in accordance with what we know from regressions.

To me, Arthur Ingalls seems both credulous and ill-informed (Psychography: 126):

> *Those who have had incarnations in Bible times and places give valuable insights concerning the life and conditions of the era. If one was incarnated in Palestine during the ministry of Jesus the Christ, the firsthand observations are always helpful. It is interesting that early Christians accepted reincarnation as did other religions of the time.*

CHANNELLED PAST LIVES

An early book with mediumistic information about past lifetimes is Cecil Palmer's *Reincarnation: The true chronicles of rebirth of two affinities, recorded by one of them* (1921). The writer channelled the memories of his past lives from one of his spiritual guides, Cedric, high priest of Heliopolis. It yields thrilling and dramatic stories, very moralistic and overflowing with vanity (1921: 112):

I was ushered into the presence of the King. Although I had never had anything to do with royalty, I was cool and self-possessed. His Majesty eyed me with curiosity from head to foot and told me he had heard of my great abilities as a public speaker and organizer, my profound knowledge of social and political problems, my firmness and the esteem in which I was held by Government officials as well as by the leaders of the people. He was desirous of adding a few capable men, such as myself to his Government and he at once offered me a fine post amongst his personal councilors on a very liberal income. My first thoughts were for Annetta . . .

Etcetera, etcetera.

Dagmar O'Connor's *The First Pharaoh* (1956) is a story channelled by a medium, and is one of the first books written on the basis of taped sessions. According to the story, the Egyptian Kingdom was founded on channelling, the first time this had ever happened in the history of the world. People lived to the age of 90 or 100, without feeling old. The first Egyptians travelled to China and sat on the temple stairways of Beijing. China was a much older civilisation and knew writing already. Before that, the book says that writing was an Egyptian art, invented by a guy called Menes. Whatever. Everything and everyone in the story is very noble and loving and spiritual.

Guides, discarnate friends and acquaintances, often somewhat older and wiser, undoubtedly exist. That we may receive their thoughts is also true. However, when they suggest to us that we divulge or publish their thoughts, there is usually a snag. The source is our subconscious, or we are dealing with people that died without the satisfaction of having been appreciated and influential. Even without such busybodies, channelling is not automatically a good thing. 'So many become enamored of being channels and good, clear channels and so caught up in the happiness of it and in the excitement and joy of it, they stop right there. We are urging Rose as an incarnate personality to become discontented with being only a channel because this is limiting her growth' (Quinn: 203).

One Gregg Tiffen has been giving life readings in Hollywood (Webb 1974). According to him, people who died young in a number of consecutive lives come from other planets. They commute a few times rapidly 'to get accustomed to earthly vibrations'. Our parents are always karmically chosen and have exactly the opposite of what we should learn, to offer enough resistance, etc. Why such pseudo-reasoning? Maybe Gregg had insensitive, but sensible parents?

*

Monica Rolfe lectures about 'cycles of reincarnation' in trance. It shows in what she produces (1975: 54): 'Those who reincarnate at the end and the beginning of a period – the end of one period and the beginning of another period – are of course given great gifts of vision and hearing, of smell and intuition and touch.' Of course.

Clarice Toyne is told by her guides about the past lives of famous people such as Winston Churchill and Charles de Gaulle (1976). Little can be said for or against the truth of those identifications. They would indicate much continuity and gradual development. Remarkably, several famous historical people have reincarnated among her acquaintances.

Armand Marcotte, an astrologer and a psychic, gives life readings with general or individual references to past lives, enriched with a lot of God. His book *Past Lives, Future Growth* (1984) gives reconstructed sessions and stories about people who wanted advice. The book is written in a popular style and illustrates well how many psychics work: usually appealing, sometimes irritating; sometimes sensible, often nonsensical.

Many of Marcotte's ideas are reasonable and recognisable, and many seem doubtful, despite his three guides: well-meaning Franciscan monks with limited views on reincarnation. According to Armand, simple negative emotions lead to repetition in next lives, while negative emotions that are part of the character, lead to boomerang karma (p. 128). I doubt that strongly, though the idea is not unreasonable. Unfortunately, the book appears to me to be full of other unreasonable ideas.

'Jim had an intercepted house, which meant that he'd died before he was thirty in the life just past' (1984: 23). First, Marcotte confuses intercepted houses with intercepted signs (signs remaining completely within a house, not intersecting with any cusp). Second, intercepted signs always come in pairs and third, intercepted signs are more frequent, the farther from the equator. In the UK, especially Scotland, it is not uncommon to have four intercepted signs. Two previous lives shorter than thirty years? Four short lives? More short lives in Scotland than in, say, Cornwall? Would people who died young return farther from the equator? At latitude 70 degrees North, some houses can contain a few degrees, while others may have two or three intercepted signs in one house. People may have six or eight intercepted houses. All short lifetimes? In my opinion, this is sheer nonsense.

Armand addresses each female client as 'honey'. A probably bisexual girl arrives with a truck, in leather motorcycle garb. She is advised no longer to pretend she is a man, otherwise she will return in her next life as a lesbian bitch. Somewhere else we get to know something about female beauty (1984: 53):

'Beauty is given to women by God for a purpose, but it was never meant to be an end in itself. A beautiful woman has done nothing to deserve that beauty – it's a gift from God. So she shouldn't try to take credit for it by demanding attention and appreciation for having it. She should use it to bring joy to others, especially those who haven't too many beautiful things in their lives. And it should be shared with generosity, instead of selfishness.'

In the unlikely event that a female reader feels touched by this, you can reach me through the publisher. And what about male beauty? Given by the devil? Or for no purpose?

ALL FUSES BLOWN

The advent of the New Age and rising interest in reincarnation opens the market for all sorts of strange theories. One author, Paul Liekens (1982), writes that somebody was smart, as he needed no microscope to find out that the solar system is an exact copy of an atom. The writer then compares the sun to the nucleus and the planets to the protons and neutrons circling around it. Elsewhere he says that almost all of the cells of our body die within a month and are renewed. The historical chapter maintains that the Council of Constantinople deleted the doctrine of reincarnation (an imprecise formulation), by an infallible papal decree. However, the Council of Constantinople did not decide by papal decree, but against the will of the pope. Papal infallibility was invented 1,500 years later. Then the writer maintains that a number of theologians, like Origen and Augustine, didn't heed the council. He is right in that. Augustine died decades before, Origen centuries earlier. He reveals that an American spiritualist told him he used too much intellect and not enough intuition – perhaps a surprising notion, considering the above.

Marcia Moore writes (1976) that she saw herself as a child trained with others in the art of levitation. Three kids in the Black Forest, playing with the energies of gods and men. They flew among the trees, raised heavy objects by mental power and took part in the design of the universe, no less. But the forces went out of control and they were smashed by a rock fall they had precipitated themselves. This explains why the design of the universe has imperfections: immature souls are allowed in.

Mission Into Time (1973) is a travel story by Ron Hubbard. In my opinion, it is Hubbard at his worst. Pretty bad. The story itself has to be stretched to fit a journal article. A group of people is on a yacht in the Mediterranean looking for archaeological traces that Hubbard had forecast on the basis of regressions. The text contains eloquent testimonies from his followers: 'As Ron said, "Is it there?" Yes, it's there! As a whole, Ron wanted to know, "Is the recall correct?" Yes, the recall was correct. That's all.' Rocks are where they should be and so on. Diagrams show how the boat manoeuvred into a bay. 'Sailing for beginners, lesson 5.' It is, I think, the most superficial and rambling travel story imaginable. The introduction contains some interesting biographical material about Hubbard, but the book itself is worthless.

Dion Dolphin wrote in the *Bulletin* of the *Association for Past-Life Research and Therapy* (May/June 1982) that during her past years as a therapist she had asked many people to go to the twenty-first century to see how things would be. They 'progress' in what she calls a 'slightly altered consciousness'. Dolphin concludes that people can see their future as easily as their past and that people's images of the future are consistent with one another. Based on this, she knows what the twenty-first century will be like. I will give you the picture. Hold on to your hats, the century has just started!

> People will have learned to stop fighting. There is no money in the way we know it now. There will no longer be separate nations, although there is still a great number of separate cultures. Most cities are much smaller. People move around in amphibian minibuses, perhaps in the air. Groups of people and children travel around the planet and stop for a while at specific cultures to learn from them. When such a group stops traveling for a while, they land on a farm and run the farm while those who have run the farm up until then, can travel. Of course, there is space-travel in space-ferries to space-cities, but the most important thing remains that people tend the earth, garden and restore our Earth to its original purpose. There may be some difficult times towards the end of the twentieth century, but immediately afterwards a golden age of love, peace, joy and harmony begins.

The author of this beautiful prose does this work as part of a research programme in the context of her academic studies. Besides this – and this explains more – she is an initiated priestess in 'the Order of Melchizedek'. Dolphin's sugar-sweet twenty-first century is, in my opinion, completely absurd. Her story only betrays that her subjects belonged to the New Age subculture and probably lived in California.

Patricia Diegel advertised the Master Sciences from an Esoteric Viewpoint (Evolutionary) in *Paradise Neighborhood News*. She has gathered these sciences in the Cosmic Mandate: a blueprint for immortality. She had done over 25,000 past-life readings – she calls them immortality consultations – and taught hundreds of people to see into their past lives by the trinity process. Her specialities are the Initiations, the Rays, the hierarchy of the White Brotherhood and the Evolutionary Path. The pamphlet's motto is: 'The Christ in me greets the Christ in you.' In one of the first editions of *Reincarnation Report* we read:

> If the Guinness Book of Records had a past-life category, Patricia Diegel might be a top contender. A past-life counselor, Patricia recently told us that she can remember 927 past lives of her own. She started with 27, including Mary, Queen of Scots. When she later met a client who also had Mary, Queen of Scots, she said 'I gave her that life. I didn't need it anymore' . . .

If that seems perhaps a little way out, may I introduce you to the writings of Sri Chinmoy? Here is a quote from his booklet on reincarnation (1974):

> When another disciple's father died, he went to a very high place, but he was not satisfied there. Her father had seen me once, in Canada, but when he had, his whole body had been thrilled from head to foot with ineffable joy. So when he left the body and was not satisfied with the plane he was in, his soul came to me and said, 'I want to go to a higher world.' So I called on one of my friends, Jyotish, to take him to the plane he was living. Now he is extremely happy there, in this very high world . . . When he takes his next incarnation, I will know about it. Most probably he will take incarnation in an Italian family, but it depends absolutely on the Will of the Supreme. And of course there will be a little bit of my interference if he wants to go somewhere which I do not approve of.

Etcetera. Unfortunately, I have never met my daughter's guru, while having an orgasm I could never tell my wife about. All this is higher than high, in my opinion written by someone who corrects the Will of the Lord when he feels like it. It seems to follow the well-known recipe of this type of writing: it doesn't matter if you cannot connect two ideas logically. Any *non sequitur* goes — as long as you have an ample supply of spiritual lubricant.

Believers in nonsense may be worse than non-believers in sense. Much worse.

Nine

INVESTIGATING APPARENT MEMORIES

We need research, as the preceding chapter will have shown. Holzer puts it politely (1985: 204): 'There is no need to disregard scientific standards in this field, where such standards are the only safeguard against delusion, whether perpetrated by others or by oneself.'

The most obvious form of reincarnation research is finding out whether reincarnation plausibly explains the ostensible memories of past lives. Most research verifies the historical correctness of apparent reincarnation memories in individual cases. As reincarnation is an unacceptable or unprovable idea in the eyes of most people, verifying it in a few cases is enough. Even when reincarnation is plausible, we might want to check the contents of a particular regression.

A second line of research produces, as Wambach's did, so many apparent memories of past lives that the plausibility or implausibility of various hypotheses can be tested statistically.

A third line of research is to look for patterns and regularities in the recall: how do we remember and forget? How is our memory organised? Where is it located? This is a virtually untouched field, although the available empirical material allows us to formulate some ideas.

A fourth line is evaluating the therapeutic results of past-life regression, which is both extensive and expensive.

Finally, we can try to find the present incarnation of deceased people. Such identification procedures can be found in Tibet and Africa, and are used when people want to find the new incarnation of a deceased Dalai Lama or tribal chief, or want to establish the past incarnation of a newborn.

ALTERNATIVE EXPLANATIONS OF PAST-LIFE RECALL

Are there other explanations, apart from reincarnation, for these apparent recollections of past lives? Stevenson, in particular, has been careful to allow for alternative explanations of his cases. Adding to his list of possible explanations for regression, I have collected thirteen possible explanations for apparent past-life memories other than reincarnation:

- Deception
- Imagination and fantasy (e.g. to compensate)
- Pseudo-recall (cryptomnesia) and *déjà-vu*
- Genetic memory
- Waking dream or psychodrama
- Imprinting by suggestive guidance (false memory syndrome)
- The collective unconscious
- Demonic inspiration
- Identification with others
- Super-extra-sensory perception
- Attachments by dead people, including obsession or possession
- Memories of experiences between lives
- Strong fantasies from past lifetimes

The first three explanations are empirical, for deception, imagination and pseudo-recall are familiar phenomena. The fourth is speculation. The fifth is a familiar phenomenon, the sixth exists, the seventh is a speculation, the eighth is a theological idea and the last five are also empirical, although many may find them just as controversial as the reincarnation hypothesis. As for hypotheses 9, 10 and 11, people who accept the reality of psychic phenomena and the likelihood of an afterlife, but reject reincarnation prefer them: spiritualists in the narrow sense of the word.

Deception may sometimes happen, but is ridiculous as a general explanation of past-life memories. Cases of small children apparently remembering previous lives have so many witnesses on many occasions that fantastic conspiracies would be needed. The work of Stevenson shows how sensible and careful investigators of such cases may check testimonies. With hypnotic regressions at a sufficient level of trance, an experienced hypnotist can use tests and instructions to exclude deception and almost exclude self-deception. One possibility is instructing the subject to traverse various episodes of various previous lives at random. To maintain deception consistently during this playing backwards and forwards without making mistakes, especially with voice changes, is impossible. Objective indicators of the trance depth – skin resistance, brain waves and muscle relaxation – also make it difficult to fake. Only paranoid laymen can maintain deception as a general explanation.

Then there is *imagination*: fantasies people believe themselves. Often this includes compensation. People fantasise interesting and important previous lives to compensate for the boredom, frustration and insignificance of their present lives. Daydreaming out of compensation is common. Proponents of the hypothesis of compensation believe people remember special and interesting lives, which does indeed happen. People who belong to spiritual movements believing in reincarnation, in particular, may identify with interesting historical personages. Many women seem to have been Mary Magdalene, Joan of Arc, Mary Queen of Scots or Marie-Antoinette, just to mention four popular previous lives. Rudolf Passian knows two women who both feel they have been Marie-Antoinette. However, that same life has already been claimed by Helene Smith (1861–1929), the famous medium of Professor Theodore Flournoy (1900). And then there is the American lady who was told by Cayce on 17 July 1925 that she had been in her last lifetime that beheaded queen. Men have their own preferences, though the proverbial Napoleon is rare.

Interestingly, people not only compensate but apparently also project present self-pity on to a previous life of a famous person suffering and misunderstood. Such people have few concrete memories, but identify emotionally with recorded events about these persons. To explain spontaneous memories by imagination is completely insufficient, as chapter 5 may have shown.

Stevenson analysed cases of children who remembered a past life under better circumstances (Stevenson 1987: 215):

A substantial number of Indian subjects recall previous lives in socioeconomic conditions distinctly different from their own. We call these promotion cases and demotion cases. Among these subjects two-thirds recall better material conditions and only one-third recall worse conditions . . . If we decide that we cannot account for all the facts of demotion cases as due to wish-fulfilling fantasies, we are free to consider other possibilities. I suggest that dim, slightly emerging memories of a previous life under better material conditions may act as a shock that brings additional memories into the child's consciousness.

Imagination does not explain regressions in general. The work of Helen Wambach (1978) killed this explanation. Every regressionist is impressed by the limitation and boredom of most previous lives. Past lives in which people were richer or led more interesting, more varied or more important lives, are just a few percent. When we relax, in a light trance, our imagination can run free, especially if we are sensitive and visual. Just as there are impressive and lively novels about imaginary characters, there may be stories about imaginary past lifetimes. As a general explanation, imagination is nonsense, but it cannot be discarded in many particular cases.

Pseudo-recall or *cryptomnesia* exists, but is uncommon and a bit psychotic: we think we remember our own experiences, but in fact have heard or read the story or have seen pictures and identify the events as our own. Hypnotic regression easily distinguishes cryptomnesia from real recall. Even in a light trance, hardly more than relaxation, the E-meter or the mind mirror easily distinguishes real recall from pseudo-recall. Sometimes we can check spontaneous or elicited historical data in a story. Quite a few previous personalities have been historically verified and many sessions have provided obscure historical data, making previous exposure to that information extremely unlikely. Pseudo-recall is almost always a very improbable explanation.

Pseudo-recall, especially when visiting places or meeting people, is related to *déjà-vu*: the sudden feeling that a situation is an exact replay of one that happened before. Hans Holzer (1985) gives good examples of *déjà-vu*. Pseudo-recall may sometimes explain spontaneous memories, especially those triggered by visiting places or meeting people; it rarely explains regressions.

What does happen often is *rescripting*: we beautify or worsen the story at points we cannot or will not confront.

Names, facts and dates are less accessible than personal and emotional experiences. Therapists or hypnotists who ask for them may elicit unreliable answers.

*

The explanation of *genetic memory* is merely speculation, as the research into the physical basis of memory does not indicate genetic coding and transfer of memories. Already with the early reptiles, brain information transcends genetic information. Carl Sagan points this out in his interesting book about evolution, *The Dragons of Eden*: 'Somewhere in the steaming jungles of the Carboniferous period there emerged an organism that for the first time in history had more information in its brains than in its genes' (Sagan 1977: 49). Sagan estimates that the human biography can be stored in a memory of 200 billion bits. In humans the genetic information is about 10 billion bits. Even if nothing of this were necessary for physical heredity, it would still be 20 times too small. It is also unclear how information would go from our brains to our genes. Meanwhile, we have discovered that people have far fewer genes than expected. 'More like a list of materials than a blueprint,' as one scientist remarked. We have hardly more genes than a mouse. Where to cram the memory of ancestral lifetimes?

The idea of genetic memory contradicts all empirical data. If memory were transferred genetically, people would convey their memories when they procreate. The seed and the egg can then only have information about the life of the parents up till that point. Apparent memories of a former life simply continue after the reproduction age. Even worse, both spontaneous recall and regression start remarkably often with memories and reliving of a traumatic death in a previous life. Genetic memory only explains this if many people still copulate after death, a proposition as disgusting as it is ridiculous. How many people recall their parents' lives before they themselves were conceived? None. Furthermore, in most cases a family relationship is impossible. Genetic memory also fails to explain memories of several previous lives with their afterdeath and prebirth experiences.

If we had a genetic ancestral memory, one-egg twins would have equal or at least similar regressions. However, this is not so, as experiments sponsored by a German broadcast company showed (Passian 1985). For spontaneous memories, the record is the same. Ian Stevenson (1987) presents examples of one-egg twins with completely different past-life memories. This refutes, by the way, the statement from the Loehr–Daniels readings that a one-egg twin is the same soul in two bodies. Even if that were possible, it is not the rule.

As an explanation of apparent past-life recall, we may comfortably discard genetic memory as pure and utter nonsense.

*

Visualising may slip into a *psychodrama*, a kind of waking dream in which we experience events that – as in a real dream – dramatise our problems, desires, frustrations, hopes and fears. When we assume we have lived before, our waking dream easily gets a historical backdrop. Waking dreams are generally rich in archetypes, poor on dull, insignificant details and poor on bodily sensations. Still, the difference from real memories is sometimes difficult to recognise. Skin resistance and muscle tension of dreams, waking dreams and regressions are the same, only the brain rhythm may differ: real regressions often contain delta. A hypnotist can induce a deeper trance to question the nature of the experience and may redirect the subject to a real experience.

An actual situation may trigger a past-life memory, which thus may have a psychodramatic and therapeutic value, just like a waking dream. Indications for a real previous life lie, then, in obscure historical details that are verified afterwards, in strong and precise bodily experiences that deviate from the present body or an ideal body, in truly novel experiences and in experiences contradicting existing prejudices.

The *false memory syndrome* is a popular explanation by psychologists and psychiatrists who reject hypnosis, regression and reincarnation. It certainly exists. It has been discovered that clients who graphically relived sexual abuse by a parent when they were very young had remembered something that did not happen. It has led to court cases and negative publicity. It sometimes leads also to extra work for us. I have had several clients utterly shaken because of the false accusations of a daughter. The therapist or psychiatrist involved worsened things by prohibiting the daughter from having contact with her denying parents any more. If memories from childhood may be false, memories from a previous life must be much more unreliable even. Though I cannot prove it, I'm pretty sure this reasoning is rubbish. Let me explain why this is most probably so.

In 1950 Ron Hubbard published *Dianetics*. In that book he wrote about his experiences with his type of regression. One of his 'discoveries' was the incredible number of abortion attempts in the United States. He had found disgusting evidence in many of his subjects of terrible experiences in the womb because of unsuccessful attempts at abortion: being stuck by needles, affected by burning poisons, hit by sticks, and kicked through the mother's belly, falls down stairs, etc. Interestingly, in all his later works, Hubbard never returns to this issue. Why? Because he discovered past lives.

Hubbard had people repeat and repeat and repeat the traumatic episode until there was no longer a galvanic skin response. He went from the present back through life till the birth experience. The idea was that if all engrams were erased, the person would be clear. And whatever clear was, it certainly included being free from fear, anger, shame and other limiting emotions. What he did find, of course, was that, even if the whole time-track from the present back to the birth had been cleared, most people were still not clear. Imagine what happened when he then found before birth vivid charges, strong experiences of being hit or cut, of falling or suffocating. He placed those experiences in the only time-period that seemed possible: in the womb. Later, of course, he discovered previous lives. What he had formerly found were in fact traumatic death experiences which he had forced into the prenatal period.

Likewise, therapists who have discovered regression, usually under hypnosis, may send their clients back to the source of a fear. For example, when they relive then a horrible rape, with full somatics, which resolves a number of symptoms, they are sure this is not imaginary. Now, if the therapist has some experience and knows what he is doing and at the same time believes that past lives don't exist, he has to project the clear and present symptoms of, for example, sexual abuse onto a repressed area of childhood. So false memories are born. And when one remembers an ordinary or happy childhood? Then this is proof of how deeply the experience has been suppressed and how awful everything must have been. Now, there are psychiatric patients who can hardly tell the difference between reality and fantasy, between their own experiences and those of others. With them, regression is not indicated.

Brute violence and sexual abuse of children occur, but these experiences are rarely as strongly suppressed as is being commonly assumed. Beyond the age of three, the memories are often conveniently forgotten, but rarely really suppressed. We forget that we remember, but when our memory is jogged, things come back.

The *collective unconscious* is an assumption made by Jung to explain what he calls the archetypal material in our psyche. To come up with a collective unconscious is as obscure a justification as explaining mathematicians' acceptance of each other's proofs by a collective mathematical consciousness. When two people are on the phone and understand each other, it is not necessary to account for this by participation in a collective consciousness and certainly not to place it outside the participants — for example, in the telephone exchange. There is a simpler explanation for archetypes: similarity between people in their physical (neurological) and psychological structure. The language of images (probably located in the right half of the brain) may have been less explored than verbal and mathematical languages, but it has its own structure and grammar as well.

William de Arteaga (1983) explains most apparent memories by *deceiving demons*. He does believe in reincarnation, but assumes that when we are relaxed and in trance, we are inspired by either the Holy Ghost or by demons – which makes regression a tricky business. Though his theological arguments fall flat for non-Christians, his book tries to be equitable and fair. It is interesting to meet such an uncommon view on the field. Unfortunately, De Arteaga needs 146 pages of metaphysics before he can talk about his experiences with Christian regressions. His catharsis consists of confessing, remorse and 'praise the Lord', not unlike what Motoyama is doing in Japan. Apparently, he presents papers about this subject at international congresses after having guided altogether two (!) regressions.

Another explanation is that people don't relive their own experiences, but those of others that have lived. This is no imagination, but *telepathy* with *identification*. A relation with or even just a genuine interest in the person involved facilitates this identification. Regressing on a problem sometimes lands us in a past life of maybe our father or mother, because we inherited the problem from one of our parents. Mother is dull and makes the life of her daughter dull. When the daughter regresses to the origin of her dullness, she relives a dull medieval lifetime that only later appears to be her mother's past life. People who prefer the explanation of telepathic identification dislike such cases, as they want to refute the idea of past lives at all. Forms of telepathy or ESP are all OK, as long as reincarnation is avoided: 'Anything else but . . .'

Sensitive people may tune in to the experiences of others, and with previous lives the chances of mistaken identity are obviously greater. Some assume that we may read these experiences from a spiritual database, the *akasha* records, and then mistakenly consider them our own. The usual term for this explanation is 'super-ESP' (*super-extra-sensory perception*). Super-ESP is a hypothesis impossible to refute; it is not falsifiable. Super-ESP, however, is flatly proposed for people who have never shown any psychic sensitivity at all. Most people who regress and young children with past-life memories have never shown psychic abilities. Stevenson (1987: 154–5) writes:

During the first years of my research, I took extrasensory perception more seriously as a plausible explanation for them, than I do now. I still consider it an important possibility, but I no longer give it the weight that I formerly did. I have two main reasons for this change of opinion. First, the children subjects hardly ever show or have credited to them by their families, any evidence of extrasensory perception apart from the memories of a previous life. I have asked hundreds of parents about such capacities in their children. Most of them have denied that the child in question had any, a few have said that their child had occasionally demonstrated some form of extrasensory perception, but the evidence they provided was usually scanty. I cannot understand how a child could acquire by extrasensory perception the considerable stores of information so many of these subjects show about a deceased person without demonstrating, if not often, at least from time to time similar paranormal powers in other contexts.

In addition, as I have said more than once already, a case nearly always includes more than the verbal statements that the child makes about the previous life. For one to several years and sometimes for much longer, most of the subjects show behavior that is unusual for their families, but that matches what we could learn or reasonably infer about the behavior of the previous personality.

Many of the subjects respond with strong emotion and in appropriate ways to stimuli related to the previous personality. For example, Ismail Altinkiliç clapped with joy when he learned that the murderers of the man whose life he remembered had, after particularly lengthy legal proceedings been judicially hanged. I mentioned earlier that other subjects . . . were brought to tears by the mere mention of some untoward event in the life of a person of whom the previous personalities in their cases had been fond. One may suppose that individual emotions may be communicated by extrasensory perception and indeed there is evidence for this; but much more is at issue in the behavioral responses that I am discussing. The child shows a syndrome of behaviors that in the more developed instances amounts to a facsimile of the previous personality's character. We have no grounds for thinking that processes of paranormal cognition can reproduce, in effect, an entire personality transposed to another person. Experimental parapsychology certainly offers no evidence for extrasensory perception of the kind required and other types of spontaneous cases only rarely offer parallels.

Regressions also exhibit no clear difference between people with and without psychic skills. A survey among people attending my lectures on reincarnation indicated that people with spontaneous past-life recall were generally more sensitive than people without. When people do have more than average sensitivity, they may assuredly receive other impressions. The assumption of telepathically reading the memory of another is a simpler explanation than the assumption of reading some general memory database, if only because impersonal clairvoyant impressions will be less likely to lead towards identification. It is easier to identify if there is somebody to identify with.

The explanation of telepathy is realistic and has to be accepted as a possibility, especially with people who are known to be sensitive. The explanation of super-ESP, because of its speculative and irrefutable character, had better be discarded. It would seem sensible to reserve identification as an explanation with people who did show psychic gifts, but even that is questionable. Professional psychics often identify with people who are missing or dead. They may feel what those people felt while drowning or being murdered. They even may assume physical or psychological traits. They have access to and share the experiences of others, but they don't identify – they remain conscious of the fact that they are sharing the sensations of somebody else (Tenhaeff, n.d.).

Some regression therapists work with sensitives or trance mediums so that they can quickly identify blocked trauma from previous lives. Therefore the hypothesis of telepathy cannot be refuted. Some sensitive persons can, even in a light trance, pick up the apparent memories of previous lives of others, especially when they know or have known them. It certainly does not happen at random.

Attachments or obsessions are the souls of deceased people who have attached themselves to living persons at their prejudice. To explain apparent memories as the past lives of attaching entities, implies also telepathy and identification. It is not uncommon to find in therapy that a previous past-life therapy that at first seemed effective, but ultimately didn't help at all, wrongly assumed that the past-life impressions where the client's own. Only when the attachment is released is the therapy successful.

Thelma Moss treated a 9-year-old boy who became terribly upset after visiting a remote derelict farm in Arizona. In the session she did with him, he felt that he had lived there as an isolated chicken farmer. He had fallen, hurt himself badly and died in pain, far from help. He had to remember all this to find release. Ten-to-one, this was no past life, but an attachment the boy picked up during the visit (Graham 1976: 94–5). In my book *Deep Healing* (1996) I give other examples of mistaken identification and its consequences. It is the most common mistake of ill-trained past-life therapists.

Some spiritualists who reject reincarnation explain all cases by attachment or obsession. Dr John Bjørkhem, a Swedish parapsychologist, concluded after more than 3,000 hypnosis experiments that regressions can all be explained by obsession – making obsession, by the way, a common human condition (Passian 1985: 41). The American neurologist Carl Wickland, the director of a mental hospital, explained in his book *Thirty Years Among the Dead* (1924) all so-called past-life memories by attached spirits. Wickland claims to have spoken with the deceased Helena Blavatsky, the founder of the Theosophical Society. During her life, she had been obsessed and realised in the hereafter that her reincarnation doctrine was in error (Passian 1985). In the early 1970s a British psychic lectures about reincarnation in the States. Before the lectures she sees the large face of a woman who inspires her to such an extent that the audience is deeply impressed. When she describes the face, a friend brings a portrait of Helena Blavatsky, who she recognises immediately as the great soul who was inspiring her. Of these two stories, at least one must be bogus. But they surely both are, as Blavatsky declared unequivocally in her articles and in interviews that reincarnation as a rule was sheer nonsense (see chapter 3).

As a general explanation, obsession is highly unlikely, but – as regression therapy practice shows – it is more common than we would wish.

Some strange cases cannot be explained easily, either by reincarnation or by obsession. K.O. Schmidt relates the next case in his *Abendländisches Totenbuch*.

> On November 22, 1963, the day President Kennedy was shot, a boy was born in Munich, named *Johann Schuler*. At an early age the young Johann had an amazing knowledge about Kennedy, events in the White House, Kennedy's office, his friends and acquaintances and details from American history in general. He told private details about the marriage with Jackie, who he recognized immediately from a picture in a magazine. He tore apart a picture of Onassis, the later husband of Jackie. Johann has a mole on the right side of his head, at the place the president was hit. However, Johann was born only 18 minutes after Kennedy died.

Schmidt thinks that possibly the descending soul of Johann Schuler had contact with the ascending soul of Kennedy who had just had his life review. Johan read it too and was so involved that he later felt he had been Kennedy himself. This Platonic idea of descending and ascending souls meeting is found, among others, in Inayat Khan. Rudolf Passian rightly considers this as an artificial explanation, but also considers all other explanations just as artificial. The immediate return of somebody who violently died a few minutes ago, and then in quite a different part of the globe, is highly unlikely. We could assume that Kennedy's soul replaced the one about to be born, as in possession. Or Johann was a deceased Kennedy-fan or personal acquaintance of Kennedy. It all remains unsatisfactory speculation.

An apparent memory of a previous life may sometimes be explained by a *memory of an intermission* between lives. Indications for this are experiences in which natural laws seem suspended; people have science-fiction or science-fantasy experiences in which mental powers play a great role and a weak bodily feeling with only vague impressions about their own aspect or gender. Often, these experiences resemble the discarnate state psychics or mediums report. The difference from the waking dream lies mainly in the absence of emotional psychodramatic material.

Joan Grant judged the first part of a girl's regression to be an imagination because the girl saw environments and situations, but did not see herself doing anything. Grant thought the girl could not envisage what she would do, as that would be beyond her experience (Graham 1976: 122). A nice illustration of Grant's critical mind, but a weak explanation. We surely can imagine what people do in situations we didn't experience ourselves. We read books; we see films. A more likely explanation of the girl's regression is hanging around after death. Such experiences are common in past-life regressions. Remigrants keep wandering in a wood for ages, while nothing happens. No hunger, no thirst, no weariness or pain, no clear thoughts, just musing incessantly. They encounter nobody, just some animals that don't run away.

Helen Roberts gives examples from the Loehr–Daniels readings of souls who between lifetimes are so interested in what happens down here that later recall seems a memory of past lives. Schlotterbeck says that, especially in group regressions and in higher-self interventions ('see it all from a distance, from above'), misidentification may occur. He gives an example of somebody seeing herself during a group regression as a German officer who is disenchanted with Hitler and cuts up his portrait. Later, in the individual regression, she appeared to be watching this scene approvingly as the unborn child of this officer's wife (Schlotterbeck 1987: 53). Rudolf Passian cites a related case from the *Zeitschrift für Spiritismus* (1914: 157):

> During a spiritist séance, an acquaintance of Dr W. Dietrich, the writer of the article, entered into a trance and revealed the most remarkable and intimate details about the

childhood of an older gentleman present whom he had never met before. If this older gentleman had died already, the story of the medium would have seemed a past-life memory. The gentleman involved could corroborate everything the medium said. The most probable explanation would be a telepathic link to the old man's memory, but the medium himself gave a different explanation: during the first twenty years of this older gentleman's life, Dietrich's acquaintance had himself been his spirit guide before being born.

An apparent memory can also be a *fantasy from a previous life*. During a regression a remigrant may suddenly find out, with deep emotion and intense satisfaction, that he has been Beethoven. He experiences himself intensely as the deaf Beethoven conducting a symphony. If such an experience is tracked and experienced several times under the right guidance, he may suddenly dissociate from the person of Beethoven and appear to be an aristocrat in the front row absorbedly listening and looking. After repeated reliving, he may even dissociate from this person and appear to be a theatre usher standing in the back of the theater, listening and daydreaming.

A man with vague pains in his whole body finds himself in a regression in France in the early 17th century as the bored teenage son of a miller. One day a horseman passes through, a typical musketeer. He likes the boy and takes him with him as a manservant. The boy learns how to be a musketeer: flashing fights, flashing repartee and flashing conquests of flashing women. The remigrant doesn't stop talking. Asked for the cause of the present-day pains he falls silent for a while and talks about heroic man-to-man fights during which he is often wounded painfully, but never lethally. The question why he carried over these pains to the present life remains unanswered. But who cares, as the pains have mysteriously disappeared during the telling.

Unfortunately, the pains return later. Finally, it is discovered that the boy was caught in the machinery of the mill when about fourteen, while he was daydreaming. We know now what about. Only after his his painful and tragic death has been relived, do the pains go never to return. And, of course, daydreaming has also caused problems in his present lifetime.

Deception, imagination and pseudo-recall in no way explain the great numbers of concrete memories of previous lives. Telepathic identification is especially plausible with people who have shown psychic sensitivity, but probably occurs more often. During regressions, the depth of trance, the technique of guidance and control equipment like the E-meter and the mind mirror are important means to discriminate cases of imagination and identification.

The explanation of a genetic memory is nonsensical, and the explanation of super-ESP unfounded and worthless. Deception may happen incidentally and is rather simple to check. Pseudo-recall may happen with apparent memory fragments coming up spontaneously, especially when places or people 'seem familiar'. Identification may often happen with uncritical and frustrated believers. Regressions may include psychodramatic waking dreams (rather easy to discern) and telepathic identification (rather difficult to discern).

Other phenomena that we will encounter, like birth marks and the transference of skills from previous lives, are – after deceit and imagination have been ruled our – strong indications against pseudo-recall, psychodrama and the common forms of telepathy.

DEMONSTRATING REINCARNATION IN SPECIFIC CASES; TESTING DUBIOUS EPISODES

A remigrant talks in great detail about a life in thirteenth-century Italy or in an unidentified, primitive village 'long ago'. Another recounts being a chambermaid in the court of Catherine the Great. How can we check the reality of such claims? We verify claims by checking them against alternative explanations. One simple example from Graham (1976: 82):

> An attempt could also be made to explain Logg's memories in terms of ESP, i.e., he may have acquired the necessary information through ESP and then formulated it into past-life recall. This explanation also does not appear to be true, because Logg demonstrates no psychic capacity. If he had, it would have been apparent on other occasions, not only during hypnosis. The hypothesis of ESP also cannot explain Logg's capacity to write in hieroglyphics. Writing in hieroglyphics is a talent, which can be acquired only through learning and practice. Information is acquired through ESP, not skill.'

The next table gives 21 indications to test the plausibility of seven different explanations of apparent past-life recollections. I leave out the explanations of deception, genetic memory, collective unconscious, demonic inspiration and super-ESP, for reasons already given. I explain the indicators in the text.

Table 5 Testing possible past-life memories

A	Reincarnation	+ :	Not conflicting
B	Attachments	(+):	Improbable combination
C	Telepathy	(−):	Probably conflicting
D	Psychodrama	− :	Conflicting
E	Deception		
F	Pseudo-recall		
G	Imagination		
H	*Déjà-vu*		

Indicators	A	B	C	D	E	F	G	H
Contents:								
Resistance & catharsis & therapeutic effect	+	+	−	+	(−)	−	−	−
New experiences, breaking through prejudice	+	−	+	−	+	−	−	−
New body sensations	+	+	+	(−)	+	−	−	−
Filmic memories	+	+	+	+	+	−	(−)	−
Concomitants								
New abilities, such as xenoglossy	+	+	+	−	−	−	−	−
Somatic changes	+	+	+	+	−	−	−	−
Indications of new abilities	+	+	+	−	+	−	−	−
Voice changes	+	+	+	+	+	−	(+)	−
Changing skin resistance and EEG	+	+	+	+	−	−	−	(+)
Weak xenoglossy	+	+	+	−	+	+	−	−
Personal characteristics:								
Birthmarks	+	+	−	+	+	−	+	−
Memories only after induction	+	+	+	+	+	+	−	−
Absence of psychic gifts	+	+	−	+	+	+	+	+
Absence of psychosomatic problems	+	(−)	+	+	+	+	+	+
Guidance:								
Varying sequences	+	(−)	−	−	−	−	−	−
Trance without regression having been mentioned	+	+	+	+	−	+	+	−
Varying hypnotists	+	+	(+)	+	+	+	+	−
Checks:								
Significant historical confirmation	+	+	+	−	−	−	−	−
Confirmation of child cases	+	+	+	−	−	−	−	−
Multiple independent testimonies	+	(−)	+	−	+	−	−	−
Weak historical confirmation	+	+	+	−	+	+	−	−

The table shows that attachment is the most difficult to differentiate from past-life memories. It also shows that the strongest indicators for a real past-life memory in a particular case are: catharsis, constancy of the memories under different sequences and the absence of serious psychosomatic problems. Historical confirmation shows that the experience is no imagination or psychodrama, but it takes time, is difficult and does not discriminate between reincarnation and identification. Opponents of reincarnation are fond of historical testing. If we can't find historical confirmation, the apparent recall has clearly been fantasy. If we do find historical confirmation, the person in question could have obtained the information in a regular way. Naturally, neither for imagination nor for pseudo-recall do they give a shred of evidence.

Clearly, we can't judge on the basis of one criterion only whether an experience is a true past-life memory. David Gershom uses nine indicators to distinguish true Holocaust memories from imagination. The more indicators, the stronger the case (Gershom 1992: 61–8):

- *Nightmares in childhood, phobias.*
- *A non-Jew, not exposed to Jewish customs, who exhibits compulsive behaviour, habits and the like that resemble Jewish customs or rituals.*
- *A secular Jew with intuitive understanding of Jewish mysticism.*
- *Feeling a stranger within one's own family.*
- *Birth during the baby boom or near-death during birth.*
- *Asthma, breathing problems or susceptibility to bronchitis; also anorexia nervosa or eating disorders.*
- *Blond hair and light eyes, especially as the only one in the family. (Two-thirds of his respondents had blond hair and blue eyes.)*
- *An extremely emotional response to the Holocaust, as a child or by an event in adulthood.*
- *The integrity of the person, the general feeling about the interview and his own impressions. Some interviews do 'click and touch the soul', while others don't.*

General indicators for authenticity are concreteness, emotional resistance, catharsis and lasting healing after the remigrant has recalled and digested difficult and burdening experiences. New experiences or experiences that run counter to present attitudes are other important indications. The remigrant may feel a noticeably different body: other gender, other age, other constitution, other size, weight or disposition. The more life recall is complete, from childhood to day of dying, the more probable it is that recall is real.

Emotional and cathartic episodes that heal serve to refute *déjà-vu*, fantasy and pseudo-recall. They also refute telepathy, as the recall relates to long-standing personal problems or characteristics. Psychodrama and attachment cannot be ruled out then. Experiencing a different body, doesn't say anything about telepathy, but makes psychodrama improbable. Filmic recall rules out *déjà-vu* and pseudo-memory and makes fantasy less likely.

Often, regressions produce voice changes: a girl, reliving a life as a lumberjack, gets a deeper voice; an aged person gets a childish voice. Hypnotic regressions show this more often, but it happens too without hypnotic induction. Bodily changes are common: breath and temperature change, muscles stiffen or loosen, skin may redden or whiten, skin marks may appear. Somatics are prominent in regressions to birth, death, pain, mutilation or deformity. In less than 0.1 percent of the cases, remigrants speak the language of a previous life, even if they never learned it (xenoglossy). More often, remigrants recall a few words, even if they don't know what language it is.

Voice changes and somatics make pseudo-recall and *déjà-vu* improbable. Strong imagination may explain voice changes, but not welts appearing on the skin when reliving a thrashing. Even without hypnosis. During a session by Morris Netherton in Brazil the remigrant experiences a concentration camp and on her arm appears a number. It was traceable to Israel: a spectacular example of historical confirmation.

In a regression a man experiences being a trader in precious stones who was robbed and killed by a fellow trader in his past life. The next morning he wakes up with a large red bump between his eyes, the place he was hit when he died. *'There was no way I could hide or explain it. I am now a firm believer in reincarnation'* (Graham 1976: 176). And such a bump disappears as fast as it emerged.

An intense psychodrama may change the voice and maybe trigger some bodily changes, but it does not make us speak in foreign tongues.

We may build checks in the regression. When trance is sufficient, we may ask a remigrant to do things requiring past-life skill: making music, dancing or singing. An important check is having a remigrant go through his lifetimes in varying order during different sessions. Among others, Wilder did this (Underwood & Wilder 1975). The results are especially impressive when the voice changes. Obsession cannot be precluded, but telepathy and clairvoyance can, as they will not lead to identical results. Psychodrama is unlikely, as it develops our ideas and emotions and so changes in replay. Deceit, imagination, pseudo-recall and *déjà-vu* are implausible when different sequences produce identical results time and again.

The skin-resistance meter and the brain-wave meter preclude deceit, pseudo-memory and imagination. When the remigrant talks with a flat voice while the E-meter shows lower skin resistance, he appears to conceal what he is seeing or about to be see. When a remigrant tells an emotional story without a response on the E-meter, he is probably just imagining.

Hypnotising remigrants, without telling them what we expect of them, precludes deception and *déjà-vu*. To preclude telepathy and suggestion, we can test remigrants with different hypnotists. We can have them repeat the events. If versions are different and imagination and leading questions are ruled out, resistance is the usual cause. Drug use is another. The remigrant may downplay his own unpleasant role, either as victim or as perpetrator. To continue, we focus on the elements that remained constant in the different versions.

Checking historical facts rules out fantasy. Obscure historical details, such as the coins used in Egypt a century after Alexander or the measuring system used by the Kirghiz in the sixteenth century, are convincing. The literature contains many examples of historical testing. Netherton gives the example of the ship *Republic* (Netherton & Shiffrin 1978: 68). Unfortunately, many convincing cases cannot be historically verified.

Confirmation is strongest when remigrants recount things yet unknown or apparently conflicting with known historical data which later are verified by new excavations or new historical research. Arthur Guirdham talks about a woman who had had Cathar memories since her youth. She described the *bonhommes* wearing blue. Historians refuted this, but years later it was discovered that dark blue was indeed worn by these people (Guirdham 1976: 10).

Somebody who is searching for confirmation of his recollections comes across a book giving the full history of the town where he once lived. He finds his own story confirmed in almost all details, except that many of the names were wrong and the three daughters he recalled appear to have been adopted girls (Schlotterbeck 1987: 43). The wrong names are important, because after place names and dates, names are the most important search criteria.

Ian Stevenson checked how much of what is told about a past life is coroborated by facts. He carefully researched the methods used in judicial investigations to check witnesses' claims (Stevenson 1975: 1) and applied them.

Two psychology students, Esteban and Titus Rivas, investigated the case of a six-year-old girl who seem to remember a past life, in which she died at about the same age, in the war. She is asked under hypnosis for her name and address. In the public registry no one of that name appears to have lived there. The researchers conclude: 'Anyway, this confirms for us that we can get no verifiable data under hypnosis, so hypnosis is a useless tool in reincarnation research.' They seem not to know the meaning of the word 'verifiable', so their conclusion is unsustainable. What is true, however, is that asking for easily verifiable data like names of places, of streets, of people, house numbers, dates and years often gets no answer or an unreliable answer. One example from Graham (1976: 164):

'What year is it?' asked the hypnotist. Arlene, as the previous personality, that of a three-year-old child, thought, but could not visualise, a date. (What three-year-old today is aware of such matters?) Again the question was asked and she blurted out, '1880.' 'No tie-in here,' thought Dan, as the regarded Massacre was much earlier, 1847. Then he realized that probably the last date registered with Arlene in her conscious state was 1880! They had been to a railroad museum that same afternoon and the plate on a woodburning locomotive read '1880'.

In the preceding chapter we have seen that many people take intuitive answers as gospel. They aren't.

Morris Netherton's story of the ship *Republic* is an example of *'multiple viewpoints'*: separate people, not knowing each other, recall in separate regressions the same obscure historical details or even the same story from different viewpoints. The highest probability of finding such correspondences is with people who feel they knew each other before. We have to keep the sessions separate and to go for details. This does not exclude telepathy, but makes attachment implausible.

Over a period of time Bruce Goldberg worked with two patients whose past-life sessions appeared to interlock. One was a sadistic goldsmith and the other the abused pupil. Goldberg wonders what would happen if they were to meet, but he did not want to bring them together. First, he says, if they were karmically destined to meet each other, they would meet anyhow; second, he does not want to play God with his patients. Bringing them together might influence their karma too strongly (Goldberg 1982: 126). Surely this view is shortsighted and inconsistent. If they were not meant to meet each other, they might never have ended up with the same therapist. Goldberg is also playing God – as we all do, with almost everyone we know – by refusing to bring them together. He also does not consider the simplest and most obvious option: to ask the two remigrants if they would be interested in meeting. If they both were, it would be at least interesting and probably meaningful for all involved.

Birthmarks exclude explanations such as telepathy and pseudo-recall. Deception, imagination and pseudo-recall remain possible, as remigrants may build stories around their marks. Absence of psychic gifts makes clairvoyance and telepathy unlikely and the absence of psychosomatic problems or identity problems makes obsession unlikely. Already by 1900 Flournoy had shown that would-be remigrants can conjure up imaginary lifetimes. Oddly, these fantasies may contain plausible material (Shirley 1924: 145).

DEMONSTRATING REINCARNATION

If we can often discard alternative explanations on the basis of the test criteria from the table, we have reasonably demonstrated the existence of reincarnation. Not proven. Only logic and mathematics offer real proof – that is, after accepting some axioms.

The most substantial anti-reincarnation book to date is *Mind out of Time: Reincarnation claims reinvestigated* by Ian Wilson (1981). He compares regressions to past lives with the symptoms of multiple personalities. Except for the historical framework, these phenomena are, in his opinion, directly comparable and caused by 'an unknown and unconscious psychic mechanism' (Wilson 1981: 157). Now, that explains a lot. Real explanations, of course, are unnecessary. For nonsense like reincarnation, insinuations are enough to refute it. Wilson's testing of historical facts reminds us of Glenn Williston's experiences. Williston tried to check the historical validity of material and wrote a colourful and humorous account of his efforts (Williston & Johnstone 1983: 137). Wilson's book suffers from the same weakness as the works of reincarnation supporters: it tries to prove something. However, Wilson did his homework better than most of the latter. This makes him obligatory reading for gullible reincarnation fans who enthusiastically gather names and dates in regressions.

Another example of the difficulties involved in historical confirmation is given by Graham (1976: 52–3):

He discovered an elderly lady, near Harriston, whose name was Eletha Helene Moore. When he telephoned her to ask her if he could meet her to talk about her family tree, she very pleasantly promised to give him all her cooperation. However, when she asked him why he was so interested in the Moore family and he replied that he was trying to find out about an Elly Moore who died in 1915 in an automobile accident, she rapidly changed her position and said that she wouldn't be able to talk to him because she wasn't feeling well. When he suggested that he could meet her a few days later when she was better, she flatly refused to do so, saying that she didn't have anything more to say to him.

It seemed that he had touched a tender spot and that there had been another Elly Moore in the woman's family. Her enthusiasm, which was very apparent in the beginning, totally vanished as soon as she heard Elly's name. It seemed that the name was too painful for her.

Jay was unable to find anything tangible about Elly in Harriston or the surrounding area. He then went to the Department of Health and Vital Statistics in the nearby town of Harrisburg to check the death certificates of all persons named Moore who had died there or in the surrounding area, in 1915. His research revealed interesting details relevant to Luft's statements.

It should be mentioned here that the most convincing part of her recollections under hypnosis was not what she said, but the way she actually relived the automobile accident Elly was involved in. Her neck and chest turned purplish blue because of the trauma of reexperiencing the fatal accident. In a state of terror, she reported how she was catapulted out of the car into a ditch and lay mortally wounded there, watching her uncle being burned alive in the flaming car where he was caught. While describing the scene, the atmosphere of death she created was so real that students who were watching her started to cry and some of them felt faint.

Jay's examination of records at the Department of Health and Vital Statistics in Harrisburg revealed that there was an Eletha Moore, aged nineteen, who had died on February 19, 1915, i.e., one month earlier than the date of death Luft had mentioned. This woman, however, had died of childbirth. According to Luft, Elly was twelve years old, blue-eyed and blond-haired; this Eletha Moore was black and pregnant. Possibly, Luft had changed her story to make her claimed previous life less embarrassing in the waking state. She might have wanted to conceal the shame and disgrace of a pregnancy out of wedlock and the fact that she was black in her past life.

Researchers interested in the study of past-life recall know that subjects sometimes do not express memories of their past lives very clearly. There are sometimes unconscious and conscious efforts to suppress unpleasant memories.

Jay also tried to trace the death certificate of George Moore, Elly's uncle. A death certificate was located for a George Moore who had died in Norristown on March 27,

1915 of cerebral hemorrhage and apoplexy-conditions, which could have resulted from a car accident. The date of his death is only eight days after the date given by Luft. Norristown, too, is less than ten miles from the route Elly and her uncle are supposed to have been on. Under the circumstances, it can be assumed that Elly may not have seen her uncle die in the flaming car. It is possible that she was unconscious while her uncle was being extricated from the car and taken to a hospital in Norristown.

The success rate of past-life therapy strongly underpins the reincarnation hypothesis. Sublimations and shifts, catharsis and permanent therapeutic effects, voice changes and bodily changes during regressions all make explanations such as clairvoyance, telepathy or a collective unconscious implausible. Effective therapy presupposes either real regression or at least a meaningful psychological process. The main arguments against the idea of a pure psychological process are being in another body, tasting things never tasted before and experiences contradicting present preferences and prejudices. Such experiences do not happen in waking dreams or psychodramas. Dethlefsen (1976) writes (I have abbreviated his text):

The idea that apparent former lives are projections is untenable. A psychodrama only exists as the result of a projection, conscious or unconscious, of inner conflicts. This cannot explain the phenomena described below.

One remigrant, a radio reporter in his present life, a textile merchant in 1755, gave the exact length of material needed for a suit measured in yards, counted money in guilders and described a famine in 1732, later verified in a historical chronicle. Another remigrant spent most of the sessions explaining everything about measurements, calculations and distances. He had been an architect. He described the minutest details of buildings he had built and only later recounted personal facts. His profession came first. I doubt whether these accounts can be explained as a projection of present inner conflicts.

When a regression counselor leads a remigrant through different lifetimes, these lives turn out to have such different contents that they cannot be the product of one life's projection. A 20-year-old student gives a precise account of an abortion she had in a past life, although she had never been confronted with abortion, reincarnation research or pregnancy now. The same remigrant experienced her menopause in a session. Afterwards, she said it was an odd feeling and deepened her understanding of her mother.

Descriptions of past lives are not conglomerates of problems, conflicts and clichés. They contain too many personal, historically specific observations and abilities to rule out the explanation of psychodrama. Remigrants tell us how long it took to travel a particular *distance by coach, how bread was baked in the seventeenth century and what herbs were used in 1687 to stop bleeding.*

When reliving situations from apparent past lives leads to catharsis and lasting therapeutic effect, this indicates either reincarnation, attachment or psychodrama. Investigating the effectiveness of past-life therapy therefore is important: because of the importance of effective therapy in general and secondly as supporting or weakening the reincarnation hypothesis. A sketchy overview of some research done in Brazil shows a table of the duration and success of each individual therapy. In the Netherlands, Johannes Cladder (1983) investigated the effectiveness of regression therapy, including hypnosis and behaviour therapy. It turned out to be a quick and effective method for people who had had no success with other methods. Eighty percent of phobics were doing better within 22 sessions, with an average of 11 sessions needed for improvement. Of the patients who believed in reincarnation, 70 percent regressed to a past life; of those who did not believe, 50 percent discovered a past life. Of clients who accepted reincarnation, 64 percent had a past-life experience; of those indifferent or sceptical, 57 percent. The patients with past-life memories had more psychosomatic and diverse complaints than the others. Their grasp on reality increased. The treatment, consisting of flooding the client with regression material, benefited phobics with compulsive behaviour very little. Ronald Van der Maesen, who duplicated an existing research design used for other forms of therapy, has done much more extensive and systematic research. Unfortunately, the results have been published in Dutch only.

The explanation most difficult to disprove is attachment or obsession: the souls of people who lived in the past haunting the living now. From the spiritist and past-life therapy literature, we know obsessions are accompanied by psycho-somatic complaints and identity problems. But many regressions are liberating and make the remigrant healthier, stronger and more self-aware. Also, the similarities between different, independent lives in comparable circumstances make the obsession hypothesis seem less likely. The pure repetition of regressions, each time in a different sequence, indicates that the remigrant is drawing from a constant, organised memory.

Another line to follow is the statistical analysis of large numbers of comparable regressions. Helen Wambach (1978, 1979) has done the most significant research in this direction. For example, she looked at the social classes of the remigrants. If experiences of past lives were compensation, then many remigrants would remember important lives. In her experiments, 60 to 80 percent of the regressions were to lives in the lowest social class. Lives in the highest social classes were found in only 2 percent (around AD 800) to 10 percent (around AD 1700) of the cases. The remaining portion were lives in the middle classes.

Wambach registered the frequency distribution of race, sex, dress, shoes, food, pottery, etc. All of these distributions reflected historical distributions. For example, she asked her remigrants what was on the table, whether they had their hands in their lap when they ate, what they ate from and with. She asked if the utensils were wooden, baked clay or metal and what they looked like, etc. Some remigrants gave answers like: there was no table, we ate with our hands, we took the food from a common pot with our hands, we ate with leaves, etc. Such answers refute the oft-mentioned 'suggestibility' during hypnosis. The frequency of lives in the five historical periods corresponded with the estimated development of world population.

RESEARCH INTO THE NATURE OF PAST-LIFE MEMORY

If reincarnation is general, we should be able to induce past-life recall in everybody, unless it is a talent slowly developed in the course of lives. The success rate for inducing past-life recall varies between 70 and 90 percent. It would be interesting to pinpoint the conditions for recall, since this could give indications about the nature of past-life memory.

People without spontaneous recall can be induced to recall with proper guidance, in a certain trance or at least in a relaxed state. The barriers seem to be ignorance, uncertainty or disbelief. Someone who has never heard of reincarnation, or thinks it is nonsense, is unlikely to try to recall past lives.

Wambach investigated ten people during her group sessions who had no past-life recall at all (1978). Of these, two achieved past-life recall in individual sessions and four resisted because they feared a death experience. When this fear was hypnotically blocked, they did have past-life recall. The other four resisted every form of psychological exploration, including free association.

Netherton found that only a few patients could remember nothing from a past life (1978). When patients said they did not see or hear anything, they were usually blind, blindfolded, deaf or sworn to secrecy. The question 'Is something wrong with your eyes or with your ears?' often led to a breakthrough. One patient was unable to remember anything from a past life. Her mother, when she had been pregnant with her, converted to a religion denying pain and negative feelings. Apparently, this was a strong shut-off command for the foetus.

Past-life recall seems to obey the same psychological laws as normal recall, though we can access past-life memories at two levels. The first level is similar to our normal memory. It seems to be subject to the same laws of association, forgetting and remembering, sublimation and shifting, and pseudo-memories as our present-life memory. The other level some call the Higher Self. On this level, memory is much more complete and objective. This memory also exists for the present life and is used in, for example, Transactional Analysis.

More women remember changing gender than men do. Psychics also see more male past lives of women than female past lives of men (Muller 1970: 277). Apparently, the female lives of men are less accessible. Men may resist remembering female lives. Male lives also tended to be more dramatic, more varied and more karmic than female lives. Lives with a lot of action and drama are more easily remembered than boring lives. This is consistent with our normal memory. In deeper trance, the difference disappears. Wambach found an equal number of past lives in both genders, even in groups with an uneven male–female distribution (Wambach 1978: 135). At a certain level of trance, we seem to tap a more objective memory.

Recall of past lives can assume different forms, with varying degrees of completeness:

- *Fragmentary recall* is feelings associated with a name or impressions of a landscape, a house, a road, a windmill or the like.
- *Episodic recall* is limited to one event or one episode, without knowing the background, history or consequences.
- In *film recall*, the most important and impressive situations (except maybe those that are too impressive) from a past life are strung together into a cohesive story. We can instruct the remigrant to bring such memories to a stop or change to slow motion, to zoom in or out or to step back to get an overview.

- *Total recall* may contain seemingly every detail of a particular life. For example, we may suggest that the remigrant go three days ahead or three weeks or three months. The memories are clear and remain consistent when repeated.
- A rare form of past-life recall is *panoramic recall*, where we oversee our entire life as if we were surveying a landscape. Probably, such recall is identical with the life review after death.

The memory of past lives is organised in such a way that we recall feelings, observations and ideas more easily than exact dialogues, names, dates and other facts. Some people live intense lives without giving a thought to dates or geographic locations. We can ask about such things, but if the remigrant did not know the answers during that lifetime, another memory has to be activated. In regressions this usually happens after the death experience, during the life review and sometimes when the higher self intervenes.

Recall, especially at the first level of memory, is easily distorted, as within the present life. Moss and Keeton (1979) describe several cases with a mixture of historically correct and incorrect facts. A few obscure historically correct details do not prove that all other information is historically correct. Conversely, a few incorrect details do not prove that all other information is incorrect. Presumably, the accessibility of the memory is connected to psychic talents. The results of the mind mirror research of Winafred Lucas support this.

IDENTIFICATION PROCEDURES

An exceptional form of investigating reincarnation is finding the present lifetime of people who have died or the past lifetime of infants. For centuries, Tibet has had a tradition of looking for the reincarnation of important lamas a few years after they have died. The present incarnation can then continue where the past one left off. The Tibetans assume that advanced souls can transpose themselves onto a new incarnation, whereas ordinary souls crumble after death. Alexandra David-Neel (1961) and Rato Khylongla Nawang Losang describe these procedures. Rato's description follows here (Rato 1977: 17):

During the lama's cremation the Tibetans establish in which direction the smoke disappears. The next incarnation will be in that direction [assuming, by the way, a primitive population I process – see chapter 12]. The lama's most prominent pupil then writes a prayer or a poem about the lama. This prayer or poem is distributed among the monks to aid in the search for the new incarnation. The most important lamas, including the Dalai Lama, are asked to pray that the new incarnation will be found quickly. Information about extraordinary children or extraordinary circumstances surrounding the birth and about the births of children in the area passed by the smoke, is collected.

One example of a pregnancy with extraordinary signs is the following: a pregnant woman dreamt that the guiding deities poured water over her head. This meant that all the child's sins would be absolved. During the last month of her pregnancy, she became nauseous when she entered a temple, but the god caught her and set her down. A third sign was a dream that the moon and the sun united, meaning the child would be extremely intelligent. During the birth, a rainbow touched the house: a happy sign.

Such indications are put before mediumistic monks who act as oracles. They choose the three most likely prospects for the new incarnation. The three cases are considered in trance and then the verdict is read. The Dalai Lama confirms the verdict and the child is brought in. The child often has to select objects belonging to the past incarnation from a large display. The procedure of selecting objects is also used in Africa to identify young children. Apart from dreams and signs, the heart of the procedure seems to be the consultation of a recognized trance medium and the child's selection of objects that belonged to the deceased.

Walter Semkiw is doing a completely different kind of research. Like Clarice Toyne, he searches for physical resemblances and checks them with resemblances in character and biography (Semkiw 2001). Semkiw recognises himself in John Adams, one of the Founding Fathers of the Unites States and its second president. Family members, friends, colleagues and acquaintances are also returned family members and contemporaries of Adams. As a bonus, we get the past lives of recent Americans like the Kennedy brothers, Clinton, Gore and Bush Jr. They were all more or less famous Americans during and just after the Revolution. It all sounds too good to be true, but Semkiw compares the portraits of then and now and – it should be said – resemblances are remarkable. Occasionally a man now was a woman then, a black now was a white then, so the research is not bigoted. Semkiw also gives examples of other Americans with past-life recall. These examples are the strongest. The analogies between past lives and present lives are sometimes far-fetched and sometimes very strong. My visual favourite: Al Gore as the reincarnation of General Horatio Gates. If it is all true, there is much more continuity between lives than we find in regressions and in children's cases.

SUGGESTIONS FOR FURTHER RESEARCH

Ian Stevenson contributed greatly to the scientific verification of the reincarnation hypothesis in his pioneer work with child cases. A comparable research programme is needed for induced regressions. Helen Wambach made important progress in this. Hypnotic regression will remain the main tool of investigation, since trance induces objective phenomena such as voice and skin resistance changes, different brain-wave patterns, etc. Using different hypnotists, inducing trance without foreknowledge and repeating the regression post-hypnotically, where the remigrants forget what happened during the regression, strengthens the research. These procedures can rule out deceit, pseudo-memories, imagination and *déjà-vu*.

Disproving hypotheses like imagination, pseudo-memory and deceit is neither useful nor interesting. Of course, every prudent researcher has to take pains to reduce their likelihood. But do not look for waterproof arguments against sceptics.

The recommendations of Maurice Albertson and Kenneth Freeman (1988) for further research are interesting. I quote some:

- *Future investigation of phenomena related to reincarnation should be undertaken only after careful planning of the research protocols. Every attempt should be made to gather data as objectively as possible, to protect against fraud or deception and to prevent contamination of sources by naturalistic information inputs.*
- *The religious and philosophical traditions, Oriental and Western, must be extensively examined to expose all of the considerations, arguments, etcetera counter to reincarnation. An effort can then be made to reply to these rebuttals and then to assess the respective cases comparatively.*
- *Near Death Experience research needs to be expanded to obtain more detailed information regarding various influences, such as cultural factors and detailed life histories, which cause a variation in the details of the Near Death Experience: the process*

of pulling out of the body (when and how); details of observations immediately after pulling out of the body such as comments, special happenings, unusual movements of people, equipment used, activities in other rooms, time clocks, friends and relatives nearby and their actions; details of the life review; details of the dark void, tunnel and white light; details of people seen such as dead friends and relatives and angels; and details of how and why decided to return.

- Unborn Child research could take the person back to pre-birth to see if the process of deciding to return is the same as that described by Wambach.

- Study of Child Memories could ask the young child to describe what happened immediately after the death in the past life being described. Are the experiences similar to those described in Near Death Experience research? What happened next beyond the Near Death Experience type experiences? What happened in the Bardo Zone? Describe the decisions to return to earth. Were guides involved? What role did the guides play? When enter the foetus? What experiences were anticipated for this life? When describing the previous life, does the young child speak and act with the maturity of an adult?

- Life Before Life research such as Wambach could be expanded to gain greater detail [and better statistical presentation and analysis]. Case studies from therapists could be collected by having a set of questions to ask when the opportunity arises without putting the client in jeopardy.

- Past-Life research and Past-Life Therapy research could be an expansion and refinement of Wambach's research by asking more specific and detailed questions about the death experience as compared to Near Death Experiences, the Bardo activities, decision-making, the role of guides, the process of deciding to return, the foreknowledge possessed prior to entering the fetus, the loss of memory, when and how and is there communication with the mother and/or father before and/or during pregnancy? The APRT members and other therapists and researchers could acquire a large amount of important data.

- Examine psychotherapy literature for therapy assessment designs. Apply these designs to Past-Life Therapy both alone and for different styles and for Past-Life Therapy versus other more conventional forms of psychotherapy. [Ronald van der Maesen did a large part of this.]

- Determine criteria to distinguish a possessing or channeling entity from an included personality. Design experiments to determine which one is present on any occasion.

The most interesting reincarnation research seems to me to find regularities and laws governing reincarnation processes and to find out more about the memory involved.

Research to establish whether reincarnation is a fact is not as promising as it seems. It is only done for people who probably will not change their beliefs anyway. Diehards have to die out. The investigation of what happens in apparent regressions to past lives is more interesting. The worst finding would be that things are different or more complicated than we expected.

Ideas about genetic memory and the collective unconscious are speculations that do not require further refutation. It suffices to point out the phenomena that contradict them. The super-ESP hypothesis is useless. More common psychic sensitivity can be shown to be plausible or implausible in analysing a particular case. But forms of clairvoyance transcending space, time and identity are speculations that may explain every human cognition outside direct observation. And regressions are no potpourri of random tidbits.

A good example of how regression research and common inquiry may combine is Dick Sutphen's story of his reconstruction of the life of Ed Morrell in his epilogue to the new edition of Jack London's *The Star Rover* (London 1915). For sceptics such a story is not convincing, but the interesting and essential point is that regression evidence can (and should) stimulate the search for hard evidence, not supplant it. Pretty often, attachment is a more probable explanation than a personal past life. Differentiating personal past-life memories from those of others, whether attached or obsessing, is practically important. Goldberg (1982) and Holzer (1985) do not distinguish the two, and, as the reader, I felt pity for their misguided subjects. In my opinion, therapists who can't find out the difference may make things worse for their clients instead of helping them.

Reincarnation research can also be of considerable practical use with problems such as:

- anorexia and bulimia
- allergies and asthma
- alcoholism and drug abuse
- transsexuality
- epilepsy
- cancer
- phobias
- suicidal tendencies
- sadism and masochism.

Our knowledge of daily life in early civilisations can be greatly enriched, even regarding such recent periods as the last century. Reading about life in the slums of Liverpool in 1850 is both very interesting and very moving (Moss & Keeton 1979: 41). Netherton's 'multiple-viewpoints' approach would be especially interesting for unknown cultures. The size of the sample and a good spread – preferably international – are important, as well as the usual precautions to preclude deceit. Wambach's reports at the end of each session provide models that may be further refined.

Pieter Langedijk (1980) suggests how regressions may contribute to historical research:

- the pronunciation of languages only known in writing
- lost civilisations
- ancient religions
- ancient civilisations that used psychic gifts.

When the idea is to do many regressions with standard questions and collect material that is both relevant and credible, we should not take broad philosophical or religious questions like the meaning of each life or the meaning of the development through lifetimes. Concrete questions will enable interesting comparisons and have practical relevance. I give some suggestions.

Questions about life preparation
- Go to the place and time that was decisive for your present life.
- If you felt any compulsion at this moment: go to the last moment you felt free and you chose freely and consciously.
- What is this choice about? Why do you choose what you choose? What do you want?
- What experiences have led to this particular choice? You will get impressions of them now.
- If you have taken talents from previous lifetimes with you, you now get an impression of the main talent that you took with you and what your experiences did to develop it.
- If you took any handicaps with you from past lives, you now get an impression of the most important handicap and of the experiences that caused it.
- If certain themes in your life have come from previous lifetimes, you now

get an impression of the most important themes and the experience that started it.

- What is the first impression you had of your parents? Who do you notice first? What do you feel when you notice them?
- Go to your first contact with your new body. What do you feel about it? What do you think about it?
- Go to the prenatal experience (in the womb) that had the most impact.

Suggestions for standard themes
- Strength and weakness, power and powerlessness
- Belonging and loneliness
- Masculinity and femininity
- Sex
- Violence
- Childhood and adulthood
- The physical and the spiritual
- Self-assurance and self-doubt
- Disappointments
- Fears
- Satisfaction and dissatisfaction
- Growth of judgment
- Growth of perception
- Growth of creativity
- Inferiority and superiority
- Loss of talents.

FURTHER READING

The oldest type of research is that of testing regressions against historical facts. Bridey Murphy's case is the first (Bernstein 1956; Kline 1956). Jess Stearn (1968) tried to confirm the sessions of Joanne MacIver in Canada. His book appeared in the USA as *The Search for the Girl with the Blue Eyes* and in the UK as *The Second Life of Susan Ganier*. Guirdham investigated Cathar cases (1974, 1976). Regressions by Bloxham (Iverson 1976), Gerald Glaskin (1979), Peter Moss and Joe Keeton (1979) and a few by Glen Williston and Judith Johnstone (1983) were also researched.

David Graham (1976) collaborated with Brad Steiger, a well-known writer in this field. It consists mainly of interviews with people involved in regressions and reincarnation and has interesting examples and observations, among others about the way false dates may surface in an otherwise credible regression (1976: 164).

So far, only Helen Wambach has done statistical research on regressions (1978, 1979).

David Christie-Murray wrote a study guide about research into reincarnation (n.d.). Related to research is formulating theory and model-building. One of the few efforts in this direction has been the work of the Brazilian Hernani Andrade (1983).

Research into child cases is dominated by Ian Stevenson's work (1966–87). Other publications come from Gupta *et al.* (1936), Hernani Andrade (1973) and Francis Story (1975). Daniel Cohen (1975) slates Stevenson among others. No arguments, just vague insinuations. A class better is Ian Wilson (1981). Walker (1981) presents arguments pro and con. A fair book, though, strangely, it adds up metaphysics and empirical evidence on both sides of the balance.

In *Hypnotically-Facilitated Past-Life Reports: A comprehensive overview of research* (2000) Thelma Freedman presents an excellent overview of research into: historical confirmation of data from regressions, the therapeutic effect of past-life therapy, and psychological and physiological aspects of regressions to past lives.

Ten

EXPERIENCES BEFORE AND DURING BIRTH

The regression material published to date gives a rich picture of how people incarnate, how they experience the pregnancy and what consequences this may have. Theological and philosophical literature on the subject presents abstract convictions that often flagrantly contradict the available empirical material. Authors whose information about the discarnate state and the incarnation process concurs with the empirical material include, among others, Allan Kardec and Joan Grant. The most informative material is from past decades. Important authors in this field are Morris Netherton, Helen Wambach, Joel Whitton, Michael Gabriel and Michael Newton.

Albert de Rochas found in his experiments that, during regression to a previous life in a magnetic trance, his subjects felt their skin about two inches outside of their physical skin (*l'extériorisaton de la sensibilité*). When he brought them back to a period between lives and they were able to report about this, their 'vehicle of sensitivity' was located in a sphere above the head.

Helen Wambach has brought a total of 1,500 people under hypnotic regression. Of the first 1,100 about 90 percent had experiences of previous lives. Of the total group 48 percent had prenatal experiences in the discarnate state and as an unborn child. The other 52 percent had no impressions or fell asleep during the group regressions (Wambach 1979).

Netherton considers prenatal regressions about experiences in the womb as essential to therapy. Wambach looked at how people prepare a new incarnation, how they experience the bond with their new body and how they experience birth and the situation immediately following birth.

From the experiences of de Rochas and Wambach I conclude that the two memory banks differ.

PREPARING FOR REBIRTH

How do people experience their return to a new body and a new lifetime? As with so many other human experiences, the general answer is: very differently. Helen Wambach investigated three questions about the preparation for incarnation:

- Did people choose and prepare their new incarnation themselves or did they feel compelled or even forced?
- Why were people going to incarnate and, if they did choose for themselves, what was their main reason or aim?
- Had people chosen the gender in which they were born?

Some of her respondents experienced nothing during the preparation for their incarnation or they simply felt that they were sucked into a foetus. Some compared it to going down a slide or being sucked up by a vacuum cleaner. Dethlefsen and others report similar experiences. Other people prepare themselves elaborately, usually in cooperation with friends and counsellors. Some are resistant or afraid and have to be persuaded. Others again apparently do it all by themselves, some even in a hurry or against advice. The answers Wambach (1979) received:

  8 percent felt nothing
 11 percent were resistant and more or less afraid
 56 percent had at least some hesitation
 23 percent prepared themselves actively
  3 percent were too hurried to plan or went against advice.

This means that about 20 percent felt obliged to return and about 80 percent more or less accepted their rebirth. Some wait for the inevitable, others regard it as a matter of course, 'something everyone does'. Someone compared it to a completely organised trip recommended by a trustworthy travel agency. Some have to be persuaded; others are enthusiastic about 'descending' again. Others again act on personal initiative and may make extensive plans. Many people report deliberating with others, mainly friends and 'relatives' who are also about to return. Often, shared plans are made and future meetings and collaborations arranged. Of the people who reported counsel with others, more than 60 percent had more than one adviser; some even had a circle of advisers.

Although Wambach found that advice from others was the rule, McClain states 'Only in very rare, very extreme circumstances does it appear that any type of guidance or suggestion is made from outside sources' (McClain 1986a: 22). Probably, she registered only spontaneous remarks, while Wambach asked everybody explicitly. Considering the common practice down here to ask professional (or less than professional) advice in many matters, I guess Wambach is right.

One remigrant reports that before birth he stays around his parents. He has no sense of warmth or cold, but knows when it is day or night (Webb 1974: 126). Many that hang around witness regressions of afterdeath experiences and perceive the difference between day and night.

> *A woman remembers dying as a small Jewish boy in the war. Later she sees herself as the boy with his mother standing in a long queue of people before the beautiful gates of heaven. The men in the queue — orthodox Jews — wore hats. He thought it strange that they didn't take off their hats before entering heaven. He became tired of waiting and wandered into a lower sphere where a male 'angel' told him 'Now you have come down so far, you have to return to earth.' He didn't want to and kept asking for his mother, but the angel told him they would find another mother for him. He saw a ray of light, which he followed to a woman's womb. (Gershom 1992: 45)*

Of Wambach's respondents, the 60 percent that had prenatal memories under regression could give a reason for coming back. The other 40 percent often had not themselves chosen to return. Wambach (1979) categorised the reasons for rebirth as follows:

27 percent came to help others and to grow spiritually themselves
26 percent came to acquire new experiences as a supplement or correction
18 percent came to become more social
18 percent came to work out personal karmic relationships
12 percent came for miscellaneous reasons.

Examples of special aims in life were: learning to overcome fear, learning to assume leadership, learning humility and leading a political group. Some quotes:

- 'I had a lot of work left to do in the relationship with my mother.'

- 'Actually, I didn't have any urgent karma to work out.'

- 'I had to tie together and round off all the loose ends from the life just before.'

- 'I wanted to expose myself to a weak and indulgent life and to overcome this.'

- 'I went back to be able to feel things and to touch them.'

- 'I wanted to come back because I just had died young.'

- 'I knew that my parents needed me because they had lost a 18-month-old girl in a fire.'

We can apply for special assignments and request special missions. When people are needed for special developments and we are able and willing to contribute, we can apply for those to our counsellors. Karmic considerations have an influence, but are not decisive.

Our gender is important for our life plan. The course of our life still differs today depending on whether we are born as a man or a woman. Wambach found that 76 percent of people chose their gender. The other 24 percent had no choice or paid no attention. Next to the choice of gender, the choice of parents is important for the life we will lead. People who plan their life, also choose their parents. Those who experience their rebirth as something that happens to them do not know why and how they got their parents. But many choose. We may choose our future parents even a long time beforehand.

> A little boy tells his parents that he had already chosen them 'long ago, when I was still with God'. He was allowed to choose who would be his father. He looked around and finally saw a boy playing the violin during a concert. A string broke, but the boy played on as well as he could. Then he said to himself: 'That will be my father!'

The incident with the string had in fact occurred when his father was still in school (Muller 1970: 66). Usually we know our parents from previous lives. Sometimes we choose them for the opportunity they offer for the task we have taken upon ourselves, exceptionally because of appropriate genetic material (Wambach 1979: 164). One woman says that the karmic links with her mother were much more important than the probability of a genetic deficiency (Alzheimer's disease). She was told she would learn from being raised without a father and she would be in the ideal area for meeting the man she was destined to marry (Whitton & Fisher 1986: 42). Sometimes people do not like the prospect of parents with whom they have a karmic relationship. 'Oh no – not her again!' groaned somebody who was told that his personal evolution would be served by being reborn to a woman he had murdered in a previous life (Whitton & Fisher 1986: 42).

Some people change their minds at the last moment and then are born somewhere else or they err out of haste. Someone wanted so much to return to a body that he approached a very large family, though his friends and relatives advised him that a small family would suit him better. Another remigrant realised immediately after his birth: 'Wrong time, wrong place, wrong parents, wrong sex!'

Other literature confirms the impression that a coming life is not fixed in detail, but limits itself to general outlines, general developments, general challenges (Kardec 1857: 325–31). When people remember a *life preview*, a preview of the coming life, only the important moments, the great assignments stand out. We embroider and elaborate these by our efforts in life. Strongly immoral acts like murder are never predestined. At most it is predestined that we will grow up in such a manner, in such an environment, with such a personality, that very probably something like this will happen. But nobody is destined to murder.

Some people remember a strong desire to return because they had previously died young. According to a widespread belief, people who have died very young return quickly. In their following life they use up the remaining life energy, so that they die rather young again. The quick return is generally right; dying young is not a correct assumption. On the contrary, such people are often twice as energetic.

It also happens that we incarnate after a previous attempt has failed, for example, a few years before with the same parents, sometimes in a body of the other sex. Carol Bowman (2000) gives many convincing examples.

THE DESCENT AND PREGNANCY; BIRTHMARKS

When does the soul enter the foetus? Only 11 percent of Wambach's remigrants joined the foetus somewhere in the first six months of the pregnancy, a very few during the conception. About 12 percent connected themselves with the foetus at the end of the sixth month and 39 percent during the last three months. Finally, 33 percent descended shortly before birth and 5 percent avoided experiencing the birth and descended immediately afterwards. Probably they hardly influenced the development of the unborn child (Wambach 1979). So the probability that the foetus is inhabited increases rapidly after the end of the sixth month. After its entrance, the child is aware as an individual – its gender, its position, its body and its age.

Asked about their prenatal experiences, 11 percent of Wambach's remigrants felt themselves to be inside the foetus, 78 percent outside the foetus and 11 percent sometimes inside and sometimes outside. Those who descend early feel themselves often inside. Most, however, float around the mother, while connected to the foetus with an etheric cord, presumably the same as the 'silver cord' that is mentioned in out-of-body experiences and in dying (Crookall 1961, 1978). When birth approaches, the cord shortens. Some visit the foetus every now and then to inspect it and to adapt the unborn child to themselves. Some report that they sometimes left their body after birth. A few could even leave at will during their first year of life.

The Loehr–Daniels readings say that often other souls guard and stimulate the growing body, so-called *body sitters* (Quinn: 67). After birth, at least one stays around, because the soul of the child easily slips in and out till about the second year (Quinn: 68). My guess would be that this depends on the age of walking.

Of the remigrants, 86 percent said that they were aware of the moods, thoughts and emotions of their mother. The other 14 percent presumably all came to the foetus in the last moment. Unfortunately, Wambach presents the statistical material in her second book so poorly that we cannot correlate the answers between the different questions.

Joan Grant explains nausea during pregnancy as a warning from the child that the mother is living wrongly in some respect. However, as Wambach found that only 11 percent of the souls had entered the foetus before the end of the sixth month, nausea in the first months should be an exemption. Nausea seems to be a psychosomatic reaction of the mother, not a signal from the incarnating child.

An unborn child may be alive, but not animated, as long as no soul has descended and connected with it or entered it. A child that has just been born and is already breathing can be like a house ready for the occupant just before he moves in. Although this is an odd idea, other regressionists report similar cases (Hubbard 1950).

The most extreme case of being reborn hurriedly and unplanned is taking over a newborn. I have encountered this a few times in my practice. It seems not credible, but more cases are known, also outside regression therapy. Hubbard gives an example of a man who is assassinated. He is furious and will show his murderers that they cannot get rid of him just like that. He rushes to the nearest maternity ward 'to grab a body'. It is likely that he had to push out another soul by sheer force. This is probably only possible with newborns who have little strength of mind, little motivation to start a new life and little control over their body. An immediate return in a body already born and inhabited by another makes for an official birth date before the date of death of the previous life, creating a negative intermission period. The story of Hermann Grundei in chapter 5 is a case in point. Ian Stevenson encountered several cases (1987: 124):

> In a small number of cases, the subject was born before the person whose life he remembered died. (The intervals vary between a day or two and several years.) In a case of this kind, taken at face value, it would seem that the subject's body was fully made and presumably occupied by one personality before another one took it over. We may be talking here about a type of body theft, often called possession.
>
> The quickest way to rid oneself of such awkward cases is to suppose that errors have been made in recording the dates and in some cases vagueness about the exact dates supports this conclusion. I have satisfied myself, however, that in at least ten cases of this type we have obtained accurate dates and the anomaly remains.

When incarnation occurs in the body of a child of, say, three years, this usually happens after a grave illness and results in a marked personality change, as in the case of Jasbir (Stevenson 1966).

In even rarer cases, this may happen in adults. Cyril Scott (1953) gives the example of a man who is replaced by another after shell shock. According to the writer, such things are only possible as the result of negative forms of mediumship in previous lives. In her later books Ruth Montgomery has popularised the idea of *walk-ins*. She got the idea from an experience of Joanne Garland (1988) and has spun it out uncritically. I find her ideas implausible, even perverse, but this area is outside the scope of this book.

Like many other regression therapists, Morris Netherton (who, by the way, was annoyed when he heard Ruth Montgomery declare him to be a walk-in, without a shred of evidence) found that reliving traumatic experiences in this life is often insufficient to remove the origins of problems and complexes. Events in this life often restimulate the unresolved wounds and knots from previous lives. Netherton found that restimulation during pregnancy or birth always precedes restimulation during life.

Roger Woolger gives examples of how difficult or painful birth experiences can restimulate past-life traumas (1988: 264):

- *Choking on the mucus mirrors death by drowning, strangling, suffocation or sometimes live entombment.*
- *Hemorrhaging and blood transfusion evokes memories of bloody deaths or of bleeding to death.*
- *Caesarean section triggers violent death memories of being hacked or cut by swords or knives, child sacrifice, too. 'Please don't cut me' may be the mother's words which resonate in the infant's unconscious.*
- *Breech birth recalls painful deaths where limbs have been pulled or stretched, as in racking and other grim tortures.*
- *Prolonged labor inevitably mirrors traumatic deaths of being trapped or dying slowly, as in avalanches, fallen trees, bombings, etc.*

Chapter 6 has already mentioned that mother and child have a connection similar to the one between magnetiser and magnetised in the trance depth called 'sympathy', in which almost complete identification occurs. Morris Netherton and Michael Gabriel give many examples that show that the unborn child registers the experiences of the mother as its own. When a girl tells her boyfriend that she expects his baby and he yells, 'Get lost! I don't want to see you any more!', the unborn child may easily register this message as if it were meant for itself. If the soul of the child has unfinished business with being refused, sent away or cast out, this will be restimulated.

> An American girl under narcosis goes into a delirium and speaks Spanish, although she does not know that language. The mother, who is called in, is astonished to recognise sentences that her Mexican guide said to her when she was fleeing from a revolutionary situation in Mexico while pregnant with this girl. (Muller 1970: 135)

According to Netherton, the most sensitive moments are the conception, the discovery of pregnancy, the first communication about the pregnancy and the birth. A striking example of the registration of the unborn child and its 'sympathy' with the mother is the following case (Netherton & Shiffrin 1978: 84).

A woman with sexual problems sees during regression her mother, pregnant with her, being visited by her father. She reads him out loud a passage from a book by the Marquis de Sade that had struck her. Although the patient does not know the book, during regression she can cite the whole text verbatim. It becomes evident that this text influences her life as a postulate, because its contents restimulate traumas from previous lives.

I know the case of a remigrant who, when reliving her birth, started to giggle and to laugh. Her mother was watching a famous comedian when the first birth pains started. Michael Gabriel (1992) starts his book with a case of a girl who not only copies her mother's feelings, but sticks to them afterwards, while her mother has already released them.

Birthmarks or stigmata are examples of the influence of the entering soul on the fetus. People can be born with physical marks such as spots or scratches on the skin or even birth defects corresponding to fatal wounds from the preceding life. The Tlingits in Alaska used birthmarks to identify the preceding life of the child. With them, as with other groups, some people announce before they die with whom they want to be reborn and by what mark they can be recognised (Stevenson 1966: 225). Stigmata in the form of skin marks are usually memory aids for the returning soul, consciously made after the descent in the new body. Birth defects and birth scars have to do with traumatic death experiences that have not been digested, especially with people who return quickly, enter the unborn child quickly and have a self-image that continues from the preceding life (Stevenson 1966: 34; Fiore 1978: 175).

Wijeratne had a malformed right arm much shorter than the other, only half as thick and with only rudimentary fingers. When he started to talk, he explained this by his having stabbed his wife to death with this arm in his preceding life. He did not repent and when he was 15 he said that he would still do the same. (Muller 1970: 56)

Stigmata may indicate at what stage of foetal development the soul has entered the body. Skin marks can grow late in pregnancy and early after birth. Defective fingers and toes will have developed much earlier.

The Turkish doctor and professor Reẑat Bayer collected 150 cases of infants with birthmarks (Passian 1985). His material justifies the conclusion that skin spots usually indicate a violent death in the past life. I give three examples.

In 1970 Bayer heard about an 8-year-old boy, Achmed, who lived in a village in the south of Turkey and had nine birth marks: scars on the chest, arms and one on the neck. There was no medical explanation. Bayer wrote to all police precincts in the region if they knew about a murder in which the victim was shot nine times. The police in Adana wrote that 15 years earlier a man was murdered by nine shots and they sent a newspaper clipping from those days. In the market place, a man was shot nine times by a jealous rival. Professor Bayer got permission to dig up the body. An autopsy revealed that the shot wounds of the murdered Mustafa and the skin marks of young Achmed were on the same spots.

A newspaper reported the case of a young man whose right thumb carried the scar of the bite of a poisonous snake common in the frontier area near Syria, though he had never been bitten. Professor Bayer visited this Semir. His mother said that her son already had the scar at birth. This time, Bayer wrote to the hospitals in Antiochia. In a provincial hospital, a 40-year old baker called Kashambash had died from a snakebite on his right thumb. He was interested in snakes and kept some. One day a snake had escaped, hidden in the oven and bitten the baker, first in his right thumb and then in his left hand. Only the first bite of a snake is lethal, as it empties the poison glands. A few hours after his arrival in the hospital Kashambash died.

In Adana in 1951 a boy was born who was going to be called Malik. Three days before his birth, the mother dreamt that her baby wanted to be called Necip. She forgot the dream, but the next night a similar dream reminded her, so she told her husband. As there was already a Necip in the family, they called the child Necati. The boy was born with eight strange birthmarks on his body. When he started to talk, he insisted on being called Necip. He claimed he had lived as Necip Budak in Mersin (80 km away) and had had five children. He gave the names of his wife and kids and said he was knifed by a shoemaker. One day Necati's grandfather visited him. He lived in a village, 9 km from Mersin. Necati again talked about his preceding life, and after much crying and begging got his grandfather to take him with him. In Karavudar, the boy appeared to recognise things. His grandfather took him to Mersin. Necati had correctly described his former wife and children, minus one girl who was born after his death. He said to his widow: 'If you don't believe that I am your husband, then remember the day we had such a fight that I stabbed you in the leg.' Bayer's female assistant was allowed to inspect the leg and confirmed it had a scar.

The widow had remarried a few years before, which the boy deplored. He lived alternately in both families. Rezat Bayer visited both families for years, sometimes with

Ian Stevenson, and recorded their interviews. He even spoke with the murderer, who was released nine years earlier. The man remembered where he had stabbed his victim. Bayer checked this with the inquest report he obtained from the Mersin court. It listed eight wounds. The birthmarks of Necati were at the same places.

Birthmarks can also be aids to the memory for the returning soul, and even for others. The next case is a moving example (Passian 1985: 117–21).

In 1915 in Vienna, one Leonard Reisinger several times dreamt of the face of a blond girl and felt nostalgic. In his dream he lifted the hair from her neck and saw a small scar, slightly inflamed. He felt he had caused the scar. Then images came fast: fire, people in animal skins, painful goodbyes and war. In his dream he asked the girl to forgive him. She responded: 'Now you know how you can recognise me also in this life, even when you don't recognise my face any more. A year from now we shall meet.'

One year later, Reisinger was sauntering in the Neubaugasse in Vienna, when he stopped in front of an institute for typing and stenography. Though he disliked both, he got the strange urge to register as a student. He entered, paid the tuition and could start right away. The date on the receipt confused him: shouldn't he have an appointment today? But he couldn't remember. He entered the stenography class and was soon bored. Though he sat in front of the class, he took Zarathustra out of his briefcase and wanted to start reading. The teacher told him to go to the office to get a pencil and paper.

'When I closed the door of the classroom behind me, the door of the opposite classroom opened and the girl of my dreams appeared. I gave a start and she blushed. She walked towards me and shook my hand.

'"Let's get out of here," I said. "But I just registered," she laughed and took my book. When she saw the title, she showed me the book in her hand. Also Zarathustra! We couldn't utter another word and walked out, hand in hand.

'"I have dreamt about you", she said "and when I just saw you, I felt I knew you. But you wouldn't believe that, would you?"'

'I was shaken, couldn't control myself and blurted out: "Do you have a small scar on your neck, under your hair?" "Yes," she responded, surprised. We looked at each other with tears in our eyes.'

The definitive work on past lives and birthmarks is Ian Stevenson's book *Reincarnation and Biology* (1997), an astoundingly documented collection of researched birthmarks that correspond with mortal wounds of the preceding lifetime.

✻

We do not carry all our traumas with us into a new life. What enters this life depends largely on restimulation during pregnancy and birth. Choice of parents is involved too. How do we choose? In what state of mind do we return? We assume a personality when we are going to incarnate. In child cases and cases of birth defects, we come back with the personality of the preceding life and so enter the new body. When we have retained a strong sense of self or when we didn't digest our past life and death, our preceding life will put a strong stamp on the present one. When we also enter early, even our appearance may resemble that of our preceding life. But what about genes? They provide the material rather than the blueprint.

We may also choose a lifetime before our last life as the matrix for our coming life. We may resemble, not our last life, but an earlier life. Karl Muller gives examples. Joan Grant also says that it is not always the 'supra-physical body' of the immediately preceding life that enters and influences the unborn child.

Based on Crookall's conclusions about out-of-body and death experiences (1961, 1978), we may expect that the psychic (or astral) body does not immediately enter the foetus, but that there is a link of ether or vitality plasma between them. How this new 'vehicle of vitality' originates is as yet unclear. Probably, a core part remains connected to the soul, to which new plasma is attracted. The vehicle of vitality of the mother will then provide for an unborn child who is not yet adopted. There may be a temporary fusion or interface between the plasmatic body of the mother and that of the incarnating child. This may explain the 'sympathy' between them.

In all psychosomatic phenomena, in every link between the psychic body and the physical body, including birthmarks and stigmata from the preceding life, an etheric link is there. Each unresolved trauma from a previous life probably still has an etheric charge that is unloaded during catharsis. This explains why every catharsis produces somatics and why every sure-fire induction includes the use of a somatic.

According to Hubbard (1950), each trauma register contains physical pain or some other somatic. This explains why we cannot resolve karma after the dying processes are completed: we get rid of some ethers and the rest wait on us until we come down again. Restimulation opens these etheric registers.

In the beginning of pregnancy I don't know for sure, even if I contact the spirit of the fetus, if it will be a boy or a girl. A male soul may this time be born as a girl and the reverse. Also, the soul may be not yet in the fetus, but hang around to guide its growth. Sometimes the soul speaks to me. It tells who it was in a previous life and which karmic relationships have brought it to these parents. The causal and astral psyche and the causal and astral body decide the physical structure. First the soul chooses the parents, either for karmic reasons or out of free will. The parents fit karmically its character, disposition and skills. Then it decides which genes from the sperm and the egg it accepts, selects nutrients from the mother's body and builds its body. The growing fetus creates the disposition of its organs and their corresponding properties conform to its karma. (Motoyama 1992)

According to Joan Grant, a fertilised egg has to be adopted by an incarnating soul within a few days or it will be rejected and die (Kelsey & Grant 1967). Netherton claims that registration takes place from the moment of conception. Wambach's research (1979) shows that few people enter the foetus in the first six months. The experience of regression therapists is diverse. Some, like Netherton, find that many souls are involved from the conception on. The remigrants of Wambach were just interested in past lives; the remigrants of Netherton were seeking therapy for personal problems. Probably, the shorter the intermission and the earlier we enter, the more chance we have to take over phobias, complexes and psychosomatic problems from the past. People who enter the foetus earlier might have more chance of restimulations, and the younger the foetus, the deeper the repercussions of any imprint.

Bruce Goldberg concludes that the soul is connected to the foetus during the whole pregnancy, but is free to come and go. The definite descent ('the grand entrance') occurs within 24 hours before or after the birth (Goldberg 1982: 181). This differs from the experiences of Netherton and is true for only some of Wambach's respondents (1979). Because of the size of her sample, I prefer Wambach's data, but more and better data on this point would be desirable.

Goldberg found, like Netherton, that during pregnancy the soul apparently enters and leaves the unborn child at will. On the other hand, there seems to be an unconscious mind that is in the embryo right after the conception, registering everything that is happening to the embryo and the mother and often identifying with the mother. After the definite entrance, the two experience tracks seem to blend. This may explain a great part of the divergent findings so far.

Whitton speaks about soul memory and brain memory, the last functioning from about three months. Whitton reports the same findings as Wambach: first awareness of actually being in the body ranges from several months before birth to just after birth. He also finds remigrants who experience hovering over the mother. He reports that they may encourage behaviour that is good for mother and child and discourage drinking and smoking. In several cases they communicate what they want to be called (Whitton 1986: 50).

It seems to me that Schlotterbeck, after first stating that there are two memory tracks (1987: 85), then resolves this problem by identifying three memory tracks (1987: 139). Thus in the final analysis we have:

1 The psychic memory of the discarnate personality entering the body in the last months, during birth or just after birth.
2 The etheric memory, which is there right from the beginning, at first indistinguishable from the etheric body of the mother; and during the rest of the pregnancy the immediate link with the psyche of the mother and so the channel for identification with the mother.
3 The physical brain memory from about three months. (A developed nerve system seems a prerequisite for real incarnation: the psychic body entering the physical body.)

THE BIRTH

Prenatal experiences are less diverse than discarnate experiences. Individual birth experiences are even less so. We are very aware of our birth. We do feel, hear and see everything that happens and we also sense what the people present are saying, feeling and thinking. We feel the great gap between our own adult, telepathic awareness and our small, helpless body that is being welcomed – or not. The mother, the father, the doctor or midwife and the nurses usually have no idea of our awareness. This experience is sometimes funny, but usually painful, especially if we are treated roughly or wrongly.

Being born is often less painful and traumatic than is commonly believed. A fair number even regard it as a pleasant experience. A normal, uncomplicated birth is not traumatic or even troublesome to the child. Few retain, for example, a fear of constriction from this experience. Of course, there are many traumatic births: children who begin to breathe before they are well out of the womb and almost choke to death, breech deliveries, etc. Netherton and Fiore conclude that the experience of the birth process is decisive for stress resistance in the rest of life. A good birth leads to strong stress resistance, and a difficult or complicated birth makes us prone to stress (Netherton & Shiffrin 1978: 133; Fiore 1978:

14). The birth itself may restimulate traumas from past lives or reinforce traumas already restimulated in the prenatal phase.

A few circumstances are unpleasant for almost all newborn children. The most common complaint is that the light is too bright and hurts the eyes; the second complaint is that it is too cold. A third complaint, already mentioned, is being treated more like a thing than a human being. That babies have to cry when they are born because this is good for their breathing is nonsense. A remigrant describes her indignation and rage at being held upside down in the cold and receiving a slap on her bottom to boot, superfluous since she was already breathing, and also insulting. A child may cry because the birth was trying or the reception is disappointing or as a natural release of emotion as in extreme laughter, great joy or great exertion. Crying is also an expression of helplessness, evoking a natural desire in adults to receive the child in an attentive, friendly and helpful manner (Kardec 1857: 156). A fourth, frequent complaint has to do with the newborn's strong desire for physical and emotional contact with its mother. Many remigrants describe their disappointment when they found their mother to be 'away', in other words, unconscious, usually under anaesthetic. In this respect, local anaesthesia is better than loss of consciousness.

Birth can be traumatic for reasons unrelated to the birth process and treatment of the newborn. During regression a patient, who felt all the time that he had to change his name, related that the doctor at his birth kept mixing his mother's name up with the name of a nurse in the presence of the newborn child (Netherton & Shiffrin 1978: 173). This will only traumatise people with a weak or impaired sense of identity.

All birth regressions are one great plea for modern, natural birth care. There is one exception: in a few cases people describe the amniotic fluid (perhaps under the influence of the air?) burning and making their skin itch. They scream with misery because they are washed too late. Some authorities recommend not washing the newborn child, because it is natural to let the skin soak up this nutritious moisture. But if a child is crying, better to wash it right away. Furthermore, there should preferably be no spotlight once the head comes out, but the warmest possible room and, especially, a welcome as a full human being.

THE MOMENT OF BIRTH AND THE
NATAL CHART; KARMIC ASTROLOGY

People who believe in astrology will wonder how the life preparation and life plan relate to the natal chart. The first question is what the astrological moment of birth is. If the moment of birth influences our character and life plan, then this moment is probably no coincidence. But what is this exact moment? And do induced and Ceasarean births interfere with our fate? Or is everything so well-inspired and well-organised that we end up being born at the predestined moment anyway?

A German obstetrician, Dr Diehl, instructed assistants to measure the various moments of birth with a chronometer as exactly as possible in thousands of cases (Dean & Mather 1977: 467). First, they noted the moment the cervix had dilated sufficiently; second, the appearance of the head; third, the first breath; fourth, the first cry; and fifth, the cutting of the umbilical cord. Between the appearance of the head and cutting the cord the interval is sometimes 30 minutes, but usually less than 2 or 3 minutes. The last four moments in particular follow each other closely, sometimes within a minute. The first cry often occurs 5 seconds after the body has emerged. In a few hundred cases, the five moments were so far apart that the natal charts for the various times differed. Years later Diehl compared the development of the lives of the children with these natal charts to decide which chart fitted best. He concluded that in every case the chart of the moment of the first breath was the right one. Just as the first breath is the first moment of independent human existence, so in drawing a chart of a marriage, a business or a country, the moment of becoming independent is the astrologically relevant moment.

What happens with induced births? In this question, the experience in Denmark is interesting because it has long been the practice there to induce almost every birth. Research of the charts of thousands of Danish births has led to the conclusion that the chart of the first breath after an induced birth is just as valid as with natural births (Dean & Mather 1977: 171). If the right birth moment is important for someone, the people who are involved in inducing the birth may be influenced. But this might be true in only the minority of cases — and the influence may sometimes fail. Gauquelin, a French researcher, compared children's charts with those of their parents. The charts of children who had been born naturally resembled those of their parents more closely, especially in corner planets (of proven relevance), than those of children with stimulated births (Dean & Mather 1977: 392). Very likely this means that a stimulated or induced birth upsets the fate of the person to some extent. With induced births, people enter the world under an astrological constellation less appropriate than in the case of a natural birth. Induced births, therefore, seem not advisable. It depends whether an intervention is necessary because of risks attending the birth or whether the intervention is customary, as in Denmark, because of the working hours of doctors and nurses. Once again recent tendencies towards natural childbirth are supported, this time by astrological studies.

Dr Heinz Fiedelsberger has researched astrological twins: two people born at the same time in the same maternity ward from different mothers. He found few similarities and many differences in character and biography (*Meridian*, No. 3, 1984: 55) (Passian 1985: 72).

Karmic astrology has further-reaching claims: it assumes that the natal chart not only unlocks the present life, but also says something about past lives or karmic lessons. The number of karmic astrology books grows, their quality doesn't. As we see how differently people come back to a new life and how very differently karmic factors enter into the equation of the next life, the mechanical assumptions of karmic astrology seem a farce. Statistical analysis of correlations between natal charts and regression contents would be a welcome change. Sometimes we can investigate the relationship the other way round. When a recent past life has been identified and its birth registration found, we might compare natal charts from both lives. Florence McClain writes (1980: 48): 'As proficiency builds, some individuals will be able to remember such detailed information as exact birth date and time in some of the more recent lifetimes. Astrological birth charts of past lifetimes often provide interesting insight in the present lifetime.' That seems an overstatement. When the common natal chart already offers few insights (as empirical research has shown), that of a past life will surely not be enlightening for the present life. And why calculate and interpret when there is a more direct and infinitely more concrete way of finding out: regressions to life reviews and life plans?

The earliest book about karmic astrology I have found is the Chinese *Three Lives*, written around 1600 and translated and edited by Martin Palmer *et al.* (1987). It is poppycock from first to last. From the hour of birth it concludes what life we will have, what life we had before and what our next life will be like. If we were born in a year of the Cock (1 out of every 12 people) in our next life we will be a steward in a large, rich family. Even taking large to mean just 1 wife and 2 children, this claims that more than 8 percent of all people will be stewards to such families, so more than 33 percent of all people living will be in rich families. One out of every 12 will be a concubine in the next life or 1 out of every 6 women. One out of every 12 people will die on a snowy day, an amazing feat for people living in warm climates (Palmer *et al.* 1987: 105–9). The editors give an example of a reading. First line: 'You will lose your home and your fortune'; second line: 'You will be wealthy and never suffer financial trouble' (1987: 48). There is no explanation given for this glaring contradiction.

Since the works of theosophical writers on astrology, many astrologers have accepted karmic interpretations of natal charts. In 1943 Joan Hodgson published *Wisdom in the Stars*, later reprinted as *Reincarnation Through the Zodiac*. Her book gives general reflections about the karmic background of the twelve zodiacal signs, especially what karmic lessons should be learned from them. Her arguments are based on a notion of karma that is as mechanical as it is lofty, but fortunately leaves our free will intact. Her notions of the zodiacal signs suggest that she has not heard of the southern hemisphere, as she associates the signs with the seasons of the temperate climate in the northern hemisphere, a narrow-mindedness other astrologers are also guilty of (Dean & Mather 1997: 79). Sun sign astrology is, apart from the lucky stars business, the most meaningless and most disproven branch of astrology. Addey says of it: 'I have yet to see a single piece of statistical work (and there have been many now) . . . which gives the slightest indication that the twelve signs, in either zodiac, are valid unities in the sense they are normally thought of' (Dean & Mather 1977: 88). Dean and Mather quote research showing that the probability that the zodiac signs are relevant is about 1 in 1,020. Joan Hodgson will be of little help.

Martin Schulman sees the lunar nodes as astrological indicators of karma. Astrologers have diverse ideas about lunar nodes – as about almost everything. There are two methods for calculating lunar nodes, the so-called average and real lunar nodes. Schulman does not even say which method he uses. According to him, the southern lunar node registers the complete history of past lives and the northern lunar node points to the future, the prospective, the not-yet-tried. How an abstract geometric intersection point without any physical reality can register lives of people remains a mystery. Schulman refers to the southern node as the climax of 100,000 years of our work on ourselves. A page later he describes this same node as often the weakest point in every chart (Schulman 1976). Perhaps Schulman's own southern lunar node has something to do with logic.

In later books (1976, 1977, 1978) Schulman deals with the retrograde planets and the *pars fortunae*. The types of karmic missions related to particular positions remain general. In the cases I am familiar with, I find no relation at all between the contents from regressions and such positions. Such reflections on astrology are gnostic speculations about astrological factors based on abstract views about karma and reincarnation without any relation to actual reincarnation processes. Schulman is not too much help either.

Stephen Arroyo (1978) looks at all psychic phenomena from a karmic point of view. His astrological karma indicators are a lucky dip: squares and opposites; Virgo, Pisces and Scorpio; the fourth, the eighth and the twelfth house; the Moon, Saturn and Pluto; the aspects of Saturn, Uranus, Neptune and Pluto; and the transits. Why the Moon indicates karma, but its aspects do not, why Uranus and Neptune do not indicate karma, but their aspects do, belongs to the riddles of the universe. And nowhere do we find any relation with empirical understanding of karma and reincarnation.

The first regression therapist who talks about karmic astrology is Adrian Finkelstein. He asserts that subsequent lives always have the lunar nodes in the same sign. So in all of our lives we have the lunar nodes in the same signs. Later he says that it is the same sign when the previous life was not properly completed. So all of our lives are not properly completed. He gives no data to support his assumptions (Finkelstein 1985: 54). My research suggests that his notions on karmic astrology are copied from the only books on karmic astrology he refers to: Joan Hodgson's *Wisdom in the Stars* and Martin Schulman's first book. He reads out what he read up on.

Yott (1989) has written a book about karmic astrology full of lofty, abstract, mechanical associations.

Penny Thornton (1990) is an astrologer who also knows something about regressions. Her book seems written for astrologers who don't know yet about regression and reincarnation. Thornton asserted that crown Prince Charles would strengthen the British monarchy and that cold fusion would be demonstrated before 1994, as Pluto was in Scorpio till that time.

She is rightly critical about the speculations of Robert Powell, who discovered correspondences between horoscopes from succeeding lives: the aspect between the Sun and Saturn is equal (or opposite) as at the moment of the preceding death. Then follow much more complicated relationships with exceptions and alternatives, and finally he says that the rules he discovered cannot be used to find previous lives, as 'the mystery of reincarnation is inaccessible to intellectual speculation'. Ramblings under the title of *Hermetic Astrology*.

The *Astrological Reincarnation Time Scale* of Tadd Mann, also mentioned by Thornton, is even more astounding. Each zodiacal degree corresponds with a historical moment. By looking at the degrees in which your planets are at birth, you will know when you have lived. As humanity now lives in the 24th degree of Pisces (how? what?), everybody who ever returns will have a planet in this degree. In the future this will lead to wild planning problems in delivery rooms. Around 14 March, when the Sun is the 24th degree of Pisces, huge baby booms will occur: all strong men living now will return.

Thornton herself analyses the birth and death charts of a child case investigated by Stevenson. I know this case, as Hernani Andrade, the original Brazilian investigator of the case, gave me the Portuguese report. The case is very strong, so it makes an interesting example. Thornton's analysis feels familiar: when you take fourteen astrological factors in twelve times twelve positions (both zodiacal and mundane) and in all their mutual relationships (aspects), adding for good measure progressive positions and transits, you always find something.

Anyway, this case contradicts her idea that the Moon at birth is in the same sign as the Sun at the birth of the preceding life. Imagine having the Sun and the Moon in the same sign (1 in 12 people): you will return all your lifetimes in this sign. The charts of this case also refute the idea of Rudolf Steiner that the constellation at birth resembles the constellation at the preceding death.

Thornton herself describes her ideas on astrology and reincarnation: 'fluid rather than fixed and absolute.' Very sensible, but difficult to combine with a discipline based on exact calculations – and difficult to chime with writing books about it. This confirms that good astrologers are empathic, sensitive and wise, which is quite different from astrology being true.

The German Baldur Ebertin (1986) is much more interesting. He compares natal charts and the content of regressions. For people convinced of the value of karmic astrology, his book is one of the very few worth reading.

Matthijs Kamphoff (2000) is a Dutch astrologer and past-life therapist. He sees twelve patterns of evolution through lives, corresponding to the twelve signs. His book tells twelve stories of developments through lives, based on regressions. The stories from the regressions seem realistic and lifelike. The patterns he sees are illuminations that make us see more and see less at the same time. I would rather look with glasses that are not pre-coloured. From the natal chart, he takes the position of Saturn in the zodiacal sign as indicating the karmic assignment. This means that we would have Saturn in the same sign during a number of consecutive lives. Could be. But it would also mean that worldwide, in a period of about two or three years, all people born would have the same karmic mission. So if you miss out this time, you have to wait 30-odd years. Or change your karmic mission? Highly improbable.

Karmic astrology is a field so slippery that all writers I read lose their footing all the time. If open-minded research leaves little of natal astrology standing, how about karmic astrology? The best approach is to combine a technique like Wambach's — regression to the prenatal stage and asking questions about the aim in life and life plan — with aspects of the natal chart that have proven empirical relevance: the mundane positions of planets and aspects between planets. Planets at least do exist; signs and houses are geometrical fantasies.

THE NEWBORN; INFANCY

The personality of a newborn child is especially clear during the first hours after the birth. Sometimes it stays clear for weeks and months. Often, a baby face shows an adult personality. Maria Penkala gives an example (1972). The adult personality shimmering through at this time is always the personality of the past lifetime that is the dominant influence on this life. Joan Grant describes a mean old man she sees looking out of a little face in the child clinic (Kelsey & Grant 1967). This adult and telepathic consciousness usually decreases rapidly after the birth, at the latest at the end of the first year, when children start to walk. Somewhere in the third year, when vocabulary is rapidly extending, reflection appears and the self-aware personality of the new life emerges.

The souls of young children often manifest themselves through a medium more easily after birth than before the birth. Many people who are going to be born cannot make themselves known via mediums or more directly, because they need their energy to influence the growing body. After birth, less energy is needed and the soul can more easily manifest itself to others (Shirley 1924: 165). This may apply only to children who easily leave their body, but that is fairly usual in the first year.

Also, Helen Wambach found that some children still leave their body regularly in the course of the first year of life. A few retain this ability for a longer period. Eugenie, de Rochas' first subject, felt during regression that she was going to be born again. She felt attracted to a mother who had just become pregnant. She hovered above the mother until the moment the child was born. After that, her consciousness was slowly taken up into the child's body. According to her, she entered the body definitely and completely only at seven years (Shirley 1924: 140).

Anyway, the adult awareness of the newborn fades in infancy. We have to work our way back to self-awareness during our childhood. Some of us have an early sense of destiny, but most of us have to find our direction again amid insecurity and confusion. Why do we have to go through such a long period of awkwardness each lifetime? Childhood, ideally, is a relaxed period of careless play, a 'bath' of spontaneity and innocence – and a receptive period for education. Although we are often more open to education when discarnate, to incorporate the results when incarnate is difficult. When the parents are as wise as their children, childhood is a period of relaxation and carefree existence. If the parents are wiser than their children, childhood offers a particularly good opportunity to develop further. If parents are less wise than their children, childhood is a struggle to come out of an often dangerous swamp, sometimes for karmic reasons, sometimes to gain strength and sometimes as an inevitable consequence of the social and cultural level of society. Finally, restimulation of karmic problems during childhood is very probable. Not nice, but a condition for resolving them.

We have to accept that in every lifetime we start being dependent on the wisdom and goodwill of other people. If we refuse this, the only alternative is to become autistic. Or not coming back. Some people feel a great resistance to a new long childhood. Helen Wambach found this to be a cause of autism (Wambach 1978). Wrong reactions by others worsen the problem.

Some esoteric schools see the first 21 or 28 years (3 and 4 times 7 years respectively) as a continued incarnation process. These esoteric schools imagine that at birth the soul floats around the body and enters the body only slowly over the years. The findings of regression research in no way support this image. We may conclude from birth experiences that almost the opposite is true. The soul is powerfully present in the body and its self-image usually becomes only gradually entangled in it during the first year. The lowest point of incarnation is in the period between the loss of the adult identity early or late in the first year after birth and the reattainment of a new identity and self-awareness around the third year.

Some children retain an uninterrupted memory of their previous life, as discussed in chapter 5. They almost always remember the directly preceding life. Usually the memories of past lives fade when they go to school, sometimes in puberty, and only idiosyncrasies remain as silent witnesses of past lives. During adolescence, from about 15 onwards, many of us experience the unconscious urge to remember ourselves again. Much of the inner confusion and the ostensible romanticism of adolescence is based on the urge to rediscover ourselves. Some people get recall, usually before the age of 30, but for most people regression is necessary.

We may have direct contacts with our own discarnate friends from before in dreams, especially vivid ones, and in out-of-body experiences. Some of Wambach's remigrants reported that the consultants or guides whom they saw in their prenatal regression were people they had dreamt about.

Barring death through primitive medical conditions, death in the first three years is more often a matter of the parents' karma than that of the child. It may also be the child's own decision. One man recounts that he realised immediately after his birth that he had chosen the wrong parents and he knew things would go wrong, so he left. Presumably, something like this is rare.

TWINS

Ian Stevenson investigated cases of twins. When twins have memories of past lives, they always appear to have known each other then, at least in all cases where both previous lives could be identified:

> In 26 of the cases of twin pairs a previous personality was satisfactorily identified for both twins. Among the other twin pairs one or both of the twins' cases remained unsolved. Among the 26 solved cases, the previous personalities had had a familial, sometimes marital, relationship in nineteen cases and had been friends or acquaintances in the remaining seven cases; in no instance had the previous personalities been strangers. (Stevenson 1987: 187)

In the case of an identical twin the differences were remarkable:

> From their early childhood Indika and Kakshappa manifested markedly different behavior, which I shall describe below. When they became able to speak, Indika gradually narrated details of a previous life that he said he had lived in another town of Sri Lanka, located about 50 kilometers from where the twins were born. The life he recalled was that of an

innocent, studious schoolboy . . . At about the time Indika began to talk about the previous life he remembered, the twins' family asked Kakshappa whether he also remembered a previous life. He said that he had been an insurgent. The other members of the family thought that Kakshappa's claim to have been an insurgent was amusing and they ridiculed him, so that he stopped talking; they thus learned almost nothing more about the life he said he remembered. Before Kakshappa's family unintentionally suppressed him, he had not given enough details to permit verification of the previous life to which he had been referring. He had, however, mentioned the name of one town that figured in the life of the insurgent about whom he had tried to talk. This town was well known to have been a center where the insurgents had gathered and some of them had been killed there. It is also only a few kilometers from the town where Indika said that he had lived.

Indika was a gentle, bookish sort of boy. He had a definite dignity and expected respect from others that seemed more appropriate for the life he remembered than for the circumstances of his family, since the previous family in his case was more prosperous than his own. Kakshappa, on the other hand, could fairly be described as tough. His talk was likely to focus on guns and bombs, never on books; indeed, he resisted going to school (when he first went). He also showed a pervasive fear and he ran away and hid from strangers, behavior that reminded observers of the way the Sri Lanka insurgents of 1971 tried to conceal themselves from the police until they were ready to strike. It is possible that once Indika and Kakshappa had spoken about the two quite different previous lives they remembered, they became cast by their family in two roles to which they then tended to conform more and more. This might have led to some further polarization of their behaviors and of informants' reports about them. Although this may have happened to some extent, it seems reasonable to suppose that some of their disparate behavior expressed behavioral memories from the different previous lives that they remembered. In 1982, when Indika and Kakshappa were just ten years old, I met them again and learned that the differences in their personalities had become much less marked. For example, Kakshappa was enjoying school and doing almost as well there as Indika was. However, in a dispute Kakshappa was inclined to resort to violence, whereas Indika was not.

Finally, Stevenson talks about the even larger personality differences of Siamese twins (1987: 190):

Before leaving the subject of twins, I wish to mention the opportunity for further investigations along these lines provided by cases of conjoined (often called Siamese) twins. An early investigator of twins, Newman, observed that members of Siamese twin pairs tend to differ in personality even more than do the members of ordinary (separated) one-

egg twin pairs. Chang and Eng, the original Siamese twins, who lived in the middle of the nineteenth century, showed vivid differences in personality. Chang was inclined to be cross and irritable; Eng, good-natured. Chang drank alcohol, often excessively (especially in their later years), whereas Eng was a teetotaler. What one liked to eat, the other detested.

PREBIRTH ATTRACTION

People who consider themselves spiritual may be very self-conscious about having children. They want to do everything right. But how? Can we attract an entity consciously? Or do we attract a better entity by living a better life? People are attracted to each other because they know each other, because they have something to do with each other, because they have gone through common experiences or have created a bond between them, often a bond of sympathy, sometimes of antipathy. A temporary change in lifestyle will hardly change these bonds. So, noble attitudes during conception and pregnancy are pious deceit. The procreative act becomes especially odd when we feel we should have noble feelings during intercourse and limit animal lust.

If you want to have children, do not bend over backwards to attract as suitable entity, but trust the choice of parents to the children who come to you.

While you are pregnant you can often contact the entity that is going to be born to you. As mentioned, souls connect to the foetus in different stages of the pregnancy, but usually rather late. If you concentrate on a soul not yet there, you make the foetus an even stronger magnet, increasing the probability of an impersonal descent, rather than the arrival of someone with whom you have a personal relationship. People who pray incessantly to have a child have a greater risk of getting someone inappropriate: a wandering soul. But when we feel someone is with us, we can strengthen and elaborate this feeling – but not too much. When an earlier pregnancy has led to a miscarriage or a stillbirth, we can address that unknown child and tell it that is still welcome. Anyway, don't pull; invite.

Some therapists help mothers to communicate with the unborn child. Winafred Lucas dedicates a whole chapter to this (1993b, Vol. II: 257). Most examples are communications before a planned abortion. But there are also examples of asking the foetus to turn around and assume the proper birth position. Which then happens. A coming soul may also announce itself in dreams, as the following examples will illustrate:

In August 1905, in Rome, the wife of Florindo Battista was four months pregnant. When she was resting in bed, awake, suddenly her daughter Bianca, who had died three years before, appeared. With a happy face, she said: 'Mama, I am returning!' When her husband came home, she told him and proposed to call their next daughter Bianca too. Battista was convinced death was the end and thought her deluded, but didn't want to take away his wife's belief in Bianca's return. In February 1906, they had a daughter who was in every respect just like the former Bianca. The mother saw this as proof that she had given birth to the same daughter twice. The down-to-earth father remained sceptical, though the ever more obvious similarities made him start to doubt. Until the second Bianca was six years old.

At the time of the first Bianca, they had a Swiss housemaid who only spoke French. She used to sing a French lullaby that always made the little girl sleep. After the child's death, the Swiss maid had returned home and the lullaby, which would have aroused painful memories, was never heard in the house again. Nine years later, the parents heard that song as an echo in their room. When they entered the bedroom next door, they saw it was Bianca who was singing the long-forgotten lullaby. Her mother asked: 'What is that you're singing?' 'A French song.' 'And who taught you that?' 'Nobody, I just know it.' And she sang on.

In November 1943, a man is invited to a spiritist séance. In a darkened room a circle of people sit around a table. The medium, not in trance, recites the alphabet and, at certain letters, the table moves. The table moves towards the man. The medium asks who is there, and 'Rudi' is spelt. That was the name of his second child, a boy who died form abdominal diphtheria at the age of two years and three months. Then come the next sentences: 'Death was my fate. I will return on February 12 next year and would like to be called Hans. Mama doesn't need to be afraid. Everything will be normal during my birth.' His pregnant wife had not come to the séance. She had had serious complications during her first two deliveries. Her husband did not tell her about this, but on that day in February she gave birth to a son they called Hans. Afterwards, the mother came back to the séances and, not knowing about the earlier session, asked for contact with her deceased son Rudi. 'Rudi's spirit is no longer among us – we have to take care of him in Hans.' (Passian 1985)

The mother of a man who had died, dreamed that her son appeared to her and said: 'Help! I have got myself in a poor family. Come and rescue me.' She obtained sufficient information in the dream to trace the child, who later had memories of her son's life. In two other instances the presumed previous personality of an infant communicated in a dream (had by a member of the previous family) his dissatisfaction with the infant's situation. In one of these, the previous personality complained that the infant's father was drinking alcohol excessively; in the other, the previous personality alleged that the infant's

mother was feeding him at her convenience rather than when he needed feeding and this was
making the baby hungry. (Stevenson 1987: 100)

RECEIVING OR REJECTING
THE NEWBORN

The evidence from regressions has practical lessons for pregnancy and birth care. The mother's behaviour has consequences for (1) the development of the foetus, (2) sometimes for the choice of soul coming and (3) in any case for the prenatal experiences that will influence the personality of the child to be born. The foetus registers the experiences of the mother as its own during the pregnancy, especially in the beginning. These experiences may restimulate karmic problems, traumas and sensitivities of the entering soul. Beginning life as a crack baby would be a bad start on all three scores.

Most important of all is the birth itself. There are three kinds of people on this planet: those who got an entry ticket, those who didn't and those who don't know. One who has no ticket has to get it from somebody else or has to give it to himself or herself, often after a long struggle. So receive the newborn, protect it, empathise with it and, most of all, welcome it deeply. If you had hoped for a boy, don't pretend you are very glad it is a girl. Get over it and welcome the child – for God's sake.

What happens if a woman involuntarily gets pregnant because of a mistake or, even worse, as the result of rape? Does this affect the kind of entity attracted? If a woman has been raped and impregnated, then a house is under construction that may, like any other house, be interesting to those looking for a home. For a future dweller, the construction of the house is more important than the reason for construction. How the impregnation happened is less important than what happens later. If the mother projects her abhorrence, aversion and hate for the rapist onto the foetus (and who can blame her?), it becomes unpleasant to move into this house. Souls feeling strongly connected to the mother or her circumstances will move in, in spite of this. For the rest, attracted souls either have a karmic affinity with this kind of situation or are unaware and indiscriminate. However, the mother's reactions to an undesired pregnancy are decisive, not the manner of impregnation. Rape is brutal for the girl or woman, not for the incarnating soul.

The quality of the growing body depends on the genes of the rapist. Perhaps the risk of inferior genetic material is larger with rapists, but people may do bad things with good genes. Not everyone who lives in a poor and neglected house is a scoundrel and not everyone who lives in a beautiful, well-kept house is noble. The soul about to be born, often aided by 'incarnation brokers', will look at the body, the family and the circumstances he or she may be born into. Rape may also lead to sympathy for the mother and provide a stimulus to come.

What does all this information imply for abortion? Kardec's informants, who are, on the whole, sober and reasonable, reject abortion as criminal. Only when the choice is between the life of the mother and that of the child do they advise giving the life and health of the mother precedence over that of the child. A life already formed is more important than a life not yet formed. Let us look at it dispassionately.

A body is a house we are stuck with for the rest of our life. Abortion destroys this house while still under construction. Is this bad? Sure, but how bad? First of all, this depends on the moment of destruction. The closer a house is to completion, the more its demolition is unkind and destructive. Secondly, it depends on whether we have already made an offer on the house or worse – have paid the first mortgage instalments. To what extent are suitable and attractive alternatives available? How strongly had we looked forward to living in a house in this neighbourhood? How much of a hurry are we in? How strong-minded or how tender-minded are we? How understanding or how enraged or how smitten? To what extent have we been involved in designing and constructing the house? Finally, and this is the crux, are we inside when the house is being demolished? Then demolition turns into homicide.

People who have an abortion or want to have an abortion, usually do not know if the foetus is already inhabited and so do not know if, by aborting the foetus, they are really killing someone. So the question is whether the soul of the coming person is already connected, and more significantly, whether it has entered. According to Wambach, in about 10 percent of cases this occurs before the sixth month. Most abortions are long before that. Murder is committed in probably around 5 percent of cases. Shock is involved in probably more than 50 percent of cases, because the soul is already connected. So, the growing practice of therapists helping mothers to communicate with the unborn child is great. Maybe they can help to talk them into leaving before the axe falls. I refer again to Winafred Lucas's chapter (1993b, Vol. II: 257). One of the therapists in that chapter says that abortion is no murder, because only the body is destroyed, not the soul. Serial killers, mass murderers and bombing crews will be happy to hear this.

Finally, it is not uncommon for people to have psychological problems that started in the womb because of a previous abortion by the mother. And, understandably, regressions show that unsuccessful abortion attempts have repercussions on the later psychological well-being of the newborn.

FURTHER READING

Original work on the experience of the foetus has been done by Thomas Verney (1981).

Prenatal experiences are as yet sporadically covered in the regression literature, probably because their therapeutic value is insufficiently realised. The most important book on this subject is *Life Before Life* by Helen Wambach (1979). Morris Netherton's work (1978) is also significant. He and Schlotterbeck (1987) give examples. Stevenson (1987) contains interesting chapters on this subject. Michael Gabriel (1995) gives many good examples of memories from the womb and the birth, though his therapy is rather limited. In the Netherlands, Henri de Vidal de St Germain has published many examples of regressions between death and rebirth, including preparing life plans (1998).

Supplementary information can be found in Joan Grant's (Kelsey & Grant 1967) and Allan Kardec's work (1857). Muller (1970) and Passian (1985) give examples of prenatal experiences and announcements.

The literature on karmic astrology seems meaningless to me. Kamphoff (2000) and especially Ebertin (1986) are the only interesting writers I have found.

Eleven

THE DEATH EXPERIENCE AND BEYOND

The literature about life after death is so extensive and its vocabulary so diverse and imprecise, that this subject warrants a complete study of its own. So I will limit myself here to material from regressions and a few general works, especially the books by Robert Crookall (1961–78).

Past-life deaths figure prominently in regressions, but the best-known source of death experiences is those people who have been briefly in a state of apparent clinical death and had vivid experiences during this time. Next there are the deceased who report about their world through trance-mediums or psychics and finally there are the psychics, who have described their perception of the process of dying.

The various sources fit together surprisingly well. I approach them with an open mind, but critically. There is no reason to assume they are not true, unless there is a reason. Each account without inner inconsistencies may be true, but the strong similarities between the accounts of people with accidental experiences are particularly convincing. I will also quote some information that at least does not conflict with the general pattern. A few of the examples from regressions are taken from my own experience as a therapist.

WHAT HAPPENS WHEN YOU DIE? CROOKALL'S WORK

Robert Crookall (1961, 1978) provides the best insights into the process of dying. He summarises a substantial body of empirical material. He is overly repetitive, but he may be forgiven for this as he painstakingly collected and analysed spiritist literature, accounts of out-of-body experiences and psychic perceptions of dying people and came to a clear and consistent picture of the dying experiences and events.

When we have died, we still feel we are present in some kind of body. Crookall calls this the psychic body, roughly equal to the (vaguely and conflictingly defined) astral body of the occultists. The appearance of this psychic body follows the image we have of ourselves. Often, this is how we looked in our recent life, initially how we looked just before death, later usually how we looked at the age when we felt ourselves strongest and best. Our appearance can change, depending on how we feel and whom we meet. Our psychic body is 'ideo-plastic', or, more precisely, 'psycho-plastic'. It shapes itself in accordance with our ideas, or, more broadly, in accordance with how we experience ourselves. Our consciousness in the psychic body is similar to that of lucid dreams: dreams in which we know we are dreaming are able to influence the course of our dream and often have vivid and brilliant perception. Our consciousness in the psychic body has paranormal abilities such as telepathy and foresight. In the psychic body we move around by imagining, as concretely as we can, the person or the place we want to go to or by marshalling our feelings about them as concretely as we can. We may create our own surroundings, visit an existing environment in the psychic world or ideo-plastically decorate an existing environment.

The physical body, the vehicle of vitality and the psychic body occupy the same space in a living person. They permeate each other. Yet there is a distance between them in a fourth dimension – perhaps better called the first dimension. The best label for this dimension is 'throughth' (Scott 1953). Considering time as the fourth dimension, as, among others, Ouspensky does, in accordance with the physicists, is in my opinion misleading and fruitless.

The ordinary physical world may be our environment, but usually we need extra effort, and an extra vehicle in this case, as someone who wants to go to the bottom of the sea needs a diving suit with an air supply. This 'diving suit' Crookall calls the vehicle of vitality. It corresponds to the occultist's etheric body. The vehicle of vitality is an intermediary between our psychic and our physical body, not a vehicle of consciousness. We cannot be conscious in it. It has little structure of its own, but gets its structure largely from the physical body and partly from the psychic body.

At death our psychic body and this vehicle of vitality disengage from our physical body. During out-of-body experiences the psychic body can either leave without this vehicle or take a part of this vehicle with it, shrouded by it as by a thicker or thinner veil. This veil dulls the awareness and so gives dull rather than lucid dreams. Frequently we enter twilight states resembling common, chaotic dreams. In this twilight zone are many deceased people who have retained a part of their vehicle of vitality, either by a strong attachment to the physical world or by an addicted or obsessive lifestyle. The following paragraphs will discuss falling asleep, hanging about, wandering about, haunting and twilight existence, all results of dying processes in which the etheric body is insufficiently cast off.

When the greater part of the etheric body accompanies us during out-of-body experiences, the physical body remains cold and stiff, more or less cataleptic. This gives more chance of unpleasant and disturbing experiences in the twilight world. Many regions of this twilight world are populated by petty, narrow-minded, jealous spirits who like to scare the wits out of people who have left their bodies semi-consciously, for example by giving them nightmares. Some of them act as parasites when we let them.

The deceased often describe misty or watery surroundings, indicating that the vehicle of vitality is still present.

When we die of old age, our psychic body departs together with the vehicle of vitality and hovers briefly above the physical body. A cord of vitality plasma (the Indian term is *prana*) remains connected to the physical body, usually at the solar plexus, becomes thinner and then snaps. This is the moment of irrevocable death. Then the psychic body disengages from the etheric double floating above our corpse and gets up into an erect position. When the psychic body is freed from the etheric body, we become aware of our surroundings. Before this, we lose consciousness for a brief moment. If we are already out-of-body, but the cord is still unbroken, we can be simultaneously aware of ourselves inside and outside of the body. Sometimes we lack energy to pull the psychic body out of the etheric casing and we fall asleep. The heavier parts of the etheric body slowly evaporate and we wake up.

When we die in the flower of life, for example in an accident, our etheric body is so strongly attached to the physical that only a small part of the vehicle of vitality comes along. In such a case, we are immediately out of the body, fully conscious and, although few ethers have come along, see the material surroundings because of our unchanged mindset.

When only the psychic body leaves, we usually leave by the top of the head; if the vehicle of vitality also leaves, we usually leave at the solar plexus or from the whole body. The psychic body may already be out of the physical body and perhaps has even departed, while the vehicle of vitality still animates our material body. Then, the body is like a deserted machine still running. Dying can look unpleasant, for example, with lengthy rattling, but the soul may be gone already. According to some psychics this can happen years before death, for example with extreme senility, giving a grubby, rundown aura with hardly any colour left (Scott 1953: 101). The psychic body is then permanently outside or has already left.

When the silver cord is broken, the vehicle of vitality has left the physical body. After the psychic body has left it, the vehicle of vitality in turn decomposes, in a period that may vary from four hours to over sixty days. For many people this may be a period of restful sleep. When Florence McClain instructs remigrants to go to a point in time about six weeks after death, most people describe a feeling of just being or just feeling safe, secure and contented (1986a: 120).

Sometimes the moment someone dies other people are suddenly strongly reminded of him. Psychics sometimes see an apparition. This telepathic leave-taking usually happens with people who know they are going to die. This contact is known as the call. The clarity of the call depends on the strength of mind of the dying person and the strength of the relationship. When we die suddenly through heart failure, stroke or an accident, we only establish telepathic contact if we really think of someone, for example a child calling its mother in its last moments.

The next experience is the review, the life panorama. Apparently we have two reviews. The first is like a high-speed movie of our whole life or like a tableau in which we view all the images simultaneously. This experience is reminiscent of Mozart, who sometimes saw the complete piece before he began to compose. One subject of Whitton's gives this vivid description: 'It is like climbing right inside a movie of your life. Every moment from every year of your life is played back in complete sensory detail. Total, total recall. And it all happens in an instant' (Whitton & Fisher 1986: 39).

Next, we experience the departure from our body, giving a sense of either sinking or of rising, depending on how our consciousness is distributed in the moment of transition: in the physical body that stays or in the psychic body that goes. We have the sensation of going through a door or a tunnel or we feel we are rising out of ourselves. The moment the psychic body is free, we feel larger and freer. We get impressions of deceased relatives and friends or just of many people; we see our own body and feel the connection – the 'silver cord'. Sometimes we may see two bodies beneath: our physical body and just above it the etheric copy. We observe impartially the possible death cramps of the body below. Then the silver cord is broken, sometimes with the help of others. Often we fall asleep with a sense of great peace. After some days or some weeks, we wake up and continue on 'upwards'.

The second review is more about feelings. We feel both what we ourselves felt and what people we met felt. Probably we first have a global review and then elaborate part by part. Florence McClain suggests that we look back at our life after the first rest period of a number of weeks, apparently referring to this second review. After the second review the next step may be either holiday or school. Or both: an enlightening journey. As mentioned, when the deceased talk about a misty or watery environment, part of the vehicle of vitality is still around.

When we die violently, we lose consciousness only briefly and often do not realise that we have died. For example, a dead soldier recounts that he continued to fight for about fifteen minutes before he realised that his acts had no effect and a bullet could go right through him without hurting him. Often we only realise our death when recognising our own physical body. A soldier, who was suddenly killed in an attack and mentally kept on running for a while, compared it with discarding a warm overcoat while running. Another deceased soldier characterised dying as: 'The soul jumps out of the body like a schoolboy jumps out of the school door: suddenly and with great joy.'

Compared to natural death, we feel even more compassion for relatives left behind. We often desperately try to convey to them that although we are dead, we are okay. We sense the emotional reactions of our friends and relatives when they hear of our death, especially when we died suddenly. We feel burdened, when their grieving sinks into depression. Sometimes we try to make ourselves known through dreams or through poltergeist activities, or we queue up at the doors of mediums and psychics to pass on a message. Remarkably, many people who die young find it a pity to have to leave behind a good body. A healthy body is a valuable asset we do not have in every life. Its loss is saddening. If we had put our body at jeopardy or had killed ourselves, we may be severely admonished, right after death, for squandering such a good body.

People who were briefly clinically dead have fairly similar experiences. Often, while leaving the body, they hear an unpleasant ringing or buzzing while screeching through a tunnel at accelerating speed. Then they are suddenly out of it and they find themselves outside their physical body, floating around in a volatile body, often near the ceiling. The volatile (psychic) body is experienced in various ways, from sensing oneself as transparent and shapeless, via a round or egg- or pear-shaped presence, to a vague outline of a body with a head, hands and feet, to an outline of the body as it was at the time of death.

We often see or feel the presence of others, sometimes deceased relatives or friends, sometimes someone we recognise as an invisible guide during our lifetime. Then there is a light that becomes stronger and grows into a being emanating love and warmth. Some may see an angel in it; some see it as Jesus, others again as the Maitreya, the future Buddha. This being asks if we are prepared to die. What do we have to show for life? What gave us satisfaction? Was it worth it? At the same time the life review appears, not backwards, like some esotericists claim, but starting with birth or the first memory. This quick life review is more or less continuous and sometimes already full of feeling. Sometimes we perceive situations through the eyes of others. The images are clear, life-like and three-dimensional. The light-being emphasises themes of love and knowledge in his questions about and comments on these reviews. 'Was it worth it? What did you learn from it?' Presumably, we can work out the lessons from this life review later on, when we feel like it or when it is suggested or we are encouraged to do so.

We experience a border or barrier, a definite separation, pictured as a stream, a road, a fence, a river, a mist or just a line. As we approach this border, we feel joyful, loving and peaceful. However, the border is never crossed, at least not by those who came back and gave these accounts. This near-death experience is between an out-of-body experience and a death experience.

PAST-LIFE MEMORIES OF DYING

Many children who remember their past lives, remember how they died. What do they all have in common? The incompleteness of their past life: unfinished business.

One group of these deceased persons who died naturally did so suddenly, that is, within twenty-four hours of being apparently well or not expected to die in the near future. Another group of the deceased persons figuring in these cases who died natural deaths were those who died young, by which I mean under the age of twelve. Still another group were those of persons having what I call 'unfinished business'. The best examples are mothers who died leaving infants or young children needing care. Also in this group are some persons who had debts to pay (or to collect) when they died. In another group of cases we can characterize the previous personalities as engaged in 'continuing business'. Typical examples of this group were prosperous businessmen intently absorbed in their businesses and in the accumulation and spending of the wealth associated with these.

If we now consider these five groups of persons who died either suddenly (whether violently or naturally), in childhood, with unfinished business or with continuing business, we can see that all their lives ended in a state of incompleteness. At the time of death they might all, for different reasons, have felt entitled to a longer life than the one they had had and this in turn might have generated a craving for rebirth, perhaps leading to a quicker reincarnation than that among persons who died replete with life, so to speak and at its natural end. (Stevenson 1987: 212)

In regressions to past lives it is often important to let the remigrant look back on his life and identify its main themes. Questions about dying and afterwards should never be suggestive. The best questions are ones like: 'What are you experiencing now? What is happening now? How do you feel?'

Remigrants seldom mention an extensive life panorama, as the clinically dead do (Moody 1975). But we can always ask them to look back at their life and get an overview. People can review their whole life remarkably well in such regressions. We may ask them what they think of their past life looking back on it. What made the strongest impression, what was the most important, what were its purposes? Usually, answers are direct and global; apparently the dominant themes from this life surface. Such life aims are very divergent. One remigrant says that the main purpose of his life was to learn to laugh, because he had been too serious in lives before. Another remigrant had been enormously rich during his life, but died as poor as a church mouse. He simply stated he had to learn that wealth and poverty do not determine humanity.

A clerk in an old-fashioned business office, fused with his desk for over 35 years, refuses a promotion because he prefers to stick to his current work. In the review of his life he sees his lifeline in front of him as a thin, glowing thread snapping at some point and become dark grey. When the therapist asks him which situation caused this, the remigrant immediately sees the refusal of a promotion. He renounced a chance to develop and so renounced himself.

The normal pattern of looking back at our previous life in perspective has many exceptions. The most common alternative is when we realise we are outside our body and stay there. Or we don't see our body and hang about it half consciously. When such a remigrant is questioned about his past life, he usually repeats the strongest feelings and opinions of his last years. If the therapist asks about the meaning of this life, he may receive an answer like: 'Nothing. It did not matter at all. [Pause] I had had this feeling, by the way, for a long time that nothing mattered at all.' Then the remigrant may be regressed to the age just before having this feeling, to proceed to the specific event that imprinted this feeling

> In about 95 percent of my sample the dying personality floats above the body and eventually on up, way beyond the earth to some realm of peace. A few subjects see brief visions of light. Of the remaining 5 percent, about half report being reabsorbed peacefully back into the earth and the remainder fall into strange vortices or dark places. Compared to hellish states on earth, classical afterdeath images of hell have been rare in my practice, but they do occur.
>
> Roughly 80 percent quickly find themselves back in another life. They either report being immediately inside a womb or in the body of a young child. Often a particular last thought will catapult them directly into an adult drama in this or another life, bypassing childhood altogether. One woman dying with the thought, 'I was too selfish. I need to care about others' went directly from dying as a fat old Semitic patriarch to finding herself as a nun in a leper colony. I could cite hundreds of examples.
>
> Of the few who are not thus thrust back on earth, some see spontaneously (as opposed to being directed by me) non-embodied or spirit figures in the realm above or beyond the earth. These will frequently be departed companions or family from the life just remembered, often a spouse or lover or beloved child or parent who died earlier. Encounter with an enemy or enemies who have been killed does sometimes happen spontaneously, but more often adversaries will be encountered in the next life. Many meet teachers or gurus from the life just lived or from an earlier one. Some return to the same teacher over several lifetimes. (Woolger 1987: 294)

A common experience is to meet after death some robed figure in white who radiates love and wisdom. Several of these figures may come in a kind of 'karmic committee'. This group helps review and advise the departed personality about the lessons of the life lived (Woolger 1987: 294–6).

Like all human experiences, dying experiences are diverse. Figure 4 distinguishes

Figure 4 Overview of types of death experiences

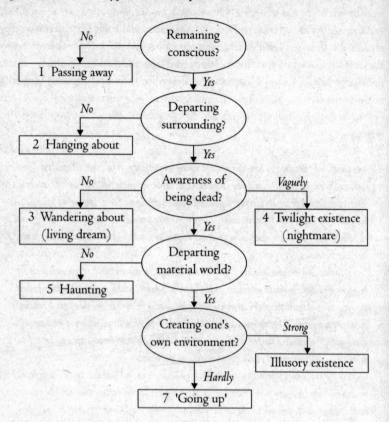

seven different afterdeath states, differing in degree of awareness and degree of disengagement from earth life. I will characterise and illustrate these seven states with examples from regressions, largely from my experience as a therapist.

The first form of dying is *passing away*. We remember nothing, feel nothing, are not aware of our surroundings; at most we experience 'just being around'. This state becomes apparent from the remigrant's simple remark that he cannot see anything. Every question is answered negatively, except when he is asked whether he has the feeling that he exists. This response can be confused with someone who did experience his death, but cannot relive it on account of some block. In this case, the remigrant becomes irritated because he cannot see anything or because the therapist's questions bother him. In passing away the remigrant keeps saying in a calm and relaxed way that he experiences nothing.

Eugenie, the first subject of de Rochas, sensed during her regression that she was no longer on a material level, but was floating around in semi-darkness without thoughts or desires and apparently in a subjective state (Shirley 1924: 140). This is the first description of passing away during a regression.

The next type of dying experience is *hanging about* the place we died. We perceive the ordinary physical surroundings vaguely. We may feel attached to places or even objects or may feel ourselves floating in the air. Some identify with an animal that comes near. Usually, we have little sense of self. When the hypnotist prods, only a vague, misty presence emerges.

> *A remigrant relives a life as a servant girl who is sent into the woods because she is considered useless. After solitary wanderings, she finds a deserted charcoal burner's hut and lives a terribly monotonous and miserable life there for a few decades. When she dies, she is glad to be out of it, but otherwise little happens to her. During the day she feels herself hovering above the forest and when the night falls, she sinks down among the branches. When light comes again and it gets warm, she rises a bit again. Apparently, she keeps up this pattern for quite a number of years, until she incarnates again after an undefined period of sleep. Further inquiry shows that she lacked any self-image while she was floating around. Asked about her self-image while she was alive, it appeared that in all those years she never looked at herself and never thought of herself. After all, she knew she was ugly and useless. So why bother to picture herself?*

Other therapists also report this experience of rising during the day and sinking at night (Langedijk 1980: 116).

> *In a regression, someone relives how, after a long schooling in a Maya-like community, priests lead a selected group of 12-year-old boys up a mountain via a long stairway. The boys feel tense because they have heard rumours that sometimes boys do not return from this ritual. They have to sit in a circle in a cave and sing ritual songs. One by one, they are called away and then they hear terrible hollow screams. However, they are not supposed to show fear or disturb the ritual. Their reactions are observed closely. When it is the remigrant's turn, he is brought into the adjacent space. The high priest is sitting on a huge throne, unrecognisable because of a large mask representing a god. Two priests grab the boy*

and hold him by his feet over a dark pit. The high priest gives the sign whether they should drop him or not. The boys who have proved themselves good pupils, by being both harsh and obedient, are spared. The bothersome, untrustworthy types are dropped. (This is one of those rituals that originally were only a test of will power and of faith in the priests, but degenerated into power politics and terror.) The remigrant feels himself suspended above the pit in mortal fear (and it has taken the therapist much trouble to get him here) and is dropped. He falls through what seems an unfathomable darkness and smacks down on the bottom, probably on top of a few others, breaking his bones in various places. The other boys are dead, except for one or two who moan terribly – or is he himself moaning? He remains alive for a few days in a pitch-black world of unbearable pain and mental derangement. After he dies, he remains surrounded by blackness. After a seemingly endless time – about 700 years – he arrives at the surface and is struck by the blinding, beautiful lushness of the outside world.

A Roman dies during the eruption of a volcano. He murders someone in a dining hall, runs out and is killed by a toppling pillar. He sees the sluggish flow of lava cover his dead body. He regards the volcano eruption and the tumbling pillar as punishment for his misdeed and remains bound at the spot. After 1,426 years [scientologists are keen on exact dating] thieves come, looking for treasures. The corpse has been turned to stone and they throw the pieces in a pit. After 100 more years, grass and flowers grow on this spot, and, still later, a little pond has formed. A bird comes, reawakening his perception of living nature. His apathy begins to disappear and the spot starts to bore him. However, he continues to stick around for a while, because he feels terribly guilty and thinks nobody will ever want him. (Hubbard 1958)

A woman relives a male life somewhere around Lake Aral, just outside Alexander the Great's empire. He is a solitary hunter who stayed behind alone after the other members of his tribe departed, succumbing to the promise of civilisation. His most important experiences are walking in the deserted plain checking his traps and at night looking at the overwhelming starry sky. After his death, he hangs around in the same area without any contact with humans, more or less sleeping during the day and during the night looking at the starry sky passing by. This gives him a feeling of majesty, but it is impersonal and sterile. This death experience is so strongly etched that after each following incarnation the soul keeps hanging about, without contact with other people.

The literature (for example, Hubbard 1958) gives instances of people who are stuck on top of a gate or in a ritual object after their death. In further regression it turns out that these people have been tortured to death and had strong post-hypnotic suggestions implanted in their confused and dulled minds, binding their souls to such objects or buildings. Apparently, this is done to make the place more impressive or ominous or as a sign of warning. The pack of priests performing these hideous acts may be long dead and gone and the whole cult extinct, while the soul remains bound until the object crashes, the gate caves in or the walls tumble down

The next type of death experience is *wandering about*, which happens when we do not realise that we have died. We leave the corpse quickly and ignore it and shut off all further evidence of our real state. We visit places and people from our past life and dream that we keep on living. It is an innocent and fairly common form of psychopathology, especially in young children who have died in an accident, for example, and who wander around until they find people by whom they feel accepted.

> *A little girl is playing on a construction site, up to some mischief. The owner of the construction site, one of two partners, who is having difficulties because business is going badly, has a particular grudge against the girl. He chases her away. The next time, he stalks her and gives her a firm push. She hits her head against a machine and is killed outright. He is shocked and drags the child away to a little mud bank close by, where he buries her and covers the grave with turf. The girl is missed, but the body is never found.*
>
> *The remigrant who is reliving this recounts that a man drags her to a mud bank and leaves her there. She feels strangely lethargic and dulled and does not know what to do. She does not realise she is dead. This only becomes clear later on in the regression. Why doesn't anybody come to pick her up? She feels more and more lonely and sad. She cannot answer the question why she does not get up and try to go home. After all, she is not hurt and can move freely. But she feels oddly dull. She just keeps repeating that they do not come and pick her up. She stays there for the rest of the day and the night until people appear on the construction site on Monday morning. Weakly, she tries to attract their attention, but to no avail. She gets weaker and sadder. Why has everybody left her? Since nobody cares about her any more, she wanders around the edges of fields and woods witlessly and at some point finds a farm. Inconspicuously, she moves into the farm family and dreams she is a part of it. This condition continues for many years, until her mother dies and starts looking for her daughter. The daughter has not aged in the meantime and looks exactly as she did at the time of her death, only a bit duller. In the regression she describes the joy of the reunion. Her mother takes her with her to what looks like home. Only later does her mother tell her that they are both dead.*

A girl of almost 3, the youngest child in a barge family, falls overboard into the strong current without her parents noticing. She is only missed an hour later. She herself has no idea what is happening. She floats through the water and lands in a city park where some boys are playing. One of these, who later turns out to be psychic, attracts her because of his open aura, and she moves in with him. Forty years later she is still a 3-year-old girl who hugs her doll tightly and sucks her thumb. Only when others see her, does she let go of the now older man. She feels coddled and falls asleep.

Neither girl refused to realise she was dead; they were simply not able to understand it. This is probably also the result of the parent's apparent inability to direct concrete thoughts to the children and to attract them. Such children are reversed orphans.

A man dies of pneumonia. He leaves a wife and three children behind. He hangs around at home and tries to comfort his wife. His children grow up and have children of their own. His wife gets old and senile. Only then does he have the feeling he can do no more there. Immediately afterwards he has the sensation of coming into a room with a pregnant woman and feels that he is slowly becoming attached to her. (Langedijk 1980: 116)

Hanging about can turn into wandering about:

Katsoguro, a Japanese boy, remembered he used to be called Tozo and had died of smallpox. He was put inside a large earthen pot and buried in a pit at the foot of a mountain. He heard the sound of earth falling on the pot. An old man accompanied him back to his house, flying through the air. After that, he was vaguely 'turning about in the air as if he had wings'. He did not see his environment; it was neither day nor night. He had no clear sense of time. He only heard the vague voices of his living relatives, especially when they prayed for him in front of the family altar. When his mother made a sugar-rice offering to him, he was able to breathe in the hot steam and felt content. Then he floated through the air and came to a village, to the doorstep of a house. An irresistible sensation made him slip in through an open window. He remained sitting next to the fire for three days and suddenly felt the warmth of the fire change into the lovely warmth of a person. It was the 'honorable blood' of his mother. For the rest, he knew nothing. (Muller 1970: 41; Penkala 1972: 59)

Interestingly, the ritual his family members performed did attach him to the place. Perhaps such a ritual binds, and possibly nourishes, the deceased who hang about. The old man accompanying him seems to indicate that staying close to the parental home is beneficial for people like him.

Another category of wandering is people who refuse to realise they have died. This happens with people who are sure that death means the end of everything or who died intensely dissatisfied, because they cannot accept they have to stop whatever they were doing. Initially, they stay in the body, perhaps they are at their funeral or cremation and then they shake the experience off, regard it as a strange dream and merrily get cracking again. They go and sit in their study again, continue writing their book, take part in business meetings. Their experiences are an odd mixture of the physical environment they perceive, interwoven with the fantasies they produce themselves. For example, they will sit invisibly in a real meeting and imagine that every now and then someone speaks to them, that everybody listens to them and that they have an important say in the running of things. This condition is pathological, but disturbs no one and is usually rather innocent for the deceased himself. His environment may gradually turn into dreamed-up surroundings without any relation to the physical environment and physical events. Then this condition develops into a kind of twilight existence.

> *A Thai monk remembered that after dying he had attended his funeral. He had a sense of lightness and moved easily about. He thought that he was in charge of the ceremony and was receiving the guests; though the participants went on with the ceremony with no suspicion of his presence. (Stevenson 1987: 110)*

Many examples of *twilight existence* can be found in the literature about spiritism and out-of-body experiences. People end up in a limited, dusky world with capricious and sometimes nightmarish elements. They may wonder if this is the real world and only vaguely realise that they have died. They just keep on dreaming, half-aware of themselves and of the surroundings. The others they meet in this condition are sometimes subjective projections and sometimes people living in the same half-conscious state. Usually they are too weak to procure lighter surroundings, so they remain in this dusky, half-isolated and half-populated domain: the twilight zone. This condition can be compared to a long, fairly structured dream. Joan Grant gives unpleasant examples (1937). The 'vital world' Lenz describes clearly corresponds to the twilight zone: dark, dirty, ugly and dangerous, 'like a polluted, run-down city' (Lenz 1979: 106). The other worlds Lenz describes are also recognisable, but seem rather too patterned by religious concepts.

We may also be well aware that we are dead but still want to stay in the physical world. This is the condition of *haunting*. We try to communicate with incarnated people, to manifest ourselves to them and to have experiences that are as earthly as possible. This can result in spiritual contacts, poltergeists and other mediumistic phenomena, and sometimes in taking advantage of the mediumistic accessibility of people who are sleeping, drugged, ill or otherwise. An important subcategory of this death state is described more usually in the esoteric literature: people who are so attached to pleasures and addictions that they haunt and stimulate people who still enjoy these pleasures physically. Typical examples are drunks, gluttons, the oversexed and people playing the devil: brutes and sadists. These experiences are uncommon in regressions. Presumably, such people have no interest in regressions or will block reliving such experiences. Only rigid methods, like Hubbard's, which force people to confront their experiences and feel responsible for them, elicit such stories.

> *A remigrant describes herself as a discarnate who apparently tries to repeat her past pleasures by bringing a married couple to more and more intense perversities. The woman gets pregnant, but she keeps on inciting the couple, so that the foetus is hurt. She wants to kill the child. She enters the body herself, lives for 14 years and then dies while riding a horse wildly. Even after this her fury has not yet spent itself. (Hubbard 1958)*

Occasionally subjects claim to have engaged in poltergeist activity while discarnate. One said he had broken the plank of a swing on which people were playing and another said he had thrown a stone at the man who later became his father (Stevenson 1987: 110).

People who are fairly self-aware and are able to disengage themselves well but have strong, dogmatic views about life after death can get what they had expected. They enter a *dream existence* or pseudo-existence, a state more like a lucid dream than a common dream. Our condition after death can contain many dream-like elements. What we experience depends much more on what we want to see and can see than on our life here. The perception of the environment and of ourselves depends predominantly on what we make of it. The mixture of objective and subjective in this 'psychoplastic' environment is an essential aspect of our discarnate condition. As after death our mind largely shapes our environment, autism and solipsism are the ultimate dangers. 'Some spirits get thought-bound like birds get egg-bound' (Scott 1953: 105). Devout, narrow-minded spirits and fanatics arrive at their own little heaven in this way, at best with a few fellow believers. Once in a while our feelings of guilt, remorse and fear lead us into the real thing: a traditional pitch-and-sulphur Christian hell. Wambach gives a lighter example of a dream existence (1978: 149–50):

> After his death in a prehistoric South American incarnation, someone experiences himself flying in the sky above the jungle. He lived in a culture where it was believed that the soul became a bird after death. Two others reported a death in old Peru, where the spiritual sun was worshipped as a god. Both experienced standing in a golden spray of light after their death.
>
> One girl told of her stay in such a place after death. Clothes were rich and elegant and needed no washing. One could have food, which appeared when one wished for it, but there was no need to eat. She met a 'kindly ruler', who eventually advised her to get herself reborn, but did not tell her where. (Stevenson 1987: 110)

If we have any overview at all in this state, we see a bright world above the twilight world. This world has various gradations of reality and human understanding. We may see the next stages, but not the return. Many deceased do not believe in reincarnation. Cyril Scott (1953) has a discussion about this with his deceased grandfather.

Complete awakening is a calm and liberating experience. We are glad to leave our body, and perhaps glance back at it, but our heart goes out to the people we know who went before us. With a profound feeling of recognition, homecoming and happiness we join them in a shining, often park-like environment and depart from this physical world.

> A remigrant experiences herself as the wife of a magistrate in a provincial town at the beginning of the French Revolution. An excited crowd drags them out of their home, kills her husband and takes her two children, a boy and a girl, to be put to work as serfs. She herself is put out on the street without anything. She has lost her senses, is incapable of doing anything and wanders on the road. In the next years she is a tramp, drinks heavily and is abused until she is too worn out and ugly even for that. Her only human moments are when she thinks of her husband and children and feels pangs of pain in her heart. Later, she is dying by the side of the road. A man kicks her to see if she is still alive, but she no longer cares. Then, all of a sudden, she feels incredibly relieved and is out. She sees the

shining figure of her husband and they embrace each other long and speechlessly, feeling consolation and healing. All her present life, without realising it, she has worked at a successful synthesis of being a grande dame and a simple, hard-working woman. In this life, she has suffered from heart fibrillations.

Crookall's work provides the framework to interpret the differences between death experiences. With complete awakening, the psychic body leaves the etheric shell almost immediately. With passing away, the psychic body is presumably too weak or too underdeveloped to disengage itself from the stronger vehicle of vitality. Self-suggestion can amplify this: we know we are dead and therefore no longer experience anything. All death experiences where we remain more or less attached to a place or to the earth, as in hanging about, wandering about, and haunting, indicate that the vehicle of vitality has not been cast off, or only partially so. The same is true for the deceased who end up in twilight existence. If people wander around and do not realise they have died, the etheric body may nevertheless be largely disintegrated. Only a minimal 'diving suit' is left to maintain contact with the material world. In conscious awakening, the psychic body is liberated; in passing away, it remains immersed in the vehicle of vitality; and in all dream-like situations, the psychic body perceives its surroundings through the filters of the vehicle of vitality.

THE ROLE OF INTERMISSION IN THE REINCARNATION CYCLE

The different post-mortem and prenatal experiences are related to each other. People who awaken completely make real contact with other deceased. Experiences discussed in the preceding chapter, such as deliberating with others and receiving advice from others, presuppose complete awakening. People who are still dreaming, experience birth as involuntary: they feel sucked in, pulled in or blown. Those who have simply passed away and slept do not recall any prenatal existence. People who haunted may be aware of entering a body. Those who wandered will first have to become aware of their condition or they will get more and more sleepy and find themselves, vaguely surprised, inside a new child. Often, wandering souls instinctively look for a living body, because of their sense of loss.

*

What do these different types of death experiences imply for the reincarnation process? The main function of complete awakening is that the past life can be evaluated and the coming life can be prepared, by conferring with others and receiving counselling, guidance and sometimes support. According to Whitton (1986), people are helped to evaluate their past life and receive recommendations for their next life by a judgment board, usually of three, sometimes of four members and up to seven judges. When we are aware of ourselves between lives, we continue to live and to love and to learn.

Edgar Cayce gives the example of a couple that reincarnated as husband and wife again and again (Cerminara 1950). The man was dominating and the woman servile and submissive. In her most recent intermission, the woman finally developed her independence, so she was able to break out of this vicious circle.

Discarnate learning is based on incarnate experiences and leads to motives and plans for the coming incarnation. On the other hand, passing away is a natural consequence of a self-awareness still too weak to maintain itself out of a body. Many people can only experience themselves because they feel themselves, see themselves in the mirror, hear themselves speak and are approached by others. We realise we exist because we bump into things, are hurt, get tired, are kissed or receive a tax assessment. All of this is gone when we die. A positive function of passing away lies in the swig of forgetfulness, being able to start afresh.

The conditions in between passing away and awakening are more complex and often pathological. The main consequence of hanging about is that nothing is digested, nothing is prepared and the next life takes place fairly close to the location of the last death. The dream life or wandering, can digest the past life to some extent, but provides no preparation and leads to a fairly large chance of being born in a family related to friends or relatives of the past life. The same is true for the condition I disrespectfully call haunting, but which can be peaceful and comfortable. In this case, choice of parents is conscious.

Twilight existence and pseudo-existence are usually psychodramatic conditions in which our psychic peculiarities determine our environment. So these states are solipsistic (all that we experience is ours; we don't experience anything outside ourselves) and, for outsiders, autistic. Pseudo-existence is largely compensation. People experience what they want to experience, as a gratification. The good side of it is that it helps healing. Someone who was cold feels wonderfully warm. Someone who was destitute is surrounded by comfort and luxury. Someone who was imprisoned roams about freely in beautiful, natural scenery and in interesting, exotic cities. Someone who was sickly and weak feels heroically strong and healthy. The other side of it is avoidance of further development and challenge. A vacation is fine, but after too long a vacation it can become very difficult to return to work.

Sometimes the twilight existence can be remedial, either spontaneously or planned. Joan Grant provides a few striking examples (Grant 1938).

When someone has tortured others in several lives and after his death is still impervious to the misery he has caused, a forced rehabilitation is called for. Experience is the best teacher. To experience torture, or to see those dearest to you being tortured, makes it more difficult afterwards to remain indifferent to the suffering of others, to forget to see them as fellow humans. Does this mean that each torturer has to be tortured in his next life? This would cause an endless cycle. Therefore, an alternative is to shut someone in the illusion that he is being tortured during a twilight existence, until the lesson is learned. With stubborn, callous people, this can take a pretty long time: years, decades or longer. This long duration is because experiences without a body make a shallower and less lasting impression than physical experiences. They work with fine sandpaper and smooth with a fine plane. Such situations remind me of the story by Roald Dahl (one of his few true stories) about the man who found the famous Mildenhall treasure. He does not want to notify the authorities about the enormous treasure, buys a carton of bottles of silver polish and gets to work on the accumulated oxidation of sixteen centuries. After more than sixteen weeks of polishing one plate, the first glimmer of silver appears. For two years, he spends every evening polishing, but he gets there.

A man, probably a Nazi, performs vivisection on babies and infants, sometimes while their mothers are forced to look on. After his death he finds himself in a grey, volcanic landscape as a screaming, crying child who is dehydrated and starving, thrown onto a hard, uneven stone table and with his own screaming ringing in his ears. He sees a monstrous man with razor-sharp claws bend over him and grin at him sadistically. He feels flames leaking out of the face and feels the deep cuts of the dagger-like claws slice him to pieces and tear him apart. When he loses consciousness, he finds himself in the arms of his mother again, screaming with thirst and hunger, but is torn away and the scene begins anew. Apparently, this surgeon was doing 'research' on the consequences of hunger and dehydration on the tissues of small children.

Later, this situation changes. Now, he experiences himself as the mother. The same scene takes place but in a hot, dry cave without an exit. The mother feels spent, physically and psychically wasted, and has desperately to watch her child being taken away and torn open. Again and again. These two situations together last more than fifteen years, interrupted by periods of unconsciousness.

Then he sees himself once again as a man. A spread of heather with a narrow path leads through dark woods. The sky is sombre and oppressive, and a low, sallow light gives a surreal shine to the scene. A poorly dressed woman walks on the path with a shawl covering her head. Frightened and whimpering, she walks bent over, pressing her young child against her breast. He himself walks behind her, naked and empty-handed. The frightening oppression becomes more and more intense, until a roaring monster attacks the woman and the child. The only thing he can do is to attempt to defend the woman by throwing himself in between the mother and the monster. His attempt is in vain and he is torn apart in terrible pain. He realises his helplessness and powerlessness, and finally until he loses consciousness. Again he feels himself behind the woman and the frightening oppression increases once more. This is repeated over and over again. Then, after an eternity, as an incomprehensible grace, somebody behind him, whom he cannot see, puts a simple cape around his shoulders and gives him a white wooden staff. He has the vague impression that, as time goes on, the staff will harden and his clothes will become more protective and, after another eternity, he will reach the end of this road with the woman and the child.

The duration of the nightmares is not because of punishment, but results from the relation between the hardness and thickness of the cape on his etheric body and the polishing effect of the (purely psychic) experience. Luckily, twilight existence is seldom as extreme as this, but then the preceding deeds are seldom as extreme. I have taken this example precisely because it is so extreme and the rehabilitating mechanism is so explicit. At the end of his road, the man will have the feeling that he puts his arm around the woman. Then, it seems he becomes one with her, then one with the child and then he will find himself safe and warm in a new womb.

What happens to the victims of torture? Pain, along with intense feelings of despair, hate or guilt (for example, if we have betrayed somebody) and a disturbed mind, can make it difficult for us to come to ourselves after death. However, when we die with a clear mind, we are immediately detached from the fate of the body left behind. Hubbard gives an example (1958):

A remigrant experiences being captured along with a group of others suspected of heresy and witchcraft. The prisoners' guard terrorises them with his fearful appearance and behaviour. She, however, does not feel the least bit of fear or awe, mainly because she has heard from a reliable source that underneath all his showing off he is impotent. In the presence of the other prisoners, she laughs at him and mocks his impotence. Beside himself with fury, he drags her to a separate cell and visits her there at night. While she scorns him again, he throws her down, with her head against the floor and chops off her arms and legs with an axe, a horrible, but still fruitless substitute for an erection. The remigrant says that standing next to her body she still laughed at this stupid man.

On the other hand, sometimes we get stuck in a normal, peaceful death. It turns out that a claustrophobic patient had been buried in her past life, but had stuck so thoroughly to her body (although she was liberated from it) that she had the feeling she was buried alive. This can also happen with cremations. Edith Fiore found a cremation experience to be the cause of the complaints of a patient who often felt hot and nervous. Another patient, with a dislike of roses, sees and smells her own body and that of others decomposing in a concentration camp, producing a sweet, rose-like scent (Fiore 1978: 230).

What does this mean for the old question: burial or cremation? For people who wake up completely what happens to their body is unimportant. With a burial, some leftovers from the vehicle of vitality hover above the grave for some time and slowly disintegrate. With a cremation the connection between the etheric and the material is burned, and perhaps a remnant of the etheric shell will roam about more freely. Decomposing polyps still attached to something or floating about hardly matter. However, when we identify with our corpse and project ourselves within it, we will have a nasty experience. Fortunately, this is rare.

When we died traumatically we may be brought into a healing pseudo-existence. A therapist can do the same during a regression. In such a renovation a gradual shift to complete awakening is possible. People who are imprisoned or who have imprisoned themselves in a nightmare or a negative dream, live in the illusory world of their own consciousness. A true healing environment is at most half illusory, because the growing presence of other people and increasing contact with them are essential for recovery. Many of the other dream conditions – twilight existence, hanging about or wandering about – are forms of 'consciousness degradation', a waste of time and energy. The motley collection of spirits hanging around physical people, objects or situations, either stupefied or shuffling around dejectedly, are a despicable and depressing sight.

A strong conviction may not only influence the afterdeath condition, but also the next birth. Stevenson (1987: 176): 'Premortem beliefs, held tenaciously enough, may influence postmortem events, including the circumstances of the next incarnation. Such beliefs may resemble posthypnotic suggestions and be implemented with the same compulsion.' Apparently, such experiences have led to the *Tibetan Book of the Dead*, though it has gone over the top by building a system and by scaring people, the two universal sins of priesthoods.

According to Netherton, a part of the fear of death comes from associations with previous traumatic death experiences: 'It triggers replay.' However, many death experiences are so peaceful and liberating (dying is often more pleasant than being born) that Netherton's explanation can be only partially valid. Many patients have had traumatic death experiences. One of Netherton's patients always hung around the place of his death until the body had decomposed (Netherton & Shiffrin 1978: 59). I have also come across such repetitions.

An easy or difficult death may be related to an easy or difficult birth. After all, how we are born is an important indicator for our stress resistance in life. As dying can be stressful, a difficult and painful birth may increase the chance of a difficult and painful death.

FURTHER READING

The most important author on this subject is the already frequently mentioned Robert Crookall (1961, 1965, 1966, 1967, 1978). Much has been published in the past years about the temporarily clinically dead. Of the books I am familiar with, I prefer Raymond Moody (1975, 1977). Spiritualist testimonies on the subject are virtually unlimited. Fairly broad information can be found in Tenhaeff (1936). Other books were mentioned in the references for chapter 4.

Death experiences during regressions can be found scattered in the regression literature. Joan Grant gives many examples of pathological conditions of the deceased and the therapeutic interventions of the living (Grant 1937; Kelsey & Grant 1967). She also gives a nice example of a dream existence in which the person involved only becomes aware of his true condition after a long time (Grant 1947).

Twelve

THE DISTANT PAST, THE FUTURE, PRE-HUMAN AND NON-HUMAN EXPERIENCES

Regressions are most interesting historically when they detail events and living conditions in important times of which we know little. As Wambach's research shows (1978), the further remigrants go back, the more primitive the circumstances, but there are exceptions. A few of her subjects went back to lives in South America in about 1500 BC, describing a fairly advanced civilization.

There are many examples of regressions to lives in a higher civilisation, much longer ago, associated with Atlantis. Edgar Cayce, too, mentions Atlantis frequently, often as the first environment in a series of lives. His statements are collected in *Edgar Cayce on Atlantis* (Cayce 1968). Even more interesting are remigrants describing lives on other planets or events in space.

Other strange experiences are people who describe being an animal or a plant. Or even 'lives' as a stone or an object. In scientology, regressions as a robot occur. Then there are quasi-human experiences as a discarnate humanoid, for example as deva or nature spirit. Finally, some have impressions of the future. Apparently, not only regression but also progression is possible.

This chapter contains the most incredible and so least plausible kinds of past-life memories. To the extent that they are real, they betray the dynamics of our evolution. To the extent they are not real, they may betray the dynamics behind them and support other explanations than reincarnation. Though I accept many of these exceptional experiences, I am sure many of them are not what they appear to be.

When we lead remigrants ever further back, where do they arrive? Fitting evolutionary ideas, we might expect even primitive humans and before that possibly ape and animal lives. Theosophists would expect a spiritual existence before the first incarnation as a human being. Others think we come from

Atlantis and before that from other planets. The regression material shows all these lines of evolution or involution and even more, in a dazzling variety. We seem to have travelled down many different roads from many different starting points.

EVOLUTIONARY PATTERNS OF SOULS

In regressions, we may come across experiences related to problems of our first life on earth as a human being. Past-life therapists talk about the primal trauma. We may even enter experiences before that first human life on earth. The transition we experienced founds our attitude to being human, to nature, to society, to having a body, to who we are, what bothers us and what we really want. Those primal experiences are very diverse. There is a moment that we first had a human self-consciousness. There is a moment we first had a human body. Those moments may be wide apart. There is also the beginning of individual existence, often still earlier.

Apparently, there are different kinds of souls with different worries, different sensitivities, different self-images, different attitudes to life – and different primal traumas. Past-life therapists should beware of lumping people and their problems together. They have to be open to unexpected, strange experiences and be able to recognise, understand them and deal adequately with them. I will discuss the different types of souls that seem to emerge in regressions, to the extent that these differences are relevant for self-understanding and for healing.

When we incarnate for the first time on this planet as a human being, we may know some aspects of human life already, while other aspects may be new to us, may even be repugnant to us. What is the core challenge for souls who became human? To have self-consciousness? To be in a physical body? To be tied to one spot at a time? To have to speak and listen and be exposed to misunderstandings? To experience walking as slow and tiring and cumbersome? Or to experience gender differences and sex? What is new is not necessarily traumatic. It may produce rather a hangover: exhausting, limiting or disappointing. Or it could be weird, but stimulating.

In Table 6, I present an overview, a more or less systematised list, and then explain and illustrate each 'family' at a time. I distinguish four families. For each

Table 6 Soul families

Family 1. Originally self-conscious, in a physical body: *extraterrestrials*

1.1 Human extraterrestrials who arrived freely: to contribute (maybe entangled since), for their own development or with aggressive intentions

1.2 Human extraterrestrials who arrived compulsorily: exiled, lost or wrecked

1.3 Non-human extraterrestrials (aliens): visiting or lost.

Family 2. Originally self-conscious, without a physical body: *spirits*

2.1 Living on this planet: *nature spirits*
   - living in and below the ground (dwarf-like)
   - living on the ground (brownish, sometimes housebound spirits)
   - common nature spirits (above ground and water, elf-like)
   - air spirits (high in the air)
   - site spirits (from below the ground to high in the air).

2.2 Living on non-physical 'planets' elsewhere

2.3 Living in a non-physical cosmos
   - gradually waking up among many, in a shining primal 'soup' (hatched)
   - part of shining planes and structures (*light people*)
   - individually created (modelled).

Family 3. Originally not self-conscious, in a physical body: *mammals*

3.1 Through general evolution (wild animals)

3.2 Through attachment to individual people (tame animals)

3.3 Through being killed, slaughtered or eaten by people

Family 4. Originally not self-conscious, without a physical body: *starters*

---

family, I will point out key challenges and typical problems. I distinguish these families according to their state before the first human life on this planet. Before that first life, we may have been either self-conscious or not and either in a physical body or not.

FAMILY 1. *Originally self-conscious in a physical body: extraterrestrials*

The first family consists of people who find themselves back in a physical human body on another planet, in a spacecraft or in a science-fiction civilisation, but not here. They were people elsewhere, normal people with a head and arms and legs. Sometimes they sense themselves in stranger bodies: heavier, lighter, bigger or smaller, or with other proportions. Probably all are related to us; we could mate with them. They resemble us; perhaps they lack ears or teeth, perhaps they have fewer toes, perhaps their proportions are different, but they have a similar body structure. With all these differences, they are clearly human. Today, they are often brilliant, scientifically minded people who also are cultural and have liberal arts interests. Or they are interested in science and technology on the one hand and on the other hand in hypnosis, altered states of consciousness and paranormal things, without feeling any contradiction.

Charles Fourier, who lived between 1770 and 1840, believed that we would reincarnate here till the end of the development on this planet and then all of us would go together to a new, higher planet. The informants of Allan Kardec say that people may descend from other, higher planets to help lower planets in their evolution or because they had trouble keeping up with the development. We can also change to other, higher planets, once we have learned whatever we can learn here. The picture from regressions is very diverse.

> In a session somebody found herself in a dinosaur. She was in it only temporarily; she could not sustain her presence there. Then she saw people in silver suits who left a bunker. She was one of them. Apparently, she experimented with how it felt to be in a dinosaur. She did not live and evolve as a dinosaur. She tried to enter, but she already had a human consciousness.

Some people came from elsewhere out of their own free will. Others were wrecked, entangled or exiled for punishment or forced education. Yet others came freely to this planet. They arrived here in a spacecraft. After they had died here, they were reborn here. Sometimes they first went back and died on their home planet before being reborn here. Souls from elsewhere rarely seem to be directly born here.

Some feel they have come to a primitive planet that needed help and education. They have come on a mission and have become entangled here. They were wise and could do much and stood so far above normal people that they gained positions of power and influence. But power on a primitive planet brings its own problems. We may be very wise, but fools are dangerous bedfellows. What from the outside may look easy, often appears more difficult once we are inside. Today, those souls often feel revulsion towards this Earth. They see ordinary people as dumb or dirty or cold or limited or unreliable, etc. They carry no primal trauma, but rather a primal postulate. This planet is primitive (they knew that before) and treacherous (they found that out later).

Others have come here by accident. In a regression they may see an exploding or crashing spacecraft. They are shipwrecked or stranded. Still others are exiled here or have fled here.

Sometimes people find themselves before the first earthly incarnation in a body of a completely different build, remotely lobster-like or grasshopper-like. These I call aliens, though that word carries weird associations. These people have no trouble with being in a body, but they have trouble being in a differently organised body. They feel their body to be wrong; they feel like strangers in their body. They are far from home, very far. They feel alienated. For them, we are aliens.

Probably, whole groups of souls have come here from elsewhere. This may have been demotion or a chance to rehabilitate themselves. Few planets will be much more primitive than ours, though they may be less complex. A world that is more primitive than the lower ends of the spectrum here, could hardly survive, would exterminate itself. My guess is that we have an incredibly mixed planet, with very diverse souls of very diverse levels. The Earth seems a free-for-all planet.

The primal problem of most extraterrestrials is that they got stuck here. What was their first feeling? Have they arrived on a dirty planet, a dangerous planet, a staggeringly beautiful planet, a primitive planet or a heavy planet? With people who come from elsewhere, their first story is surprisingly often not true. Even the third or the fourth version may not be completely true. Often they feel superior, stuck among inferior people. Dealing with such primal postulates is heavy stuff.

The therapist has to seek the emotion that is coupled with remaining on the Earth. That primal emotion can be impotent rage. Despair can be attached, as well as confusion and incomprehension. Maybe, after a dark, forgotten period, the first thing they notice is that they are walking around here on Earth.

Often they seem to remember a civilisation that most call Atlantis. The feeling of being grounded in a primitive society can be a result of having experienced Atlantis, or rather the time just preceding it. Atlantis seems to have been the first extensive civilisation on earth. Before that, space colonies or outposts may have been here. Some regressions suggest that the first efforts to populate this planet more extensively were tried in the time of the dinosaurs, but failed. The traumas from that deep past seem to haunt some of us still. Most probably, there has been a Lemurian age, in which the civilised and the barbaric were strangely mixed. Even the spiritual then could be very physical and very violent. The scientific and technological explosion of the last two centuries has been connected to the return of Atlantean groups. That might well be true, though many regressions to that time are doubtful, distorted by popular occult lore.

Ancient lifetimes before Lemuria or in early Lemuria, 'when the world was still young', were neither primitive nor civilised. They are remembered as we may remember our childhood. Regressions to this time become simple, but almost enchanted and less and less detailed, until we seem absorbed by the landscape we lived in. – as if we hardly can remember our infancy as a soul. Large, hairy bodies, moving gracefully and trancelike, like dancers in a silent world. Observant, but wordless. Lifetimes from this era feel wide and large, passionate and childish.

FAMILY 2. *Originally self-conscious, without a physical body: spirits*

A second family of souls consists of people who experience themselves before their first incarnation without a physical body, but with an individual, thinking consciousness. They feel themselves, they think about themselves, they are themselves; they know others and they communicate. Their primal trauma is not getting stuck in an island-consciousness, but getting stuck in an island-body, in a well-defined animal organism.

They feel like prisoners in their body. They dissociate easily. When experiencing great problems or under great pressure, they tend to leave their body. If there is a primal problem, their primal hangover is to be imprisoned in a human, material body. They perhaps still haven't accepted the need to eat, to defecate and urinate. These activities seem strange and dirty. Their body has other uneasy, animal properties, such as sex.

Nature spirits perceive the natural environment, orient themselves in it and perhaps influence it, but they are not material. Many avoid people, abhoring them; some seek people, finding us interesting. They live anywhere from in the ground to high above the world. The higher they live, the larger they are; the less circumscribed they are, the more space they assume; the calmer they are, the more individual they are – and the more often we encounter them in past-life therapy.

In and below the ground they live very busily in whole groups. They give the impression of being about 12 to 16 inches high. They are interested in us only when we do something in the ground. Their transition to becoming people seems rare – if it ever happens at all.

On the ground live humanoids that are somewhat bigger, about 20 to 30 inches high. Often these humanoids live in groups, sometimes with a few others and sometimes alone. They are not very intelligent, but most are curious. In human terms they are weakly gifted. If they have an interest in us, they imitate us. They can even become house spirits, and sometimes they appear in sessions as personal attachments, but rarely with adults.

I once I encountered a truck spirit, one who joined truck drivers, travelling through half of Europe, because it couldn't find its way back to its land, having once left Ireland with a truck.

These spirits don't know exactly if they have a gender. If they imitate people, however, they also want gender and they project protuberances to the area of the sexual parts. In imitating clothes they succeed better. They often have a love--hate relationship with people. If they avoid people, they don't become born as humans, and for us they are of little further interest. Yet they can sometimes attach themselves to a human and later become human. If they ever become human, it is often out of admiration or personal attachment. They are souls who have inferiority feelings. Their primal postulate is that they are less.

The third species floats above living water, over plants and shrubs, lives in trees or flies over the treetops. We may call them elf-like. These nature spirits are also humanoid, but thinner, transparent and more drifting. They have arms and legs, but these are vague.

They love living water, small animals, simple things like grass and flowers and insects and birds, and they dally deliciously among them. Wind and clouds are important to them, just as are rain and sunshine. Almost all of these souls find it heavy to be in a human body. If they ever attach to people, we get the problem of Andersen's mermaid.

Still higher, we come among and above the clouds. Here live souls that feel themselves high and clear and imperturbable. They see over the world and are all mind. If we ask if they are alone, they realise that there are others, but these others are distant. These beings feel connection only to high-flying birds such as eagles.

Remigrants sent by Pieter Barten to their earliest lifetimes found themselves to be large, hairy ape-men walking on all fours (TenDam 1982b).

When a human soul descends into them, they walk upright for a while. When they tire, the soul rises from the body and has a glorious view of a beautiful landscape. It knows it comes from some higher place. It still has contact with that origin, but cannot return, 'like there is plexiglas in between'. When it has recharged itself, it returns to the body of the primate, who walks upright for a while again. In a next reincarnation, maybe thousands of years later, the human soul still has to leave to recharge. This time, when the soul is out of the body, it gets no higher than the tree-tops, while the ape-man sleeps near a tree or in a cave until the recharged soul returns. The connection between the human soul and the animal body has already become more intimate.

Air spirits complain about their heavy body in their first life and mainly about walking. It takes too long to get from A to B. They often have problems with bones and muscles, particularly legs and feet. In regression, bird's-eye view is easy for them. They can easily watch events from above. They become people who tend to look rather than talk, who are intelligent, but don't like books and are not very social. Once I encountered one who was very good at making maps and atlases – panoramic, spatially and structurally good.

Site spirits are nature spirits who are wide and spacious and associate themselves with a part of the landscape, a valley or a rock. They extend from deep in the earth to high in the sky. They experience everything that happens in their surroundings. They are slow and deep. There is tremendous power in these souls, but our fast modern life makes them nervous. We live in another frequency; we have another clock. They are, and they remain, slow and deep.

Air spirits and site spirits are called devas by some. These angel-like nature spirits may perceive us, but usually remain aloof, as they have little affinity with us. Some, however, out of interest or compassion or through a personal connection with a human soul are born as humans. People who once were devas see death as less dark and hold on less to life. They are often idealists, noble people, connected to nature and wide-open spaces. They have a strong sense of beauty and tend to be clairvoyant. In the harsher aspects of life and society they are at a loss. They are typically *Schöngeister*. Cyril Scott (1953) describes seeing a deva in someone's aura, and later his guide tells him he was once a deva himself.

A woman has problems with people. Asked whether she belongs to them, she answers, 'Not really.' 'Go back to the first time you met people.' 'Oh, what funny brown dolls!' She senses herself as large and hardly circumscribed, somewhere in the atmosphere over the Pacific. Far beneath her, she sees a beach with moving small dolls. Out of curiosity she comes closer. One doll looks upwards, feels her presence and calls something to the others. They bow deeply and throw themselves on the ground, because they feel that she is some goddess. She is surprised. How strange that she never saw these before! She comes even closer and explores where those brown dolls live. Then suddenly — zap, and the next thing she notices is that she is caught in a belly — so small and so dark! Traumatic. Her first experience with people was not negative, but the second was. Since that experience she has not got over having been sucked in.

Many people experience themselves on other planets that are not real. Society and natural surroundings look as they do here, but on closer inspection the environment appears to be immaterial. They have no body, but are already accustomed to a human consciousness and a human society. They have few problems here, except that they now have a body with all its shortcomings. It is awkward to have to live with such limited parapsychological functions. Power, influence and communication exist in such worlds, but money and food and drink do not. They are not good cooks. They cannot deal with money. In politics and in the church they can succeed. They also feel at home in the writing professions.

Goldberg was the first to describe 'light people'. These souls live in a world of shining dots or planes or structures, a world of geometry and music. They are self-conscious, but not sharply separated as entities. They feel themselves to be parts of bigger wholes, of bigger structures that have a kind of collective consciousness.

Their primal trauma is that they have broken away from that bigger structure or become torn away or sent away by stronger beings they call Planners. Independent existence means that their original harmony and links have been broken. They have become amputated, not as if their hand had been amputated, but as if they are the amputated hand.

They also find talking and listening awkward. Telepathy is much easier. Before, they were almost as one brain. They discerned themselves, but they did not separate themselves. The way they are isolated and have to communicate here is maddening for them.

Others seem to have arrived complete and ready from the hands of a Creator — their Creator. Many others slowly grew and developed in a shining primal soup and gradually awakened. The first ones seem to have been made by Fathers and the second ones to have been hatched by Mothers.

FAMILY 3. *Originally not self-conscious, in a physical body: mammals*
The Loehr–Daniels readings say animals never become humans (Smith: 248).

Many experiences contradict this. Some persons in regression see more primitive lives as hunters and gatherers, sometimes in the Stone Age. Several have found themselves in lifetimes before primitive people, in primates and before that in higher mammals. Though genetically we are closer to chimpanzees, until now I have encountered almost exclusively gorillas. Moving to the higher mammals, monkeys are remarkably rare. They seem to have little affection for people; rarely do they cross the line. Regressions into lives as dolphins are rare, but they happen. Animals like elephants and tigers seem less exceptional.

These souls had already experienced themselves as physical individuals before they had individual self-consciousness. They seem to have progressed through the higher mammals, often toward primates, in the normal evolution.

The notion of individual animal souls taking on a human life contradicts the idea of group souls that some esotericists assert, but fits the numerous observations of mediums and psychics who see deceased pets waiting for their owner. Regression somewhat resembles dreaming. Mammals do dream, just like people. Birds have dreams lasting about one second (Sagan 1977).

The first bridge between animals and people is increased brain volume. The second bridge is company with people by domesticated animals – horses, dogs and sometimes cats. Quite often, the last life as an animal ends in meeting people, as in a hunt or a trap. One gorilla is killed, pursuing hunters. She incarnates in a human body, because the last she saw of her infant was that it was among humans who had caught it. It seems reasonable to assume that one of the most copious sources of new human souls is the mass slaughter of especially the more intelligent mammals, like pigs, for human food. In human lifetimes too, violent and sudden death may raise awareness, and victims often return among their oppressors or predators. Their revulsion or their hate may be strong, but their fear may lead them to the only safe place: among their enemies. Or they are filled with revenge, which also leads them to return among their enemies. So slaughterhouses may be the third bridge. Being slaughtered a few times may be enough to lead a soul across the divide. Of course, we will rarely get such people in past-life therapy.

The next example is, given the virtual absence of an intermission between lives, probably no animal past life, but at least illustrates the extent to which humans and mammals may identify.

Two friends are going to visit a country seat in Prussia, in the first half of the last century. At the railway station they take an open horse-and-buggy. They enjoy the sights. One of them gets restless. 'I have never been here before, but everything seems familiar. I could swear that this road will continue to the right after the next hill. And behind that hill at the left is a small wood with a village behind it. Three streets meet at the village square.' Everything is confirmed. In the village he jumps from the cart, excited, and runs into a street. His friend can't keep up with him. He enters a farmhouse and returns in confusion. 'I have been here before. I know each house, each tree. In this farmhouse, I lived for a long time. Come on, I need to speak to the people who live here.' The people there don't recognise him and he doesn't know them. Yet he can tell them many details about the place. 'There, at the right, behind the large horse stable, should be a kennel.' There was. In front of the kennel he falls down on his knees and with a trembling voice calls out: 'Here I lived, as a dog! From here I saw the shepherds with their flocks, the maids carrying water and the farm hands putting the horses to the carts. The children called me Potzky when they played with me or put me to a small cart that I had to pull through the village with them.'

An elderly woman who had worked as a maid for the previous owners tells that 28 years ago, in the autumn, a large black dog, called Potzky, had died in the kennel. The boy was born on 25 September of the same year. (Passian 1985: 137)

Since 1977, José Gruber has regressed some patients to prehuman experiences. He calls this evolutionary therapy instead of past-life therapy. Patients experience themselves as nebula, rock, plant, animal and finally human. Whatever the nature of these apparent regressions, they are therapeutically effective. Gruber discovered this with a 40-year-old man with psychosomatic complaints that resisted specialist treatment. After regressions to childhood and birth, his condition improved, but did not heal completely. Gruber regressed him to prehistoric times. During four sessions he relived being a nebula, lava and a rock that had melted by intense heat and later congealed into semiprecious stone. Still later, he feels himself to be moss, growing on a rock. It felt dry, but compared to the stone more lively. He feels sunlight and ice that melts after some time. He lives for 230 years. In his next existence, he is a small frog that lives a few months. Then he feels a strong pressure from above, as if his tongue is pressed to his palate. He cringes and is relieved when the moment of being eaten is over. Later again, he lives for 30 years as a seal in a polar landscape. This is 10,000 years or more ago. His next lifetime is as a male monkey 7,000 years ago, somewhere in Africa. Gruber suggests that he talks with his female. He assumes a curious sitting position and utters some sounds. 'What did you tell her?' 'She has to look after the young ones better. She left them behind on the ground and just walked away. There are lions and such.' Finally, he enters into human lifetimes: in India (4700 BC), Africa (2000 BC), Italy (400 AD), eighteenth-century France and Germany 1867–1927. True or not, the therapy was successful. (Passian 1985: 141)

One A.F. Knudsen experimented from 1892 till 1896 on a South Sea island with hypnotising animals. On the stud farm, some horses were difficult to break, because they were either too stupid or too clever. These animals were unsaleable. One by one, Knudsen hypnotised them and broke them. Even the most difficult animal was now saleable. Neighbouring farmers asked him to break their difficult horses too.

One day, about 60 horses of every age were in the field. There was one 3-year old horse Knudsen wanted to break. By hypnotic suggestion he commanded the horse to raise a front leg and make an eight. He succeeded and repeated the command a few times. Then he noticed how an older mare in the field neighed and did the same. He discovered two other horses doing it too. He found out that every suggestion he gave to one of them, the other three would copy. The horses were not related.

Systematically, Knudsen now took each horse separately and checked what other animals were influenced. All the horses appeared to be in groups of at least three and at most 18 animals. The more intelligent the animals, the smaller the group. Later, Knudsen extended this experiment to cattle. The results were the same, though because of their lesser intelligence, the cattle reacted more slowly than horses. The group size of cattle was between 50 and 100 animals. Altogether, he experimented with hundreds of horses and thousands of cattle.

Knudsen now took one animal from each group, while the others of the same group were led out of sight, at distances of up to 8 kilometres. Each animal was given an attendant, who noted what happened. Distance played no role; the contact remained. Animals that seemed to share one group soul could be dispersed over several farms, even at great distances. Gender, age and parentage played no role in this.

Knudsen further observed that: When the subjected animal followed hypnotic orders, the others followed them too, but always with some delay and less perfectly. When the hypnotic suggestion worked well with an animal and the animal was not distracted, the group consciousness was clearly present. With intelligent horses, rapport was established within five minutes. A strange voice or an unexpected movement of the hypnotist could break the rapport with the other group members, without lessening the rapport between the subjected animal and the hypnotist.

When one group consisted of both wild and tame horses, hypnotising a tame animal made the wild group members more amenable, though they remained unruly. When a hardly tamed horse was given a saddle, it could react wildly, Even the tame group members would get wild at that moment.

When Knudsen suggested pain to an animal, the other members of its group felt nothing. The same was true when one animal fell or hurt itself.

From the experiments of Knudsen, Passian concludes that animals living together with people learn and develop and individualise faster (1985: 145). I would add that pain and probably the death experience also seem to be strongly individualising.

People who had animal lives, even long ago, rarely come to our couch. They have fewer problems with physical life, as they are used to that already. Such souls may also shirk from more mental games such as therapy, and certainly from ideas about non-physical existence. Their primal trauma is that they became imprisoned in a sharp, intellectual, human ego-consciousness. The higher mammals are conscious, but their self-consciousness is vaguer; they lack intellect. Our thinking self-consciousness is difficult and painful for them, sometimes even maddening.

Today, we may feel accustomed to and at home in a body, but physical survival becomes less important in our society. We have the luxury of mental problems, at least in the Western world. For still simple souls, mental problems are a great burden. Many problems arise from simple souls who do not yet have the required level of refinement and so with the advance of modern societies come from their strength in their weakness.

FAMILY 4. *Originally not self-conscious, without a physical body: starters*

This is probably the most frequent species of souls, yet we rarely or never get them in past-life regressions. If we get them in past lives at all, they have had but a few such lives. If we regress them to before their first lifetime, we get the same sensations as they had before birth or after death – only a faint feeling of being around. They somehow know that they exist, but that's all. Before their first incarnation they had no conscious individual existence. Independence and individuality seem to have begun with their first human life.

When a woman is pregnant and no soul is around, there seems always one to be scooped from a general psychic mass, a kind of soul cake. By intervention or by natural process? Either might happen.

Probably many people who are now alive are walking around for the first time here, with freshly individualised soul substance. The population explosion puts many immature souls in this world.

People who have had no experiences before their first incarnation are still individual. Just as marble cake has dark and light patches, soul cake can be mixed. From where does that soul cake come? Possibly it grows through the physical evolution in plants and animals. Don't ask me how. Almost surely, it comes in part from human souls who weakened or degenerated, who didn't make it. We can lose ourselves or hurt so much and for so long that our soul becomes subcritical and no longer survives. The remaining soul substance then goes back into the general fund. Therefore soul cake is not homogeneous.

For the third and fourth soul families, the function of the human body, that living robot, is to develop self-consciousness. Their primal trauma is the shock of self-consciousness, an enormous burden indeed.

According to anthroposophists, everyone who has a problem is insufficiently incarnated. That is almost by definition true, but the idea behind it is that humans are spiritual beings. That idea is true only for people who were already self-conscious without a body. Such souls feel better between lives than in lives.

Starters and people who come from animals have to develop awareness during the intermissions between lifetimes. First they will just sleep, later they may remain hanging around after death. Only after several incarnations do they retain enough self-consciousness between death and birth. We can encounter a deceased who misses coffee, let alone other bodily pleasures. It depends on what we are accustomed to. The last two main families easily become stale during their incarnations and the first two main families easily become wounded. This difference does not depend on personal responsibility and personal behaviour. In past-life regressions to prehuman conditions, 80 or 90 percent percent of people were spirits. Maybe 10 percent were extraterrestrial and only a few were animals. Probable starters are even more exceptional. Past-life remigrants are no random sample of the world population.

Our prehuman origin lies before the watershed of the primal trauma. If we were banished or abandoned or left behind, our home world is hidden behind betrayal or guilt or grief or confusion. Some people feel that they don't belong with their parents. The liberating experience is then to relive what happened just before this life. Something similar can occur on another level. Why did I become human? How did I get into this world? Then we explore what feelings are involved, what charges are connected with being in a human body for the first time or with coming to this planet for the first time.

Many remigrants report experiences in prehistoric advanced civilisations.

These experiences are usually identified with Atlantis and, in at least some places and at some times, the Atlantic civilisation is seen as having contact with extraterrestrials. On the other hand, instructions to return to Atlantis lead to diverse situations. Our subconscious appears to interpret the word 'planet' not only as an astronomical planet but also as a discarnate state or any other parallel reality. Some remigrants may go to such planets as Mars, Venus or Uranus, but their descriptions make it absolutely clear that these planets are not the astronomical ones. These experiences may have some meaning, but should make us wary of using such names as 'Atlantis' or 'Uranus' in regression inductions or interpreting them as physical environments of past lives.

Pieter Langedijk finds experiences of higher civilisations on other planets when he sends people back to their first incarnation (Langedijk 1980). These experiences often resemble the discarnate state. A world called Uranus, after further questioning, turns out to be a non-physical environment. According to some remigrants, humans incarnated for the first time in the Atlantic age. Others remember lives in colonies of extraterrestrial origin, which stimulated the primitive people in this world in their development, often a difficult task. Langedijk places memories to technically more advanced civilisations more than 10,000 years in the past (1987: 8). People with impressions from lives on other planets, independently of each other felt that to have been more than 30,000 years ago (1987a: 8).

Barten tells of someone belonging to a space society in an Atlantic incarnation, leaving his body while he inspects the primitive Lemurians here (TenDam 1982). If that were true, it would contradict the theosophical idea that Lemuria was far earlier than Atlantis.

Ron Hubbard and the scientologists often encounter lives on other planets, in technically more advanced civilisations and science-fiction environments. Scientologists strictly date the beginning and end of each trauma. They get lives on other planets up to millions or billions of years ago. Bruce Goldberg suggests that between 100,000 and 50,000 years ago many souls from other planets began to incarnate here (Goldberg 1982: 45). He talks about a remigrant who, during regression, experiences himself as a labourer involved in the construction of a pyramid. He describes the supervisors as people more than six and a half feet tall, with large heads and long fingers. They do not talk, but send out compelling telepathic signals (Goldberg 1982: 90).

Some remigrants regress to ancient primitive conditions with an apparently modern body, to the time of the dinosaurs. Desider Mockry-Meszaros, a

Hungarian, painted his prehistoric memories, scenes that went back to the beginning of a barely cooled Earth. He had still earlier memories of the underworld of another planet. His paintings were bought by, among others, Maxim Gorkyi (*New York Times*, 9 February 1930).

During his out-of-body experiences Robert Monroe got into one of three environments. The first environment was our physical world, but seen and explored without a body. The second environment was like a dream world, corresponding to the astral world of the occultists. On a few occasions Monroe ended up in a third, parallel world. After he had passed some vertical screen, he sped straight through black space for a long time, on every occasion ending up in the same person, in what seemed to be another life on a somewhat similar planet. Every time he was disoriented, because he had no idea of the occurrences just before his arrival. When he returned from time to time, he realised that the man whom he entered was getting into difficulties in his personal life and in business because of these odd periods of disorientation. The other world of his 'environment III' was real, physical and consistent. It resembles a parallel incarnation on another planet (Monroe 1976).

NON-HUMAN LIFETIMES; IDENTIFICATION INSTEAD OF INCARNATION

Historically, one of the greatest disputes between reincarnation believers has been whether or not people return in animal bodies. In other words: is there reincarnation or metempsychosis? Regressions to animal lives are uncommon compared with those to human lives, but there are examples of spontaneous memories as well as regressions. Ron Hubbard gives a few examples of animal incarnations (Hubbard 1958). A psychotic girl remembers being a lion that ate a zookeeper. After the customary treatment of these experiences, she was cured. Another example is a remigrant who describes being thrown out of a spacecraft hovering above the ocean. A huge ray eats his body. He then experiences himself as that ray. According to Joe Fisher (1985: 136), many of Joe Keeton's subjects regress to animal lives, and Helen Wambach (1978) also had some subjects who found themselves on four legs. Ian Stevenson also found a few examples (1977: 7; 1983: 6, 167).

A Chinese slave walks up to a governor's mother and asks her if, as a little girl, she had had a wild fox as a pet and wore a yellow petticoat under her red and white striped dress. When she acknowledges this, he tells her he was this fox. He had run away and had lived in an old grave until a hunter killed him. After this, he met the 'Lord of the Other World', who told him he was not a sinner and should take a human body. He was reborn as a beggar and died of hunger and misery when he was twenty. After this, he appeared in front of the same Lord, who said he would be a slave in a house of a prominent notable; the term slave was not attractive, but he would not be hungry and miserable. (Penkala 1972: 49)

Marcia Moore came across two animal memories among many hundreds of people. One woman thought she had been a cat in a temple and one man that he had lived as an owl (Moore 1976: 235). Frederick Lenz found six persons, or 5 percent of his cases, with animal incarnations before human incarnations. His examples are an owl, another bird, a sea turtle and a whale. Experiences as plants are rare. Somebody remembered one life as a tree (Pisani 1978). Morris Netherton, tracking down traumatic chains, often finds the root problem to be the traumatic injury or death of an animal. However, he found nobody backsliding to animal lives during the traumatic chains (Netherton & Shiffrin 1978: 183). An American boy thought he had been a hippopotamus in a past life (Langedijk 1980: 114).

Margot Klausner describes her oldest memory, from perhaps 100,000 years ago, as being a kind of flower growing on a rock. It was not yet a real flower, but a more primitive plant without a stem. Instead of leaves it had a kind of moss and the petals were rough and prickly. The heart of the flower form was golden-yellow and the petals were violet. She describes herself amid many such flowers on top of a high mountain. Later, she realises this is somewhere in Atlantis and she briefly describes the development of mankind on Atlantis. Apparently, she has had human lives in the place where she was first a flower. (Klausner 1975)

Someone feels he is a stone statue at the bottom of a stair cut out of the rock. Later, it turns out that priests have killed him in a hypnotic ceremony. He feels himself being stuck inside the stone next to these stairs. He is only freed when earthquakes and erosion burst and pulverise the stairs.

A prominent and fierce Egyptian dominates many people and liquidates his opponents. The priests seem interested in this forceful personality and manipulate him by hypnotic rituals.

During another ritual they kill him and put his soul in a ceremonial lamp with the instruction 'to light forever the gates for the Lord of Darkness', a rather paradoxical assignment. His consciousness fades inside the lamp. The next thing he knows is the lamp shattering somewhere in sixteenth-century France. Apparently his unconscious state lasted 4,800 years. (Hubbard 1958)

Scientologists give many examples of people pulled out of their body by science-fiction hypnotic machines and then being put in a bottle or vase or implanted in a robot. Other therapists report such psychic voidings also, though rarely. Once a soul has become human, can it return to having animal lives? Such an evolutionary degradation seems unlikely. The preceding chapter gave many examples of people remaining stuck in the material environment by etheric or mental bonds. They awake incompletely, which prevents liberation and meeting other people. Such people often hang about or wander around, dimly perceiving the physical world. They can enter into living people, who may remain unaware of this. They put themselves in the same spot in three-dimensional space, but a distance remains in the fourth dimension, the 'throughght'. There is no reciprocal contact, as in obsession. People who feel themselves within objects, identify hypnotically with the object until it is broken. The example of the Roman who was plagued by feelings of guilt and rejection shows that someone may be stuck at a location without a specific material counterpart.

None of this is reincarnation, where we are born into a physical organism with senses, nerves and everything else, an organism in which we are self-aware and active. A soul stuck in a lamp or a statue has been made psychotic, often by 'black magic', to induce fear and awe in living people. Animals also react to such haunted objects. Similarly, someone floating around aimlessly may be attracted to any physical entity seemingly offering shelter. He may attach himself to a fox, a bird or whatever animal he feels an affinity for, but also a living person. He may follow the animal or person around, identify himself with it and even make some contact ('crawl into the aura'). With animals this is only partially possible and is often pathological, unless it is a conscious choice as an educational or sometimes therapeutic experience (an extreme form of vacation).

The story of the man who falls into the sea and is eaten by a ray proves how pathological this may be. Subsequently, he is the ray. This is no incarnation, but identification. Interestingly enough, people who remember a 'life' as an animal, which clearly was a psychotic identification, are cured of present psychological problems when this experience is worked through and 'erased'.

I have already given the example of the psychotic girl who remembers a life as a lion who eats a zookeeper. We have to be on our guard against seeing this as the first cause of the psychosis. Presumably she was not the lion, but the zookeeper, psychotically trying to come to terms with the experience, like the man with the ray. She could have had an aggressive, animal self-image before. Through such a self-image, she could have been pulled towards a similar emotional occurrence and subsequently have identified herself with it. Either she hated the zookeeper, hung around him and inspired him to act carelessly and through the emotion and responsibility identified herself with the lion; or she felt the tension of her own more general hate—guilt feelings and identified herself with these. It may be more specific: perhaps she was torn to pieces by a lion some time before, for example in an arena, and has been left with so much hate that she wants to cause it to happen to others. And so on. Anyway, some psychosis was the cause of this identification.

Margot Klausner's experience as a flower-like plant can also be better explained as the identification of a discarnate person who remained attached to the physical world than as a real incarnation. It is a persistent self-hypnosis. Self-created surroundings are a dime a dozen among the deceased. The only extraordinary thing about the cases here is that they do not create the surroundings themselves, but perceive the material environment and imagine themselves to be a part of it as an object, a plant, an animal or a person.

PROGRESSIONS TO THE FUTURE

Albert de Rochas, the first to reach past lives by regression, discovered progression by chance. He sat the remigrant down in front of him and made magnetic passes with his left hand along the length of the body from the head down, while he held his right hand on the forehead. This caused a magnetic trance and, with silent or spoken suggestions, a return in time: age regression. To bring the remigrant back to the present, de Rochas used magnetic passes across the body, moving both hands horizontally from the middle of the body out to the sides. If he continued this long enough, people ended up in the future.

Eugenie, a subject of de Rochas, was the first who was brought into progression. She arrived two years into the future and showed signs of pregnancy and shortly afterwards, signs of drowning. De Rochas quickly brought her to two years later and again she was pregnant. When he asked where she was she answered, 'On the water'. De Rochas thought she had started to flip and brought her back. Two years later, she had a child from her lover and shortly afterwards threw herself desperately into the Yser. However, she was rescued in time. In January 1909, she had a second child on a bridge over the Yser, where she had suddenly gone into labor. She was indeed 'on the water'. (Shirley 1924: 140)

A female subject of De Rochas aged during the progression. She was aware of her future burial and heard people say that death was a blessing for a woman her age. She also reported that the priest was passing round the coffin, keeping evil spirits at bay. Then everything darkened. She saw spirits around, but couldn't communicate with them. Later, she felt she had to return to Earth. The next life was short: she died of angina at the age of three. She then came into a friendly environment and was happy. She was surrounded by good spirits, but recognised none. In her next life, she was 16 years old in 1970.

De Rochas also progressed one Josephine. During the experiments, in 1904, she was 18. In the progression, at the age of 30, she conceived a child out of wedlock. She was disconsolate at being abandoned. She felt she had to atone for what she had done in a previous life as a man. She said it wouldn't help her if de Rochas warned her after the trance what was in store for her. In a later session, she mentioned the name of the future father. De Rochas had her remember that name after waking from the trance. He told her this could happen, but was not bound to happen. After all, a job offer forecast in a previous progression had had not materialised. Josephine moved to another county and de Rochas lost contact. Much later he wrote to her and she responded that she had got a job as a seamstress and was going to marry a butcher's man called Rougier. This name differed from the one she had mentioned during her progression. De Rochas: 'So the sad event that she foresaw at the age of 30, will not happen. Maybe she has avoided it, because she was warned by me.' (Passian 1985: 40)

Glaskin gives the example of somebody who used the Christos procedure and ultimately ended up in his own life several years hence rather than in a past life (Glaskin 1974: 76).

The remigrant found himself in the cemetery of a neighborhood in his own city. Along with about fifty others, he was attending his mother's funeral. He recognized his brother and sisters, his father and his stepfather. The funeral 'had taken place, but not yet'. He said he was 24 years old and was wearing a black suit he had bought in England. Stephen had never been to England, but was planning to go in the coming year. He was far from happy with the prospect of the funeral. He did actually go to England and after eighteen months had to return suddenly because his mother had contracted a dangerous spinal disease. Intentionally, he did not buy a black suit. After his return, his mother improved.

Dethlefsen also guided progressions in the present lifetime, but wasn't enthusiastic about them. His remigrants were much more tired than after regressions. He advises regressions rather to the prenatal period. He claims that the foetus has a life preview, a foreknowledge that only disappears at birth (Passian 1985: 41). Helen Wambach's work seems to place the life preview rather before the entrance into the foetus. Both Joel Whitton's and Michael Newton's work confirms this.

Bruce Goldberg has worked regularly with progressions (Goldberg 1982: 151ff.). According to him, in progressions to future lives, the images shift suddenly.

Chet Snow has followed up Helen Wambach's work on progressions and completed it with material he and other collaborators of Wambach collected later. The title *Mass Dreams of the Future* (1989) is precise: it is no more and no less. Snow finds that all those impressions of future lifetimes, between 2100 and 2200 and after 2300, can be summarised to four different environments. Some environments are conflicting, and both economically and technically the speed of advance of space travel and space colonisation is highly improbable. Snow relates the contents of these progressions to predictions of Edgar Cayce and of a motley collection of all kinds of channels and psychics. If those had been true, before 1998 large parts of California and Japan would have been submerged.

Parapsychologists such as TenHaeff have shown that precognition exists, but the material of Wambach and Snow, though psychologically interesting, is no precognition of a future reality. If many people subconsciously have such images, what they tell us is about present hopes and fears.

When we drive a car on the highway, we can look forwards and backwards, but I am afraid time is a quite different kind of dimension. In time, there is no looking forwards or backwards; consulting records differs from imagining expectations. Scrying the future is probably possible up to a point: to the extent that the future is contained in the present. But even if we can do that, distortion is even more likely than with memories. In recall, we can add or subtract elements, we can whiten or blacken things, we can even indulge in fantasy, but there is still something like the real memory. In precognition, conscious expectations and subconscious hope and fear are even more distorted.

De Rochas' and Glaskin's experiments are interesting because they indicate that progressions may be meaningful without being an accurate picture of future occurrences. In *Winged Pharaoh* Joan Grant writes an analogy consistent with this notion (Grant 1937: 130):

The past is fixed, that which has happened cannot be changed. But every action changes a future that is fluid and can be modified in a past that is lasting. Your next day or the next life you will be born in, is like your mirrored image in a pool. At any moment you can check what the pool of your future looks like, but through your own free will you can make storms rage over it or make waves on its peaceful surface. That is why so few forecasts bear out. Just look at the gardener with his watering can. I can foretell that he is going to cross the courtyard without spilling anything because that is the future that his present acts are making. But if he trips or throws down the can of his own free will, then his present future has been changed, because through his act he has brought about a different effect and so my forecast will not bear out. But this is an image that only few people are allowed to see, because you could then influence someone's deeds.

Now, just as with the gardener who begins to walk through the garden with his watering can, there may be patterns in the development of humankind that have been designed and will be worked out in more detail on the way. For this reason, people can have impressions of the future of society. Perhaps they have even designed their own personal future in it. However, Wambach's research makes it clear that many people do not even plan their coming life, let alone have already made preparations for lives in the further future. It is questionable whether they are at all able to pick up images of this future.

PROVISIONAL CONCLUSIONS

1 When we regress ever further, we find different origins. Souls seem to develop either by evolution (probably the most fundamental and most frequent method) or involution. Human souls may evolve from animal souls or kick-start directly as human souls. Spirits may involve into humans. Extraterrestrials will have had one of the three origins before. All this is no metaphysics, but an inventory of regression experiences, subject to new insights.

2 Atlantis, Lemuria or other planets are probably open to multiple inter-pretations in the subconscious. Affixing a label that does not correspond to the concrete experience of the remigrant is risky. For example, when we ask someone to go to the 'twenty-second century', the subconscious may interpret this as the twenty-second century from now or the twenty-second century according to a different calendar. Although special states of consciousness

generate interesting and valuable information and may give us confidence in the seemingly unbounded potential we have, this remains a field that is neither transparent nor familiar. The experiences of the human subconscious (and conscious) teach us that we have to instruct it just as carefully as a computer, otherwise unintended leaps may occur.

3 Experiences as animals, or even as plants, rocks or objects in between human lives, are no incarnations, but identifications of people who did not release themselves from the physical world after death, a kind of dream existence.

4 The future is only partially predestined by the past and by plans. Impressions of the future are usually extrapolations of existing tendencies and plans, often distorted by either hope or fear. True precognition seems to exist about key events. The seemingly accidental contains planned and predestined moments. But objective, detailed progressions to future lifetimes are contradicted by what we know about afterdeath and prebirth experiences.

FURTHER READING

First, there are Edgar Cayce's books (especially 1968), cited earlier. Hubbard's book (1958) is riddled with extraordinary experiences: in the ancient past, on other planets, in science-fiction worlds, in animal lives, in attachment to objects. Perhaps this results from his selection (although his examples vary considerably in quality and are summed up carelessly, hardly implying selection), perhaps it results from the method, and perhaps also from expectations within scientology. Or people with such experiences may be attracted to scientology.

Other examples are scattered in the literature. Marcia Moore (1976), Pieter Langedijk (1980) and Bruce Goldberg (1982) mention more than others. Perhaps such stories are less common under deep hypnosis or other authors are more critical or more afraid of criticism.

Thirteen

KARMIC AND DHARMIC CONNECTIONS BETWEEN LIFETIMES

Even without a clear memory of past lives, we exhibit traces of them in our idiosyncrasies, our preferences and our character (Van Ginkel 1917: 60). The same is true for our relationships: 'Love is an eloquent witness.' And so, I add, is hate. Our past lives stir in our emotions, our fears, our habitual reactions and problems, barely beneath the surface of consciousness. With most people, just the right mental or emotional key makes these past lives surface.

Edgar Cayce hardly ever gave information about past lives without pointing out the karmic connections. As chapter 4 of this book illustrated, sensitives and psychics include a lot of karma when they talk about past lives. Helen Wambach found karmic obligations in 30 percent of her group. Another 30 percent felt they had been free in designing their life and the rest were unclear or somewhere in between (Wambach 1979: 42, 75). On the other hand, Ian Stevenson found, to his surprise, hardly any indications of karma in the cases of children with spontaneous memories (Stevenson 1975: 34, 65).

These differences probably result from the different samples of people that Cayce, Stevenson and Wambach worked with. Stevenson researched children who had ended a life – often prematurely – with only a few years' intermission and a fairly short distance from their present birthplace. Cayce advised people with psychic and physical problems. He moved into past lives when someone's present fate and present suffering remained incomprehensible within the framework of the present life. Wambach's subjects were people interested in reincarnation and curious as to whether they would be able to remember.

NATURAL AND MORAL
INTERPRETATIONS OF KARMA

The existing views of karma contain three fundamental antitheses:

- Is everything determined or only a few things?
- Does karma work as a natural law or does it involve some kind of judgment?
- What is decisive? Our intentions or what we actually did?

The first antithesis is that between karma as determining everything versus karma as one influence among others, such as heredity, astrological constellations, extra-sensory influences, coincidence and free will. We come across the deterministic view of karma mainly in the early theosophical literature, where karma is praised in mystical and abstract prose (Anderson 1894). Karmic justice means reaping what we sow, picking the fruits of our own efforts. However, this is only meaningful when we have responsibility and choice. A fully deterministic view means predestination, reducing human history to a puppet disco.

The second antithesis is that between karma as a spiritual law of nature versus karma as evaluation or jurisdiction. In the last case we speak about administering karma. An intermediate position is that the consequences of our acts naturally form a karma fund, but that allocation of karma in our future lives depends on evaluation or even free will. We can postpone or roll over the debt, but we cannot cancel it. Which karma is worked out in which order depends on the evaluation of the karmic judges (we ourselves always being one of them) and the karmic administrators. The theosophical view in this respect is ambivalent: karma is regulated by the Lipika or Lords of Karma, beings so powerful and objective that they work as a spiritual natural law. Concrete conceptualisation of such views is difficult. Adherents of such thoughts assume that this is because the nature of the subject is beyond our understanding. Such an argument can never be disproved. This is classical mythology: personifying natural powers and natural laws.

The third antithesis lies in what decides karma: the actual consequences of what we did or the intent we did it with. Our legal system distinguishes murder and manslaughter. In chapter 2 we saw that, according to the Jains, it makes no difference whether, by opening a window, we have caused someone to fall off the ladder and die by accident or out of vengeance or to lay our hands on the inheritance. Most views on karma put greater weight on the intent behind our acts.

A deterministic view of karma fits the notion of karma as a natural law and may fit with both the factual and the moral view. If somebody pushes us over by accident, this may irritate us, but we react differently when we realise it was done on purpose. The view of karma as jurisdiction can only correspond with a non-deterministic view and a view where intention is more decisive.

The classical Greeks had three goddesses of fate who wove people's destinies: Adrasteia, Nemesis and Themis. Adrasteia decreed the natural consequences of acts. With her, there was neither providence nor redemption. Adrasteia corresponds to karma as natural law. Nemesis decreed the rewards for good deeds and the punishment for bad ones. In our terms, she corresponds to the jurisdical view of karma. Third was Themis, who decreed the correction of consequences of acts. She constantly tried to restore order and harmony, to heal and to educate. She corresponds to karma as corrective and therapeutic.

The karmic repercussions of an immoral act have Adrasteia putting the burden of the immediate consequences on us. We may then have to undergo Nemesis' karmic punishment, and Themis arouses the desire in us to make up for this act. Our capacity to place ourselves more or less under the influence of either Nemesis or Themis is consistent with this subtle Greek view. If we want to compensate for our imperfect deeds, we place ourselves under Themis as it were, and Nemesis is less necessary. When Themis is busier, Nemesis gets more of a rest. They do job-sharing. Adrasteia has full tenure.

FOUR PATTERNS

Chapter 2 saw various reincarnation philosophies distinguishing between people who return for karmic reasons and those who return of their own free will. To assume that reincarnation may be more or less obligatory or voluntary is consistent with Wambach's results. I distinguish four levels in the reasons given for reincarnation. Any particular incarnation may contain a mixture.

- Level 1 *Natural:* Incarnating according to natural laws. The reincarnating soul has neither guidance nor choice. This will happen when we fall asleep after death and experience nothing before our rebirth except feeling 'sucked in'.

- Level 2 *Educational:* Incarnation based on karmic obligations and the need to learn. Here, we are guided, sometimes forcefully, and to some extent have a life plan. Our say in the matter varies from little ('detention work') to substantial ('choice of essay subject').

- Level 3 *Volitional:* Incarnation on the basis of our personal interests and resolutions, with a personal life plan. We have complete say in the matter and choose our own guides if we want them ('promotion research').

- Level 4 *Mission:* Incarnation based on a contribution to the development of others. Our life plan fits in a larger plan.

Buddhists assume that Bodhisattvas, the Lords of Wisdom and Compassion, return to help advance mankind out of free will. According to Mahayana Buddhists, the Bodhisattvas appear as world teachers according to a fixed schedule. The Ismaelites share this notion. They use the terms *hukul* or *burut*: the periodic return of the perfected. Among Wambach's subjects, mission considerations are sometimes dominant in ordinary active and well-meaning people who lack any aureole of being world teachers. Apparently, voluntary return is less exceptional and less of a sacrifice than world escapists believe.

I divide causal patterns, that is, relations according to natural law, into retention, repercussion and fruition. *Retention* or persistence is retaining experiences and skills as they are, unchanged; repercussion is the effect of undigested, haunting experiences; fruition is the digestion and transformation of experiences.

In *repercussion*, a piece of the past lies undigested in our stomach, such as a childhood trauma that influences our later life. Reactions to traumas differ greatly. If a child catches his parents in a sadomasochistic act, he may see the world as a capricious, inhumane and frightening puppet show; or he may become withdrawn and vulnerable; or he may act out sadism by twisting the legs off spiders and flies.

If we subject ourselves to an authoritarian father, we may remain submissive as adults, even to our deceased father. This is retention or persistence. If the father's authority resulted in fear and this in turn to an inferiority complex and psychosomatic problems, then this is a repercussion. *Fruition* here could mean that we had an authoritarian father, internalised this authority and transformed it into our own authority. Or we had to develop our own authority against all odds.

Educational patterns involve upbringing, guidance, therapy and correction. If we have to change schools because of our behaviour, are sent to a youth custody centre, are banned or put in jail, these are not cause-and-effect relationships, but interventions from evaluating second or third parties, intended to punish or reward us, to advance our development or change our outlook or attitude. We may also punish or educate ourselves. Every experience we consciously seek is also educational. Educational relationships include all the ordeals, tests and masterpieces others require of us or we require of ourselves.

Free patterns mean following our own preferences and interests. As these choices are never completely arbitrary, but related to what we have done before, I still use the word 'patterns'.

RETENTION: CONTINUITY THROUGH LIFETIMES

From the literature and from regression experiences we know of retention in (1) habits, (2) characteristics, (3) talents, (4) appearance and (5) relations. Habits, or what Stevenson calls behavioural memory, may remain when conscious memories have disappeared (Stevenson 1987: 116). Such remarkable habits may be peculiar ways of preparing food, doing household chores or performing religious acts. We may also retain bodily habits from the last part of our preceding life in our new life.

> *Presumably, someone like Lord Nelson who became left-handed by necessity would, if he were reborn, have a congenital disposition toward left-handedness. I assume that the hand that was more practised at the time of death would become dominant in the next incarnation. I know of only one case that directly supports this conjecture. It is that of a young girl in Burma, Ma Khin Sandi, who was identified as the reincarnation of her maternal grandmother. Ma Khin Sandi was left-handed, but her grandmother was not; nor was anyone else in the family. However, the grandmother had a stroke with paralysis*

of her right arm for the last several months of her life; and I conjecture that a behavioral memory of a useless right arm may have led Ma Khin Sandi to use her left arm preferentially. (Stevenson 1987: 198–9)

Addictions and substance abuse, such as alcoholism and opium addiction, may also be retained (among others, Netherton 1978: 94). A drug user has become addicted to morphine. In his preceding life he was an opium addict. In the life before that, as an infant in a rich family, he was given opium by the servants to keep him quiet. That situation may or may not have had a karmic cause. The addiction started there and continued in following lifetimes. When dealers recruit junkies, this may or may not have past-life causes, but it will certainly have next-life consequences. An alcoholic is locked away in a mental institution after his wife discovered he had an affair. Brandy is his only escape. He dies a wreck. Here too, there might well have been a karmic clue, but the addiction, once started, continued in the next lifetime. Joan Grant, Morris Netherton and Florence McClain give examples of addiction that came from insufficient doses of alcohol or morphine as anesthetics in battlefield surgery (Kelsey & Grant 1967; Netherton & Shiffrin 1978; McClain 1986a). Stevenson finds the retention of cravings and addictions also in his cases.

Some subjects have surprised and amused their elders by requesting – even demanding – an intoxicant, such as alcohol, tobacco or cannabis derivatives. They claimed to remember previous lives in which these substances solaced them and they saw no reason why they should not resume their use. Their tastes for the intoxicants seemed in no instance explicable by imitation of their parents, who either did not take the drug demanded by the child or did not approve of a young child's doing so.

What kind of characteristics may we retain in next lives? The most amusing example is that of a good or bad memory.

Perhaps the most obvious category of persons likely to remember a previous life might be that of persons with unusually good memories . . . Suzanne Ghanem was one of the leading subjects in the total number of details of the previous life recalled, especially names . . . Saada (the previous personality) was recognized in her family as having had an unusually good memory, especially for the names of people . . .

Said Zahr was making statements that his father thought referred to the life of a well-known Druse sheikh. One of the sheikh's sons learned about the case, made some study of it himself and took me to meet the subject and his family. The sheikh had been an eminent person and greatly venerated. Much about him was common knowledge among the Druses; moreover, a family's prestige would mount if its members could say that the sheikh had been reborn among them. For these two reasons the sheikh's son adopted an attitude of extreme reserve toward the case and could not shake a suspicion that the subject's father had coached his son, although there was no direct evidence of this . . . I commented on the paucity of the subject's statements; he seemed to remember extremely little about the previous life. To this the sheikh's son replied: 'That might be a feature in favour of the case's authenticity; my father had a very bad memory.' (Stevenson 1987: 213)

Temperament can also be retained from one life to the next.

Students of temperament have found that infants even a few days old show marked differences in this respect; indeed some expressions of temperament, such as the level of activity, may manifest and be observed in foetuses. The causes of differences in temperament have received comparatively little study and no expert claims full understanding of them; some experts admit to bafflement about the differences. In several cases I have investigated, informants emphasized similarities of temperament — such as a high level of physical activity or a quick temper — in a subject and in the person whose life the subject claimed to remember. (Stevenson 1987: 184–5)

Self-confidence or feeling insecure, extroversion or introversion, mystic tendencies or common sense, may be brought along from past lives; so may all kinds of special preferences and interests, such as a strong desire for particular kinds of food (Fiore 1978: 6), an interest in Regency architecture or a predilection for natural gardens.

We may also take important aspects of our mentality with us from past lives. One man became more tolerant after the Crusades, when he discovered the 'heathens' to be more civilised than the ragamuffins that came to devastate the Holy Land. That tolerance lasted in later lives. Another, after a similar experience, was left with a healthy distrust of external religious display as a measure for inner religious quality.

Less pleasant tendencies also continue. A Samaritan is maltreated by Jews and develops a hatred of them. He takes his anti-Semitism with him to a following lifetime. Someone with a hatred of blacks turns out to have been taken prisoner as a Phoenician sailor and to have suffered as a galley slave under brutal, dark-skinned overseers. Some authors carry things too far, explaining anti-

Semitism and the like as always resulting from past lives. These examples indicate only that at least some events have specific causes from past lives.

Each life may lead to associations with the country or the time in which we lived, with our gender or with our trade in that life. A happy life in Greece gives happy associations with Greece in later lives, maybe a preference for Greek music or Greek food. A difficult life as an Irish land labourer in the nineteenth century may lead to a dislike of potatoes.

We may take skills with us from one life to the next, though seldom completely. Usually, a certain aptitude remains (Stevenson 1987: 239). Arbitrary examples from the literature are: organising skills, debating, singing (a nice example in Penkala 1972) and being a good puppeteer (Fielding 1898: 336; Muller 1970: 44). A less common but remarkable retention of ability is xenoglossy or glossolalia, speaking a language from a past life. Examples of this are Shanti Devi, who could speak the Muttra dialect without having learnt it, an American woman speaking Coptic, an English sports instructor speaking ancient Egyptian and Therese Neumann (known for the appearance of blood on her hands and feet on Good Friday), who spoke a few sentences of Aramaic. The Aramaic may have been (pious) deceit, since it is possible to memorise a few sentences.

Child prodigies are examples of exceptional intellectual or musical ability. An exceptional intellect does not appear out of the blue, and it grows out of the brain mass inherited from the parents just as little as command of the violin grows out of a violin received from the parents. Although such gifts are undoubtedly a stimulus, especially when the parents play the violin well themselves, there is no substitute for practise. We develop intelligence through many lifetimes, though with large fluctuations. Natural skill in meditation, imagination, out-of-body experiences, clairvoyance, telepathy and every form of sensitivity, mediumship and other paranormal gifts, can often be traced back in regressions to temple training in past lives.

Besides abilities and tendencies, physical features may continue. I have already given the example of birthmarks. Racial characteristics may also be carried over to some extent to lifetimes in other races. These can most usually be expected in the face. Sigurd Trier, a Danish spiritualist, concluded that, though the parents provide the material, the soul individualises and shapes its face from that material, according to its will and its capability (Muller 1970: 247). Hiroshi Motoyama concludes the same for the whole body. Chapter 6 mentioned Francis Lefebvre, who remembered his life as Vasco da Gama. When his wife saw a small painted portrait of Da Gama, she remarked that it resembled her husband when angry.

> *Alexandrina was the reincarnation of a sister who had died before her. Except for the hair and the eyes, which were both a bit lighter, the second Alexandrina looked exactly like the first one. There were considerable physical similarities, like hyperemia of the left eye, eczema behind the right ear and a slight asymmetry of the face. Naturally, there were also strong psychological similarities. (Shirley 1924: 46)*

> *Paulo was his deceased sister reincarnated. Emilia had taken cyanide one-and-a-half years before Paulo was born. She was dissatisfied being a girl. At a spiritist séance, she announced her return as a boy. The boy Paulo was confused about his gender. He refused boy's clothes till he was five and pants were made out of a skirt that had belonged to Emilia. He began to accept that he was male, but still felt female. He remained a bachelor and avoided female company. (Steiger 1967: 78)*

Such maladjustment to the present gender may lead to homosexuality or transsexuality.

> *Doctors are unable to discover the cause of the stomach cramps of a 49-year-old man. After concentrating for a week on the reasons for his pain, he has a lively regression with sounds and scents. He has been sentenced as a heretic and his intestines are being pulled out with glowing irons. While being sentenced he hears his name: Jan van Leyden. He is exhibited in an iron cage, still alive. His stomach cramps began after he had been staring in fascination at the monkey cage in a zoo for a long time. He finds a portrait of Jan van Leyden and sees, among other details, the same beard he himself had when he was younger. (Muller 1970: 161)*

Carol Bowman presents in her books several examples of remarkable likeness with the preceding lifetime. If we may believe Walter Semkiw, this even is the rule.

When we feel immediate and strong acceptance or rejection, respect or contempt, trust or distrust, we may have retained a similar relationship from a previous lifetime. Sometimes this may result in fruition. A good business relationship of long standing may lead in a next life to immediate trust and intimacy and possibly to a more personal relationship.

REPERCUSSION:
UNDIGESTED AFTER-EFFECTS
FROM PREVIOUS LIVES

Repercussions are the remnants of experiences of pain, terror, shock or chronic misery, often not understood, misunderstood or undigested because of sudden death. Repercussions may be mental or emotional or even physical, as illustrated by birthmarks that correspond to mortal wounds in the preceding lifetime (see chapter 5). Stevenson says there seems to be a 'template'; older occultists would speak about an etheric matrix.

> *Suppose an old man was hacked to death with a sword. The marks on the body in which he reincarnates do not (usually) bleed, but the baby may have a hand missing where one of the old man's hands was struck off before he was knocked unconscious and died. The wounds on the old man therefore do not persist unchanged; instead, they act like a template and, as part of the psychophore, they subsequently influence the form of the new physical body with which the psychophore becomes associated in its next incarnation. (Stevenson 1987: 239)*

Traumas from past lives work out just like traumas in this life. Netherton finds the cause of stuttering in harsh punishments experienced either in childhood or previous lives. When we cannot digest a shocking experience, we suppress it or seemingly digest it by a fixed explanation that works not unlike a rule in a computer program and becomes part of our character. I have called such conclusions or decisions *postulates*. Examples are: 'I have tried everything. It is in vain.' Or: ' I am stuck.' Or: 'I will never betray my feelings again.' Or: 'People ignore me.' Or: 'Love is just a dream.'

Traumatic death experiences in particular give repercussions in next lives. First, because mortal fear and intense pain are traumatical and, second, because death precludes digestion while in the body. When we die without waking up properly, the pain and confusion and shock may stay with us unremittingly. After death we digest the most incisive life experiences, but experiences that include physical pain or other strong physical sensations can only be completely digested in a new body. As explained in chapter 11, this probably comes from undiscarded ethers of the vehicle of vitality. Incomplete dying has also its own repercussions. Agoraphobia may be one of them (De Jong 1983).

Stevenson finds in his children's cases phobias caused by traumatic death experiences. Of 252 cases in which the preceding personality died violently, 50 percent had a phobia now (Stevenson 1987: 114). Of 47 cases of drowning, 30 (64%) were now afraid of submersion and of 23 deaths by snakebite, 9 (39%) were now afraid of snakes (Stevenson 1987: 179).

The repercussions of traumatic experiences reveal themselves not only in phobias, but also in psychosomatic complaints, complexes, nightmares and compulsions. A woman who was a nomad and died in a sand storm is now afraid of wind. A sentinel, falling asleep and thus causing the deaths of himself and his comrades, is now a woman with amnesia. An overweight man starved to death in his last life. Sexual traumas from abuse or maltreatment, or from chronic and degrading discomforts such as chastity belts, may cause menstruation problems or frigidity in the next life. Often, chronic headaches can be traced back in regressions to being decapitated, guillotined, shot through the head, hanged or scalped. Such traumas contain both mental and physical pain.

> *A woman with migraine experiences in regression that her life ends when three men club her on the head, rape her and leave her dying [similar experiences are common enough to make any sane man a feminist]. After a few repetitions of this experience, she can look back on it calmly, but the headaches stay. After some further digging, it turns out that she feels guilty because she had cheapened herself in this life. She saw this death as a well-deserved punishment. Only when she was able to see this life more in terms of choice and responsibility and less in terms of guilt and punishment, did the headaches stop. (Fiore 1978: 16)*

> *A phobic girl remembers a life as a male beggar. He is imprisoned and beaten to a pulp with a metal ball with iron spikes. Subsequently rats nibble at him and he dies. She can only disengage herself from this experience when she realises that the killer's anger and hatred was a reaction to her previous persistent harassing. (Cladder 1983)*

Such a terrible death is not even remotely justifiable or understandable as punishment for harassment. Still, incomprehension holds us and comprehension frees us. People reliving concentration camp experiences who get stuck in 'But why did this have to happen to *me*?' do not find catharsis.

Fear of the dark is an unconscious memory of terrible experiences we once had in the dark. Being overweight is often the result of previous starvation. Edith Fiore found that people who were more than five kilos overweight had, almost without exception, starved to death in a past life (Fiore 1978: 6). Anorexia may be a reaction to a previous life as an amply endowed girl who constantly heard remarks about their body while being sexually harassed or molested. As with other sexual traumas, the symptoms usually appear in this life at puberty (Fiore 1978: 33).

Homosexuality is retention when we had a previous interesting and gratifying life as a homosexual. In some cases, homosexuality vanishes as the result of past-life therapy. This shows that homosexuality at least sometimes has a traumatic cause (Kelsey & Grant 1967: 138). Homosexuality may only be a repercussion when the present life is unhappy and unsatisfactory. A homosexual who leads a happy, gratified life may be stigmatised, but otherwise is just as little a case for therapy or reincarnation therapy as is a heterosexual. And if stigmatisation becomes oppression, society should be in therapy.

FRUITION: THE FRUITS OF EXPERIENCES AND ACTIVITIES IN NEXT LIFETIMES

Exertion in one life results in capabilities in the next. Practice leads to development; neglect leads to atrophy, to backsliding. Wrong practice leads to wrong development. Passive lives in which we did little wrong and little right, in which we buried our talents, are worthless. Inactive lives, even under the banner of asceticism or contemplation, weaken the spiritual muscles. Someone who had deeply experienced how easily words can wound and be misinterpreted resolved to say nothing in his next life. Such isolation and silence does not lead to phenomenal oratorical talent (as Steiner claimed that esoteric clergymen – if those exist – believed) but rather results in stammering, stuttering and poor speech. Unsociable lives lead rather to isolation, even amid people, than to social wonders.

Active lives, applying our talents, develop our willpower and exercise our faculties and so develop our independence and individuality. Passive lives accomplish the opposite. Spiritual disciplines, in which we subjected ourselves to others and practised opening up, lead in later lives to negative mediumship and to hypersensitivity to (psychic) influences. Susceptibility to obsession and some forms of mental illness can probably be traced back to this. Scott gives the example of someone taken over by another person after shell shock (1953: 231).

This brings us to *precipitation*: a form of fruition in which a psychological characteristic of one life becomes a psychosomatic or body property in the next. Being plagued by obsessions may come from passivity in past lives; weak intestines from gluttony in a past life. Surrendering to negative emotions may lead to lymphatic or nervous diseases in a next life. Past-life sadism may lead to present-life epilepsy.

OVERVIEW ON CAUSAL CONNECTIONS

Repercussions are the consequences of physically and psychologically shocking and painful experiences, especially traumatic death experiences, that have been suppressed, not understood or misunderstood and so remained undigested. Fruition gradually blends into retention. If personal contacts lead to a personal relationship (fruition) then the personal relationship continues to exist (retention). If practice makes perfect (fruition) then this state of perfection may be taken further (retention). If someone has a natural gift for playing the piano, this may be the result of an ability already existing in the previous life (retention), but also the result of persevering practice in the past life, even if it did not then lead to a satisfying result (fruition). So we may persevere even if we sense that we will not make it in this life.

Retention:
- Abilities
    - intellectual and musical talents (child prodigies)
    - glossolalia (speaking unlearned foreign languages)
    - psychic talents (through temple training)
    - other special talents (like puppeteering, organisation skills, etc.)
- Tendencies
    - habits
    - temperament
    - mentality
    - addictions
- Appearance
    - facial structure and facial expression
    - racial characteristics (skin colour).

- Relationships
  - immediate friendship
  - immediate animosity.

Repercussion

- Physical idiosyncrasies (like birthmarks)
- Psychosomatic complaints (epilepsy, anorexia, frigidity, migraine, phantom pains, allergies, asthma, hyper-activity)
- Phobias (fear of heights, agoraphobia, fear of strangers, fear of snakes)
- Postulates (engraved conclusions or decisions, such as prejudices, character neuroses)
- Obsessions and pseudo-obsessions.

Fruition

- Experiences lead to interests and preferences
- Interactions lead to relationships
- Exertion leads to abilities
- Practice leads to development
- Neglect leads to atrophy
- Dubious exertions lead to dubious properties (culminating in psychic susceptibility through negative mental training and practices)
- Perversion leads to psychosomatic complaints.

All those connections are unrelated to any outside judgment, influence or intervention.

EVOLUTION, EDUCATION AND SELF-DEVELOPMENT; DEVELOPMENT AIMS

Our development continues across lifetimes. Three kinds of process play a role: evolution, education and self-development.

Evolution is natural development from continuous experience in challenging circumstances. We are not spectators looking at our lives. We make decisions, exert ourselves and take risks. We bump and hurt ourselves. We work or dance or make love. We learn from our experiences, even when we are unaware of it. We may avoid experiences, we may shield ourselves from new experiences with prejudices and ideologies and we may prefer to get stuck in the rut. The postulates mentioned earlier, like ingrained, mechanical commitments, arrest our personal evolution by imprisoning us in fixed formulas.

But there is no escape from experience: avoidance, flight, repetition and shielding in themselves also lead to more experience. Even suicide provides experience. We have an innate drive to gain experience. When circumstances remain the same we get bored and look for new stimuli. Although this may lead to passive consumption reactions such as addiction, there is a general powerful drive pushing us on to new experiences. Curiosity, restlessness and a desire for variation are evolutionary drives. Experience is the source, the driver and the destiny of our evolution.

A second process is *education*, comprising all forms of support and influence from more developed people, our fellow 'evoluees'. Education may vary from noncommittal suggestions to powerful interventions we can hardly withstand. Education through lives is mainly helpful in reviewing the past life and in preparing for the new life with a life plan.

The third process is *self-development*. Freedom begins with unrestrained impulses. Self-development begins primitively, in incarnating in a hurry or disregarding advice. Then comes makeshift planning and ultimately self-development, culminating in the sovereign shaping of personal destiny. This transcends self-development by contributing to others and society. When we develop, we emancipate: we make choices and we are responsible for them.

The wealth of individual goals and pedagogic, therapeutic and correctional karmic processes, are anchored in five general educational aims. The most fundamental aims of development seem to be *intelligence, morality* and *competence*. The 'light being' in the experiences of the clinically dead emphasises knowledge and love in the life review. Much of our development, during as well as in between lives, has to do with the development of knowledge and cognitive faculties, powers of judgment, insight, ability to see the whole picture (helicopter view) and discernment. A deep, comprehensive and realistic insight is *wisdom*, practical rather than theoretical wisdom.

The second general development aim is *morality*. This is about developing attentiveness, friendliness and good will to others, and to some extent to nature. It concerns feelings of empathy, solidarity and sympathy. Ultimately, this grows into *love*. We learn to bond with the reality around us, especially with our fellow humans. According to Allan Kardec (1857), we evolve to develop intelligence and moral sense. Usually, intelligence develops before moral sense. This is obvious: love without understanding remains sentiment. It makes us blind and so is dangerous. Love with understanding makes us see.

The third aspect is the collection of diverse abilities, skills and faculties, which differ for each person. I call the bundle of abilities built in the course of our lives *competence*. We could also call it talents.

Some people like to see themselves as driven by feelings versus others who are 'only' driven by thinking. Alfred Adler showed long ago that people often use this 'primacy of feeling' to manipulate others and to shirk responsibility. But all feelings are tied to mental images. We can elicit or dampen feelings by changing the mental imagery. People who say they just cannot help feeling in some particular way suppress their judgments and images. They cheat. People are only turned on if they turn themselves on. People who see themselves as driven by will, simply turn a blind eye to the ideas and the emotions underneath.

When developing intelligence and talents, we are tempted to neglect emotions, especially empathy. Morality is based on seeing and accepting other people as fellow beings. Morality without empathy and intelligence is just a good habit, which may turn into a bad habit in a different culture.

The effect of the bad things we did in a previous life depends much on the good things we did. Just as one light in a dark night makes a great difference, one constructive act can change the effects of many destructive acts. Lenz gives a nice example of the difference that makes during the life review (1979: 70). Wisdom without love is sterile, wisdom without competence is impotent. Intelligence with competence but without morality leads to guilt and karma, and so pushes us to develop our moral sense.

So we are reincarnating to become wise, loving and competent. But to plan a particular life, two conditional aims are added to those three evolutionary aims. The first is *karmic correction* after stagnated or distorted development: not to develop intelligence, but to heal self-inflicted stupidity; not to develop moral sense, but to heal immorality; not to develop abilities, but to correct disease and weakness. The second is the *alignment* of ourselves, our aims and our karma with the life circumstances.

DEVELOPMENT STAGES AND DEVELOPMENT DISORDERS

As mentioned in chapter 2, the Hindus distinguish four stages of human development: *kama, artha, dharma* and *moksha*. According to Huston Smith (1958), the four phases have the following characteristics.

1 *Kama* is a stage in which we consciously or unconsciously seek pleasure and avoid pain. We evolve through the experiences of pleasure and pain and we are educated through reward and punishment. Self-development is scanty. *Kama* at its best makes us connoisseurs of the pleasures in life.
2 The second stage is *artha*, in which we strive for success, in terms of possessions, influence, respect or fame. *Artha* at its best is a good life with success in all these areas.
3 The third stage is *dharma*: social and religious virtue and righteousness. Beyond success, we seek honour. We try to be a responsible citizen, a tender mother, a good family man, an honest merchant, etc. We try to make something of our own life and to contribute to society. We look back on our life in terms of what we have meant to others, whether we have left the world a little better than we found it. *Dharma* actually means law and I take this to mean voluntary obeisance to moral, human and social laws necessary for a humane world. On the *artha* level we differ more than on the *kama* level, and on the *dharma* level we differ more than on the *artha* level. It makes a big difference whether we have been a successful village grocer or the founder of an international company. There is an even greater difference between people who did their best on the community council and those who helped to end a protracted and senseless war.
4 The fourth stage is *moksha*. The most practical and probably the original meaning of the word is rising above the limitations of being incarnate. We partake of the spiritual world, but we do not need to renounce the physical world.

How do we advance from one stage to the next? The *optimistic* view trusts evolution. Satisfaction on one level drives us to the next. This resembles Maslow's hierarchy of needs: when one need has been satisfied, the higher one emerges. When we have sufficient pleasure and comfort, we get bored and want a new challenge; we move to the level of personal career and later to the level of social activity and moral criteria. And after having satisfied these needs, the need for *moksha*, for a spiritual life emerges.

In the *pessimistic* vision, advancing to the next level requires lifetimes of discipline and self-control, and the seduction of backsliding always remains. We need the help of the souls who have already reached *moksha*: Avatars, Bodhisattvas or Buddhas. In the disciplinary vision, a well-organised and civilised society stimulates people to go on to higher levels. The most difficult step is that from *dharma* to *moksha*, requiring renunciation of the world and stringent religious discipline. Moksha then means that someone is freed from this world.

The more optimistic view of *moksha* does not contradict the disciplinary vision. In the latter, our exercises to accomplish *moksha* are only more psychological and we may do them in the middle of everyday life or in merely temporary retreats.

How are the four stages of development related to the goals of intelligence, morality and competence? Surrendering to *kama* makes us sly: we have to become clever to find pleasure and avoid displeasure. *Artha* develops intelligence further because the acquisition of possessions, influence, respect and fame makes demands on energy and intelligence. With *dharma*, the scale tips over to moral sense. The two golden rules of dharma are: 'Do not unto others what you will not have them do unto you,' and 'Do unto others, what you will have them do unto you.' Our evolution stimulates us to develop intelligence, moral sense and competence, but free will remains. The most primitive form of free will is laziness. 'Sedentariness, *the* sin against the Holy Ghost!' Nietzsche called it (1889).

The numerous forms of unwillingness combined with inability (usually a lot of unwillingness and a little inability, while being convinced of the opposite) give rise to four fundamental developmental disorders:

- *Fixation*: wanting to stay where we are, getting stuck.
- *Regression* (in the sense of development psychology): wanting to return to a former stage.
- *Overstretch*: going too fast, trying to skip intermediate steps.
- *Perversion*: not developing as a human, but becoming beast-like, plant-like, thing-like, demonic or god-like.

The development from *kama* to *moksha* seems to be evolution, increasingly changing into self-development, with education and therapy all along the way. Education stimulates others in their development; therapy and correction help others to overcome fixation, regression, overstretch and perversion.

PSYCHOLOGICAL AND EDUCATIONAL CONNECTIONS BETWEEN LIVES

We find four kinds of psychological and educational connection between lives:

- Carrying over good things
  - positive inversion (externalisation)
  - precipitation.
- Responses to the life review
  - wanting to try things out again
  - wanting to do and to experience things differently
  - wanting to compensate for things
  - wanting to experience new things
- Delayed assimilation
  - replay, second chance
  - inversion of negative experiences (internalisation or 'boomerang karma')
  - indirect inversion.
- Retention and fruition of fixed will or desire
  - reinforcing postulates
  - discharging fixed intentions.

Carrying over good things When we meet consideration we tend to be considerate as well. If we receive love we tend to give love. This also happens between lives. When we look back on a life as an invalid and realise how much love and care we received, this may arouse us to care for others in our next life. This is *positive inversion* or externalisation: wanting to do good to others because others did good to us.

When psychic experiences in one life lead to physical conditions in the next life, we call that *precipitation*. Edgar Cayce gives a number of examples of women who devoted themselves to beauty in music, dance and bodily care and were themselves beautiful in their next life. Apparently, this is no reward from a karma authority, but a natural consequence. Patient endurance of an undeserved fate (not in the life plan) may lead to a surplus of energy in the next life. According to various authors, a conscientious lifestyle leads to health and beauty in a next life. According to Rudolf Steiner, patiently enduring lengthy physical suffering leads to beauty in the next life. Examples from Edgar Cayce support this idea.

Responses to the life review When we look back on our past life after death, with or without a guide, we may want to experience things again or to undergo or do things differently. We may want to make up for things or experience them ourselves. Somebody looks back in shame on a life of primitive atheism and the next time he becomes an extreme Muslim (Van Ginkel 1917: 93). This is a good example of a psychological rather than a natural connection. His reaction is a response to a personal evaluation. Because the evaluation is tainted with a negative emotion (shame), he tends to overreact (fanaticism).

Other examples: an overly protective father had deserted his family in two past lives; a workaholic discovers that a few centuries ago in Greece his family had starved to death (Goldberg 1982: 56). When soldiers look back at their lives, they are not ashamed of the violence they committed or the deaths they caused but of fanaticism and cruelty, especially if they have enjoyed it. Kardec also indicated this.

Florence McClain found that some of the young protesters of the late 1960s and the 1970s were casualties of the Second World War and Korea, while others of that time had come back eager to return to the military. A couple of the more militant of the anti-nuclear protesters were casualties of Hiroshima and Nagasaki (McClain 1986a: 131).

Homosexuality seems often to be a response to the life review. Morris Netherton found that homosexuals had usually had several previous lives in which they had been homosexual or had homosexual episodes – freely, reluctantly or forced. The key was in the life immediately preceding the first homosexual life. It usually concerns very aggressive sex with women. For example, men raid a village, kill the men, rape the women and then kill them too. While being raped beside a dying child a woman gets a knife and kills the man. Now sexual intercourse with a woman is associated with pain, bloodshed and death. The deceased man is ashamed of himself and vows he will never do that to a woman again, or rather, have it happen to himself. Homosexuality then begins as a defence mechanism. Williston and Johnstone (1983) give comparable examples of men watching their wives bleed to death in great pain while trying to give birth. The woman may scream and blame and curse her husband or lover as the cause of her misery. The man vows he will never do this to any woman again. In the first instance the guilt is never about sex itself, but about the violence. In the second instance guilt is associated with perplexity and helplessness. In both cases the women involved may make similar vows, possibly resulting in lesbianism in the next life. Impotence and frigidity may have the same origin.

Delayed assimilation usually leads to a repetition or a second chance, or else it may lead to *inversion*. After a suicide we may enter the same state of mind in a next life. A suicide with honourable motives, for example to prevent treason, does not have a repercussion. According to Edith Fiore (1978: 164), suicide may lead to an optimal desire to live in the next life. This may happen, but rarely.

Why do we accept such educational interventions, either willingly or unwillingly? Because our soul wants to undo, to conquer, the limitations, scars and imperfections of the personality. We have an in-built urge to develop. As long as that evolutionary urge remains intact, we accept bearing correcting karma.

Indirect inversions often are symbolic. Abuse and cruelty or enjoying watching abuse and cruelty, without remorse, may lead to multiple sclerosis, polio or deformity in a next life. The readings of Edgar Cayce give examples. Precipitation is also possible with both retention and inversion. Someone partially blind had abused people by his hypnotic eyes in a past life. Cayce gives examples of asthma coming from having tortured and strangled others in a past life, anaemia from spilling other people's blood in a past life and bed wetting from drowning witches. Such indirect, symbolic inversions are less effective, because the feedback is veiled. Apparently, the people involved resisted looking in the mirror, so a more constructive compensation or therapy was impossible.

Cayce also gives examples of people suffering because of their height as the result of haughtiness, superiority and contempt in a previous life. The same behaviour may also lead to being painfully short in this life. People who are ashamed when they look back at their haughtiness, may accept a life in a small body. People refusing this may end up in a large body and only afterwards realise how annoying this is. Our incarnation designers and consultants (among which we should not forget our own soul) are very creative.

The inversions from negative reactions via internalisation are well known. Gina Cerminara (1950) calls this *boomerang karma*. Someone quick to condemn others is condemned by others in his next life. Someone who exploited others is exploited. Someone who killed another's child experiences the death of his own child. A man who made his wife wear a chastity belt while he was on the Crusades becomes impotent in a later life (Cerminara 1967: 107). A man who had gouged out people's eyes becomes blind in his next life.

Such inversions are so common that they are almost synonymous with karma. But they are not a natural law. If they were, the cycle of repercussions would be endless. If someone has to be mocked now to make up for his own mocking in a previous life, the others who mock him now have to be mocked in their next life, and so on *ad infinitum*. In my opinion, this is the common educational principle, 'He that will not be advised must suffer'. If we refuse to deal with the effects of our acts on others, then we need to feel these effects ourselves sometimes. The remedial twilight existence, of which chapter 12 gave examples, is based on the same principle.

Compensation doesn't need to be personal. If we mock somebody, we don't need to be mocked by the same person. That would be a vicious circle. Besides, the mirror is far from perfect and what returns often differs. If somebody's child died because of our carelessness, our child will not necessarily die from carelessness next time around, let alone from the same kind of carelessness or from the same other person. That death may already deeply affect us during our life, leading to care or worry or becoming overprotective or wanting to make it up to other children. Or we may close ourselves off and 'He that will not be advised must suffer' becomes operative to prevent our degradation. Then our child may die either through somebody else's carelessness or through our own.

Retention and fruition of fixed will or desire If we have confided in someone who betrayed us afterwards and then resolved, from the bottom of our heart, that we will never show our feelings again, that resolution may continue to operate in following lives, even if working against us. The consequences of such 'postulates' depend on their formulation. A man who witnesses his wife dying in childbirth bearing a dead child, resolves 'never to go through this again'. In his present life he is impotent (Goldberg 1982: 71). Another impotent man relives a hunting episode with a friend. By accident, he shoots his friend, who dies, calling him an imbecile, wishing he had never met him and refusing to be touched by him. In this life the deceased friend is the man's wife and his reluctance to touch his wife translates into impotence (Goldberg 1982: 79). This is an example of registering somebody else's words as a postulate. Another example of such a postulate is the girl who is murdered while being told that, being a woman, she is just stupid and irresponsible (Hubbard 1958).

Frigidity and impotence can be found among people who have sworn to celibacy in a past life, as well as in people who broke this vow. Either the vow remains effective or breaking the vow causes such shame or such fear of breaking the vow again that we want to prevent this at all costs. Women may have suffered so much in labour or with a primitive abortion that they want to quit the propagation business altogether. This may lead to impotence and frigidity, but also to lesbianism or homosexuality in a next life. Here, too, we have to look for personal reactions, not for impersonal mechanisms.

The diversity and unexpectedness of the effects of karmic causes is clear from the following example, (Kelsey and Grant 1967: 63).

During the War, Joan Grant is nursing a soldier who has been wounded in the foot. For months the wound refuses to heal. She has an impression of the soldier's previous life. He is a Catholic priest who prays incessantly to receive the holy stigmata (the bleeding hands and feet as a sign that he has attained mystic union with Christ's suffering). His subconscious took the wound in his foot to be an answer to his prayers. It is almost funny to read how she tricks his subconscious and makes the wound heal.

Linear postulates lead to the recurrence of particular situations, for example, never showing your feelings again, doing everything that is asked of you, etc.

Antithetical postulates are intentions to do the opposite from now on. They result in a pendulum reaction. Gina Cerminara devotes a chapter to this subject (Cerminara 1967: 174). Warriors storm a valley, kill the men and take the women prisoner. One warrior has several women, but their eternal quarrels get on his nerves, so he resolves firmly to never have more than one woman again (Cerminara 1967: 176). In the next life, he marries the first one available and gets so frustrated that in the following life he may try one after another. The pendulum swings back and forth, until the oscillations get smaller.

A weak, unattractive woman in Palestine prays for strength and beauty. During the Crusades she was a powerful man and in the American colonies an attractive woman. However, as a beautiful woman she was so vain and proud that in this life she is small and weak again, with strong feelings of inferiority. (Cerminara 1967: 178)

We may also overreact at the life review, especially when we look back unguided.

A remigrant finds out that in his last ten lives he alternated between extremes of sanctimonious and licentious behaviour. Watching himself fluctuate from one extreme to the other, he becomes annoyed and perplexed to the point of dismissing physical life. Suddenly the incredibly vivid face of a woman appears explaining to him that eroticism is an elemental force, provoking interaction and intimate involvement and so may develop conscience, altruism, benevolent concern. Until then he had seen sex and spirituality as separate worlds, not knowing how to choose between them. (Whitton & Fisher 1986: 73)

Pieter Langedijk and Agnes van Enkhuizen wrote (1987a) that the spiritually inclined are often born among down-to-earth people, to be confronted with the facts of daily life. Or they have to learn about them, after a lifetime of theory and superiority, having taught and berated common people from their ivory tower.

INDETERMINISM

As mentioned above, Ian Stevenson found many similarities between the past and present personalities of the child cases he examined. However, he rarely found karmic connections. The new family and new living conditions appeared to have no relation to the past life. The apparent reason for this is the absence of a life plan in falling asleep, hanging about, wandering and haunting. No reflection, no self-education, no teaching. When planning is absent, coherence will be weak. Characteristics simply continue and there are some repercussions and some fruition brought into a life unconnected to the previous one.

In most children's cases Stevenson found that one person knew the family of the preceding life as that of the present life. That person didn't need to know that a child had been born with past-life memories. Considering the afterdeath experiences of hanging about, wandering around and haunting, the soul may follow, either consciously or unconsciously, living people. Then the relationship between both lifetimes is not karmic, but the consequence of natural needs and affinities until the soul finds a pregnant woman. This fits in with the experiences mentioned in chapter 11 and the tendency of wandering souls to identify with something in the physical world, as noted in chapter 12. This also explains the short intermissions, the limited distance between place of death and place of rebirth and the absence of karma.

Partial intervention may only determine where we will be born. As mentioned before, the Chinese man who remembered a life as a fox, recalled the 'Lord of the Other World', saying to him: 'You are not a sinner, take a human body.' After a life as a beggar he died when he was 20. The same lord said to him: 'You will be a slave. The denomination is not beautiful, but you will not suffer hunger and misery' (Penkala 1972).

Wijeratne's case is an example of negative somatic precipitation in a child (Stevenson 1966: 149). Wijeratne was a boy with deformations on the right side of his chest and his right arm. Between the ages of 2 and 5 he talked a lot to himself about a past life and said that his malformed arm was a punishment because in his past life he had stabbed his wife to death with this arm. Francis Story correctly notes that this case differs from most birthmark cases because the deformity it appears to be a punishment. Most birthmarks are what he calls psychokinetic consequences of people having internalised their physical wounds after their death (Story 1975: 277). This relates to the psycho-plastic character of the psychic body (see chapter 11). Linked to a conclusion such as 'This is how I am' or 'This is how I have become', the image may be engraved in the growing foetus.

Thiang San Kla was a Siamese sergeant, claiming to be his uncle Phoh reborn. He was born three months after Phoh died, but had a large birthmark that corresponded exactly to the knife wound Phoh died from. Phoh had a festering wound on his right big toe. Thiang's right big toe was slightly deformed. Phoh had been tattooed on both hands and feet. Thiang was born with tattoo-like markings on hands and feet.

This last detail is interesting because it indicates that the self-image is decisive. Skin marks, therefore, do not imply that the body has been entered early in its development. Ravi Shankar's mother noticed his stigma (a 'cut' in the neck) only when he was three or four months old (Stevenson 1966: 92).

Child cases show a lot of retention, some aspects of repercussion and incidental precipitation or some other psychological or psychosomatic reaction, and, without a life plan, much that is undefined or accidental.

If we incarnate mostly because of karmic relations with others and these others are in a particular culture in a particular social class for reasons of their own, then a birth in their vicinity will entail the same culture and the same social class: living conditions possibly unrelated to our own past lives. Each culture, each situation has its own openings and limitations for our development. This is a natural consequence of social development and not of our personal past lives.

Even well considered incarnation choices have consequences unrelated to our own direction.

FREE CHOICE: SUSPENSION, SELECTION, PREFERENCE AND MISSION

We cannot do everything at once. Each life presents only so many opportunities to work off our karma. That is the difference between the general karmic fund of repercussions, complications in relationships and moral obligations and the karmic package for the coming life. This package is also called 'ripe karma', an unfortunate expression, because it implies a purely natural process. Besides maturing, other psychological and educational factors play a role, as well as adaptation to the particular body and the circumstances of the coming life. We have to postpone settling some karmic accounts. Or we set priorities. In education, overload is well known: wanting to teach too much at once. The geography project has to teach the children geography, accuracy, group work, composition, awareness of the problems in the Third World, newspaper reading and improvement of the pupil–teacher relationship. Karmic overload is like teaching a wounded person to use his right arm while his left leg is being amputated, his head wound is still fresh and his blood production needs stimulation.

Morris Netherton describes karma as 'a debt to ourselves, to be repaid by us at a time we choose and in a way we choose ourselves' (Netherton & Shiffrin 1978: 184). This description is correct, but underestimates the dependence on educational conditions and the social aspect. We may well feel a debt to others.

Another freedom is choosing on the basis of our own wants and preferences. We feel affinity with people, circumstances, activities, peoples or cultures. We choose from our fund of experience, relations and capabilities. We choose who and what we associate ourselves with and by whom we want to be guided. Or we choose a calling or task that contributes to a wider development.

Fewer than half Wambach's respondents could answer her question about their aim in life. The causal processes of retention, repercussion and fruition affect them, but do not decide the coming life. Retention, repercussion and fruition determine the material and tools with which they work and from which they choose.

			Spiritual growth and helping others	27%
Evolution	Education	Freedom	Special developments	12%
			Learning love and compassion	18%
			Karmic relations and obligations	18%
			Supplementary experience	25%

Natural evolution gradually moves into education. Education gradually moves into self-development. Self-realisation gradually changes into contributing to the evolution, education and self-development of others. Unfortunately, the way Wambach published her material prevents analysis of interrelations between, for example, self-development and helping others as a goal or planning and actively preparing the coming incarnation. They probably correlate strongly.

Most of the people who could not answer the question about aims will have had lives that were more causally determined. Eighteen percent (or less than half) had to work on karmic obligations and relations. Their karma will be educational or self-educational exercises rather than simple repercussion of traumas in relationships.

The life aims that Wambach's respondents mentioned clarify the relationships between causal, psychological and free patterns. Most probably, direct repercussions don't lead to encounters with the same people who traumatised us or whom we traumatised – unless something truly personal was involved. Phobias and postulates are impersonal. Of Wambach's group, 23 percent felt no compulsion but could plan freely. Many reported that they chose a mission or applied for certain tasks. So this freedom is certainly not limited to advanced souls such as the leaders of humankind, as theosophists have assumed.

FREEDOM AND ARBITRARINESS

We may incarnate unplanned, unprepared, on the spur of the moment, without supervision. Our new life then will have little connection with our preceding life, not as a result of sleepy dependence on natural processes and chance circumstances, but as a result of impulsivity. This may lead to noncommital, drifting lives or to lives too arduous for us. This also happens to stubborn people who, against all advice, overstretch themselves. Those who don't want to be advised, must suffer. However, the will of a stubborn pupil must also be respected. Breaking our will is worse than letting us fail. Decent incarnation guides know that.

When we prepare our life, deep and lasting wishes and resolutions from our preceding life are retained, but supplemented and often supplanted by choices and preferences built up during the intermission. Edgar Cayce gives an example of a diseased relationship between a dominant man and an oppressed woman. This relationship was repeated throughout a number of lives and kept getting worse. 'Not only did her weak subjectiveness cause her misery, but it made her husband a monster of egoism. There was cowardice under the mask of patient and gentle suffering.' In the present life she was able to break this vicious circle because she had developed more during her intermission than her husband had.

Education or development during the intermission loosens the attachment to our past. Apparently, we may learn to plan our own coming life better during the intermission. After death an archdeacon who had believed a bit in reincarnation during his life was hardly surprised to find out that he had lived many times before and would live many times again. What did surprise him were special training courses for the subject. There, people learned to analyse their past lives, to arrive at conclusions on the basis of this and to make plans (Shirley 1924: 161).

Our preferences influence the choice of development aims, the kind of work we want to do, the role we want to fulfil and, especially, the people we want to meet, and live and work with. We want to do something again or to experience it from a different side. Social developments too may influence our preferences, when we as discarnates keep track of them. Some of us bide our time until we can make the contribution we want and have the role we want. Moreover, we often have preferences for peoples or cultures. There are hundreds of examples of people in, for example, Britain, the US or France, who have lived several times before in that same country. Many people seem so faithful – or bonded by habit – to their gender or their field of occupation (such as trade or agriculture or religion or medicine) that they hardly choose. A Jewish life may lead to more Jewish lives, a Japanese life to more Japanese lives. One peculiar finding by Wambach is that of many Americans suddenly having a life in, for example, Asia in the last life before this one, after a whole series of European and American lives (Wambach 1978: 131).

For most people, the choice of gender is derivative. In cases of spontaneous memories (seldom with a life plan) 13 percent had changed gender, 4 percent of the men remembered a previous life as a woman and 24 percent of the women remembered a previous life as a man. In regression cases (usually with a life review and life preparation) 80 percent of remigrants appear to have changed gender at least once. Here, too, the main conclusion is: patterns, but no fixed rules. A few of Wambach's examples (1979: 75–7):

- *'I did not choose my sex. It was just time to go back, so I took what was available.'*
- *'My sex was not important for my purpose.'*
- *'I chose to be a man because that would make it easier to participate in the advance of science.'*
- *'I preferred to become a woman, but I chose to be a man anyway because the trials would be greater.'*
- *'I wanted to be a woman because my female half is better able to love, is more expressive and has a better sense of herself.'*
- *'I wanted to be a woman, so I would be better able to give.'*
- *'I chose to be a woman because my parents would accept that more easily.'*
- *'I chose to be a woman because my partner wanted us to have the same sex as we had in 1503.'*

People who fall asleep after their death, or hang around, wander or haunt, often incarnate in the vicinity of where they died, even if it was far from their place of birth, in a land where they had only stayed temporarily, and outside of personal considerations. Think of the examples of the Burmese children who remember dying in the Second World War as an American pilot and a Japanese soldier. Incomplete dying often makes a reincarnation in the country of death natural. After dying completely and waking up, the desire to return to the same country or the same people depends on personal preference and 'faithfulness'. If we consider it important or pleasant to be Jewish, the chance is greater that we will be Jewish in our next life, from either a rational or an instinctive choice. People differ in their need for continuity and change. A scientist may want to bring out a different aspect of herself the next time and become a rock star or a jet pilot.

LIFE PLAN AND COURSE OF LIFE; THREE REINCARNATION PATTERNS

In regressions, most people are fairly aware of their condition after their death. They look back on their past life, continue to learn and prepare their new life deliberating with others and hearing advice. Capabilities, attitudes, preferences and so on continue. Traumas and postulates have left their repercussions and the influence of psychological reactions with more or less drastic educational interventions continues. The length of the intermission differs considerably, but is seldom less than a few years and averages about 60 years. Helen Wambach found a 52-year average, and Karl Muller, using a smaller and more diverse sample, slightly under 80 years.

A reincarnation process likely to be much more common, but less frequently found in regressions, is of people with little or no awareness of their inter-mission: of sleep, hanging about or wandering. The best examples of this are the child cases Ian Stevenson researched. They experience being born as entering a foetus or as just sliding off something or being sucked into something. The intermissions between lives are usually shorter, varying from a few months to almost ten years. They hardly have karma in the usual sense of the word, because psychological or educational considerations in preparing the new life are lacking. Evolution is the general pattern: gaining experience, condensing this into a slowly growing understanding, humanity and competence, and sometimes the repercussions of traumatic experiences. Ultimately, experience leads to more awareness, until people remain more and more awake between lives and more receptive to contacts with other people.

When we learn and develop more independently, we get the urge to do some real work: contributing to the development of others, incarnate or discarnate. This resembles finishing school, doing an apprenticeship and getting a job. We learn to help others to evaluate their past life and to plan a new one. We have less urge to return and become more selective in choosing a new life. I suspect, but the scant data makes this no more than an educated guess, that then the average intermission between lifetimes is a little under 200 years, with large differences. Some people will reincarnate more often, others less, depending on the circumstances on earth and what kinds of people are needed.

So, there are three populations as far as reincarnation is concerned:

1 *Population I*: General evolution; no individual life plan; undirected and short intermission; a new life close to the old in time and distance.
2 *Population II*: Personal development; a personal life plan with mainly personal development goals and personal settlement of karmic relations; some review; some consultation and some foresight in the intermission; awareness of the intermission; personal ties with other people.

3 *Population III*: Personal contribution to greater developments; personal learning and working objectives; conscious deliberation in the intermission; at times a guide for incarnates; a new life linked to those of friends and associates; reincarnation as a free choice.

In practice, there may be exceptions, various shades and combinations of these three patterns. Someone from population II or III may hang around after a particular death and be reborn within a few years. Someone from population I may receive personal help and some preparation for his new life, as the example of the Chinese slave shows.

We think about our coming life and make a life plan. This life plan may contain work aims and certainly will have personal development aims. In these personal goals we will consider our karma: traumas, postulates, complicated relationships, negative psychological reactions and remedial interventions.

Karma is nothing more or less than the liabilities of past lives that we carry with us. On the asset side is *dharma*: developed intelligence, moral sense and competence; and relations consisting of respect, acceptance and trust. After the 'profit and loss statement' of each life, we have an adjusted karma–*dharma* balance, at least in populations II and III. The life plan may contain global or detailed indications of when karmic items will come up and when particular abilities will wake up. We then have a *karma–dharma clock* as a part of our life plan. I know only one example that describes this mechanism explicitly. A remigrant relives how he prepared his life, working on the things he wanted to change. He worked with a piece of machinery, 'a sort of clockwork instrument into which you could insert certain parts in order for specific consequences to follow', planning his forthcoming life on earth (Whitton & Fisher 1986: 43).

I suspect that *dharma* as well as karma is etheric potential, the karma potential obstructing, delaying or obscuring us, the *dharma* radiating light or providing power. Think of intuitive talents such as mana and charisma.

In the life plan, a part of the assets and a part of the liabilities are taken along to a coming life; in accounting terms: fixed and liquid assets; in theosophical terms: not all karma is ripe karma. *Dharma* and karma we can personally select – except the karmic consequences of lifetimes that have not been reviewed properly after death. Elaboration of the life plan begins with the choice of parents, determining largely our constitution and the environment we are born into. The course of the whole or the remaining pregnancy and the birth also influence our starting conditions.

Choices made in the course of our life are about whether we do something, how we do it and to what we respond and how we respond. The review determines how we work out our life and so what consequences this life has for us. It differs depending on whether a difficult life is ended in hate, with a shrug or with compassion.

In population II, guides do much of the planning and life aims are mainly about personal development. In the absence of guides, in emotional or intellectual seclusion, usually a one-sided, impulsive and roughly sketched life plan follows an incomplete review. The most important differences among people in population II are the weight of the karmic burden, the energy of the dharmic potential and the wisdom of their guides.

Souls of population I have neither a life plan nor a life review. They do not choose their parents, but are naturally drawn to the available foetus of a more or less fitting mother. It is probably the condition of the vehicle of vitality or etheric body of both mother and returning soul that determine attraction.

Whitton (1986: 45) says that people committed to their own evolution, study and prepare themselves. Uncommitted people will often fall asleep after their preceding life has been reviewed. 'Materialistic' souls (on the borderline between population I and II) often rush back to a body when they realise their discarnate state.

Help from guides, colleagues or friends may continue during our life as inspiration and guidance. When we deviate from the planned course of life, they may remind us silently about our life plan. More spectacular interventions have led to the notion of guardian angels, guardian saints and spiritual guides. Thus, our life plan affects us during our life in three ways:

- As forgotten prenatal post-hypnotic suggestions urging us to do something or avoid something in reaction to particular signals.

- As meaningful 'coincidences' of meeting people, arriving somewhere or finding books.

- As inspirations and intuitive impulses.

Many people are convinced of this, so much so that they see everything as preordained. The evidence shows that no life plan is specified completely. The plan presents the patterns; we fill in the details here.

A woman, who was raped, discovered that the rape was not planned, but that her karmic script indicated that she would make herself vulnerable to a random personal tragedy that would effect a great change in her life. (Whitton & Fisher 1986: 47)

Another woman sees that her life is planned in detail up to her early thirties, in order to overcome negative karmic influences. After that, she can practically decide what to do with her life. People can also forget or refuse to plan, often because of a reluctance to reincarnate.

'I originally planned to be a doctor. I started in that direction, but I did something very different. I've always felt a little guilty about it. But I see now that being a doctor was not the best choice for growing into my blueprint. Somewhere along the line my subconscious must have realized it wasn't the best route for me to take.' (McClain 1989: 129)

A man gets a father who has done him wrong in several lifetimes. In a situation in which he can easily let his father die he decides to get help. Later he himself has an accident and is lucky to survive. However, his life plan had assumed he would let his father die and that the accident would kill him. After the accident the plan was at an end. He learned that 'sketchy plans for future lives had been brought forward to operate in the current life' (Whitton & Fisher 1986: 45).

According to Whitton and Fisher this happens more often than not (1986: 99). 'There are also people who appear to be placed precariously between destiny and fate, between scripting their lives and taking the stage as impromptu players. They have a plan, but the plan is open to an inordinate amount of improvisation' (1986: 99). Applying *dharma* and avoiding karma is good work. But producing *dharma* and settling karma is the real thing. Evolution throughout incarnations leads rather to fertile contribution than to sterile contemplation. A good plan before life is a great asset. Decisiveness and responsibility during life are even better.

And it can go wrong. We can go wrong. Downward lines are possible. Nobody forces us to evolve. When we really want to sabotage ourselves, we can. The Loehr–Daniels readings are the only source openly discussing the sometimes irrevocable degradation of souls (Roberts 1987). Graham gives one example (1976: 142).

There seemed to be a deterioration of consciousness that carried over from one life to another. Most importantly, this case tends to give substance to a statement that a colleague of mine once made regarding a similar case: 'It must have taken more than one life to get that bad!' In my experience, serious psychological problems all have a record that extends into the distant past and this record contains the roots of serious problems. For example, there was the episode of the congenitally deformed body, suggesting that the mental patterns for a healthy body were damaged. The severe confusion, possible hallucination and hint of possession in the current life seem to be the result of severe abuse to the mind and emotions in this life and in several of the previous ones. The mental damage of both alcoholism and hateful rebelliousness seems to be cumulative. Dr Leichtman's direct investigation into the mechanism of consciousness verifies this matter.

But most of us stumble along. Till we discover we have become dancers, inexhaustible.

FURTHER READING

The literature contains many general considerations of karma. In the esoteric visions, reincarnation and karma are inseparable. References to these are given at the end of chapter 3. Relatively the best book is by Virginia Hanson (1975). A first attempt at refining the concept of karma, using concrete cases, is the book by Gina Cerminara (1950), based on the life readings of Edgar Cayce. In *Predestined Love* (1988) Dick Sutphen presents reasonable views on karma. I think his analyses in his next book (1989) are more sloppy and at some points inaccurate.

The work of Ian Stevenson gives important insights in the incarnation processes of population I. Helen Wambach (1979) is important. Joan Grant and Denys Kelsey, Thorwald Dethlefsen, Morris Netherton, Edith Fiore and Bruce Goldberg give examples of past-life therapy regressions that contain the life review or life preview. Joel Whitton (1986) especially gives important examples. Much in this chapter has been fed by my own experiences and those of fellow-therapists.

Fourteen

THE SOUL AND ITS PERSONALITIES

To believe in reincarnation has it pleasant sides. Our good-bye to this world is not final. We will meet again the people to whom we feel close; we have more than one chance, etc. But to what extent is it really us who had past lives and who will have next lives? To what extent are we different in our different lives and to what extent are we the same?

IDENTITY AS SELF-IMAGE

In our daily life, we are sometimes ourselves, sometimes not and sometimes we are not sure. How we experience ourselves depends on our thoughts and feelings, our physical condition, other people, the circumstances, our age. Sometimes we are quick-tempered, sometimes calmness personified. One moment we may say, 'I am cheerful. I am hungry.' The next moment, 'I want to stop. I am dead tired.'

Sometimes our self-image shifts considerably. We thought we were clumsy and now it turns out we are dexterous. We thought we were misunderstood loners and suddenly it turns out we are popular. We thought we were lucky and suddenly we have a streak of bad luck. We thought we were clumsy with girls and now we know we are homosexual.

To say 'I' now, differs from saying it ten years ago. In another ten years we will have changed again. Ten years ago, we could say: 'I am insecure. I have acne. I am good at French. I do not have a boyfriend yet. I love my father.' In ten years' time we might say: 'I am divorced. I have two children. I love my job. I have contact lenses. I have fallen in love again.'

Stage hypnotists can make people believe they are chickens or famous singers – or even that they are famous chicken singers. Similarly, our day-to-day identity, our normal self-image, may have become interspersed with almost hypnotic suggestions by ourselves and others. We may talk of delusions or self-deceit and in serious cases of megalomania or paranoia. Psychiatrists and psychologists know all about identity problems (apart from their own identity problems). The old adage 'know thyself' implies that our self-image usually contains mystifications. Our identification also changes with our experience of success or failure (a basic theme in Alfred Adler's Individual Psychology), with our experiences of satisfaction and frustration (a basic theme in Freudian psychoanalysis), with the growth of understanding or perplexity, and with our physical condition.

The picture is even more complicated. We also have differing and sometimes conflicting identities at the same time. Faust's lament, *Zwei Seelen, ach, wohnen in meiner Brust!* ('Two souls, alas, live in my breast!'), is the classic example of this. Transactional Analysis speaks of the Parent, the Adult and the Child in each of us as three sides of our 'I'. In the Parent, we identify with others whom we see or saw as our superiors. In puberty, we may idolise other examples and identify ourselves with heroes, whether from the past, from the silver screen or living around the corner. In *Play it Again, Sam*, Woody Allen tries to identify himself with Humphrey Bogart, and we may identify in turn with Woody Allen.

A Jerusalem hospital has a special intake for Christian tourists who get smashed, only to discover that they have been Jesus or John the Baptist, and for Jewish tourists who find out they have been King David. And now there are past-life regressions to help us identify with interesting or satisfying lifetimes.

Besides all these changes, inner conflicts and identifications with others, we have much inside that we do not realise: the subconscious. The subconscious is a chapter, or rather a library, in itself. Our life may even split into different strands of experience with different subpersonalities. One of the first books about the multiple personality syndrome was *Sybil* (Schreiber 1973). To some extent, everybody's personality is a community of relatively independent parts. We may be aggressive in business and a patient and friendly father – or the reverse. Psychotherapy uses this community in Ego-state Therapy (Watkins 1979; Edelstein 1981). It is also found in Gestalt Therapy and Psychosynthesis.

Finally we may have loss of memory. Many people cannot recall large chunks of their present life. Maybe we can't remember the times we were angry or the times we had to endure scorn. Parts of our experience and our personality remain 'underground'. When subpersonalities combine with loss of memory and emerge uncontrolled, we near psychosis.

Our personality is like a family, members of which may interact, consolidate or furcate. We have sensitive and insensitive members, older and younger ones, conceited wiseacres, vague copies of other people, black sheep and criminals who are seldom at home (at least, in most of us). That a soul is an individual, an indivisible entity, may ultimately be true. It is certainly true for our body. That persons are individuals, indivisible entities, is a myth.

PATHOLOGICAL SELF-IMAGES

We have a healthy identity when our subpersonalities live together as a harmonious and considerate family; when we are parent, child and adult simultaneously; when our male and female sides are balanced (preferably a man in the lead in a male body and a woman in a female body). Our self-image becomes pathological when the various family members ignore each other or even forget each other (for example in the case of Sybil) or when suppressed identities break into the parental home. Even without obsession we may legally be psychotic: unaccountable.

Many people see their 'Higher Self' as their perfect self, able only to reveal itself partially. Such people populate sects or adhere to noble world-views. Their ideal of humanity is to lay off the all too human and become a kind of angel. To me this is evolutionary overstretch: not wanting to be who you are, but who you think you ought to be. An angel image is a shining robot identity, a mechanical and infantile attempt to rise above the reality of the world and ourselves. Successful identification leads to inhuman robots, unapproachable people, smiling, caught in their self-righteousness, play-acting exaltedly in their own decorated little heaven. Their inherent morbidity shows in the suffocating atmosphere for outsiders. People with sufficient self-hypnosis see the world as being light. Pain, sickness, doubt, misery, meanness and hopelessness are absent or unreal, imaginations of the as yet unawakened soul. When the self-delusion is a less potent, the exterior world is dangerous: full of tempters, false Messiahs (from other clubs), cynics, blockheads and sleepwalkers. The outside world may also be dark: the world is a dangerous and bad place, a hell even. With even weaker self-hypnosis we have to acknowledge our own imperfections. Then we become actors in the classic melodrama 'oh, woe is me', yearning for the angel in us (or outside us) and eternally struggling with the beast or devil in us. An overview of the non-human identities we may assume is given in Table 8.

When we identify with something superhuman, we ignore or suppress the subhuman, the animal. The animal within us then degenerates. Powerful

Table 8 Non-human identities

	Angel	Devil	
	HUMAN		
	Plant	Animal	
Robot	Thing	Stone	

personalities who are ashamed of their weaker and 'lower' subpersonalities deny them entrance. Some people fight with a raging wolf that is parts of themselves, instead of calming it and turning it into a faithful and watchful dog. The exorcised animal becomes a monster; the accepted animal becomes a totem, sometimes a pet. Wanting to ascend into the light creates the suction of darkness. A concentration camp inmate may naturally think of his wife back home as an angel. A torture victim may naturally experience the world as hell. Only self-made heavens and hells are pathological. All kinds of projections, shifts and reaction mechanisms may happen. In Victorian times, boys might dream of angelic girls and feel themselves to be masturbating beasts. Life is difficult. And that is just what makes us grow up. The imperfect is the womb of the perfect; the permanent grows out of the transient, peace out of war, health out of sickness, calm out of nervousness, wisdom out of folly.

Next to disassociation and inflation, the most important identity diseases are: depersonalisation, derealisation and what I will call 'deseparation'.

Depersonalisation means losing our sense of I while staying fully conscious, no longer feeling an identity, a personality. The memory of 'having been around' does not bring back the feeling of 'being there'. We are an empty bottle of fleeting thoughts and colourful shadows. *Derealisation* works the other way round. We experience ourselves as surrounded by and trapped in, unreality. Everything is decor, cardboard, grey paste with the bewildering, disgusting, wholly impossible pretension that it is real. Jean-Paul Sartre calls it *La Nausée*. Solipsism, the doctrine that only I exist and that others are just apparitions of my own consciousness, is the intellectualised dummy of *derealisation*.

Mysticism transcends our human self-image by identification with an object, another person, other living beings or a landscape. We may even transcend the separation between ourselves and the world around us, pouring ourselves out over the world, becoming one with all (thus, with God), the *unio mystica*, the mystic unity. Clinically speaking, such a state resembles depersonalisation or derealisation. In the first state we no longer experience our own reality, in the second we no longer experience the reality of the other and in the third we no longer experience any separation between ourselves and the other. A clinical translation of the *unio mystica* is *deseparation*: the disappearance of separateness. Propagators of deseparation prefer to become one with the world, with God or with everyone and seldom with their wife, their neighbour or the cat across the street. A tree or another being or object without danger of responding – or not responding – to their passion for oneness is more acceptable. In truly intimate human relationships, moments of healthy and valuable deseparation may occur. It can be of the most attractive ingredients of sexual intercourse, though people are often more interested in losing themselves than in finding another.

Our identity, our being ourselves, our 'I', then, is not a fixed and indivisible fact, but rather the result of shifting identification processes, open to influences and arbitrariness. Identification is a natural and essential characteristic of our consciousness. It has its own morphology and its own pathology. In depersonalisation, identification halts, resulting in an identity 'nil', while our body and consciousness remain intact. In practice, our body awareness anchors our sense of self. Usually, we experience ourselves spatially in our body with the focus in our head, behind our eyes.

OUR DISCARNATE IDENTITY, LARGER SELF AND LIFE PLAN

Crookall's work and regression experiences show that after complete release from the body and waking up well, we are free from confusion, inhibition and defect, but not all-knowing and infallible. Many deceased who communicate with us admit that and yet forget it. Discarnate people, feeling free and having easy access to much information, tend to be over-enthusiastic.

Fully awake discarnates usually present themselves as they were best in the incarnate state, but adapting to the subject they consider and the people they meet. Immediately after death, most take on the appearance of the last time they felt good, and later of the age and the condition in which they felt best. Still later, many assume an aspect less tied to their past life. In general they appear to others in the form most familiar to them. When interested in subjects that particularly concerned them in a particular life, they may take on the personality of that lifetime. Thus, the self-image of a discarnate is both more flexible and more stable than that when incarnate. The personality remains untrammelled. People who get stuck in the etheric twilight area indulge in their pet emotions and pet thoughts and pet environments. Or they sink into their own dreams – sometimes nightmares.

When we have truly become ourselves, we have a freed personality. Theosophists speak of the Higher Self, but this term implies a separate entity from our ordinary or lower self. Some talk about 'my Higher Self' and 'my lower self'. Like 'my self', these expressions are misleading, because they suggest identity in terms of having something rather than being it.

Many see the Higher Self as all-knowing, all-wise and never changing from the beginning to the end of incarnations. This is only partially true. Of course there is a continuity of entity. I will call this entity the 'soul' from here on. Christopher Bache (1990) first talks about the 'oversoul', but says later that just 'soul' is a better label for our essential identity throughout lifetimes and intermissions. I call 'spirit' all the phenomena of consciousness, including self-consciousness. The content and structure of this self-consciousness, the self-image, grows out of our experiences in a body. Physical, incarnate experience, much more than psychic, discarnate experience leads to awareness and self-awareness. The soul awakens and focuses itself in its incarnations. Once we have self-awareness, it can blossom out in the discarnate state. The body is the vehicle for spiritualisation. The beginning soul only has awareness thanks to the organism it inhabits, and after death it sinks into forgetfulness (falling asleep). Gradually it learns to dream after death. The dreams become more vivid; subsequently the soul awakens in meeting other real discarnate people and finally is self-aware and self-responsible.

When discarnate, we are as the personality we were in our best lifetime, but without physical limitations and with access to all our other personalities. The various personalities of the different lives resemble the various subpersonalities we know during one life. When we die, we continue the personality of the past life, but soon enough we gain access to past personalities and thus, after reviewing our past life, we grow into this larger personality, usually focused on the most aware and the most mature lifetime. This comprehensive sense of self disappears during each incarnation, as in sleep: we experience a break of consciousness, but not a break in personality.

According to the Loehr–Daniels readings, the growing number of personalities triggers a growing need for integration (Smith 1975: 233–4). That seems logical, but regressions neither confirm nor deny this.

> After a series of lifetimes, perhaps forty or fifty with a personality representing each lifetime, the soul no longer resembles one individual, but a crowd of people. Then it is time to reorganize itself back to individuality. Dr John calls the new individual produced by this reorganization a solity. The solity could, perhaps, be thought of a superpersonality, for it is created by integrating and absorbing a number of past-life personalities who have been already fully utilized . . . The solity is still just part of the soul, but it represents a much larger portion than any single personality . . . The solity does not reincarnate . . . It represents forces already developed that would prove too much for one human personality to carry.

We see the opportunity of a future life from the vantage-point of the larger self, and we design our new life based on our experiences, characteristics, development needs and preferences. At least that is the usual state of population III after a complete death experience. We know we will lose a large part of our awareness and will be able to express only a part of our abilities. In making our life plan, we draw from all the personalities of past lives. In each new life, one past lifetime provides the dominant, feeding personality, usually decisive for the character, the capabilities and often the looks of the new incarnation. Without a conscious intermission, personal formation or choice, as in population I, the dominant personality is simply the personality of the past life. With a conscious choice this may be quite different. We can reach personalities from quite a few lives back. We do have less choice in lives and episodes that carry unreleased tensions or 'karma'.

The consciousness we have in our larger personality is the consciousness of our psychic body, which Crookall calls 'psychic consciousness'. When we are shrouded in ethers, we have a dream consciousness. Apparently, there is one stage of consciousness above the 'psychic consciousness' called 'cosmic consciousness'. Whitton uses the terms 'dissociative consciousness', 'affective consciousness' and 'meta-consciousness' (Whitton & Fisher 1986: 7). His definitions do not seem very apt. His dissociative consciousness, as he defines it, is more a state of being than a state of consciousness. Out-of-body experiences may be a dissociative state, but we have a dissociative (what I called 'elliptic') consciousness only at the moment of exit or entry. Out of the body we may have either dream consciousness or psychic consciousness. A sleep consciousness is a *contradictio in terminis*. In sleep we are unconscious, while subliminal perceptions may be called subconscious. Further, Whitton's definitions of affective consciousness and metaconsciousness overlap. Affective consciousness may have 'oneness with the universe' and in metaconsciousness we lose all sense of personal identity. This is unclear terminology. I propose, therefore, to use the following terms:

unconsciousness:	sleep, loss of consciousness, catalepsy
dream consciousness:	dreams, incomplete awakening outside the body
consciousness:	perception of the outside world
self-consciousness:	self-perception within the outside world
psychic consciousness:	complete awakening outside the body, lucid and vivid dreams, higher self-consciousness, spiritual self-perception
cosmic consciousness:	permeable boundary of self and not-self, perception of larger, cosmic whole of which we are a part, without loss of personal identity.

Our present personality is more than nature and nurture. First, we have often chosen our parents, and so our genes and environment, ourselves. Second, we often have a life plan we designed or accepted, and have compiled a fund of capabilities and characteristics from our past personalities. David Cliness concludes that between three and fifteen lifetimes may influence the present life (Bache, 1990: 124). At any given moment in our life we have, besides our personality developed so far, the yet unrealised potential of our life plan. Our personality is not only what we are, but also what we want to be according to our life line. Thus, we have:

- our present personality (with a number of subpersonalities)
- our traumas and postulates (often related to problematic subpersonalities)

- the unrealised personality potential of this life
- the discarnate part of our larger personality
- the as yet unexplored potential of our soul.

Therefore, our personal development entails:

- resolving traumas and postulates
- liberating and incorporating problematic subpersonalities
- harmonising and connecting the other subpersonalities
- realisation of our life line
- contacting our larger personality
- developing more knowledge, understanding and wisdom; more morality, empathy and love; more independence, competence and creativity.

THE REALITY OF PERSONALITIES FROM PAST LIVES; PSEUDO-OBSESSIONS AND OBSESSIONS

Past lives are not mere memories, but the personalities from past lives continue to exist as such. A regression to a past life more or less animates the past personality. With a life directly related to the present life, we experience this past personality simply as an aspect of ourselves. A life that is less related we experience not unlike a lucid dream: we are as easily inside as outside.

Our soul never incarnates completely and probably remains conscious, apart from our present ego, in the discarnate personalities of our past lives. Some personalities sleep. They are empty balloons that we have to fill and wake up. After that, they return into the fold of the larger self, because their lives have been completely worked through. They have become free roles of the larger self. Other past personalities retain their own charge of undigested experiences or of dammed-up capabilities that they could not fully express in their life.

In our phobias and complexes, past personalities may blend in. Less conspicuous, but often stronger, postulates (compulsive ideas and attitudes) from past lives have seeped into our present character. In this limited sense, we may speak of a return of the same personality. *We are always a reincarnation of our soul and only partly a reincarnation of past personalities.* We can easily identify with them, but also disidentify and communicate with them, like with close family members or friends. They may mingle, even blend, but they do not get wrapped up in each other. Unless they form what the Loehr–Daniels readings call a solity.

In daily life, these past personalities may come up at different moments and in different ways. Some of us have a different face in different circumstances or behave quite differently at a different age. Many such changes come from the choreography of subpersonalities, but some may come from past lives. When we explore past lives related to our present life, we recognise themes in our present life, sometimes coinciding with a subpersonality. Psychics and mediums also imply that personalities of past lives can stand on their own. Chapter 2 mentioned the African who had a pleasant and easy life because he was always advised by his best friend – himself in a past life. Past lives that are released and integrated are our best guides.

In séances contacting the dead, some spirits announce that they are the past personality of somebody who is now living and want to help the present personality. This occurs without the latter knowing anything about it. Chapter 4 mentioned the example of the spirit who appeared during a séance and said that she was the previous incarnation of a woman who at that moment was sleeping peacefully in another country. She said she often wandered around in a nunnery where she had died in a previous life. When asked whether the ordinary personality knew about this, she answered it was just a vague dream and a certain feeling (Muller 1970: 172). Here, we see a previous personality that only appears when the present personality is asleep.

The negative example of ill-integrated personalities is that of 'pseudo-obsession', where we carry a past personality in our body or aura, not integrated into the larger personality. Often it was a short, traumatic life that never arrived at full self-awareness or in which self-awareness was lost, crippled or stultified. Pseudo-obsessions usually produce shifting psychosomatic complaints. The Brazilian spiritualist doctors regard autism as a symptom of pseudo-obsession. I would add to this anorexia nervosa, bulimia, persistent migraines and phantom pains together with emotional instability.

Past-life therapy regresses to that traumatic life, and then the therapist leads the haunting, restless personality through a complete dying experience, guided by the present personality or, if necessary, the therapist. After that, the pseudo-obsessor becomes an integrated 'family member', either in the present life or in the larger self. Healing a pseudo-obsession is interesting, satisfying and often has spectacular results: a revolution in general well-being and a dramatic disappearance of the psychosomatic complaints.

Such unintegrated, haunting past personalities may sporadically disturb ordinary age regressions, when a different personality suddenly appears to manifest itself. This may scare the inexperienced therapist because it looks like an obsession. To find out if the intervening personality is a past life or an attachment, is rather easy.

A Brazilian had worked hard for his family all his life and has put everything aside for them. When he was 63 years old, after an accident, he started to get nervous and to reproach his wife for adultery. The family laughed about it since they found it a silly assumption. However, he became more and more agitated and finally psychotic. He became aggressive towards his wife and later also to other people and had to be kept under constant surveillance. Finally, he was put into an asylum. After a few days of agitation he was calm and friendly to everybody again. After three months, he was sent home healed. But there all the symptoms returned immediately. He wanted to beat his wife and screamed day and night. He was brought back to the asylum, where he became calm and happy again for two months.

A psychic reading said that in his previous life he had been a rich Spanish merchant. He was a widower with a number of older children when he got married to a young girl who had lived a carefree life as an embroiderer for the bullfighters. He caught her in the act of adultery and sent her out of the house. Later, he met her in the company of one of his sons, when she mocked him. This resulted in a fight with the son, who was seriously wounded. He forgave the son and took him home, but the son died of his wounds. Thereupon, the father committed suicide. Apparently, as the man got older and weaker in his present incarnation, the personality of the past life was freed and produced the shadows of the past along with its feelings of distrust and hatred. Here we see someone acquiring a pseudo-obsession at a later age through the personality of his own previous incarnation. It seems that a weakened constitution and a strong emotional charge in the past personality may suffice for this to happen. (Ferreira 1955).

As this man grew older and weaker, his preceding lifetime emerged and produced the shadows of the past with their confusion, distrust and hate (Muller 1970: 210).

Also when the preceding lifetime is the feeding personality, without a proper life review it may be present as an almost separate personality. Preceding lifetimes may also disturb us, when they are still vital, but hardly realise that they died. People who are uncommonly active or hyperactive as children, often regress to a preceding life as a soldier who died young. Now they have the energy for two. Motoyama tells about someone who reincarnated as the child of one of his siblings (Motoyama 1992: 103):

> Indeed, the uncle had been reborn as the nephew. The uncle had been a heroic figure. He had been an excellent practitioner of the martial arts and had sacrificed his life for his country. He did not regret dying. His desire to beat the enemy continued after death and he went on fighting in the astral dimension. Even after his rebirth, he remained strongly attached to his warrior personality. He overpowered the normal consciousness, provoking the epileptic fits of the nephew.

> A four-year old Viennese girl is apathetic for four days. She stares, doesn't move, throws up all food and medicines and does not sleep at all, so her condition worsens by the hour. A friend of the family, organises a spiritist séance. The trance medium, who can incorporate entities, suddenly rises and angrily calls in an Austrian dialect, 'Let me out!' 'Where do you want to go?' 'Outside. Get out of my way!' 'No, you stay here till you have told me where you want to go.' After some more discussion, the entity says that he is called 'Jogl Stoanbauer' (Georg Steinbauer) and comes from Grimmenstein. After much effort, it appears that he died in 1827 and has finally found his wife Leni again. He says that at this moment his wife is waiting in the next room. Five days ago, he saw her leaving the body of a small child. He had grabbed her and never wanted to let go of her. The little girl was the farmer's wife reborn. The friend of the family explained the situation to poor Jogl. When he understood that the little girl would die if he didn't stop, he crossed himself and assured the friend that he had never intended that. He turned to the room where the girl was lying and said, apparently to his Leni, 'It is okay, now for God's sake return into the little one.' Suddenly the door opens and the little girl bursts into the room with rosy cheeks and calls: 'Mama, I'm very hungry!' From that moment on she was completely healthy again.
>
> A check at the registrar's office confirmed all the details of the farm family. The last member of that family had died 55 years before. (Passian 1985)

A less dramatic sudden personality change, this time ephemeral, is this example from Goldberg (1982: 66):

> A young American woman on holiday in Germany is planning to depart for Belgium. She runs into a twenty-four-hour delay. To pass the time, she visits a castle turned into a museum. In the castle she sees the portrait of an inhabitant from the thirteenth century. She

goes into spontaneous regression and relives the woman's complete life. She is unable to move a muscle during the experience, which lasts about forty-five minutes. Later she goes to a therapist to confirm a few details.

Goldberg justly says that this is not classic *déjà-vu*. Here we have a temporary obsession where the deceased tries to catch someone's attention, either through the woman's accessibility or because a personal relationship exists. This may also be a previous incarnation of herself and so a pseudo-obsession. Anyway, it is clearly a case of a separate personality intervening. The rigidity and maybe even the twenty-four-hour delay, are clearly interventions.

An intelligent and attractive anorexia patient finds herself in a past life as a fat and extraordinarily unpleasant man who likes to keep attractive little girlfriends and abuse them (Goldberg 1982: 127). The difference between these two lives is so extreme that I wonder if the patient might be a previous girlfriend who is obsessed by this boor. It would fit in much better with other anorexia cases. If this is true, the regression therapy has ingrained this obsession further and the author's conclusions are prematurely optimistic.

Muller gives the example of a medium who is treating an obsession and receives the message that in this case the disturbing personality should not be removed, since this was a past personality of the same person and is to be integrated (Muller 1970: 213). The previous example from Goldberg appears to be the reverse: an obsessing personality that should not be integrated but separated. Past-life therapy without insight into obsession and pseudo-obsession may be counterproductive. Another reason for laymen to refrain from it.

THE APPEARANCE OF PERSONALITIES DURING REGRESSIONS

When regressing to a past life, we feel these experiences as our own, in spite of large differences in body, habits, emotions and opinions. During a regression we can be our present and our past personality simultaneously. Joe Keeton's regression technique results in the double presence of both past personality, who is in contact with the therapist and the present personality as a powerless but conscious observer. I have characterised this as an 'elliptic' consciousness, a consciousness with two focal points. This is what a personality is: a focal point of our consciousness, a sense of self connecting and centring a string of experiences.

All recollection, reliving and regression experiences contain some elliptic consciousness. You can remember being beaten when you were 6. You remember it, you re-experience it and at the same time, you feel sorry for the 6-year-old from the vantage-point of your present age. Many forms of self-reflection dissociate the focus of awareness somewhat: self-pity, self-judgment, narcissism and so on.

Colin Wilson points out that multiple personalities seem to have a hierarchy. That hierarchy may be complex. Not all subpersonalities know about each other. 'Carla' may discuss 'Jennie's' attitude, but 'Jennie' doesn't know 'Carla' exists. In the regressions with Joe Keeton, the present consciousness perceives the previous consciousness, but not the other way round. Still, the present consciousness is powerless. So there is another difference between subpersonalities: having access or not to the driver's seat. The third difference is in the order of 'birth'. In the case of 'Sybil', the other subpersonalities had split off. She didn't know about them and could not control them. Though Sybil was the weakest personality, she was the main stem, the original. Splitting off, or furcation, resembles the condition of a mother who faints at times and produces babies that diminish her energy and size.

The personalities of different lifetimes have a similar coexistence. Some have access to the larger personality and so can find the rest. Other personalities are more inward-looking or have isolated themselves. They may be caught in their undigested experiences.

When regressing someone to a past life without a clear problem focus we will probably get one of the feeding lifetimes, most likely the central feeding incarnation, the main root of this life. Each life plan is connected to a few past lives, usually three to six. With a particular issue, we end up in the lifetime most immediately connected to this issue. Often, we first hit a traumatic death. We first enter lives with clear karmic or dharmic connections. Other lives are only accessible via the larger self.

Chapter 6 gave examples of 'identification': the past personality taking over the driver's seat. Strangely, the opposite can also happen: the present personality may enter a situation relating to the past personality. Shirley gives an amusing, but disturbing example of this (1924: 58). Robert Monroe had a similar experience just as amusing and just as disturbing. His experiences take place in what he call 'environment III' and give the impression of a parallel incarnation in another planet (Monroe 1977).

Often, contact with the larger personality speeds up the therapy. But sometimes the therapist is trying to pass the buck. She might doubt whether a regression to a particular episode is desirable and asks the larger self or a guide for advice. Or the remigrant is reluctant to relive something and prefers to experience it from a more stable, a more objective point of view. Contacts with the larger self are helpful when they encourage working through the experience, not when they help to avoid it.

During a regression an alien personality may come up. Obsessors and pseudo-obsessors may emerge either unobtrusively or demonstratively. A short regression with an obsessing entity is always good and often liberating and clarifying.

Addressing subpersonalities and other personalities in the consciousness of the remigrant as separate persons is therapeutically effective. The present personality may be asked to intervene in a traumatic death scene or childhood episode. This last is Inner Child work. Remigrants can comfort the newborn they have been or rescue a past personality from the hands of henchmen. They can provide the comfort, understanding, love, security and relief that was once lacking. In this way, we don't rewrite history, but change its repercussions. Personalities and subpersonalities can be imprisoned in undigested experiences and totalitarian postulates blocking psychic energy. Technically, this resembles the static twilight existence described in chapter 11.

Can an obsessor enter someone during a regression? Mediumistic people may regress in an uncommonly deep trance and can stare, stiffen and cool down. We can easily prevent overly deep trance. Physical contact and calm instructions are sufficient. If a remigrant leaves the driver's seat, an alert therapist will protect that space.

An insecure or scared therapist should let the remigrant return. Psychic sensitivity and ability in a therapist are helpful, but not necessary. Calmness and professional skill are more important. The remigrant may reckon that a therapist who inspires trust will be good enough.

PARALLEL PERSONALITIES

Exceptional cases in the regression literature may sharpen our understanding of the relation between the soul and its personalities: overlapping lifetimes, simultaneous lifetimes and furcating personalities. When the previous personality died after the present personality was born, the intermission is negative. This may be from a few days to three months and, in rare cases, up to three years. During a regression into this life, a break may occur at the age of eighteen months and suddenly the remigrant shifts into the dying experience of the previous lifetime.

When someone withdraws after birth, this may lead to early death or to a change of personality. The person who enters the body usually just died rather nearby. This may happen quite directly and the memories may cease on the same day as the previous personality died. Sometimes a confused soul has been wandering about for some time, looking instinctively for a body. Almost always it finds a growing foetus, but on rare occasions it apparently finds a living body just being abandoned or about to be abandoned by the inhabitant.

Pieter Langedijk (1980) writes of a remigrant who relives sitting and eating in a high chair when she is two years old. When he asks her to go back to the age of one, she says: 'There is nothing. I am not one-year-old.' Every time he brings her back to the age of two she has experiences, but at the age of one there is nothing. Then, instead of telling her to go back to age one, he tells her to go one year back. 'Now where are you? You are somewhere, aren't you?' 'Yes, I am in a concentration camp in Germany and I am being shot.' A few weeks later she entered an eighteen-month-old child.

Langedijk also reports the case of a woman who relives looking for a new family after her death. She sees a mother with a beautiful little daughter. Her desire for beauty is so strong that she hangs around until illness exhausts the girl and then she pushes her out and takes over the body. Her further life was difficult because she did not fit in with the family. The beautiful body entranced her, so she did not realise that the parents had a terrible relationship (TenDam 1982).

Apparently this is not karma, but what Rousseau called 'natural punishment'. Such lifetimes overlap in terms of the registrar's office, not in terms of psychological life histories. Such negative intermissions or apparent overlaps also occur in child cases. Stevenson found a few cases and investigated them. The example of Jasbir is the most well known (Stevenson 1966: 34). Jasbir died when he was three. Immediately after that, he came back to life, like someone who has been temporarily clinically dead. A new personality had taken over the body who remembered his previous life. Another well documented case is that of Hermann Grundei (Muller 1970: 122). His previous life ended thirty-five days after the birth of this life. The striking resemblance is interesting. Perhaps here there really is an overlapping incarnation. Anyway, negative intermissions have been sufficiently demonstrated. They usually occur when the young child is weak or ill or has little will to live. The intruding personality normally has a strong drive to return right away. Change of personality may also happen after, for example, shell-shock. According to Cyril Scott, this only happens to people who have practised dubious forms of magic in their past lives and have been trained to open themselves to the will of others (1953: 231). I would add: or it happens to those who did that to them.

Can we have simultaneous incarnations? Regressions give some tricky indications. According to 'Seth', our soul is simultaneously incarnated in a human body and in an animal or in several animals of different species. Regressions don't show such parallel animal lifetimes. Dick Sutphen (1989) gives examples of parallel human lifetimes. He even gives instructions for this in group regressions. These parallel lifetimes complement what the remigrants themselves miss, so they seem to indicate compensation. I am not convinced. The only other example I know from the literature is Pat Roberts (Moss & Keeton 1979: 171). Pat relives the life of a woman in Liverpool around 1900. Many obscure data were later verified in the archives and from gravestones. Even the names and the birth dates were correct. The only problem was that many facts, though true, appeared to be in conflict. Further investigation showed that two women with almost the same name had lived rather close together. Facts from these two lives had been mixed up in the regression. This could be a parallel incarnation or perhaps an obsession.

Bruce Goldberg speaks of 'simultaneous multiple incarnations', but does not give examples from his regression practice (Goldberg 1982: 43). The idea that a soul can incarnate in several bodies simultaneously is supported by the case of English twins who were infamous criminals and who seemed to share the same personality and the same consciousness. Rather than a split personality in one body – as with obsession – it looked as though this was one personality in a split body.

Wambach's prenatal regressions (1979) contain some mysterious cases. One remigrant was a small girl with long hair before she was born (Wambach 1979: 53). She said that she 'had to find her other half to make a whole'. Another remigrant says that she and her mother were the same person until her awareness entered the foetus. At this point, they separated. She herself remained virtually unchanged, whereas her mother changed considerably. She felt as though she was in control, while her mother felt helpless (Wambach 1979: 119). This could indicate that the mother's personality split, the strongest aspects of her personality going to her daughter, where they became a separate personality.

Strange as it seems, this may be possible. Cases like Eva and Sybil and other multiple personalities show how independent subpersonalities may become. We ourselves are subpersonalities of our soul, so maybe we could 'furcate' further and our subpersonalities could incarnate separately. According to the Loehr–Daniels readings a soul never has two incarnations simultaneously, except in the case of identical twins (Smith 1975: 241). We have seen that this is certainly not always the case. Cloning humans will give new evidence. I bet that with few or no exceptions, regressions will uncover a preceding lifetime different from the 'parent's'.

A PRELIMINARY SUMMARY

We are souls who often stay in human bodies, not always and not necessarily self-conscious (we may sleep or be deeply entranced). Self-consciousness is the product of a 'radiant' soul and a 'reflecting' body. The more this reflection is focused, the more self-aware we are. Different bodily experiences produce different foci and consequently, different identities. Sooner or later, self-awareness can be retained after death. In the course of its incarnations, the soul collects more and more personalities in which to experience itself. Each personality is developing (sometimes temporarily stagnating or degenerating) until it finds peace – finds its place in the large house of the field of consciousness – in the light of the soul.

In one of the first reasonable books on reincarnation, Ralph Shirley writes (1924: 35):

> It is difficult to determine just how much individuality exists in a human or animal life. Perhaps a rudimentary form exists even among the simplest forms of animal life, although this is speculation. We have but few leads. Among even the most developed people, individuality is less constant than we like to believe and it may be broken in extreme circumstances.

Expositions on reincarnation and identity often speak of the higher and the lower self. This chapter will have made clear that those ideas are misleading especially the frequently used comparison of the Higher Self as the actor and the lower self as the present role. If consecutive lives are different parts of the actor, then we are actors who identify so much with our part that we forget we are acting. Furthermore, we lack an audience in front of the stage, unless we assume that some cosmic beings are manipulating us. As this assumption cannot be disproved, it is more suitable to science fiction and paranoia. Also, we do not perform the same life a number of times. A successful performance is not re-run. On the contrary, we are more likely to repeat the bad performances and the early exits. Rehearsal, if any, is done a little just before life and then we are sent onto the stage with a good smack of amnesia, a clumsy little body and the prospect of a lengthy dependence on older actors who have been sweating on the stage for many years before us. Finally and most importantly, an actor plays characters that have nothing to do with each other on consecutive evenings, while our lives are clearly related.

We are more than just our present personality. Behind, above and around our present personality we find a freer and larger self, usually remaining latent during our lives, probably lacking a separate awareness, existing rather as a matrix or womb.

We have subpersonalities: waking, dreaming or sleeping. We also have some feeding personalities, chosen or recommended or just continuing. Besides all these, traumas or postulates from other lives have often become linked to this life through restimulation. Because there are often traumatic chains, whole series of lives may connect in this way to the present life. The primary feeding personality is the most interwoven with the present personality. Usually, the secondary personalities are easier to identify separately because they are more distinct; they relate to particular moods, attitudes and aptitudes.

FURTHER READING

The little that has been written about the subject of this chapter is theosophical, gnostic or mystic. Little work has been done on personality theory using regression material. The most advanced, as far as this subject is concerned, are the spiritist reincarnation therapists in Brazil, cited by Karl Muller (1970). The Kardec spiritists and psychics in general have ideas about the relationship between the reincarnating soul and its incarnate personalities, as familiarity with the discarnate condition is necessary to have such ideas. Joan Grant offers a few indications (1937, 1952; Kelsey & Grant 1967). An interesting and extensive treatment is *The Meaning of Personal Existence, in the Light of Paranormal Phenomena, Reincarnation and Mystical States of Consciousness* by Arthur W. Osborn (1966). The often cited Loehr–Daniels readings are on this score much more explicit and extensive than Edgar Cayce. Where we can test them against the evidence from regressions, they agree on almost all points.

Fifteen

AN EMPIRICAL VISION
OF REINCARNATION

The first four chapters listed and discussed ideas about reincarnation. The following eight chapters were about experiences: the research of spontaneous memories and a review of the results of regressions. Chapters 13 and 14 contained my general conclusions about the empirical literature, the practical experiences of therapists and my own experience as a therapist. This chapter compares traditional ideas about reincarnation with the empirical evidence and the conclusions based on this evidence. Reincarnation as an empirical field is young and chaotic, but many ideas can be disproved already by the evidence we have.

GENERAL IDEAS ABOUT
REINCARNATION

What reincarnates? The soul. But what exactly do we mean by that? The Tlingits, West African tribes, the Burmese and many other peoples believe that reincarnation is the return of a person who lived before, with all his preferences and peculiarities. He has a preferred family in which to be born, he sometimes announces his new birth and he usually resembles his past personality.

The Hindus believe rather that the soul is divine and always stays the same. Leibniz's monad doctrine and theosophy contain similar ideas. Each life is like a character in a play (lower self) in which the actor (Higher Self) loses himself.

Reincarnation beliefs may diffuse into pre-existence beliefs or become mixed with psychic transference, the belief that we bear the traces of the lives of past people without having been one of them. Thus ideas vary from the notion that the same personality returns to the idea that the personality is lost at the end of a life and only the Higher Self remembers the lifetime.

The evidence from past-life therapy, especially with pseudo-obsessions, shows that the reality is more complex. The preceding chapter discussed 'the larger self', 'feeding personalities', 'furcation', etc. Past personalities are usually quite independent, even if entangled in the present personality. They continue to exist: sleeping, dreaming or awake. They may stimulate or inhibit the present personality. When we have vivid memories of a past life while our self-image is still weak, as in Stevenson's child cases, a considerable portion of the past personality is apparently transferred to this life. How much it fades as time goes on and how much is incorporated into the new life depends on character and circumstances.

Maurice Albertson and Kenneth Freeman concluded from their analysis of all the sources (1988) that little research into reincarnation has been done under experimental conditions, but that the consistent pattern of the hundreds, thousands and even tens of thousands of cases enables us to draw many conclusions about many aspects of reincarnation. According to them, almost all the datas support the basic tenets of reincarnation: humans have both a body and a spirit; the spirit survives bodily death and later may enter a new body.

- The research of death experiences, out-of-body experiences and earthbound entities shows that the spirit can exist independently of the body, can move freely outside the body, can perceive the physical world and can remember these perceptions.

- The research into prenatal memories shows that something in the foetus has a mature and adult awareness.

- The spontaneous recall of infants, the memories of a discarnate state before birth, past-life regressions and past-life therapy show that our spirit remembers previous lifetimes and the periods in between and that we can recount them in detail, though not always precisely. Our spirit also carries old behavioural patterns and bodily and psychological complaints into this lifetime. Some problems remain resistant to any form of therapy, till past-life therapy uncovers the cause in a past lifetime.

Of the 25 hypotheses they tested to the agglomerated empirical material, the authors could refute only one: the assumption that the goal of reincarnation would be unconditional love. Growing independence appeared to be a more likely aim.

*

Many visions assume that souls evolve from unconscious, passive and primitive stages into conscious, creative stages. Human souls may once have been animal souls and perhaps had plant and mineral stages before that. Superhuman stages are often assumed, running from angels to gods. An alternative concept is that humans were originally spiritual, incorporeal beings, developing particular proficiency during incarnations, becoming creative in the physical world and perhaps developing more qualities too. In this view, the incarnate state is basically educational. Many schools of thought emphasise that this education is tenuous since we are wont to forget our descent and get wrapped up in ourselves, in karmic complications or in physical pleasures, pains and limitations. 'You are a lost son before you know it.' In chapter 12 we saw that we have evidence for both lines of development. Many remigrants end up in primitive conditions when they go further and further back in time, making reincarnation look like a slow and volatile process of becoming more human, more civilised, more cultural and more aware. Other remigrants end up in more advanced civilisations and in discarnate states when they go a long way back. The reasons they give for reincarnation here are more vague and more diverse. Often, they talk about helping the less gifted primitive folk down here.

Others schools view the incarnate condition as the result of succumbing to temptation, the fall of man or the punishment for misdeeds in the discarnate state. Diverse, often paradoxical philosophies are built on these thoughts: we attain self-awareness through incarnations with the aim of losing it again or we leave God with the aim of finding Him again. The evidence refutes these views fully and completely.

Florence McClain rightly looks critically at the 'old soul' business, in which people make differences between old and young souls, usually placing them selves in the old soul category, looking more or less benevolently on the primitive, still materialistic, extrovert (and often more successful) young souls around. She says instead: 'Regression evidence (our own as well as that of other researchers) indicates that all souls were created at the same time – a very long time ago' (1986: 8). Yet thinking of the very different origins we find in regressions: animals, devas, 'light people', other planets, this seems a bold statement. Her paragraph on the 'Origin of man' (1986a: 132) remains abstract. McClain should tell us more about that evidence and about those other researchers.

When we are incarnated, we do, experience and learn things differently from when we are discarnate. When discarnate, we live in a 'psycho-plastic' world: we experience that our body, our environment and our inner state always correspond. In the discarnate state, the mind is truly its own place. Incarnation means entering a world of more objective conditions and events. An imaginative glass of water does not quench our thirst. It may help us feel less thirsty, even depressing our body's need for water, but in the end, we may still die of thirst. Wishing our lover to be just around the corner does not make that happen. Our piano playing is only impressive after impressively long practice. 'Real is what makes a difference.' In the physical body, in the physical world, perception and imagination differ much more. This also enhances the reality of other people.

Incarnation is anti-solipsistic: it forces us to have experiences, to learn and to develop. And our physical structure triggers self-perception (seeing, feeling, touching and hearing ourselves) and so makes self-consciousness unavoidable. Our nervous system is the scaffolding around our growing self-awareness. At some point, this self-awareness is so strong that it does not dissolve when it leaves the scaffolding after death. We take this self-image with us into the discarnate state and so we learn to remain self-aware after death.

Incarnation is no banishment or imprisonment, but scaffolding, runway, nursery. So we alternate between the initially sleepy and later lucid existence of discarnate citizens and the simultaneously wakeful and drugged existence on the incarnate 'battle front'. Each incarnation tests our insight, our compassion and our competence. The goals of recurrent lives appear to be continual evolution and emancipation:

- growing intellectual capacity: intelligence, knowledge, understanding, insight and wisdom

- growing emotional capacity: sympathy, compassion, joy, peace and love

- growing capacity for independence, freedom and responsibility

- growing capacity for action: doing, making and creating.

Recurrent incarnations with intermission periods of reflection enormously increase our potential for growth:

- more time for experience, including repetition of growing up

- more variation: gender, health, family, position, culture and circumstances

- more recuperation: refreshing, recharging or recreational intermissions

- more justice; this argument is so obvious and well known that it needs no elaboration.

Visions warning about the dangers of the incarnate condition have a point. People with active, balanced and fulfilled lives, with fruitful and meaningful work, all too commonly go on to experience all kinds of difficulties, ending up in lives of confusion, misery and even degeneration. It then takes a lot of time to get a handle on ourselves again.

The empirical evidence demonstrates that human relations and compassion play an enormous part in our lives and in the connections between lives. The traditional reincarnation philosophies are remarkably weak on social themes, although life aims such as individual religious or spiritual development are far less common than social themes.

What do the traditional views say about the number of incarnations and about intermissions? The number of incarnations varies from just a couple in Persian-type views, to hundreds of thousands in Indian-type views. Persian thought sees a good life as increasing the chances of an even better next life and a bad life as increasing the chances of an even worse life. In other words, it sees positive and negative developments as self-reinforcing. Consequently, in a few lives the person will either elevate himself above human status or sink below it. Indian thought presumes that it may take a long time for a person to attain the full experience needed to develop from simple, limited feelings to the realisation that the main reason for being here is to get out of here, as a process through lives from *kama* via *artha* and *dharma* to *moksha*.

And what does the empirical evidence say? The evidence confirms both mechanisms of slow, gradual development and self-reinforcing development at the same time and therefore refutes both extreme positions. Anyway, it refutes completely the idea that people usually have only a couple of lives. A problem during therapy can normally be followed through a number of lifetimes. About 90 percent of regressions take place in the past 3,000 years and the rest in undatable primitive circumstances or in cultures reminiscent of Atlantis. Virtually everyone who has some experience with regressions believes in at least dozens of lives and possibly hundreds. Higher estimations are speculative because of difficulty in dating and discriminating old lifetimes.

According to the Druse, we are reborn the moment we die. According to the Jains, after death we immediately attach to a conceived foetus, so the period between dying and being reborn is about nine months. In Africa intermissions of one to three years are assumed. Allan Kardec (1857) says intermissions vary from a few hours to many thousands of years. The theosophists started out with intermissions of more than 8,000 years and ended up with Leadbeater's classification, in which intermissions vary from five to more than 2,000 years. Rudolf Steiner began with an incarnation cycle of 2,600 years and ended up with intermissions of about 700 years.

Based on the empirical evidence, we can be fairly precise about intermissions. The diverse cases of Karl Muller (1970) ranged from immediate incarnation (and even negative intermission) to a number of centuries, with an average intermission of 70 years. Helen Wambach's work (1978) is more exact and more reliable. She found intermissions varying from four months to more than two centuries, with an average of 52 years. Joel Whitton (1986) found intermissions ranging from 10 months to more than 800 years, with an average of about 40 years. Stevenson (1966) normally found intermissions of a few years and a maximum of 12, in child cases.

Thus the Africans are right, the Druse and the Jains are wrong. The Druse have invented a temporary reincarnation country 'somewhere in China' where children can live for a few years and then die prematurely to return as real Druse. Poor China! This is a familiar kind of argument: impossible to refute. Kardec is right and the theosophists and anthroposophists are wrong. Their ideas are at complete variance with the empirical data and are based on such abstract considerations as an astrological era lasting 2,160 years and 700 being a beautiful number. Chapter 13 gives a possible explanation for the discrepancy between regressions (a few decades on the average) and child cases (a few years on the average).

The population explosion is often explained by a drastic reduction of intermission times. Whitton says that intermissions have been steadily diminishing over the past several hundred years. I tend to agree, but as yet we lack statistics. If intermissions are not shorter, then many souls are incarnating for the first time. That seems likely, but we have no data to corroborate this.

Some theories claim that incarnations follow cycles. For example, everyone is born once (or twice) in each astrological age (the age of Pisces, the age of Aquarius, etc.). Other astrological speculations are that we are born first as Aries, then as Taurus, then as Gemini, etc. Most regressions are weak in that kind of information, but existing data do not support this claim. Naturally, it always remains possible to assert that between an incarnation as Taurus and an incarnation as Virgo you died three times as a young child. Whoever believes such unfounded claims may join the Druse.

There is no evidence at all that the natal chart of one life is connected with that of the next. If we look at regressions and at the indications of how a new life is prepared and how a choice of parents is made, such a connection seems unlikely. Unless Helen Wambach's collection of birth experiences is one great fraud, it refutes these astrological theories. As uncertain and unclear as Wambach's material may be, the regressions of 750 people are an incomparably better foundation than the speculations of 75 astrologers.

Chapter 13 collected patterns of relations between lifetimes from the empirical evidence. This material flagrantly contradicts the idea of cosmic clocks relating the place and the moment of birth of one life directly to the place and date of birth of another life. Karmic astrology, like most astrology, is not the result of discovering patterns in series of data, but of deducing relationships from abstract musing about the meaning of astrological factors and then reading the conclusions in the material at hand. As much research witnesses, this is a very unreliable road to take. The only option would be to correlate the content of regressions of very many people with planetary aspects and planetary positions from their natal charts.

SIMILARITIES AND DIFFERENCES BETWEEN LIVES

What about change of gender? The wildest nonsense comes from Cabbalists, who warn men not to be petty or stingy, otherwise they will return as women. Theosophy and anthroposophy believe in cyclical alternation and allow only limited deviations. According to Van Ginkel, the average person alternates seven male lives with seven female lives (Van Ginkel 1917). Regressions give a crystal-clear answer: gender change happens often, but not according to fixed schedules. The probability of a gender change between two consecutive incarnations is about 20 percent. The probability of any gender change in a series of consecutive lives approaches 80 percent. Some people seem strongly to favour one gender rather than the other. Which gender we are born with depends on diverse factors and considerations. Population I people (general evolution, no life review or life plan), for example, usually are born in the same gender as before.

Another subject is that of physical resemblance. According to the theosophists, the more we approach the level of Master, the more our appearance, especially our face, remains the same through the incarnations. If this is true, there are many more Masters in the world than the theosophists have realised. How much two incarnations look alike differs greatly. Probably, the resemblance is greatest when the soul has been in contact with the foetus from the moment of conception. We may carry particular features with us, for example in the face, for several lifetimes. The central feeding incarnation has the greatest effect.

Ideas of return into the same family, nation, culture and race are common. Druse return as Druse; Jews prefer to return as Jews. Rudolf Steiner asserted that people never return in the same nation and the same culture, except central Europeans like himself. Other theories assert that a whole nation may reincarnate *en masse* in another nation. For example, the ancient Greeks would have reincarnated in the French and the ancient Romans in the British. These tunes have all kinds of variations. Where families are important, ideas about return in the family prevail; where nation is important, people believe they return in the same nation.

We find no such fixed rules here either. Certainly in population I, people tend to be reborn close to the place of death of the preceding life. In this type of rebirth, proximity decides, not national or cultural identity. The Burmese children who remembered being a Japanese and an American respectively, both of whom died in Burma during the Second World War, illustrate this.

More than half of regressed Americans did live in the United States in their one, two or three preceding lifetimes. The British often lived in England before and the French in France. In my practice in the Netherlands, fairly often remigrants did live in the Netherlands around a century ago. Some lived in the Netherlands in the sixteenth and seventeenth centuries. But most past lives were elsewhere.

There are no large reincarnation waves through nations or cultures. Reincarnation is personal, guided by individual preferences and by personal relations. Attaching importance to a birth in a particular family, country or religion, or in a particular region or city, increases the chances of being born there. Regional, national, religious and cultural identifications increase the chances of return. Japanese may well return as Japanese, especially if they value that. The converse also happens: if we lived in Italy and were terribly bored all our life by the same view of the Apennines, we are unlikely to be reborn with the same view. In other words, local, national, religious and cultural identifications enlarge the chance of returning to the same turf.

People bonded by living or working together tend to meet again the next time, because of karmic entanglements, reciprocal sympathy or trust or being kindred spirits or sharing some task. We encounter people we know from previous lifetimes in almost any life. Personal feelings and entanglements are stronger dharmic or karmic connections than correction for misconduct or compensation for good conduct in a past life. Rarely is someone from population II or III is born among people with whom he has no relation at all. In almost every lifetime we meet at least a few people we know from past lives. People who recognise each other at first sight or who fall in love at first sight, may indeed know each other from past lives.

Since Plato, a prevailing idea is that of soul mates or twin souls – androgynous souls who have been separated into male and female halves. The idea of a twin soul fascinates people, especially lonely romantics tired of their partner. It may give them a glow in their eyes, as others have who know Jesus loves them.

The empirical evidence does not support the idea of a twin soul, though people may become so attached to each other that they continue an intimate relationship life after life. In some instances, two people may have been married to each other in more than half their past lives. In others, they may have been brother and sister, father and daughter or business partners. Lenz found examples of twin souls in 15 percent of his cases, but he defines twin souls as 'persons who have similar interests, capacities and attitudes', which stretches the concept beyond meaning (Lenz 1979).

The idea that most of us have soul mates, people to whom we have grown close in our lives and with whom we can be at ease (especially outside the restrictions of the body), is an idea as stimulating as it is true. People who have the same origin, the same 'roots', might also feel a deep affinity, even without shared experiences. According to Hans Holzer, we may have several 'potential' soul mates, always of the opposite gender. This invalidates the first word of soul mate. I propose to establish a clear terminology:

- *twin souls*: souls who have the same origin, who began their individual existence at the same moment, who normally are together when discarnate and who often share experiences when incarnate

- *soul family*: souls who have the same origin
- *soul mates*: friends who have shared many lifetimes, often as partners.

A twin soul is thus an original sibling and a soul mate a friend of many lives. Twin souls went out together and soul mates have come together. Just as your sister may be your best friend, a twin soul may be a soul mate. Of course, people are especially fascinated by the idea of meeting a twin soul or soul mate of the opposite gender (or of the same gender if they are homosexual). But it is immediate familiarity and deep mutual trust that count, not immediate sexual attraction.

'Reincarnation waves' are large groups of kindred spirits reincarnating close together. For example, Arthur Guirdham's books (1970, 1974, 1976) are about a group of people remembering Cathar and other lifetimes. Reality is difficult to distinguish from illusion here, but the idea seems valid. The common misfortune of the Cathars probably considerably strengthened their cohesion. The process in which people begin to realise that they once all lived together is called *ingathering*. Many enthusiastic testimonies will continue to come from people who found their spiritual home in this belief before they found themselves. Spiritually dominant people who are convinced they know about their previous lifetimes can easily convince nice people they immediately like, that they belong to the same circle.

What about metempsychosis or having intermittent animal lifetimes? We have only limited indications of metempsychosis and these can be explained more easily as intermission identifications. Some people believe they see animal characteristics in some of their fellow humans or point out what they see as a pathological love of animals. There may be more obvious explanations for men with thick necks and beady eyes, for example, than previous pig lives. Besides, would any pig with an ounce of common sense want to become human after going through the slaughterhouses a few times? Or are the slaughterhouse experiences precisely what confused them? Victims of torture and terror sometimes begin to identify themselves with their persecutors. And this in turn is a nice explanation for the underhand tricks the man with the thick neck and the little eyes plays on his environment. Which brings us neatly to the next subject: karma.

KARMA

Views of karma are rather diverse. What does the evidence show? There is no direct, mechanical karmic relation between facts and events in this lifetime and facts and events in past lifetimes. Undigested traumatic experiences cause phobias, problems and complexes in following lives. Past lives can also cause deeply rooted, rigid attitudes and views. Karmic patterns do exist, not as natural laws, but as psychological and educational patterns. Chapter 13 tried to classify these.

We can discard the deterministic views. Clearly, occurrences and deeds from past lives are neither unequivocally ingrained nor have an unequivocal effect. On the contrary, a deterministic view in which action A always has karmic repercussion B is nonsense, much as it may satisfy people who like to feel embedded in a computerised superhuman order. We can also discard the view that the actual deed, regardless of the intent, determines karma. Our psychological reaction determines what we take with us to a next life. After all, our soul is what goes from one life to the next, and psychic reactions are semantic; that is, the effect of an experience is never direct, but always depends on our interpretation.

All other ideas about karma seem to be more or less true. There is jurisdiction to the extent that we ourselves, alone or with others, sit in judgment on ourselves. *The mind is its own place.* People only appear in front of Moses or Our Lord God when they create such a thought. We judge ourselves from our own, sometimes narrow, point of view. We can only conquer ourselves if we accept ourselves. External judges exist, but they don't make overtime. They may pressure us to look in the mirror, even trap us in a pseudo-existence after death or offer a life plan we hardly can refuse. But nobody is coerced.

Karma can best be defined as a collective term for every kind of liability we take with us from past lives. We need a term then for assets as well: I have proposed in this book *dharma*. The notion that karma can be postponed is true, as well as other notions that give a human perspective on karma. Karmic mechanisms work just like the mechanisms within our life. The only difference is that the life review and the life preview are more powerful than most reflections and plans during life.

Still, each day we can look back on our life and every day we can prepare the rest of our life. We are less at liberty because we have more or less forgotten our life plan. But we can take new initiatives, change attitudes and choose new directions. Those supplements are not always improvements, because we usually have a better overview — and better advisers — before birth. However, we may have decided before birth too hastily, overreacting to an experience from a preceding life, and we may come to our senses during life. This is particularly true for people who reincarnated quickly and emotionally. We may always go beyond our incarnation preparations. *Today is the first day of the rest of your life.*

Chapter 12 contained many examples of how karma works. Karma and dharma are probably etheric potentials, connected to the vehicle of vitality. In our psychic body we are free, we are ourselves, except when we have a narrow-minded perception of ourselves, which is to some extent our own choice as well. At any rate, it contains nothing inhibiting change. Reorientation automatically and immediately changes our psychic body. But we are confronted with the vehicle of vitality and our physical body, although they are part of us, because we cannot change them immediately and at will. Karma and dharma are old burdens and old strengths within us. Meeting someone whom we know from a past life is hardly karmic or dharmic by itself. The karmic or dharmic factors are what we ourselves bring to that encounter. And what the other brings towards us.

Karmic or dharmic charges may be inactive or active. They may be located in our body or in our aura. Catharsis during therapy heals a karmic wound or dissolves a karmic gnarl. Every moment of acceptance and liberation resolves karma. Do we redeem or discharge karma when we are helping someone we have harmed in a past life, out of a sullen sense of duty? In our next life review we may feel less guilt at best, and when the other has appreciated our help, it is yet easier for us to release any remaining negative energy. When our relationships with others deepen, we absorb more of them and they absorb more of us. But whatever the interaction, each of us is doing her or his own 'housekeeping'. Karma and dharma are within us, 'nearer than hands and feet'.

A thorough conviction that we will or should return quickly, surely increases the chances that we will. Ideas about the importance of last thoughts etc. come from powerful religious traditions and institutions scaring powerless, insecure people. Many beliefs, usually religious, contain the idea that our last thoughts, the way we die or the kind of funeral or cremation we have will affect our condition after death and sometimes our next life. Here, too, the mind is its own place. If we are convinced of that, what happens may conform to our expectation.

Undoubtedly, many people panic when they are about to leave their body without the Extreme Unction and many more couldn't care less. We may be convinced we will go to hell, so we may go there, at least ain the form of a period of dream existence. If we are convinced that we are doomed to wander forever because our children failed to perform the right burial rites, this does not promote our peace of mind.

> In sixteenth-century Italy, a lonely woman is known to the people of the surrounding villages as a witch. She does in fact perform disgusting rituals with the blood of animals and exceptionally of a baby, either stolen or bought, to retain her youth. These rituals only make her older and uglier. When her end nears, she panics and begs a chaplain for remission of her sins. He refuses to absolve her because she is a child of darkness, a servant of Satan, eternally doomed. The woman dies in great fear, knowing herself to be evil. Although she does not go to hell, her fear leads her into darkness and causes her to lose consciousness. Although she is properly reborn again later, this whole life remains undigested. In a regression her experiences resurface and she finally receives absolution.

From whom, do you think, she receives absolution?

The idea that a failure to perform rituals and duties to a T dooms us to an unpleasant next life is either narrow-mindedness or plain terrorism. Some Cabbalistic and Tibetan ideas are less sadistic, but just as totalitarian as those of the old-fashioned preachers of hell-and-damnation. Gruesome and cruel practices continue up to the present day by fanatics, just for kicks, as a sport and even as part of research. After all, you may torture people just to find out how they react to torture. Many people die in circumstances that make it impossible to think and feel properly. What a mess it would be if a mother who was gassed with her children got a bad next life just because she had no peace of mind at the moment of death!

Rituals can bring peace and order, and may make us conscientious and foster feelings that we easily lose in the wear and tear of daily strife. They may express spiritual loyalty. Life is often so chaotic, tough, harsh or depressing, that rituals restoring peace of mind are important. But they may also be instruments of repression. Religion is beyond common sense and normal civility, so religious power may sooner or later, subtly, turn into totalitarianism and finally into exploitation, extortion, inquisition and terror. Many religious and spiritual thoughts have nonsensical, totalitarian and even cruel twists. 'If you do not convert and become an active member of the right club, you will have to start a new cycle of perhaps thousands of incarnations.' I have heard otherwise decent, well-meaning people utter such threats. This is not giving stones for bread, but fungus.

Another example is the Dutch Neoplatonist Van Helmont, who was warning us in the seventeenth century that perjurers will be reborn forty times as a bastard (Van Ginkel 1917). We no longer fall for this idiocy, because the shame of being a bastard is out of fashion. But some people still seriously declare the annihilation of millions of Jews to be the karma of the Jewish people.

I do not claim that all that was mere coincidence. Some people who feel an intense personal hatred for a particular group may have had nasty experiences with that group in a past life. Think of the example of the anti-Semite who was disparaged and treated as an inferior by Jews in his past life as a Samaritan. Spending long years as a galley slave with sadistic Negro overseers may easily make you a Negro-hater. Certainly the hatred of many feminists for males is not without reason, either. But it is dangerous to extend individual dynamics to explain mass phenomena. Mass phenomena do not result from personal karmic knots.

Understandably, someone who has been maltreated by men in several lives may become a man-hater in a next life. Still, it is a primitive reaction, showing lack of insight and mental health. If somebody with a wart on his nose beats people up, it is not true that all people with warts on their noses will do the same. This is as true for warts as for gender, race or membership of any group or culture.

Some esoteric writers see illness as karma from past lives. Chapter 3 gave examples from Rudolf Steiner. A later writer is Douglas Baker (1977), who explains the karmic origins of psoriasis, anorexia, breast cancer, mongolism, etc. These writers presuppose that everything seemingly accidental happens for a reason. These diseases may even be necessary.

We have no empirical evidence for this at all. Research in this area is possible by regressing people who had a particular disease and checking similarities – and differences – with a control group. However, it is unlikely that significant relationships will be found. Steiner tells us that the frustration and hatred of industrial proletarians results in tuberculosis in a next life. People do harbour or digest feelings of hatred in many different ways. Someone who choked to death in a mine, may retain his hatred in his throat or chest. Another person who once starved may now have intestinal problems.

Finally, the idea that we carry positive results from past lives, like talents, into following lives is less widespread and elaborated, and it is generally true.

THE PROCESS OF INCARNATION

The religious views of reincarnation say little on this subject. The main differences are about when the soul actually descends. Some say during conception, others during birth and a few in Africa say it is during the ritual of name-giving.

The regression material presents a miscellaneous picture. Souls may be attached to the foetus from conception; they may even provoke a conception. Something important to one person, for example the choice of parents or the choice of gender, may be unimportant to someone else. People differ in the extent of their life plans, as in the aspects that are important to them. The widespread belief that birthmarks and prophetic dreams can identify who a newborn child was before, is generally true. But hope and fear may distort the evidence. Identification at a later age, as in Africa and Tibet, when an infant has to select objects belonging to his preceding incarnation from among many other objects seems more reliable.

Another common belief is that children who remember a past life will die young. This is one of the reasons why parents are not pleased when a child recalls a past life, even when they believe in reincarnation. Other reasons could be that the child wants to return to his preceding family, continually compares his home with his preceding life or rejects the limitations of being a child. That children who remember a past life will die young is untrue; it is rather the reverse.

The children Stevenson investigated had a shorter intermission and were born closer to the place where they died in their past life than people in regressions. Children with spontaneous memories frequently died young in their preceding life, often in accidents or by violence. Apparently, most of them belong to population I. They hardly realise they are dead; they barely remain aware and their personality enters the new incarnation virtually unchanged. This explains why child cases have fewer memories of the intermission. About 50 percent of remigrants have such memories (Wambach's research), while in child cases the number is less than 25 percent.

Why do fewer children in the West remember a past life than in the East? In areas where such cases do occur in the East, about 1 in 500 to 1 in 1,000 children have such memories. A rough estimate is that in Western society this percentage is about half as large. The main reason is probably that neither the materialistic, nor the agnostic, nor the Christian views in the West encourage parents to accept these memories and so make ignoring or repressing the child's recollections more likely. A second reason may be that incarnations of the population I type are relatively more common in non-Western countries. If such cases were recorded better, it would be interesting to find out if the frequency were the same as elsewhere. It probably would be.

Many infants say things that indicate prenatal memories. Some of these statements indicate a sense of a pre-existence and a sense of reincarnation, even without personal memories of the past life. Karl Muller was one of the first to collect cases of children with perceptive remarks about the prenatal state and reincarnation (Muller 1970: 70).

MEMORIES AND REGRESSIONS

Is it common or uncommon to have memories of past lives? Spontaneous explicit memories of a past life are certainly uncommon: most people do not have them. But are past-life regressions commonly attainable? Between 70 and 90 percent of those interested in remembering past lives are able to do so simply, as many have found out to their surprise. Esoteric circles caution against an easy and gullible road to past-life memories and argue in favour of a solid esoteric schooling, because the experiences of past personalities can only be reached via the immortal part of the soul, which is, of course, quite something. Esoteric schools object because of their concept of the higher and lower self and (I suspect) because lay regressions topple their precarious monopoly on the only right way to develop.

Theosophical and anthroposophical circles are ambivalent towards people who remember past lives or regress to them. They fear imagination instead of memory, especially as people with apparent recall relate shorter intermissions and less karma than their doctrines postulate. Finally, they object to hypnotic regressions. Hypnosis makes people passive and is creepy. What is especially creepy about it is that it is much faster and more effective than their meditation and concentration exercises. It isn't fair. It is wrong being so easy.

This reminds me of Henry Ford's rejection of the automatic starter. He said it would corrupt the masculine character of the American male: 'Cranking up the car in the morning is good for men.' And so countless people drive out of the present with the automatic hypnotic starter – or with the newer, more effective non-hypnotic starters – and leave regular people standing next to their cars, because starting with a manual crank is tiring and seldom works if you do it half-heartedly and the crank is made of rubber. Of course, true and serious drivers deny that the other drivers really went anywhere. Besides, the road drivers are not members of the Automobile Association and cannot drive at all, and are a menace to themselves and others. A real automobile driver stays in his driveway.

The mind mirror research also indicates that classical meditation of the kind esotericists usually recommend might rather inhibit past-life recall: it stimulates alpha and theta waves, while we need beta and delta.

Some esotericists claim that the historical decline and resurgence of the belief in reincarnation and of past-life memories are providentially determined. The advent of their esoteric schools hails the new age. Some time in the future, which Rudolf Steiner saw as being around the millennium and the theosophists much later, more and more people will remember past lives. Doubtless, this coincides with the expectation that these schools will grow in numbers and influence.

Rudolf Steiner says that knowledge about reincarnation was lost in the Kali-yuga (according to him from 3101 BC to AD 1899). But almost all reincarnation ideas we know are from this period. His statement implies that all of that is false knowledge. Only after 1899 does real knowledge about reincarnation emerge, a date that neatly separates the founding spiritist and theosophist publications (before 1899) and Steiner's own publications (after 1899). Further, Steiner claims that there was an absolute low in the knowledge of reincarnation during Christ's time. This is certainly incorrect for Africa and Asia. For Europe and the Middle East it is inaccurate, because the actual low was almost a century earlier, after which a resurgence of Platonism in the Hellenistic world brought a return of reincarnation ideas.

Elsewhere Steiner claims that concrete memories of past lives were gradually lost in the third post-Atlantic age (from 2907 to 747 BC). Historically, nothing backs this up. Regressions of people who remember lives in which they remembered past lives or were aware of reincarnation, indeed usually return to a period fairly long ago, but seldom more than 2,000 years ago. Steiner's notion that memories of past reincarnations were lost because the priests drank too much wine attributes a staggering influence to wine and to priests – both serious misconceptions, especially the second. He takes the wedding at Cana as a symbol for this. I fail to see the connection.

Steiner believed that reincarnation ideas returned during the eighteenth-century Enlightenment in a Christianised form, that is to say, in the light of the development of humanity, whereas earlier Buddhist ideas had concentrated on individual development. This is rather an odd idea, considering that the Buddhist *anatta* doctrine can hardly be interpreted as individual development and also considering that reincarnation thoughts re-emerged precisely because the ancient Indian culture became more known. According to him, in the eighteenth century, Christianised ideas come up that are preparing the new age, beginning after 1899. The only conclusion is that Christ revealed to an in-crowd, after proper preparation by the German Enlightenment and less proper (Buddhist-inspired) preparation by the theosophists, a secret that no one before Steiner could reveal correctly in public. This view is inconsistent and does not correspond with historical facts.

SUMMARY

A view on reincarnation that is in line with the present evidence is as follows:

- Everybody probably reincarnates dozens of times or over one hundred times.
- Intermissions vary greatly, usually from a few months to several centuries. A few years to a few decades is most common.
- At least 80 percent of people change gender, with varying frequency and without fixed rules.
- Many people have some form of life plan, which is never a completely detailed blueprint.
- We may be born with people we already know. When we have a life plan, we will probably also meet some (or many) people we have met before.
- Recall of past lives can be enlightening, past-life therapy can be healing and both may be part of a life plan.

Sensitive people appear to have more past-life memories. Typically, their memories and the information they give about others and about reincarnation in general contain more karmic relations and gender changes. They often remember or see more than one life. They are usually more interested in understanding causes and effects than in demonstrable proofs of reincarnation. However diverse the sources, the information they give is similar. Psychic people can clearly distinguish their own memories from those of others. This weakens the telepathic explanation of apparent past-life recall.

Previous personalities are reanimated in apparitions, in pseudo-obsessions and in therapy sessions.

Next to specific undigested experiences of reviewed and otherwise digested lives, whole previous lives may be unreviewed and so undigested. Both retain their energies and can become activated in the present life. Also the personality from a previous life may influence the preparations for the present life. *Anatta* theories are therefore untenable and the reincarnation idea itself has to be more precisely defined.

The present empirical evidence contradicts most religious and esoteric views. The intermissions are normally shorter than believed. Related ideas such as the *anatta* doctrine and metempsychosis can be discarded. The workings of karma are far from universal and mainly psychological. The relation between a transcendent individuality and ever-new personalities is viewed too rigidly and schematically, resulting in the idea that past-life memories can only be found through esoteric exercises or initiation. Fulfilling religious duties is not half as important as some would like it to be.

The main differences between the empirical evidence and classic esoteric theories are:

- karma works less as a natural law, is more psychological and knows many different patterns
- intermissions are shorter
- gender changes follow no fixed rule, and
- no special education or initiation is needed to recall past lives.

Some practising regression therapists see regression evidence confirming religious or gnostic authorities. Although there are some correspondences, the differences are so striking that I doubt the intellectual integrity of the authors involved. There are even people who consider the *Tibetan Book of the Dead* a good guide, confirmed by regression evidence. You must close more than one eye to be able to say that.

RECOMMENDED READING

There are as yet few attempts at a comprehensive empirical vision. The first book in this direction is by Allan Kardec (1857). Broad, reasonable treatises on reincarnation have since been published by Van Ginkel (1917), Ralph Shirley (1924) and, above all, Karl Muller (1970). Gina Cerminara (1950 ff.) developed a theory on the basis of Edgar Cayce's work. The general discussions in Stevenson's research (1966 ff.) are excellent, though limited to cases of spontaneous memories in young children. The two books by Helen Wambach (1978, 1979) are an important first step towards a statistical framework. David Christie-Murray's book (1981) is reasonably comprehensive. Christopher Bache (1990) has written essays on the subject that are well-founded in the empirical material available.

Ian Stevenson has written one of the best books ever on reincarnation, in which he draws conclusions from a lifetime of researching children's cases (1987).

Karl Muller introduces his book with Allan Kardec's epitaph: '*Being born, dying, being reborn and always advancing, that is the law.*' The same law holds true for the development of knowledge – something esoteric writers often accept when looking back, but tend to forget when looking forward. Scientific curiosity is a better guide than gnostic insight.

Sixteen

PAST-LIFE THERAPY

Past-life therapy is regression therapy accepting that scenes from apparent past lives may emerge. Regression therapy derives its name from its method: recovering and reliving past experiences cathartically. Though reliving cathartically is sometimes sufficient, regression proper often has to be complemented by working with subpersonalities, sometimes called ego-state therapy: having the present personality communicate with the child or the past life that had the traumatic experience. In the present lifetime, this work is called Inner Child work; in past lifetimes, this is called working with pseudo-obsessors: treating and integrating disturbing past-life personalities.

The second complement of regression is bio-energetically discovering and processing old residues – including those from past lives – that clutter our system and that we still may experience physically. Regression therapy in the wide sense includes Inner Child work and bio-energetic work, and the same holds for past-life therapy.

So past-life therapy is an expanded and specialised form of regression therapy. What is special? What does a broad regression therapist who works only in this life have to learn additionally to become a broad past-life therapist?

- Guiding death experiences, including what happens immediately after death up till the life review, if any.

- Guiding the life preparation, including planning, preview and choice of parents.

- Discovering and processing past-life elements in experiences from this lifetime, including prenatal experiences in the womb, which explain mental and emotional responses in this life.

Both working with subpersonalities and working bio-energetically can lead to discovering what those two fields respectively call attachments and foreign energies: charges, subpersonalities and even complete personalities of others. In the last case, we are dealing with attachment by deceased people. Sometimes attachments appear to come from people we knew in a previous lifetime. Consequentially, past-life therapy includes removing karmic attachments.

In regressing to infancy, birth and the time in the womb, children often respond, consider and decide in a way that betrays an adult background, an adult awareness. As adults have Inner Children, children have Inner Adults. Past-life therapists take those Inner Adults seriously and discover in them previous lifetimes or conclusions and decisions from the intermission between death and rebirth. When processing an apparently relevant childhood trauma gives only half results, past-life therapy will go further back.

I have given my own vision of past-life therapy in *Deep Healing: A practical outline of past-life therapy* (1996). In this chapter, I limit myself to some general considerations and an overview of the publications in this field.

Past-life therapy is generally short therapy, though the sessions are longer and more intensive than is usual in psychotherapy. Denys Kelsey, who could compare past-life therapy with his previous work as a psychiatrist and to the work of his colleagues, once said to Norman Shealy (Graham 1976: 38), 'In a maximum of twelve hours of regression therapy, I can accomplish what will take a psychoanalyst three years.'

The research of Rabia Clark (1995) shows that most therapists (74%) combine working in past lives with other methods and forms of therapy. Most frequently mentioned are NLP (52%), hypnotherapy, including the Ericksonian hypnotherapy (37%), and Gestalt (20%). Inner Child work also belongs in this shortlist. Many therapists (26%) also do past-life therapy with children, from about eight years of age. The main reasons are childhood fears and phobias. Other reasons are bed-wetting, dyslexia, depression, anger and hyperactivity. Some work with even younger children, in fact from the time they begin to speak. Carol Bowman (2000) gives examples of both mothers and young children.

How often do patients relate previous lifetimes if asked to return to the first cause of their problem? About one-third of my patients, after an open suggestion, arrive in a past life, about one-third remain in this life and about one-third relive childhood events that appear to be restimulations of older traumas. Shakuntala Modi found, with patients with more serious problems, that 70 percent had symptoms originating from past lives. Brian Weiss found that about 40 percent of his patients had to go to past lives to solve their problems (Weiss 1993: 28):

Regression to an earlier period of this present-day lifetime is usually fruitful enough for most of the remainder. For those first 40 percent, however, regression to previous lifetimes is key to a cure. The best therapist working within the classically accepted limits of the single life-time will not be able to effect a complete cure for the patient whose symptoms were caused by a trauma that occurred in a previous lifetime, perhaps hundreds or even thousands of years ago. But when past life therapy is used to bring these long-repressed memories to awareness, improvement in the current symptoms is usually swift and dramatic.

Some patients prefer to indulge in past lives while they resist confronting bad feelings and bad experiences from their childhood. In general, working in this lifetime is emotionally more taxing. Working in past lifetimes is usually mentally more taxing and the somatics are probably more intense, except where present-life work involves reliving serious physical trauma such as accidents or violence.

INDICATIONS AND COUNTER INDICATIONS

For what kind of problems do people seek past-life therapy? Or when do therapists who have more options apply this therapy? We have ample information on this: a survey in 1988 of the members of APRT, the professional association of past-life therapists and researchers in the USA; a similar survey of the members of the NVRT, the professional association in the Netherlands; and the survey of Rabia Clark in 1995. Garritt Oppenheim (1990), I myself (1996) and Shakuntala Modi (1997) also present lists. If we summarise these lists, the big four reasons for past-life therapy appear to be:

1 Fears and phobias
2 Relationship problems and problems of connecting with people in general.
3 Depression
4 Physical complaints without medical explanation or not responding to medical care.

After those four, the most common other reasons are:

5 Sexual problems

6 Addictions

7 Obesity and eating disorders.

Oppenheim mentions – as I do – uncontrollable anger as a motive and further gives some interesting very specific motives, such as writer's block and stage fright (Oppenheim 1990: 24).

What problems and which patients are unfit for regression and past-life therapy? The first condition for regression therapy is that we can communicate with the patient. We cannot do regression therapy with patients whom we cannot talk to because they are mentally too retarded, too heavily drugged or too psychotic. These patients cannot hold on to their own thoughts and feelings, or the reverse, they cannot let go of them. Or they may be too autistic. For regression we need people who can explore their thoughts and feelings and can distinguish fact and fiction. Few psychotics qualify.

Morris Netherton considers working with schizophrenics possible, but only within an institution. He starts with imagination and gradually moves to real regression. It works, but slowly and in a limited way. With autistic children he has had no success. An alcoholic has to be free from alcohol for about three days to regress successfully. People using barbiturates or other tranquillisers have to detoxify before starting regression therapy.

Roger Woolger considers working in past lives too intense for many. They have no need to reopen old sores in their psyche, but need a personal, therapeutic relationship to rebuild their confidence in life and in themselves. Others find it difficult to visualise and to internalise.

Oppenheim mentions as counter indications (1990: 23):

- patients with acute anxiety attacks
- those acutely confused
- those in acute depression
- those with severe acute psychotic symptoms
- patients who ask for hypnosis to stop smoking or lose weight or improve their golf scores or achieve similar goals – they can nearly always attain their goals without deep-level probing
- patients deeply rooted in religious teachings who back away from reincarnation

- macho patients (including women) scoffing at anything mystical or paranormal as 'crackpot' or 'weirdo'.

Patients may be neurotic, tremble with fear, hear voices, have multiple personalities, or be depressive, suicidal or murderous. As long as they want to work and as long as they assume responsibility, we can work with them. We cannot work with dependent people. Assuming responsibility is a condition for any therapy that is insight-oriented. This excludes people who don't accept that they are patients and people who want to remain patients. In both cases, they are engaged in games, not in therapy.

People with 'patient mentality', even after apparently successful regressions, hardly improve. People addicted to their suffering are rather cases for 'antitherapy', jolting them out of the standard patient–therapist relationship. Others are walking case files: they regurgitate all their previous diagnoses and can talk about themselves only in psychobabble or psychiatric jargon.

People who refuse to be patients may reject suffering in all its forms (they have forgotten to feel, as feeling is too painful or too threatening) and so are unfit for explorative, insight-oriented therapies. They refuse to relax and want to interpret, comment and rationalise anything remotely resembling a significant experience or emotion. Those who cannot live, cannot relive. Working in this way may be interesting as an intellectual ball game, but it is a dead-end road to catharsis. People who want to get rid of their problems without finding out the causes may sometimes be helped by antitherapy or paradoxical therapy and often by behavioural therapy or classical hypnotherapy.

For many, past-life therapy still has a sensational ring and so it attracts professional sufferers who want to add it to their collection of near-hits. Also, past-life therapy is mainly known in alternative, spiritual circles. Some may been told, by people who have just discovered they are psychic, that they have a hole in their aura because in a past life they dabbled in black magic. People who have visited others to hear things about themselves expect a therapist to perform for them. They don't come to produce, but to consume. Or they want psychic surgery. They want to be hypnotised and come back to their senses when everything is over. Or they want to witness a miracle healing. Some even assume they are entitled to that. They have suffered enough and they pray so hard to be healed. Others want to hear that they are a special, uncommonly difficult case. Beware of patients who trust you deeply before you have done anything. They may want to bind you: 'You are the only one who can help me.

I am completely sure of this. A psychic saw your name in my aura.' Etcetera.

Few past-life therapists like working with drug addicts. They get perceive images that are usually both chaotic and tedious. It seems as if their tapes have come loose and are entangled. Scientologists believe that each drug is tied to a specific emotion and they rigorously pursue the separate emotional lines one by one.

Back to suitable themes for regression therapy and past-life therapy. I list ten, trying to avoid jargon:

Old anguish: paralysing fear, roaring despair, waves of grief, mountains of sorrow, maddening confusion. This comes from old traumas that we can track down and resolve with straight regression.

Being stuck. Seeing no way out. Simmering impotent rage. As well as straight regression (often to death experiences or long incarcerations), bodily work (such as acupressure) and bio-energetic interventions are indicated, till freedom has been won back and the blocked energy flows again.

Loneliness and desolation. This requires regression to the beginning of these feelings and then to before they began: homing.

Inhibition. Never mingling easily. Feeling an outsider, a spectator. Feeling clumsy, shy, withdrawn. Often guilt or shame are involved, real or talked into. Personification (working with subpersonalities), mainly Inner Child work, is indicated.

Submissiveness. Over-adapting to others. Lack of assertiveness. Not being able to stand in your own space and energy.

Being lost. Having lost the way or not knowing which way to take.

The body resisting. Physical complaints without medical cause or not responding to medical treatment.

Ineffective insight. We know what the problem is, we know what to do, but nothing changes.

Relationship problems. Being entangled with somebody else. Efforts to disentangle are in vain.

Self-discovery. The search for unknown, undiscovered parts of ourselves or unsuspected talents. Curiosity. Free explorations rather than therapy.

Past-life therapy often helps where other forms of psychotherapy stop short. Its methodical basis – regression – is simple. While lay hypnotist can quickly achieve hypnosis (though objections can be made against some of the practices) practitioners have to be able to establish relationships of trust, to counsel and to deal with emotions. And they need practical wisdom. A background in psychology and in other forms of psychotherapy is desirable.

Regressions and personifications quickly uncover the source of most problems. A person who wants to work with those methods, but doesn't believe in real past-life or prenatal experiences, may consider those experiences as diagnostic psychodrama and treat them as such. As long as the experiences are taken seriously as experiences the process will be effective. A seasoned therapist can apply other psychotherapeutic insights or methods at many different moments during reliving and processing. Practical knowledge of, for example, Individual Psychology or Gestalt Therapy is desirable. Past-life therapy can be combined profitably with other insight-oriented forms of psychotherapy. Just finding, repeating and releasing traumatic experiences and closing off with positive suggestion often helps, but is, in my mind, too limited a repertory for a practising past-life therapist.

Past-life therapy always starts just as regression therapy. Traumas, postulates or hangovers also originate in the present life, and pseudo-obsessions may come from multiple personalities. The only really specific element in past-life therapy, compared to present-life regressions, is dealing with afterdeath and prebirth issues. With hangovers this is often necessary, with pseudo-obsessions always. Introductory relaxation, visualisation or hypnosis are usually a waste of time. The only thing that counts is to find the right 'bridge', the most natural entry. The simplest bridge that is sufficient as an induction is localising an actual emotion in the body. But for many people, emotions are remote or their body is remote. As many traumas, hangovers and pseudo-obsessions have some postulates tied in, and we can use these as entry points. Postulates are embodied in key sentences. Repetition of the key sentence often unlocks the underlying problem.

Over the emotional bridge, somatic bridge or postulate bridge we can uncover these four types of problems. While dealing with them, we'll find out to what extent they originated where. Sometimes we first need to resolve the traumatic death of the preceding life, before the patient can work on childhood problems, but the other way round may be more common. The trick is to start with problems of which the resolution frees the most psychic energy, and to take on the heavier or more resistant problems later.

FIVE DIFFERENT SCHOOLS OF
PAST-LIFE THERAPY

The practitioners in this field conceive of past-life therapy in five different ways:

- *Real reliving is unnecessary.* People only need to know what happened. If they cannot remember, we ask the Higher Self or interview a guide, or somebody else can see it for them. The knowledge gained is often used in a religious way: admonishment, prayer, forgiving ourselves and others, etc.

- *People have to relive, but not in full.* They only have to understand what happened. If, unfortunately, reliving becomes difficult, tense or painful, we get them out and have them replay everything from a distance, without having to feel the impact. As I heard an American lady say: 'Reliving trauma is only retraumatising.'

- *Full reliving is in itself healing.*

- *Full reliving is the first step only.* Repetitions are necessary till the traumatic episode is being relived calmly.

- *Full reliving is necessary, but only new understanding brings full release.* The original experience remains charged, but appears in a new light. People are no longer burdened. They are unstuck.

The first conception is not true past-life therapy, but a psychic consultant telling people what they have done or experienced in past lives that explains why they are not radiantly happy today. The consultation may be complemented by psychic treatment such as Reiki, aura healing or chakra healing. For people who cannot do the work themselves (autistics, psychotics, retards, infants), this is a godsend. For people who do not want to work (professional patients and professional consumers), this is an escape. For people who want to work and who can work, this is a delay — and a handicap, as they cannot enter later sessions with an open mind. I agree with Franklin Loehr (*Psychography*: 42):

> The clinician himself is not — repeat NOT — to use regression therapy of his clients for his own psychic development. The client's past-life recall is his experience. For the clinician to 'feel along with it', to psychically pick it up or even to precognitize it, detracts from the

quality of the client's experience. I learned this early. I have 40 years' experience as a psychic channel for the Loehr–Daniels Life Readings, but I scrupulously keep my work with a recall client to that of a clinician and counselor only. I remember speaking for a group of regression therapists and overhearing one boast how he could 'go along all the way' with his client. No! Your client pays you to be a skillful psychotherapist, not a sidewalk fortuneteller.

In the Netherlands, quite a number of people advertise themselves as past-life therapists, and then tell you about your previous lives. It is rarely useful, often the reverse. In Japan Hiroshi Motoyama works this way. Just like many of his colleagues in the West, he advises people to meditate and pray (Motoyama 1992). I think this is unsound psychology, and, even worse, I think it may prevent people from healing themselves. Other so-called therapists croon at every incident during the reliving that people should forgive. The clients hardly understand what is going on – they don't know the causes, they don't know the consequences – but something bad is going on, so let's forgive and ask for forgiveness! I have witnessed sessions that were interrupted every ten or fifteen minutes by visualising golden cups filled with a radiant golden liquid. Yes, your guess is right: forgiveness to the brim.

An interesting variant of this first school is exploring past lives by testing the arm or another body part. Kinesiology is using the body of the client as an oracle. It resembles swinging the pendulum, but uses variations in muscle tension. It is no therapy, but an interesting alternative as induction. Ultimately, it comes down to reliving. This method may be indicated for people who have difficulty visualising. The findings of kinesiologists such as Bert Kahnemann correspond fully with experiences from regular past-life regressions.

I don't believe that the arm test automatically tells the truth. Many questions may be imprecise or ambiguous. We are consulting unspecified parts of the subconscious computer. Much depends on the quality of the kinesiologist – I think more so than with methods. Kinesiology has all the advantages – and all the disadvantages – of consulting the subconscious by using the body. If the conscious part is done properly at the end of the session, the disadvantages may be compensated for and the advantages may remain.

Many therapists of the second school also easily consult the Higher Self of the patient and evoke spiritual guides. Guides may be asked if regression is permitted or useful and what would be a good entry point. Sessions may wobble between regression and channelling. Often, therapists let their own guide communicate with the guide of the patient. Naturally, many sessions are about the deceased, including attachments. In the better sessions, guides do not present themselves as higher beings, but as friends and acquaintances from past lives or a deceased family member of this life. Some therapists working this way add — rightly — that a guide who prescribes what you should do is not a guide but an intruder.

This approach has its limits. Real neurotics cannot be helped by this method, because it contains little psychotherapy. Evil and the darker sides of human nature also cannot be dealt with this way. This approach is not sufficiently grounded for that. But pretty often it may work and, if it works, it works simply and quickly. Sessions with children may be especially beautiful. An example of the good things the New Age can bring.

A good instance of the third conception of past-life therapy is Brian Weiss's report on the hypnotic sessions he did with one of his patients. To his immense surprise, those sessions led spontaneously to past lifetimes. In the same hypnotic condition, messages came through from guides, which explains the title of the book: *Many Lives, Many Masters* (1988). Why somebody who lacks a body is considered a master, I never did quite understand, and I am amazed that an intelligent, critical and well-educated psychiatrist drops his jaw when things are said from the Beyond that are often quite reasonable and sometimes just platitudes and generalities.

More interesting is that people may be cured dramatically, just by reliving, without any therapeutic processing. Unfortunately, in practice this is not always the case, but it is enlightening to have another extensive case study. This is an honest book from a distinguished and unimpeachable psychiatrist, who reports in wonder, but truthfully, about an experience that went completely against the grain of his profession. A convincing book by a courageous man.

An example of the fourth conception is the oldest known form of regression therapy: the *dianetics* of L. Ron Hubbard (1950). All episodes of lessened consciousness and physical or emotional pain lead to engrams, as he calls them. Identifying and repeatedly reliving these engrams leads to discharge. His ideas resemble those of Columbus: obstinate misconceptions, but epoch-making results. Like that of many pioneers, his significance is more in opening new territory than in developing a handy conceptual framework. His methods are rigid, probably effective, but inefficient. Intense opposition to his approach has led to a self-contained empire of cleared people, maintaining itself with the ample proceeds of the time-consuming clearing of others. Out of dianetics came *scientology*, operating under duress. Witness – among many others – an interview in *Penthouse* (1983), containing the most fantastic array of charges ever brought against one man. Scientology is a bastion, formed by a religious denomination, by copyrights on each sentence and a fearsome tenacity. Scientologists don't canvass at your doorstep, but harass you by mail. I will describe briefly the therapy of Ron Hubbard without his jargon and without fully justifying his methodology.

The remigrant or patient holds in his hands two tin cans or other electrodes connected to an E-meter, measuring skin resistance. The therapist, called the auditor, keeps track of the meter. The auditor counts back in time, till he hits a traumatic episode, indicated by the E-meter showing lower skin resistance. He dates this period precisely and establishes its duration precisely. By questioning, he clarifies the initial situation. He asks the remigrant what he sees. From an often insignificant detail he develops the situation in full. Then he asks the remigrant to go over the whole episode in his mind. The E-meter shows to what extent this is done effectively. Then he asks the remigrant to describe the experience. Usually, emotions lessen somewhat in the telling, but do not discharge completely. The auditor has the agony traversed many times till the remigrant remains completely calm. He then asks if there is another situation linked to this one that has to be traversed. If the E-meter shows a reaction (similar to the use of finger signals), he searches for these other episodes and processes them likewise.

Often the remigrant blocks. He prefers to avoid an experience and doesn't see anything; impressions remain vague or he glosses over things. In this case the engram is not released. Questions that open the engram are: 'What can you sense? What precisely do you see? What can you confront? What can you be responsible for?' Many engrams are anchored in postulates: the conclusions and decisions we used to deal with the situation. Examples are: 'It isn't really happening.' Or: 'I will never again show how I feel.' Remigrants can recount an episode in four or five versions before they describe what really happened, what they really did. Even then, processing may be incomplete, because the embedded postulates still have to be resolved.

Hubbard's procedures are strict. The auditor has the remigrant recount a traumatic episode till the E-meter shows no further reflections. Hubbard gives several examples of the tenacity of scientologists, including one case of forty hours of working on one situation (Hubbard 1958).

Later approaches that connect past-life therapy to behavioural therapy are in one respect even more primitive: discharge is sought by mere repetition, while scientology stresses confronting the situation and taking responsibility, be it in a mechanical way.

Stanislav Grof is an example of the fifth, cathartic school, in which I count myself. Typical of Grof's approach is strongly somatic induction (forced breathing) and strongly somatic processing. Other therapists stress mental processing: understanding and reinterpreting. I have often found that a previous therapy was effective, but had cost much time or led to inconclusive results, because mental processing was neglected or the reverse: that somatic processing was neglected. Occasionally, mental processing and somatic processing have both been done, while the emotions have been neglected. Lasting catharsis presupposes that work has been done and results have been achieved on four levels: mental, sensory, emotional and physical. Among the best examples of this fifth school I count Morris Netherton and Roger Woolger.

Past-life therapy has a sister, 'past-life mobilisation': waking up dormant talents from past lives. It does not relieve karma; it liberates *dharma*. This discipline is still underdeveloped. I have found neither methodology nor research on this topic. According to Joan Grant (Kelsey & Grant 1967), awakening sleeping talents occurs when animating the 'supra-physical' (presumably a permanent extract from the etheric body) from a past lifetime.

The possibility of waking up dormant talents is demonstrated by the experiments in 'artificial reincarnation' by Vladmir Raikov in Moscow. He told hypnotised subjects they were reincarnations of some great artist. After the sessions, their drawing or painting or musical abilities improved considerably. How much stronger the effect must be when real past lives are involved!

According to Ron Hubbard (1958), 82 percent of people clearly improve psychologically and physically after past-life therapy. General belief or disbelief in reincarnation has no influence on its success. The only condition is that apparent experiences from other times are accepted as meaningful subjective material, without continuously wondering about their objective truth. A telling detail in Hans Cladder's research (1983) is that past-life regressions diminished the psychosis scores and enhanced the reality perception scores of patients. Extraversion also increased, another indication that reality orientation had improved.

Rabia Clark writes that therapists most often report success with relationship problems and phobias and the least success with obesity, addictions and depression. Brian Weiss found (1992) that the success rate increases from 50 percent to 70 percent by careful intake and by carefully connecting past-life experiences to (childhood) experiences in this lifetime.

Success certainly is not only a question of the right methods. Past-life therapy, like most psychotherapy, is more than applying skills; it also depends on the person of the therapist. A good therapist is weathered and mild, all friendliness and scars.

FURTHER READING

Early works. Ron Hubbard wrote *Dianetics* (1950), a thick and controversial book by somebody who became even more controversial later. For the practising professional, study of this work is a must, despite the prolixity and obstinacy that seem to be inherent in pioneering works. Hubbard's later book about past-life regressions (1958) is the opposite of prolix, but unfortunately badly organised and presented.

One of the first books about the relationship between past lives and therapy, by Inácio Ferreira (1955), is interesting to read, but at the same time disappointing. Mediums identify the causes of eleven psychiatric cases in past lives. The cases seem valid and the restimulations in the present life are interesting and credible. What is being done with this? Nothing. Absolutely nothing. This is no precursor of past-life therapy. Karl Muller (1970) later gives many examples of spiritist past-life therapy, mainly about karmic obsessors.

Another early book is that of Denys Kelsey and Joan Grant (1967), but they do not give examples from sessions. Isola Pisani dedicates a whole book to someone doing regression therapy with Kelsey (1978); a romantic and philosophical, but sympathetic report of an inner journey.

Works in English Past-life therapy really starts in 1978 with the now classical works of Edith Fiore and Morris Netherton. Another good read is the book by Glenn Williston and Judith Johnstone (1983). Adrian Finkelstein gives some interesting cases, but is sloppy and therapeutically weak (1985). His induction method is ideological and his descriptions and ideas about spiritual healing are unrelated to regression work. Rightly, he considers self-help and a positive attitude as essential, but he forgets the most important thing: understanding.

Florence Wagner McClain (1986a) wrote a practical and informative brochure, an almost ideal introduction to regression therapy for potential clients. The only objection is that she suggests that anybody can experiment with regressions and that guidance is just knowing what questions to ask. Joel Whitton (1986) is interesting and illuminating, especially about the intermission period, but uses classical hypnotic induction and classical psychiatry and hardly offers specific methodology.

Karl Schlotterbeck (1987) illustrates that psychotherapeutic insight is needed to work with regressions. He approaches the subject from many different angles, but often when the reader expects a conclusion, he moves on to the next chapter. Much of his book is more journalism than analysis, but it is reported by an experienced and sensible practitioner.

Past-Life Therapy in Action by Dick Sutphen and Lauren Taylor (1987) is the best presentation of Sutphen's way of working.

Roger Woolger has written one of the best books on past-life therapy (1987). He makes it crystal clear that regression is only the beginning of therapy. His Jungian views mainly contribute, his Buddhist views mainly distract. Insufficient insight into incomplete dying makes the short-circuits he often finds between successive lifetimes rather confusing than enlightening (1987: 294 ff.). For the rest an excellent book.

The first, already mentioned, book by Brian Weiss (1988) is the report of a psychiatrist who stumbled into past lives. His second book (1992) is much more interesting. His colleague Robert Jarmon is a psychiatrist who likewise discovered past lives by accident. He later meets Brian Weiss and they collaborate. Though the regression techniques and insights in the whole process remain somewhat superficial, we have here a true, professional therapist at work. Also interesting is that he intersperses regression cases with other cases from his practice as a medical doctor and a psychiatrist, as in near-death experiences and psychic experiences of non-psychic people. A believing Catholic, a medical doctor and a past-life therapist: you wouldn't believe those three could go together, but apparently they can. Good stories, well told (Jarmon 1997). A third American psychiatrist who stumbled into past lives and wrote about her findings is Shakuntala Modi. She gives interesting statistics from her therapy practice (1997).

Garrett Oppenheim offers good examples of therapies (1990). Winafred Lucas wrote and edited two volumes in which she has ten therapists explain their way of working (1993a and b). A must for the practising therapist!

Edward Klein has written a clear story about a series of therapeutic sessions and their processing (1995). The methodology is simple, even monotonous: hypnotic induction, two imaginative bridges and the exploring the most meaningful moments of the lifetime. The death experience is also simple: leave your body, float around, answer the question about life lessons and see the connections with the present lifetime. One life, one session. Klein is startled when his client enters a lifetime that she had already entered in a previous session. This is a first for him! For experienced therapists, this book offers little; it is only one more illustration. For the student, it shows well the relationship between sessions and daily life. For people still looking quizzically at regression, this is an interesting and consistent story. Not a bad introduction.

Rabia Lynn Clark wrote her doctoral thesis on past-life therapy (1995). She inventories how past-life therapists work, what they work on, how long for and with what results.

Works in Dutch A number are well worth reading. A recent book by Ronald van der Maesen and Rob Bontenbal (2002) is written to convince academic psychologists that past-life therapy is a serious profession. The price is high: the subject is almost smothered in the usual abstract academic jargon. But it could well be a price worth paying.

Works in German The first German past-life therapist to publish was Thorwald Dethlefsen (1976). Werner Koch is another therapist, apparently experienced, but writing as if he invented past-life therapy (1992). He calls his book a first. He doesn't know the literature, or at least doesn't mention it. Medical, theosophical and metaphysical ideas are strangely mixed with regression experiences. A critical, perceptive reader may sift out a few interesting observations. Far better is the book by the Swede Jan-Erik Sigdell (1993), who worked for many years in Switzerland.

Epilogue

REINCARNATION AND THE ART OF LIVING

What does reincarnation bring as an idea or experience for daily life? It depends. Stevenson relates that an Indian monk remarked to him that belief in reincarnation changed nothing, as there were as many creeps and thugs in India as in the West. Stevenson agrees with him when thinking of people in general, but thinks that belief in reincarnation can make a large difference for an individual who accepts the consequences (Stevenson 1987: 233).

But which belief and which consequences? Motoyama considers redeeming karma, not only individual, but also national and global karma, to be our life goal. His views, to my mind, seem abstract and debatable. Take his views on marriage, for example (Motoyama 1992: 58):

> *Couples who are going to live together exclusively for physical reasons, are not prompted by karma to marry. They join because of sexual, physical passion, the most materialist human quality. A bodily relationship is an ephemeral bond, because it lacks the spiritual, psychological and karmic basis of the other categories. In the world of today, we see this kind of relationship very often and the great number of divorces shows how volatile it is. The temporal nature of a physical relationship is alarming because it is nihilistic. Human flesh does endure less than a century, so that all relationships based mainly on the flesh, have to be temporal. As such ephemeral, superficial relationships are increasing, our world is approaching decline and decadence.*

Is sex materialistic? Even the idea that sex is physical, is doubtful, when we think of the sexual out-of-body experiences of people like Robert Monroe and Waldemar Vieira. And is it true that sexual relationships miss spiritual, psychological and karmic aspects? On the contrary. Is something ephemeral nihilistic? Ever been to a concert? Ever had a peak experience? And is divorce the result of marriages that were only sexual? I can think of many other reasons. Like lack of sex. Are relationships that are only sexual at all possible? I am very glad human flesh does not endure more than a century. And as ordinary addictions already can be taken into a next life, passionate relationships certainly can. Motoyama gives many interesting examples of his extrasensory perceptions, but his general reflections are not necessarily a testimony of practical insight. The broader and the deeper the subject, the more we need common sense.

So let's face it: belief in reincarnation may mean absolutely nothing. You can use it to justify your behaviour and make your life sound more exciting. Your new girl friend is your twin soul and you met her just when the karma between you and your wife had been worked out. What about the children? Well, they have their own karma. Dad leaving is part of that. Everything gets a deep, impressive echo.

Belief in reincarnation may mean as little or as much as any other belief. Fatalistic people find an excuse for their fatalism, just as active people find a reason for their activism. Take Henry Ford (Head & Cranston 1976: 355):

> *I adopted the theory of reincarnation when I was 26. Religion offered nothing to the point. Even work could not give me complete satisfaction. Work is futile if we cannot utilize the experience we collect in one life in the next. When I discovered reincarnation . . . time was no longer limited. I was no longer a slave to the hands of the clock . . . I would like to communicate to others the calmness that the long view of life gives to us.*

Ian Stevenson sees as the main consequence of a true understanding of reincarnation that we explain less by chance and become personally more responsible. That would explain part of the resistance to the idea of reincarnation: we are left with fewer excuses. His argument is so compelling that, though long, it follows here in full (Stevenson 1987: 221 ff.).

> *I devoted chapter 2 to the belief in reincarnation. I do not propose to write another full chapter about disbelief in it, but the topic deserves at least a section of a chapter. I disclaim any aim in what follows at converting readers to a belief in reincarnation. I wish only to draw attention to a group of obstacles that seem to me often to hinder the open-minded appraisal of the cases of children who remember previous lives. The hindrances that I propose to discuss are: the unfamiliarity in the West with the idea of reincarnation; the assumption that our minds (and memories) are in our brains and cannot possibly also exist elsewhere, the belief that we cannot conceive what life after death would be like and the preference many persons seem to have for not wishing to accept the personal responsibility for their destinies that reincarnation suggests they may have.*

I approach the topic of this section with some fear that I shall be guilty — or thought to be guilty — of moralizing or even being preachy. I should like to avoid these faults. However, reflection on the many arguments in favour of reincarnation and on the evidence for it, imperfect as it is, has made me ask whether there may exist irrational — as well as rational — impediments to believing in it. If so, one irrational objection against it may be the burden of responsibility for one's individual destiny that reincarnation imposes. Reincarnation is a doctrine of hope; to be sure, it suggests that a person can profit in a future life from the efforts he makes in this one. The hope becomes fulfilled, however, only through personal effort and this may be more than most persons can accept. Passivity lies deep within humans as we now are. We can observe this easily without referring to the possibility of reincarnation. Many sick persons let themselves be cured to death — with prescription drugs rather than modify the way they live — by eating and drinking alcohol less and smoking tobacco not at all. In the social sphere a thousand will vote for legislation to correct the fault of its neighbor for every ten who will say, as I believe Beethoven did: 'Lord, cease not to labor at my improvement,' and for every one who, with Beethoven, will actually labor himself at self-improvement. If a person cannot accept responsibility for the outcome of one life, he will not welcome being asked to assume it for two or more lives. Nevertheless, it remains true that, as Baudelaire wrote: 'There can be no progress — real moral progress, I mean — except within an individual person and by the individual himself.'

The average Westerner seeks to avoid personal responsibility for his condition and conduct in a variety of ways. Christianity has offered a selection of escapes ranging from the idea of predestination to that of atonement for all our sins by Christ's death on the Cross. Modern science offers the concept of chance, but that idea began with gamblers and insurers, not with scientists. Already in the eighteenth century Gibbon could write (with some complacency, it seems to me): 'When I contemplate the common lot of mortality, I must acknowledge that I have drawn a high prize in the lottery of life . . . the double fortune of my birth in a free and enlightened country, in an honorable and wealthy family, is the lucky chance of an unit against millions.'

The metaphors used to express the concept of chance vary from time to time; and in its modern guise, the uniqueness of an individual person is said to derive, for the most part, from the random sorting of chromosomes into the germ cells of the person's parents. We use and have used many other names for the same concept: accident, luck, fate. Whatever the label, the idea serves to spare the person using it from even a share of responsibility in what happens to him. I believe that most Westerners find the idea of chance somewhat appealing; and to the extent that they do so, they may think that of reincarnation uncongenial.

Some persons find unattractive the thought that chance is the governing force in their life; and yet they may still wish to avoid personal responsibility for it. For two generations now, Western psychiatry and psychology have soothed this group with assurances that all their troubles come from the defects of their parents or from the aggregate of everyone else — what we call society.

For those whose life is not too enticing, the idea of having to return is depressing. So, many people are convinced that this is their last life on earth. When they tell me that — sometimes radiantly, sometimes conspiratorially — my standard response is that I whole-heartedly hope that too. I happen to think, however, that an active, happy and satisfying lifetime gives better closure. Better to leave fulfilled than frustrated.

A philosophical belief is one thing; personal recall of past lives is another thing; experiencing the life review after death or the life preview before birth is something else; being healed by past-life therapy is something else again. Reincarnation ideas, especially if they are fed by personal experience, can improve the way we live and add a new dimension to mental health, to education, to ethics and to public life. In the next sections, I draw first theoretical conclusions and then practical consequences.

THE MAIN INSIGHTS DERIVING FROM REINCARNATION

The experiences of the life review after death and the life preview before birth put our life into a meaningful perspective: we have been coming from somewhere and we are going somewhere. Death remains a drastic and dramatic change, but it no longer terrorises us and incapacitates us with the prospect of an unimaginable and futile vacuum. The first consequence of grasping reincarnation is the diminishment or even disappearance of the fear of death. After publishing their book *Other Lives* (1969) Brad Steiger and Loring Williams received numerous letters and phone calls from people who told them how their book had helped them to overcome their fear of death (Graham 1976: 106). Other writers will have had similar experiences.

The break caused by death is often the release from intensely limiting and intensely painful conditions. Checking out regularly maintains our stamina.

Dying well and being born well are very important. Full release and awakening after death, followed by a proper life review, preferably not alone (see chapter 11), and a good preparation of the new life, again preferably not alone (see chapter 10), will avoid much frustration and digression.

We realise we have our own life plan. We do not have to do everything at once. Every life has a main theme, a main direction. Life is less arbitrary and coincidental. We accept our life conditions better and we may feel that we are on course – when we are.

Learning and development never end. Living again and again means experiencing and doing new things and looking back on them. 'Up there' we evaluate, think and steer. 'Down here' we put ourselves and our ideas to the test and we may consolidate our gains.

Different lifetimes bring different experiences: one life a man, the next a woman; one life active, the next reflective; one life poor, the next rich; one life meek, the next assertive. We learn to see things in perspective. It makes us less dogmatic, less prejudiced, less complacent, less nationalist, less racist, less sexist.

Reincarnation means an ever-growing wealth of experience. It means a sometimes difficult and exhausting, but never-ending road to more insight, deeper feelings, richer talents and to being both more ourselves and more related to others. Imperfection leads to ever less imperfection.

Our body is not a prison, but a diver's suit to enable us to operate 'down here'. Moreover, it is a living robot geared towards self-awareness. For many people this means no self-consciousness outside the body before having developed it inside the body. For others, the body is a living robot in which they learn separateness and emotions.

We help less advanced people and are helped by more advanced people. Human relationships continue beyond death and birth. Through all the muddle, human relationships flower. We learn to be considerate to others and to empathise and sympathise with others and with and through others we learn acceptance, respect and trust, also in ourselves. Our sense of responsibility develops.

The future of this planet is our responsibility, our shared lot. We get a broader perspective of history.

RECOMMENDATIONS DERIVING
FROM REINCARNATION INSIGHTS

Start with being born well: know with whom and why. Neither shirk away from the efforts at hand, nor overburden yourself; agree to some appointments. Don't be too ambitious or too modest in planning your life. Next to what we want to do and what we can do, circumstances limit our possibilities to develop ourselves or to redeem karma. Trying to settle all accounts and clear out in one mighty sweep is usually folly. Often it is better to clear off less karma and contribute more to others or to the world at large.

Accept your fate, without becoming fatalistic. You are who you are and where you are, but you always can change something. Karma neither prescribes, nor proscribes. It is no computerised justice system. It is partly natural and partly woven from our own responses and from educational advice or interventions by others.

Receive your children as people who have to find their own route and learn their own lessons, and who have their own contributions to make. As parents we are stewards, but we are not the prime cause of the behaviour of our children. We can take neither all the credit nor all the blame.

And the acme of living well: die well, don't hang around, don't sulk or complain, don't retreat in shame or guilt or anger, but go straight to the people you belong to and – in God's name – look straight in the mirror. (You can start practising here.)

RECOMMENDED READING

Little has been written on the consequences of the belief in reincarnation. Arthur Osborn (1966) points out personal consequences, and Thea Stanley Hughes a few social consequences (1976: 66). Manley Hall (1977) starts promisingly: 'The purpose of the present essay is to show some of the ways that belief in reincarnation can be of practical daily use.' Alas, the rest of the booklet is full of metaphysical thoughts, many of which are controversial. Everything he asserts and everything he confirms, he calls Eastern wisdom or Eastern philosophy.

Violet Shelley wrote a book with the, for many, promising title *Reincarnation*

Unnecessary (1979). She has found eighteen readings of Cayce that make her conclude it is not necessary to reincarnate. From most readings we only can deduce that the person in question doesn't need to return to earth, for example: 'The present life can only add. It is not necessary, unless the entity wants to, to return to this earth for more experience.'

What are really good books? In the bibliography they are marked with (⁵). Gina Cerminara's *Many Lives, Many Loves* (1963) is a collection of essays on reincarnation – a consolidation of her *Many Mansions* and *The World Within*. Very reasonable and so much common sense! This book has much to offer as an intelligent and judicious vision of reincarnation and related subjects. The last essay explains my appreciation (1963: 206).

> *I am convinced that for any proposed reforms (of our world) to be truly effective and lasting, there needs to be a new kind of insight in human beings, insight of a psychological, scientific and philosophical nature. I would like therefore to raise my voice in favour of the widespread and immediate dissemination of knowledge concerning two things: the theory of reincarnation and the methodology of General Semantics.*

I am a real fan of Alfred Korzybski, the founder of General Semantics. I devoured his major work *Science and Sanity: An introduction to non-aristotelian systems and general semantics*, of almost 800 pages, published in 1933. To my mind, his style resembles Ron Hubbard in *Dianetics*: poor writing, rambling, full of repetitions, absorbed in his own world, but pioneering. Compared with Korzybski, Hubbard appears to be a monomaniacal, ill-educated adolescent and, compared to Hubbard, Korzybski seems a gentleman, eccentric, but a man of the world. Regression therapists will be familiar with the bastard of general semantics: Neuro-Linguistic Programming. I have realised only after many years how important general semantics has been in my approach to past-life therapy.

Christopher Bache, a teacher in the psychology of religion, has written one of the best books ever on reincarnation, *Life Cycles: Reincarnation and the web of life* (1990). Well-informed, philosophically broad and yet close to practical daily life. Recommended especially for people who find my book somewhat excessive or too critical. If you seek practical wisdom, read Christopher Bache and Gina Cerminara.

Then we have books that suggest how to discover your own past lives or to help others to discover theirs. Colin Bennett (1953) is indifferent, just like

J.H. Brennan (1973) and Michael Talbot (1987).

Bettye Binder wrote *Past Lives, Present Karma Workbook* (1985), a small practical guide to learning to distinguish which personal impressions may be recollection and which may be fantasy, to learning to deal better with emotions like anger, guilt and blame, and to learning to live more positively in general. It offers several practical exercises, but little on reincarnation.

J. Maya Pilkington and the Diagram Group collaborated on *Who Were You?* (1988), a lucky bag of interesting tidbits, clumsy summaries, random trivia, rambling lists and nonsensical illustrations. We may admire the drive to collect, but the result is more astounding than enlightening. Maybe for a beginning reader some useful details are included in this toppled bookcase.

The best books for people who want to explore past lives on their own are Gloria Chadwick's *Discovering Your Past Lives* (1988) and J.H. Brennan's *The Reincarnation Workbook: A complete course in recalling past lives* (1989). People who want to experiment with simple regressions in the living room would do best to read Gerald Glaskin (1974) and Bryan Jamieson (1976).

GLOSSARY

See the indexes for references to the main text and for words not included in this glossary.

Akasha record A theosophical idea also used by other schools of thought. Everything occurring in this world is registered in the 'memory of nature'. This memory is in a supersensory, all-encompassing etheric field: *akasha* (originally meaning 'radiant'; later heaven). How this happens is unclear. The ability to see impressions of the past is regarded as a form of clairvoyance, called 'reading the *akasha* record'.

Impressions of events before the present life may be explained as impressions from the *akasha* records rather than as personal memories. This does not explain the personal character of memories. The idea of *akasha* records is vague and general. It is worth little as an alternative explanation of past-life recall, being more speculative and complex.

Anatta (from *an-atta*; 'not-self') A doctrine in Theravada Buddhism. There is reincarnation, but not of the self. Only 'psychic patterns' are imprinted on a new person. Identity of being does not have to co-exist with identity of awareness. A person's present sense of self is not at all identical with the reincarnating soul. Historically, the idea is a reaction to the earlier unsophisticated ideas about the reincarnating self.

Art of living From the perspective of reincarnation this means developing a sense of our life line or life plan; treating others humanely; keeping negative emotions under control; accepting our fate without passivity; taking the time needed for the maturation of judgment or will; entertaining neither too many nor too few ambitions; never purposefully inducing negative emotions in others.

Awareness For most of us, awareness and self-awareness have been developed inside the body. Once we have attained self-awareness, we can learn to retain it after death, without a body. Once we are self-conscious outside the body, our consciousness may develop to an extent that returning in a body diminishes it. Self-awareness is the continually shifting result of identification processes. Trance shifts our attention inwards. We become self-absorbed and our sense of time diminishes. During a regression, this shift moves into the past. During dissociation, our awareness may split into two focal points simultaneously: 'elliptic consciousness'.

Barrier Resistance to relaxing and focusing; more specifically, resistance to regressing. Without barriers, induction is a piece of cake. Barriers are blocks to the induction itself. The induction restimulates either awful experiences related to trusting, passivity or relaxation, or the first experience about to surface is a shocking death.

Barriers may be dissolved by recognising the implicit fear, guilt or shame or the implicit shut-off commands; by going deeper into trance; by practising relaxation at home; or sometimes by improving the trust between remigrant and therapist.

Blocks Resistance to reliving specific experiences during the regression. The experiences are suppressed and resist being remembered. Usually the regression halts. The experience is sometimes blanketed by a screen memory or is remembered in a shallower form. The remigrant moves out of regression into reliving, memory or even recollection.

Other surfacing regression experiences may contain shut-off commands or are too threatening and scare us before they become fully conscious. The therapist has to get around the blocks, while respecting them. Blocks are often excellent leads: the issues that are avoided are the relevant issues.

Bodhisattva. The Hindus call the state of liberation *moksha*. They rather see a gradual ascent during many lifetimes. Before we attempt to attain *moksha*, we can grow, progress and attain wisdom through many incarnations. The Buddhist view of reincarnation as a wheel is more pessimistic. Buddhism sees the incarnate state as imperfect and unsatisfactory. The Wheel of Life and Death turns on and on without end. Each life irrevocably leads to the next life – unless we follow the eight-fold path. We may then ultimately attain Nirvana. We continue to exist, but no longer as a separate individual being. Rather than enter Nirvana, one may reincarnate out of mercy and love for not yet liberated brothers and sisters. Such a person is a Bodhisattva. Even after entering Nirvana and attaining the Buddhic state, we may choose to remain there as a Pratyeka Buddha or return as a Buddha of Compassion.

The 'periodic return of the perfected', found among the Ishmaelites, is a similar thought to that of the Buddhist Bodhisattvas and the Hindu Avatars. The suggested return of Elijah as John the Baptist or the return of David as the Messiah can be seen in the same terms. Such thoughts are found in cultures that do not believe in the reincarnation of common people. However, regressions show that voluntary incarnation with a mission is relatively common. See also *Free will*.

Catharsis Catharsis is purification, a death as well as a rebirth. A liberating experience resolving ignorance and negative emotions (e.g. fear, hate, jealousy, anger, powerlessness, guilt, shame, indifference) and replacing them with understanding, acceptance and peace, often with joy and a sense of freedom. Every therapeutic episode in a regression therapy strives for catharsis. The healing life review, as the temporarily clinically dead report, can be considered the great catharsis.

Christos experiment The most careful and elaborate induction method for non-therapeutic regressions to past lives. It has prescribed step-by-step procedures with built-in safety measures and is described by Glaskin (1974).

Compensation theory People who believe they remember a past life are compensating for the limitations and difficulties in their present life. This theory is only relevant when remigrants claim their past life was more pleasant or more important than their present one. Few remigrants believe they were important or even famous. The theory does not explain verified details from past-life regressions that could not have been known from study or communication.

Descent The shift of consciousness from outside to inside the foetus. Sometimes an etheric thread connects the psychic body with the foetus while the consciousness remains outside. As the birth approaches, the thread shortens. Often, the soul is alternately in the body and outside it. It seems that the brain has to be developed sufficiently to be in the body. The main descent or 'grand entrance' is usually in the last months of pregnancy, or during or just after birth. After the descent, the soul can still depart, but it becomes more and difficult.

Determinism Each event is predetermined by past events. Therefore present events determine future events. Coincidence and free will are illusions. A complete knowledge of the past would enable perfect prediction of the future. The religious form of determinism is predestination. In reincarnation, determinism may be part of the karma doctrine. Although regressions show that karma is not fixed by natural laws but works psychologically, the idea of determinism has not been disproven. Determinists do argue that each psychological reaction looks arbitrary; essentially, such reactions can be computed beforehand. But if each outcome results from a specific psychological constellation, how do we know this constellation? By its outcome. Jack beats John because Jack is better. How do we know he is better? Because he won. This is running in circles. The empiric refutation of determinism is impossible. This makes determinism an intellectual mood or an ideology, not a scientific or practical concept.

Deva An angel-like discarnate being inhabiting and possibly influencing nature. It resembles a personification of natural powers, but quite a number of remigrants have deva-like experiences as memories. Apparently some psychics do perceive devas.

Dharma (I) Rough meaning: inner law. Obligations that we take upon ourselves voluntarily and consciously, maybe because we owe it to ourselves: *noblesse oblige*. *Dharma* is the 'nobility' we have acquired as the strength and ability to act not arbitrarily or on blind impulse, but aligned with the situation and with ourselves. *Dharma* is the reverse of karma, which implies involuntary actions imposed on us by circumstances or the past.

(2) The assets (talents and strengths) carried over from past lives. The opposite of karma, the liabilities from past lives. Some *dharma* is activated naturally and some we activate intentionally. *Dharma*, like karma, can probably be found in the vehicle of vitality, the chakras and the aura.

Dissociation Loosening or separating, the opposite of association.

- Liberating ourselves from identification with a past experience. 'That happened then. I don't have to be afraid of that any more. Now I don't have to do that any more.'

- Making a part of ourselves that is a subjective participant into an objective observer.
- Introducing the present self into a past experience to aid healing and acceptance.

Dissociation is a temporary aid to achieve elliptic consciousness and facilitate catharsis or to break an undesirable bond or identification with the past, and is, as such, essential for catharsis.

Drugs Related to reincarnation and regression in three ways:

- Drug addiction often continues through lives.
- Drugs may be used to induce memories of past lives. They may produce interesting experiences, but these are so unstructured that they cannot be properly processed. No understanding, no catharsis.
- Drug addiction complicates regressions and therapy. Apparently, drugs confuse the retrieval system. Memories get mixed up.

Engram The registration of an undigested, sharply defined episode with all its physical, emotional and mental consequences. Engrams are connected to other engrams by association and restimulation.

Etheric body A good characterisation is Crookall's term *vehicle of vitality*, the link between the soul and the body, not a vehicle of consciousness. We are self-aware either in our soul or in our body. When the soul and the body separate at death, one part of the ethers remains in and with the body. Another part is cast off by the soul after death and slowly disintegrates. A third part probably remains with the soul and contains at least the chakras and all the karma and dharma.

Evolution (I) The experiences, lessons and emancipation we gather in consecutive lives. Many souls ascend to self-consciousness. They once started with animal lifetimes or they 'kick-started' directly into human lifetimes. Many other souls were self-conscious as spirits before descending into human lifetimes – this is more properly called involution. Some seem to have been human before on other planets, and now – either voluntarily or involuntarily – partake of the lessons a more primitive planet has to offer.

(2) More specifically, evolution is any natural development resulting from ever-changing experiences during lifetimes, in challenging circumstances, with exertion, choice and risks; it is always learning, even in spite of ourselves. It precedes education and self-development, and never ends.

Free will In reincarnation, free will begins when we are sufficiently aware before birth to have some choice in our next lifetime. The simplest forms of free will are returning on impulse, or either accepting or refusing a proposed life plan. Free will increases when we can plan and preview ourselves. Our choice widens as karmic burdens, obligations and relations lessen. In life, free will is in the choices we make in our actions and our interpretations and evaluations. For example, we can give in to a mood or get over it. We can choose to look at things pessimistically or optimistically.

Furcation A subpersonality going its own way – which may even be incarnating separately.

Gender choice The gender of a coming incarnation may be fixed by a rule, chosen arbitrarily or decided by accident. The first option usually means that the sex remains the same or alternates according to fixed rules – such as a different gender every incarnation. Many people believe in such regularities.

The published cases show gender change to be common, but not universal. Apparently gender is often chosen, but is more often determined without the incarnating person's intervention, either systematically or arbitrarily, and may sometimes be entered into rashly or mistakenly.

Genetic memory One of the hypotheses used to explain ostensible past-life recall. The personal memories of people who lived in the past are genetically stored and inherited. This hypothesis is speculative: first, because genetic memory inheritance has not been established; second, because it is usually unlikely and in many cases impossible from the contents of regressions; third, because the genetic capacity is much too small; and fourth, because only memories up until conception can be transmitted. Yet almost all past-life memories include recollections of death.

Gnosticism The doctrine that we can all, with the right development of our intellect and, above all, our intuition, find direct inner truth that will enlighten, liberate or transform us. The recommended first step is to study the works of the already enlightened. When personal experience is emphasised, Gnosticism tends towards mysticism. When formal apprenticeship within a school or church is emphasised, enlightenment is usually termed 'initiation' and the insights will be esoteric. When the development of psychic talents is emphasised, the tendency is towards occultism. These three varieties are found in any combination. Anyway, we have to rise above material limitations and common sense. In other words, we should rise above the mental limitations of the incarnate state.

Group karma The idea that we are not only affected by the consequences of our own acts, but also by those of the collective we belonged or belong to: fertile ground for generalisations and speculations. So far, regressions have presented no evidence to support this idea. On the contrary, karma appears to be personal. A group of people with a particularly strong bond may reincarnate together and develop a common destiny, but this is rather group *dharma* than group karma. The idea of group karma often coincides with ideas of national souls, collective horoscopes and so on.

Guides During an induction with visualisation the therapist can ask the remigrant to imagine a guide as an inner travelling companion and adviser. This guide may have either psychological or objective reality. Some therapists believe that in regressions to past lives discarnates function as guides. These can be called upon as protectors or consulted via psychic people or via the patient himself.

Hangover (The residue of) a past life undigested as the result of general emotional malaise: loneliness, boredom, heaviness, hopelessness and meaninglessness.

Heredity Genes are of secondary importance in parental choice. The body should be suitable for the incarnating soul. Possibly, we may influence the composition made from the genetic material of our parents. Many incarnating souls help shape the embryo, imprinting on the infant personal characteristics. Notable talents are not inherited, but brought in. The physique suitable to these talents, such as musicality, is based on genetic material.

Hypersentience The induction method developed by Marcia Moore: a mixture of relaxation and visualisation, supplemented by some magnetisation and slight hypnotic trance. Characteristic of this method are rather exalted visualisations and regression goals.

Hypnosis Inducing a trance by verbal or sensory suggestions. Like magnetisation, hypnosis often leads to real regression (level 4), while relaxation and emotional, somatic and postulate bridges often result in reliving (level 3).

Identification Adopting or determining an identity.
1 Absorbing experiences, feelings, thoughts and examples into our self-image. Changing our ideas about ourselves, so that we are able to say 'I am not a second-rate artist' or 'I can fix things just as well as my father'.
2 Deep absorption in an experience, forgetting what has happened since then and including the present occurrences in the past situation (level 5).
3 Identification with another person: the impression that we are somebody else or were somebody else in the past. In Britain, women often identify with Mary Stuart and on the continent with Marie-Antoinette.
4 Establishing which infant is the new incarnation of a deceased notable or who was the previous life of the infant. An example of the former is the identification of a new Dalai Lama.

Incarnation Bonding with the foetus, descending into the foetus or the infant, influencing the foetus or infant and increasingly identifying with the young child. The incarnation process may begin at conception but often begins much later. Its decisive moment is when the soul definitively enters the new body. Few enter before the end of the sixth month, many even during or just after birth. The preparation usually begins with the consideration or the hint that it is time to return to the physical world and ends with connecting definitely to the foetus. The most important aspects are the life plan and parental choice. Often we deliberate with others; often we are advised by one or more, ranging from a good friend who drops a hint or two to circles of professional life-designers.

Induction In general, inducing a trance. Here, more specifically, gaining entry to experiences from past lives. The following induction methods are used:
1 Magnetism: using magnetic passes. Out of fashion or even extinct.
2 Hypnosis: usually through suggestions and pseudo-suggestions followed by direct instructions to go back to a past life.
3 Relaxation and visualisation: physical and mental relaxation, concentrating on the body, evoking images, often coinciding with a swinging or floating feeling or with an imagined out-of-body experience. After crossing a symbolic border or a landing after floating, the remigrant enters an experience from a past life.

4 Evoking recollections and intensifying these to reliving. Going further and further back to the first years, the birth, just before the birth and then on further.

5 Via the emotional bridge: evoking an emotion and deepening it, then instructing the remigrant to go back to a situation that caused and imprinted this emotion.

6 Via the somatic bridge: amplifying a well-defined and localised bodily sensation and then instructing the remigrant to go back to the situation that caused and imprinted this sensation.

7 Via the image bridge: taking a recurrent image or dream, or an image coming up spontaneously at the beginning of the session.

8 Via the postulate bridge: having a charged sentence repeated, then instructing the remigrant to go back to the situation that once imprinted this postulate.

Karma Originally, action. Later: the consequences of action throughout lives. The liabilities from past lives, consisting of direct and indirect somatic effects, remedial interventions, negative and incomplete psychological reactions, entanglements and voluntarily accepted debts.

Karmic astrology Reading the preceding life, or the karma from past lives, from the natal chart. Empirical material is limited to anecdotal illustrations. Different authors have different pet theories.

Life goal When we relive afterdeath or prebirth experiences, we usually find a main goal for the preceding or the coming life. Almost certainly we usually have several goals. The generic life goals seem to be growth in understanding, empathy, proficiency and independence.

Life plan The goals of the coming life, important encounters, karma to be worked out and talents to be developed; all are set down as preprogrammed reactions and drives.

Life review This occurs after death. Probably we have two life reviews. First, a quick chronological review of the past life, with questions such as: 'What did you learn from this? Are you satisfied with it? Did you feel related to certain people?' In the second review, we empathise with the people we met. This is a deeper, more personal reliving and evaluation. The first review can be so quick that the images seem spatially arranged: a life panorama. By exception, we may see a number of previous lives as if looking in multiple mirrors.

Moksha Liberation from the limitations of the incarnate state: limited awareness, blindness to and inactivity in the spiritual world, poor psychic talents. It is often interpreted as the liberation from personal existence, as reunion with the divinity we originated from and the end of our need to reincarnate.

Obsession Used here in the original meaning: being obsessed by a foreign discarnate personality. The obsessor can be an intentional or accidental disturbance: active or passive obsession. Some obsessors have a karmic relationship with their host. An obsessor can be in the aura or in the body.

Out-of-body experience The soul's temporary departure from the body, also called 'astral projection'. With 'simple' out-of-body experiences only the psychic body departs from the physical body. With a 'complex' out-of-body experience, part of the vehicle of vitality also leaves. With a simple out-of-body experience we seem to be asleep and are incommunicado. Afterwards, we can tell what happened. A complex out-of-body experience induces catalepsy: our body cools and stiffens and breathing and circulation are slower than during normal sleep, resembling hibernation.

Many induction techniques visualise leaving the body. This is usually without objective perception of the physical environment. During such a mental trip, the therapist continues to communicate with the remigrant, who remains aware of his own body, in an elliptic consciousness.

Overlapping incarnations Most examples of overlapping incarnations are those of people who enter a child rather than a foetus. Usually this happens when the soul who had been in the child up until then is either just leaving or has only taken weak possession of the body, for example Jasbir (p. 320). The case of Hermann Grundei (p. 320) may be an exception, because he was a look-alike of his old life. A real overlapping incarnation would imply some furcation.

Parental choice The considerations involved are:

- availability of a nearby foetus (unplanned incarnations of population I (see *Reincarnation patterns*)

- karmic entanglements with one or both of the parents
- a good relationship from a past life with one or both of the parents
- an opportunity for development fitting with the life plan
- suitable genetic material.

Past-life recall This type of recollection is graced with many names to distinguish it from common recollection: pre-memory, far memory, retrocognition, paranormal memory and extra-cerebral memory. The memory can be vague, merely a feeling of having lived before, with vague recollections of some situation long ago. It may consist of images, which can be static like photographs or moving, from fragments up to an entire film memory. The visions are sometimes accompanied by sound and touch and, less frequently, smell and taste. The feelings and thoughts from that time often re-emerge as well. Memories of conversations may be without sound, as if telepathically replayed. Sometimes names, places or dates are recalled. At other times there is some kind of commentary and in rare cases one can even communicate with the commentator.

Recollection can intensify to reliving, as if we are back in the situation. We can be outside observers or participants or both simultaneously: remaining outside looking at what is happening and being in it. This sometimes happens in dreams as well. The presence or absence of identification is the main difference between personal memories and telepathic impressions.

Rarely, we may see the images simultaneously, in parallel. Such a panoramic memory of a past life may reproduce a former life review.

Memories of past lives can come up spontaneously or be triggered by particular circumstances. They often follow a sense of recognition and familiarity in a new city or region or with a stranger. Memories can emerge in dreams, during illness or in accidents and in lapses of consciousness.

Past-life therapy Regression therapy accepting and often seeking regressions to apparent past lives and to experiences after death and before birth.

Precipitation The deposit in the body of psychic (and etheric) charges from a past life (karma and *dharma*). Various forms are:

- Psychosomatic complaints resulting from dubious or perverse practices in a past life (terrorism, torture, deceit, abuse of power, sexual abuse); this includes reversals.
- Psychosomatic complaints resulting from the repercussions of traumatic experiences (severe victimisation, undigested dying experiences, etc.)
- Care, attentiveness, harmony and a sense of beauty, which may lead to a healthy, balanced and beautiful body.
- Psychosomatic complaints resulting from postulates.

Progression Sensing or reading the future of this life or a coming life. There are examples of plausible progressions in this life. Progressions to coming lives seem to be sensitive to the prejudices and unconscious expectations of experimenters and subjects.

Pseudo-obsession Obsession by the personality of a past life. If a particular life has not been worked out because of incomplete or unrealised dying, that personality will not reintegrate in the soul. In a next lifetime, this past personality will haunt the aura or the body. As with real obsession, this causes psychosomatic complaints. A treatment of this personality leads to harmonisation (it becomes a regular feeding personality) and integration. Sometimes it is altogether purged and departs to the 'light' of the Higher Self. Psychic and psychosomatic complaints typical of pseudo-obsession are, for example, autism and anorexia.

Psychic (1) The quality of extra-ordinary (paranormal) intuition and sensitivity as in telepathy, clairvoyance and communicating with entities. (2) A person having and using those qualities.

Psychodrama The visualisation of some psychological tension in the form of a story, spontaneous or induced. Many dreams are psychodramatic. A psychodrama can be induced in a waking dream. It can lead to a spontaneous trance just as intense and clear as true reliving.

Psycho-plastic The most conspicuous characteristic of the psychic (or astral) world. Our surroundings correspond to our mental state. This can be subjective: we create our environment to suit our own thoughts, feelings, wishes and fears; but also objective: we get to a place or visit a person by thinking of them intensely. The body experience is also psycho-plastic: our self-image and appearance depend on what we think, how we feel and whom we meet.

Psychosomatic Somatics heavily influenced by psychology. A person who is allergic to roses may sneeze when he sees plastic roses. Placebos are sometimes just as good as, or even better than, real medicine, especially if expensive and prescribed by somebody the patient trusts.

Diseases like cancer and cardiovascular diseases have a psychosomatic aspect: certain personality traits increase the likelihood that certain diseases will manifest themselves. Our nervous system, our hormonal system and our immune system are very susceptible to our mental and emotional state – and the other way round.

In a deep trance, blisters can appear, bleeding can start, warts can disappear, etc.

Regression In general, going back in time; more specifically, a deeper form of reliving: forgetting everything that happened after the relived situation. Reliving and real regression are usually done under guidance. Bodily reactions belonging to the relived situation may occur during regression. Regressions may be done in different ways for different purposes.

Regression therapy Reliving and processing situations that were traumatic and/or resulted in the formation of postulates, till attaining catharsis.

Reincarnation Returning to a human body many times. It can be a religious doctrine, an argued conviction or a personal experience: spontaneous memories or induced regression. Other designations are: metamorphosis, palingenesis, transanimation, transcorporation and transmigration. The three most common terms are:

- reincarnation: continual rebirth as a person
- metempsychosis: rebirth either as a person or as an animal
- transmigration: developing from mineral to plant to animal to human and higher incarnation forms.

Reincarnation patterns The various ways in which people reincarnate.

- Population I: Unaware or vaguely aware; unplanned; based on the availability of a nearby foetus; intermission of a few years.
- Population II: Reincarnation following a life plan, usually recommended and strongly educational. Intermission is normally a few decades.
- Population III: Reincarnation according to a self-designed life plan, often with some self-chosen or accepted mission.

Restimulation The awakening of an existing postulate or trauma by a situation resembling the original situation that caused the trauma or triggered the postulate. In general, restimulation reinforces the existing trauma or postulate. Restimulation results in 'chains': a series of experiences sharing a similar trauma or postulate. Restimulation during pregnancy and birth facilitates restimulation during life. The therapy situation itself may restimulate traumas and postulates, especially those connected with passivity, dependence and manipulation.

Retention Continuity throughout lives. Everything we take unchanged with us from past lives: qualities, talents, idiosyncrasies, tendencies, appearance and relations.

Soul The continually reincarnating entity, developing through its incarnations. It is who we really are.

Stigmata Birthmarks, usually in the form of blotches or marks on the skin. The best-known birth stigma is a skin blotch where the previous incarnation was fatally wounded; for example, a red line on the neck if they were decapitated or a red spot on the back where a spear entered. Presumably, stigmata are more common when the deceased felt the wound intensely just before or just after his death, absorbed it into his self-image and then entered the foetus early in its development without properly reviewing the past life. One boy, whose fingers were grown together, recalled a lengthy fight leading to his death, with hands so bloody that his fingers stuck together.

Other stigmata seem to be memory aids: facilitating past-life recall or facilitating recognition by others. Such memory aids are common in tribes believing in rebirth close to where the past incarnation died and accepting wishes for the next life and prophetic dreams as natural.

A third kind of stigma is purely karmic. Wijeratne had a shrivelled arm and felt this to be the result of having killed his wife with that arm in his past life (see p. 205).

In regressions with strong somatics, temporary stigmata may appear, for example a person who suddenly has red stripes on his back when reliving a thrashing.

Super-ESP Super-extra-sensory perception, a proposed form of clairvoyance to explain apparent past-life recall and apparent messages from the deceased. Such clairvoyance clearly exceeds the talents of the usual psychic, hence 'super'. Parapsychologists who do not believe in a discarnate existence before or after death or who think that accepting this will endanger the precarious scientific status of parapsychology normally use this explanation. As with many mental constructs, super-ESP can hardly be disproven, since everything can be explained this way. It seems an unlikely explanation for the experiences of people not exhibiting more common psychic qualities.

Temple training Ancient training in psychic abilities. Many people with psychic sensitivity or ability recall psychic training in earlier lives. Much of the temple training that comes up in past lives took place in Egypt, in the Indian cultures of Central and South America and in Atlantean cultures. Less common areas of temple training are India, the Far East and early or prehistoric Greece. Other temple trainings are difficult to place historically or geographically, especially when being done outside official institutions.

Throughth The fourth (or first) dimension. The deceased feel able to pass through objects and people. Perceived three-dimensionally, they are in the same place but in the fourth dimension they are not in the same place. Contact in the fourth dimension results in interaction: people become aware of the deceased. This is what happens with telepathy, obsession and such like. Psychics see three-dimensional sections of the four-dimensional aura. This explains why different sensitives see different things, besides reasons of common imprecision, imagination and unconscious interpretation.

Trance Originally, a state resembling deep sleep entered by a medium or subject through deep magnetisation or hypnosis; more broadly, any state of changed consciousness in which we have less attention for our immediate surroundings.

Within the framework of regressions, trance is a consciousness shifted from the exterior to the interior world and from the present to the past, and includes physical changes in muscle tension, skin resistance and brain-wave rhythms, as well as mental changes such as relaxation, an altered sense of time, reduced observation and increased imagination. Trance depth can vary during a session. A trance-medium is a person who can bring herself (or himself) into a trance enabling communication with discarnate entities. More generally, anyone whose psychic abilities only surface in trance, such as Edgar Cayce.

Vehicle of vitality. A term coined by Crookall to designate the intermediary between the psychic body and the physical body. It is often called the etheric body. Crookall preferred 'vehicle' because apparently we cannot be self-aware in this body, whereas we are aware in the physical and the psychic (or astral) body. The vehicle of vitality seems to have no independent organisation. Many observations indicate that the 'silver cord' has no organic structure, but is more like a string resulting from stretching an elastic substance.

Probably, the vehicle of vitality is the seat of all dharmic and karmic influences.

BIBLIOGRAPHY

WORKS IN ENGLISH

Abhedananda, Swami, *Doctrine of Karma*, Vedanta Press, 1944

[1]Abhedananda, Swami, Reincarnation (1899), 8th edn, Calcutta: Ramakrishna Vedanta Math, 1964

[5]Albertson, Maurice & Kenneth Freeman, *Research Related to Reincarnation*, Fort Collins: International Conference on Paranormal Research, 1988

[3]Algeo, John, *Reincarnation Explored*, Wheaton: Theosophical Publishing House, 1987

Allen, Eula, *Before the Beginning*, Virginia Beach: A.R.E., 1965

[3]Amidon, Norton W., *Cross-Correspondences among the Loehr–Daniels Life Readings*, Grand Island, Florida: Gnosticoeurs, 1985

Aivanhov, O., *Reincarnation*

[1]Anderson, Jerome, *Reincarnation: A study of the human soul in its relation to re-birth, evolution, post-mortem states, the compound nature of man, hypnotism, etc.*, San Francisco: Lotus, 1894a

[1]Anderson, Jerome, *Karma: A study of the law of cause and effect in relation to re-birth or reincarnation, post mortem states of consciousness, cycles, vicarious atonement, fate, predestination, free will, forgiveness, animals, suicides, etc.*, San Francisco: Lotus, 1894b

[3]Andrade, Hernani Guimarães, *The Ruytemberg Rocha Case*, São Paulo: Brazilian Institute for Psychobiophysical Research, 1973

[3]Andrade, Hernani Guimarães, *A Case Suggestive of Reincarnation: Jacira & Ronaldo* (1975), 3rd edn; São Paulo: I.B.P.P., 1980

[2]Arroyo, Stephen, *Astrology, Karma and Transformation. The inner dimensions of the birth chart*, Vancouver: CRCS Publications, 1978

Arundale, Francesca, *The Idea of Rebirth*, London, 1890

[1]Atkinson, W.W., Reincarnation and the Law of Karma, Yogi Publication Society, 1908

Aurobindo, Sri, *The Problem of Rebirth*, Pondicherry, 1952

Austen, A.W., *Teachings of Silver Birch*, London: Spiritualist Press, 1938

[5]Bache, Christopher M., *Life Cycles: Reincarnation and the web of life*, New York: Paragon House, 1990

[1]Baker, Douglas, *The Wheel of Rebirth*, Wellingborough: Aquarian, 1978

[1]Baker, Douglas, Karmic Laws: *The esoteric philosophy of disease and rebirth* (1977), Wellingborough: Aquarian, 1982

[3]Baker, Douglas, *Reincarnation: Why, where and how we have lived before*, Wellingborough: Aquarian, 1981

[3]Banerjee, H.N., *The Once and Future Life*, New York: Dell, 1979

[4]Banerjee, H.N., *Americans Who Have Been Reincarnated*, New York: MacMillan, 1980

Banerjee, H.N., *Lesson in Past Life Regression*, San Diego: Metaphysical Book Club, 1981

Banerjee, H.N. & Will Ousler, *Lives Unlimited: Reincarnation East and West*, New York: Doubleday, 1974

Baronte, Gervée, *You Have Lived Before!*, London: Pearson, 1936

Baronte, Gervée, *The History of the Soul*, (Chesham,1937)

[1]Baronte, Gervée, *Your Previous Life on Earth: Reincarnation simplified*, London: Jenkins, 1938

Batzel, Beth & Karl Schlotterbeck, *Lion of Satan, Lion of God*

Bendit, Laurence J., *The Mirror of Life and Death* (1965), 2nd edn, Wheaton: Theosophical Publishing House, 1968

[3]Bennett, Colin, *Practical Time-Travel: How to reach back to past lives by occult means* (1953), Wellingborough: Aquarian, 1980

Berg, P., *Wheels of a Soul*

Berger, A., *Reincarnation*

[5]Bernstein, Morey, *The Search for Bridey Murphy* (1956), New York: Doubleday, 1989

Bertholet, Alfred, *The Transmigration of Souls* (1904), New York: Harper, 1909

[1]Besant, Annie, *Karma* (1895), 10th reprint; Adyar: Theosophical Publishing House, 1975

Besant, Annie, *A Study in Karma* (1912), Adyar; Theosophical Publishing House, 1917

Besant, Annie, *Dharma*

[1]Besant, Annie, *Reincarnation* (1898), Adyar: Theosophical Publishing House, 1924; *Reïnkarnatie*, Amsterdam: Theosophische Uitgevers Mij, 1898

[1]Besant, Annie, *On Karma* (1916), Adyar: Theosophical Publishing House, 1921

[1]Besant, Annie, *The Necessity for Reincarnation*, Adyar: Theosophical Publishing House, 1921

[2]Besant, Annie, *Karma and Social Improvement*, Adyar: Theosophical Publishing House, 1921

[1]Besant, Annie & Charles Leadbeater, *Man: Whence, how and whither* (1913), 5th reprint; Adyar: Theosophical Publishing House, 1971

[1]Besant, Annie & Charles Leadbeater, *The Lives of Alcyone*. Volumes I and II, Adyar: Theosophical Publishing House, 1924

Binder, Bettye B., *Past-Life Regression Guidebook*, Culver City, CA: Reincarnation Books, 1993, 2nd ed

[2]Binder, Bettye B., *Past Lives, Present Karma Workbook* (1985), Culver City, CA: Reincarnation Books, 1992

Blakiston, Patrick, *The Pre-Existence and Transmigration of Souls*, London: Regency, 1970

[1]Blavatsky, Helena Petrovna, 'Theories about Reincarnation and Spirits', *The Path*, November 1886

Bloxham, Arnall, *Who was Ann Ockenden?*, London: Spearman, 1958

[3]Blythe, Henry, *The Three Lives of Naomi Henry*, London: Frederick Muller, 1956

Bolduc, Henry Leo, *The Journey Within: Past-Life regression and channeling* (1988), 2nd printing, Virginia Beach: Inner Vision, 1989

Bolduc, Henry Leo, *Life Patterns, Soul Lessons and Forgiveness*, Independence: Into Time Foundation 1994

Bond, F. Bligh, *The Diary of Patience Worth*

Bowen, Francis, *Christian Metempsychosis*

[4]Bowman, Carol, *Return From Heaven*, New York: HarperCollins, 2001

[4]Bowman, Carol & Steve Bowman, *Children's Past Lives: How past-life memories affect your child*, New York: Bantam Books, 1997

Box, Sushill Chandra, *Your Last Life and Your Next*, Calcutta, 1959

[3]Brennan, J.H., *Five Keys to Past Lives: Practical aspects of reincarnation* (1973), Wellingborough: Aquarian Press, 1978

Brennan, J.H., *Reincarnation*, Wellingborough: Aquarian Press, 1981

[4]Brennan, J.H., *The Reincarnation Workbook: A complete course in recalling past lives*, Wellingborough: Aquarian Press, 1989

Brownwell, George, *Reincarnation*, Santa Barbara, 1946

[3]Bryce, James, *Reincarnation Now!*, Vancouver: Fforbes, 1978

Butler, Chris, *Reincarnation Explained*, Science of Identity Federation, 1984

[4]Cannon, Alexander, *The Power of Karma in Relation to Destiny*, London: Rider, 1936

[1]Capel, Evelyn Francis, *Reincarnation within Christianity* (1980), London: Temple Lodge Press, 1988

Carr, Donald, *The Eternal Return*, New York: Doubleday, 1968

Cayce, Edgar Evans, *Edgar Cayce on Atlantis*, New York: Paperback, 1968

[4]Cerminara, Gina, *Many Mansions* (1950), New York: Sloane, 1970

[5]Cerminara, Gina, *Many Lives, Many Loves* (1963), 4th printing, Marina del Rey: De Vorss, 1987

[4]Cerminara, Gina, *The World Within* (1967), London: Daniel, 1973

Cerminara, Gina, *Edgar Cayce Revisited and Other Candid Commentaries*, Virginia Beach: Unilaw Library Donning, 1983

[4]Chadwick, Gloria, *Discovering Your Past Lives*, Chicago: Contemporary Books, 1988

[1]Challoner, H.K., *The Wheel of Rebirth: Some memories of an occult student*, London: Rider, 1935

Challoner H.K. & R. Northover, *Out of Chaos*, London: Theosophical Publishing House, 1967

Chapple, C., *Karma and Creativity*, Albany: SUNY, 1986

[1]Chinmoy, Sri, *Death and Reincarnation*, Jamaica, N.Y.: Agni Press, 1974

[3]Christie-Murray, David, *Reincarnation*, London: The Society for Psychical Research, 1975

[4]Christie-Murray, David, *Reincarnation: Ancient beliefs and modern evidence*, Newton Abbott: David & Charles, 1981

Church, W.H., *Many Happy Returns*, London: HarperCollins, 1984

[4]Clark, Rabia Lynn, *Past Life Therapy: the state of the art*, Austin, Texas: Rising Star Press, 1995

[2]Clow, Barbara Hand, *Eye of the Centaur: A visionary guide into past lives*, Santa Fe: Bear, 1989

[1]Cohen, Daniel, *The Mysteries of Reincarnation*, New York: Dodd, Mead & Co., 1975

[2]Cooke, Grace, *The Illumined Ones* (1966), Norwich: Fletcher & Son, 1985

[2]Cooper, Irving, *Reincarnation: The hope of the world* (1917), Wheaton: Theosophical Press, 1972

[3]Cott, Jonathan, *The Search for Omm Sety: A true story of eternal love*, New York: Warner Books, 1987

[4]Cranston, Sylvia & G. Williams, Reincarnation: *A new horizon in science, religion and society*, New York: Julian Press, 1984

[5]Crookall, Robert, *The Supreme Adventure*, London: Clarke, 1961

[5]Crookall, Robert, *Intimations of Immortality*, London: Clarke, 1965

Crookall, Robert, *The Next World and the Next: Ghostly garments*, London: Theosophical Publishing House, 1966

Crookall, Robert, *Events on the Treshold of the Afterlife*, Moradabad: Darshana, 1967

[5]Crookall, Robert, *What Happens When You Die*, Gerrards Cross: Smythe, 1978

[4]Cunningham, Janet, *A Tribe Returned*, Crest Park, CA: Deep Forest Press, 1994

Cunningham, Janet & Michael Ranucci, *Caution: Soul Mate Ahead! Spritual love in the physical world*, Columbia: Two Suns Press, 1984

Damian-Knight, G., *Karma and Destiny in the I Ching*, London: Arcanu, 1987

[2]De Artega, William de, *Past Life Visions: A Christian exploration*, New York: Seabury Press, 1983

De Silva, Lynn, *Reincarnation in Buddhist and Christian Thought*, Colombo: Christian Literature Society of Ceylon, 1968

[1]Desmond, Shaw, *Reincarnation for Everyman* (1940), London: Rider, 1954

[2]Devlin, Barbara Lynne, *I am Mary Shelley*, New York: Condor, 1977

DeWitt Miller, R., *Reincarnation*, New York: Bantam, 1965

[1]Dixon, Jeane, *Reincarnation and Prayers to Live By* (1969), New York: Morrow, 1970

Ducasse, C.W., *A Critical Examination of the Belief in Life after Death*, Springfield: Thomas, 1960

[3]Ebon, Martin, *Reincarnation in the Twentieth Century* (1962), New York: Signet, 1970

[2]Edmonds, I.G., *Other Lives: The Story of Reincarnation*, New York: McGraw-Hill, 1979

Edwards, Paul, *Reincarnation: A critical examination*, New York: Prometheus Books, 1996

Eichhorn, Gustav, *Heredity, Memory and Transcendental Recollection as Seen by a Physicist* (1909), 1959

[1]Encausse, G. (Papus), *Reincarnation* (1925), Rider: London, 1929

Evans, W.H., *Reincarnation: Fact or Fallacy?*, London: Psychic Press, 1953

[2]Finkelstein, Adrian, *Your Past Lives and the Healing Process: A psychiatrist looks at reincarnation and spiritual healing*, Farmingdale: Coleman, 1985

[4]Fiore, Edith, *You Have Been Here Before*, New York: Ballantine, 1978

[2]Fisher, Joe, *The Case for Reincarnation* (1985), London: Grafton Books, 1986

Floride, Athys, *Human Encounters and Karma*, Anthroposophic Press, 1990

[4]Flournoy, Theodore, *From India to the Planet Mars* (1900), New York: University Books, 1963

Fox, Emmett, *Reincarnation Described and Explained* (1939), London: Harper & Row, 1967

[5]Freedman, Thelma B., *Hypnotically-Facilitated Past-Life Reports: A comprehensive overview of research*, Canastota: self-published, 2000

[2]Frieling, Rudolf, *Christianity and Reincarnation* (1974), Edinburgh: Floris

[5]Fuller, Jean Overton, *Joan Grant: Winged Pharaoh*, Fullerton: Theosophical History, 1993

[4]Gabriel, Michael, *Remembering Your Life Before Birth* (1992), Santa Rosa, CA: Aslan, 1995

[4]Gallup, George, Jr with William Proctor, *Adventures in Immortality*, London: Corgi, 1983

Gardner, E.L., *Reincarnation: Some testimony from nature*, London: Theosophical Society, 1965

Geley, Gustave, *Reincarnation*, London: Rider, 1930

George, T., *The Lives you Live as Revealed in the Heavens: A history of karmic astrology and pertinent delineations*, Arthur, 1977

[4]Gershom, Yonassan, *Beyond the Ashes: Cases of reincarnation from the Holocaust*, Virginia Beach: A.R.E. Press, 1992

[4]Gershom, Yonassan, *From Ashes to Healing: Mystical encounters with the Holocaust*, Virginia Beach: A.R.E. Press, 1996

Glasenapp, Helmuth von, *The Doctrine of Karma in Jain Philosophy*, Bombay: Bai Vijibai Jivanlal Charity Fund, 1942

[4]Glaskin, Gerald M., *Windows of the Mind: The Christos Experiment*, London: Arrow Books, 1974; ISBN 0 7045 0117 1

Glaskin, Gerald M., *Worlds Within*, London: Arrow Books, 1978

[4]Glaskin, Gerald M., *A Door to Eternity: Proving the Christos Experience*, Wildwood: Book Wise, 1979

[4]Goldberg, Bruce, *Past Lives, Future Lives: Accounts of regressions and progressions through hypnosis*, North Hollywood: New Castle, 1982

Goudey, R.F., *Reincarnation: A universal truth*, Los Angeles: Aloha, 1928

Gould, B., *The Jewel in the Lotus*, London: Chatto and Windus, 1957

Govinda, Lama Anagarika, *The Way of the White Clouds*, London: Hutchinson, 1966

[4]Graham, David, *The Practical Side of Reincarnation*, Englewood Cliffs: Prentice Hall, 1976

[4]Grant, Joan, *Winged Pharaoh* (1937), New York: Harper, 1938

[3]Grant, Joan, *Life as Carola*, (London: Methuen, 1939

[3]Grant, Joan, *Eyes of Horus* (1942), London: Diploma, 1974

[3]Grant, Joan, *Lord of the Horizon* (1943), London: Diploma, 1974

[3]Grant, Joan, *Scarlet Feather* (1945), Columbus: Ariel, 1990

[3]Grant, Joan, *Return to Elysium*, London: Methuen, 1947

[3]Grant, Joan, *So Moses was Born* (1952), Columbus: Ariel, 1990

[4]Grant, Joan, *Time Out of Mind*, London: Barker, 1956

Grant, Joan, *Far Memory: The Autobiography of Joan Grant*, Columbus: Ariel, 1985

[4]Grant, Joan & Denys Kelsey, *Many Lifetimes* (1967), London: Corgi, 1976

[1]Gregor, Norman, *Thoughts on Reincarnation*, Turnbridge Wells: Gregory

Grossi, *Reliving Reincarnation Through Hypnosis*

[3]Guirdham, Arthur, *We Are One Another*, Jersey: Spearman, 1974

[3]Guirdham, Arthur, *The Cathars and Reincarnation*, Jersey: Neville Spearman, 1976a

[3]Guirdham, Arthur, *The Lake and the Castle*, Jersey: Neville Spearman 1976b

[2]Guirdham, Arthur, *The Psyche in Medicine*, London: Spearman 1978

[3]Guirdham, Arthur, *The Island*, Jersey: Spearman, 1980

Gunaratna, V.F., *Rebirth Explained*, Kandy: Buddhist Publication Society, 1971

Gupta, I.D., N.R. Sharma & T.C. Mathur, *A Case of Reincarnation*, Delhi: International Aryan League, 1936

[1]Haich, Elisabeth, Initation: *Priestess in Egypt*, London: George Allen & Unwin, 1965

[1]Hall, Manly P., *Reincarnation. The cycle of necessity* (1939), 7th printing, Los Angeles: Philosophical Research Society, 1978

[1]Hall, Manly P., *How Belief in Rebirth Can Enrich Your Life*, Los Angeles: Philosophical Research Society, 1956

[1]Hall, Manly P., *Research on Reincarnation*, Los Angeles: Philosophical Research Society, 1964

Hall, Manly P., *Astrology and Reincarnation*, Los Angeles: Philosophical Research Society, 1975

[1]Hall, Manly P., *Past Lives and Present Problems: How to prepare for a fortunate rebirth*, Los Angeles: Philosophical Research Society, 1977

[1]Hall, Manly P., *Death to Rebirth*, Los Angeles: Philosophical Research Society, 1979

Hampton, Charles, *Reincarnation: A Christian doctrine*, Los Angeles: St Alban Press, 1925

Hampton, Charles, *The Transition Called Death: A recurring experience* (1943), Wheaton: Theosophical Publishing. House, 1979

[3]Hansen, Paul A., 'Finding My French Past Life', IARRT Bulletin 2001

[1]Hanson, Virginia, ed., *Karma. The universal law of harmony*, Wheaton: Theosophical Publishing House, 1975

[2]Hanson, Virginia, R. Stewart & S. Nicholson, *Karma: Rhythmic return to harmony* (1975), 3rd ed., Wheaton: Theosophical. Publishing House, 1990

[4]Harrison, Peter and Mary, *Life Before Birth*, London: Macdonald, 1983

[2]Hartley, Christine, *A Case for Reincarnation* (1972), London: Hale, 1987

[4]Head, Joseph & Sylvia Cranston, *Reincarnation: An East–West anthology*, New York: Julian Press, 1961

[4]Head, Joseph & Sylvia Cranston, *Reincarnation in World Thought: A living study of reincarnation in all ages; including selections from the world's religions, philosophies, sciences and great thinkers of the past and present*, New York: Julian Press, 1967

[4]Head, Joseph & Sylvia Cranston, *Reincarnation: The Phoenix Fire Mystery. An East–West dialogue on death and rebirth from the world of religion, science, psychology, philosophy, art and literature and from great thinkers of the past and present*, New York: Julian Press/Crown Publishers, 1977

Henderson, A., *The Wheel of Life*, London: Rider, 1935

Hick, John, *Death and Eternal Life*, London: Collins, 1976

[3]Hodgkinson, Liz, *Reincarnation: The Evidence*, London: Piatkus, 1989

[1]Hodgson, Joan, *Wisdom in the Stars: Reincarnation through the Zodiac* (1943), Vancouver: CRCS Publications, 1979

[2]Hodson, Geoffrey, *Reincarnation. Fact or Fallacy?*, (1951), Wheaton: Theosophical Publishing House, 1972

Holzer, Hans, *Born Again. The truth about reincarnation*, Garden City, NY: Doubleday & Company, 1970

Holzer, Hans, *Patterns of Destiny*, Los Angeles: Nash, 1974

[4]Holzer, Hans, *Life Beyond Life: The evidence for reincarnation*, West Nyack: Parker, 1985

[2]Howard, Alan, *Sex in the Light of Reincarnation and Freedom*, Spring Valley: St George, 1980

[2]Howe Jr., Quincey, *Reincarnation for the Christian*, 1974, Wheaton: Theosophical Publishing House, 1987

[2]Howell, Olive Stevenson, *Heredity and Reincarnation*, London: Theosophical Publishing House, 1926

[3]Hubbard, L. Ron, *Have You Lived Before This Life?*, 1958

[1]Hubbard, L. Ron, *Mission into Time*, 1968, Los Angeles: American Saint Hill, 1973

[2]Hughes, Thea Stanley, *Twentieth Century Question: Reincarnation*, London: Movement, 1976

[1]Humphreys, Christmas, *Karma and Rebirth* (1943), Wheaton: Theosophical Publishing House, 1983

[3]Hussey, Helen Nethery, *Dr John Quickbook no. 1: Karmic Roots*, Grand Island, Florida: Religious Research Press, 1981

[3]Hussey, Helen Nethery, *Dr John Quickbook no. 2: Karmic Justice for Women*, Grand Island, Florida: Religious Research Press, 1981

Hussey, Helen & Sandra Sherrod, *Dr John: He Can Read Your Past Lives*, Gnosticoeurs, 1983

[1]Inayat Khan, Hazrat, *The Soul, Whence and Whither* (1923), New Lebanon, N.Y.: Sufi Order Publications, 1977

[1]Ingalese, Richard & Isabelle, *From Incarnation to Reincarnation*, New York: Watkins, 1980

[4]Iverson, Jeffrey, *More Lives than One?* (1976), New York: Warner, 1977

[4]Jamieson, Bryan, *Explore Your Past Lives*, Van Nuys, CA: Astro-Analytics Publications, 1976

[5]Jarmon, Robert J., *Discovering the Soul: The amazing findings of a psychiatrist and his patients*, Virginia Beach: A.R.E. Press, 1997

[1]Jinarajadasa, C., *How We Remember Past Lives and other essays on reincarnation* (1915), 8th printing; Adyar: Theosophical Publishing House, 1973

Jinarajadasa, C., *The History of Reincarnation*, Adyar: Theosophical Publishing House, 1919

Johnston, Charles, *Karma, Works and Wisdom*, New York: Theosophical Society, 1900

[1]Johnston, Charles, *The Memory of Past Births*, New York: Theosophical Society, 1904

[4]Jong, Marianne de, 'Agoraphobia: Trauma of a lost soul' (1983), *Journal of Regression Therapy*, Volume VI. No. I, December 1992

[4]Kardec, Allan, *The Spirit's Book*, 1857, London: Psychic Press, 1975

[4]Kear, Lynn, *We're Here: An investigation into gay reincarnation*, Atlanta: Brookhave, 1999

Keyes, Charles F. & Valentine Daniel, eds., *Karma: An anthropological inquiry*, Berkeley: University of California Press, 1983

[2]Klausner, Margot, *Reincarnation*, Ramat-Gan: Massada, 1975

[4]Klein, Edward, *Soul Search: The healing possibilities of past lives* (1995), 2nd printing, Virginia Beach: A.R.E. Press, 1996

Kline, Milton, *A Scientific Report on 'The Search for Bridey Murphy'*, New York: Julian Press, 1956

Knight, Marcus, *Spiritualism, Reincarnation and Immortality*, London: Duckworth, 1950

[2]Kolisko, Eugen, *Reincarnation and Other Essays* (1940), Bournemouth: Kolisko Archive, 1978

Krutch, Joseph, *More Lives Than One*, New York: Morrow, 1962

[4]Lane, Barbara, *Echoes from the Battlefield: First-person accounts of Civil War past lives*, Virginia Beach: A.R.E. Press, 1996

Lane, Barbara, *Echoes from Medieval Halls*, Virginia Beach: A.R.E. Press, 1997

[3]Langley, Noel, *Edgar Cayce on Reincarnation*, New York: Warner Books, 1967

Lauritsen, P., *Reincarnation and Freedom*, Gylling: N.U. Yoga Ashram, 1967

Leadbeater, Charles W., *Reincarnation*, Harrogate: Theosophical Publishing Committee, 1930

Leadbeater, Charles W., *The Band of Servers: A record of past lives and the karma thereof*, Adyar: Theosophical Pub. House, 1941

Leadbeater, Charles W., *The Soul's Growth Through Reincarnation*, Vols. 1,2, 3,4, Adyar: Theosophical Publishing House, 1941–50

[3]Leek, Sybil, *Reincarnation: The second chance* (1974), New York: Bantam Books, 1975

[3]Lenz, Frederick, *Lifetimes: True accounts of reincarnation* (1979), New York: Ballantine, 1986

Leonardi, D., *The Reincarnation of John Wilkes Booth*, Olde Greenwich, Connecticut: Devin-Adair, 1975

Lewis, H.D., *The Self and Immortality*, New York: Seabury Press, 1973

[1]Lewis, H. Spencer, *Mansions of the Soul: The cosmic conception* (1930), San Jose: Rosicrucian Press, 1933

Livingstone, Marjorie, *The New Nuctemeron*, London: Rider, 1930

[2]London, Jack, *The Star Rover* (1915), Valley of the Sun, 1987

Long, Herbert, *A Study of the Doctrine of Metempsychosis in Greece. From Pythagoras to Plato*, New Jersey: Princetown University Press, 1948

[5]Lucas, Winafred Blake, 'Mind Mirror Research on the Retrieval of Past Lives', *Journal of Regression Therapy*, No 1, Vol. IV

[5]Lucas, Winafred Blake, *Regression Therapy: A handbook for professionals*; Volume I: *Past-life Therapy*, Crest Park: Deep Forest Press, 1993a

[5]Lucas, Winafred Blake, *Regression Therapy: A handbook for professionals*; Volume II: *Special Instances of Altered State Work*, Crest Park: Deep Forest Press, 1993b

Luntz, Charles, *The Challenge of Reincarnation*, St Louis: Luntz Publications, 1957

Lutoslawski, Wincenty, *Pre-existence and Reincarnation*, London: Allen & Unwin, 1928

Luxton, L.K., *Astrology, Key to Self-understanding: A guide to karma, reincarnation and spiritual astrology*, St Paul: Llewellyn, 1978

Lynn, Denise, *Past Lives, Present Dreams*

[3]MacGregor, Geddes, *Reincarnation in Christianity*, Wheaton: Quest Book, 1978

MacGregor, Geddes, *Reincarnation as a Christian Hope*, London: Macmillan, 1982

[3]MacGregor, Geddes, *The Christening of Karma. The secret of evolution*, Wheaton: Theosophical Publishing House, 1984

[3]Mackenzie, Vicki, *Reborn in the West*, London: Thorsons, 1995;

MacReady, Robert, *The Reincarnation of Robert MacReady*, New York: Zebra, 1980

MacTaggart, John, *Human Immortality and Pre-Existence*, New York: Kraus, 1970

Manik, Chand Jain, *Karmic Control Planets*, Astrological Publications

[1]Mann, A. Tadd, *The Divine Plot: Astrology, cosmology and history*, London: Unwin Hyman, 1988

[1]Mann, A. Tadd. *The Elements of Reincarnation*, Shaftesbury: Element Books, 1995

[2]Marcotte, Armand & Ann Druffel, *Past Lives, Future Growth*, San Diego: ACS, 1984

[5]Martin, A.R., *Researches in Reincarnation and Beyond*, Pennsylvania: Sharon, 1942

[3]Martin, Eva, *The Ring of Return: An anthology of references to reincarnation and spiritual evolution: From prose of all ages* (1927), Albuquerque: Sun, 1981

[3]McClain, Florence, *A Practical Guide to Past Life Regression*, St Paul: Llewellyn, 1986a

[4]McClain, Florence, *The Truth About Past Life Regression* (1986b), 3rd printing; St Paul: Llewellyn, 1989

McDermit, Marilynn, *Reincarnation: A Biblical Doctrine*

McGill, Desmond & Irvin Mordes, *The Many Lives of Alan Lee*, Merrimuck National Guild of Hypnotists, 1988

Meyer, Louis, *Reincarnation*, Unity Village, Missouri: Unity School of Christianity, 1937

Mirza, N.K., *Reincarnation in Islam*, Adyar: Theosophical Publishing House, 1927

[4]Modi, Shakuntala, *Remarkable Healings: A psychiatrist discovers unsuspected roots of mental and physical illness*, Hampton Road, 1997

[2]Montaño, Mary, *Loving Mozart: A past life memory of the composer's final years*, Albuquerque: Cantus Verus Books, 1995

[3]Montgomery, Ruth, *Here and Hereafter*, New York: Coward McCann, 1971

[2]Montgomery, Ruth, *Companions Along the Way* (1974), New York: Fawcett, 1976

[5]Moody Jr, Raymond, *Life after Life*, New York: Bantam/Mockingbird, 1975

Moore, George, *Metempsychosis*, Cambridge, Mass.: Harvard University Press, 1914

[3]Moore, Marcia, *Hypersentience*, New York: Crown, 1976

Moore, Marcia & Mark Douglas, *Karmic Astrology*, York Harbor: Arcane, n.d.

[3]Moore, Marcia & Mark Douglas, *Reincarnation: Key to immortality*, York Harbor: Arcane, 1968

[3]Morrell, Ed, *The Twenty-Fifth Man* (1915), New York: Vantage, 1955

[4]Moss, Peter & Joe Keeton, *Encounters with the Past: How man can experience and relive history*, London: Sidgwick & Jackson, 1979

[3]Motoyama, Hiroshi, *Karma and Reincarnation: The key to spiritual evolution & enlightenment*, London: Piatkus, 1992

[5]Muller, Karl, *Reincarnation, Based on Facts*, London: Psychic Press, 1970

[2]Mullin, Glenn, *Death and Dying, the Tibetan Tradition*, London: Arkana, 1986

[5]Netherton, Morris & Nancy Shiffrin, *Past Lives Therapy*, New York: Morrow, 1978

[4]Newton, Michael, *Journey of Souls. Case studies of life between lives* (1996), 5th ed, St Paul: Llewellyn,1998

Norman & Spaegel, *Principles and Practice of Past-life Therapy*

Nyantiloka, Mahathera, *Karma and Rebirth*, Kandy: Buddhist Publishing Society, 1959

[1]O'Connor, Dagmar, *The First Pharaoh: The story of Tehuti and Menes, a new revelation concerning reincarnation*, London: Regency Press, 1956

O'Flaherty, Wendy, *Karma and Rebirth in Classical Indian Traditions*, Berkeley: University of California Press, 1980

[1]Olugunna, Deji, Karma. *Blueprint of redemption*, London: Regency Press, 1973

[4]Oppenheim, Garrett, *Who Were You Before You Were You? The casebook of a past-life therapist*, New York: Carlton Press, 1990

Pakenham-Walsh, W.S., *A Tudor Story: the return of Anne Boleyn*, Cambridge: James Clarke, 1982

[1]Palmer, Cecil, ed., Reincarnation: *The true chronicles of rebirth of two affinites, recorded by one of them*, London: Palmer, 1921

[1]Palmer, Martin, Kwok Man-Ho & Kerry Brown, transl. and ed., *Three Lives* (1600), London: Century, 1987

[1]Paramananda, Swami, *Reincarnation and Immortality* (1919), Boston: Vedanta Centre, 1923

Parameswara, P., Soul, *Karma and Re-birth*, Bangalore: Parameswara, 1973

Pasricha, S., *Claims of Reincarnation*, New Delhi, Harman, 1990

[1]Perkins, James, *Through Death to Rebirth*, Wheaton: Theos. Press 1961

[1]Perkins, James, *Experiencing Reincarnation*, Wheaton: Theosophical Publishing House, Quest Book, 1978

[2]Pilkington, J. Maya & the Diagram Group, *Who Were You?*, New York: Ballantine, 1988

[1]Prabhupada, Swami, *Coming Back: The science of reincarnation*, Los Angeles: Bhaktivedanta Book Trust, 1982

Praed, Rosa, *The Soul of Nyria* (1914), London: Rider, 1931

Priestley, J.B., *I Have Been Here Before*, London: Heinemann, 1938

[2]Pryse, James, *Reincarnation in the New Testament*, 1900, Mokelumne Hill Health Research, 1965

Pryse, James, *Reincarnation and Christianity*, London: Rider, 1909

[3]*Psychography: A Method of Self-Discovery*, Grand Island: Religious Research Press, 1990

[4]Quinn, Noreen, *She Can Read Your Past Lives*, Religious Research Frontier Books

Rama, S., *Freedom from the Bondage of Karma*

Reincarnation: Theosophical Manual No. 2, Adyar: Theosophical Publishing House 1970

[1]*Reincarnation: The pilgrimage of the soul*, London: Concord Grove, 1987

[1]Reyna, Ruth, *Reincarnation and Science*, New Delhi: Sterling, 1973

[4]Rieder, Marge, *Mission to Millboro* (1991), Nevada City: Blue Dolphin Publishing, 1993

Riley, B., *Veil Too Thin: Reincarnation out of control*

[2]Rinbochay, Lati & Jeffrey Hopkins, *Death, Intermediate State and Rebirth in Tibetan Buddhism* (1979), Ithaca: Snow Lion, 1985

[1]Rittelmeyer, Friedrich, *Reincarnation: Philosophy, religion, ethics*, 1931

[4]Roberts, Helen Nethery, *Karma, the Great Teacher*, Florida: Religious Reseach Press, 1985

Roberts, Helen Nethery, *Karmic Justice for Women*, Grand Island: Gnosticoeurs, 1986a

Roberts, Helen Nethery, *Karmic Roots*, Grand Island: Gnosticoeurs, 1986b

[5]Roberts, Helen Nethery, *Destiny of the Soul*, Florida: Religious Research Press, 1987

Robertson, M., *Time out of Mind: The past in your astrological birth chart and reincarnation*

Rogo, D. Scott, *The Search for Yesterday*, Englewood Cliffs: Prentice Hall 1985

[1]Rolfe, Mona, *The Spiral of Life. Cycles of Reincarnation*, Suffolk: Spearman, 1975

[3]Ryall, Edward, *Second Time Round*, Jersey: Neville Spearman, 1974

Sagan, Samuel, *Regression: Past-life therapy for here and now freedom*, Roseville, Australia: Clairvision School Foundation, 1996

Sahay, K.K.N., *Reincarnation: Verified cases of rebirth after death*, Bareilly, India: Privately printed, 1927

[4]Schlotterbeck, Karl, *Living Your Past Lives: The psychology of past life regression*, New York: Ballantine, 1987

Schubot, Errol, *Exploring Your Past Lives as a Pathway to Healing*

Schulman, Martin, *Karmic Relationships*

[1]Schulman, Martin, *Karmic Astrology*, New York: Weiser, 1976–78

[3]Scott, Cyril, *The Boy Who Saw True* (1953), London: Spearman, 1961

[3]Semkiw, Walter, *Return of the Revolutionaries*, unpublished manuscript by the author, 2001

[2]Sharma, I.C., Cayce, *Karma and Reincarnation* (1975), Wheaton: Theosophical Publishing House 1982

[3]Shelley, Violet, *Reincarnation Unnecessary, based on the Edgar Cayce Readings*, Virginia Beach: A.R.E. Press, 1979

[5]Shirley, Ralph, *The Problem of Rebirth* (1924), London: Rider, 1938

[4]Smith, Roy C., *Incarnation and Reincarnation: An astonishing guide to yesterday with the power to transform your tomorrows!*, Los Angeles: Religious Research Press, 1975

Smith, Susy, *Reincarnation for the Millions*, Los Angeles: Sherbourn, 1967

[4]Snow, Chet, *Mass Dreams of the Future: Featuring hypnotic future-life progressions by Helen Wambach*, New York: McGraw-Hill, 1989

Sparrow, L., Reincarnation: *Claiming your past, creating your future*, New York: St Martin's Press, 1995

[2]Stearn, Jess, Yoga, *Youth and Reincarnation*, London: Spearman, 1965

[4]Stearn, Jess, *The Search for the Girl with the Blue Eyes*, Garden City: Doubleday, 1968

Stearn, Jess, *The Second Life of Susan Ganier*, London: Leslie Frewin, 1969

Stearn, Jess, *Soul Mates: Perfect partners, past, present and beyond*, New York: Bantam, 1984

[2]Stearn, Jess, *Intimates Through Time: Edgar Cayce's mysteries of reincarnation* (1989), New York Signet/Penguin Books, 1993

[2]Steiger, Brad, *The Enigma of Reincarnation* (1967), New York: Ace, 1973

Steiger, Brad & Loring G. Williams, *Other Lives*, New York: Hawthorne, 1969

Stein, W.J., *The Principle of Reincarnation*, London: Anthroposophical Publishing, 1947

[4]Stevenson, Ian, *The Evidence for Survival from Claimed Memories of Former Incarnations* (1961), 4th printing, Fulham: Pegg & Sons, 1978

[5]Stevenson, Ian, *Twenty Cases Suggestive of Reincarnation* (1966), 2nd edn, Charlottesville: University Press of Virginia, 1974

Stevenson, Ian, *Xenoglossy*, Charlottesville: University Press of Virginia, 1974

[5]Stevenson, Ian, *Cases of the Reincarnation Type*. Volume I: *Ten Cases in India*. Volume II: *Ten Cases in Sri Lanka*. Volume III: *Twelve Cases in Lebanon and Turkey*. Volume IV: *Twelve Cases in Thailand and Burm.*, Charlottesville: University Press of Virginia, 1975–83

[5]Stevenson, Ian, *Children Who Remember Previous Lives. A question of reincarnation*, Charlottesville: Universitiy Press of Virginia, 1987a

Stevenson, Ian, *Unlearned Languages: New studies in xenoglossy*, Charlottesville: University Press of Virginia, 1987b

[5]Stevenson, Ian, *Reincarnation and Biology: A contribution to the etiology of birthmarks and birth defects.* 2 vols., Westport: Praeger Publishers, 1997

[2]Stewart, Ada, *Falcon: The autobiography of His Grace James the IV, King of Scots*, London: Davies, 1970

[3]Story, Francis, *The Case for Rebirth*, Ceylon, 1959

[3]Story, Francis, *Rebirth as Doctrine and Experience*, Kandy: Buddhist Publishing Society, 1975 (includes 1959)

Strauss, B., *Sex and Reincarnation*

Strauss, Richard, *Life Challenge: Astrology, karmic indicators*

[3]Sutphen, Dick, *You Were Born Again to Be Together*, New York: Pocket Books, 1976

[3]Sutphen, Dick, *Past Lives, Future Lives*, New York. Pocket Books, 1978

[3]Sutphen, Dick, *Predestined Love*, New York: Simon & Schuster, 1988

[3]Sutphen, Dick, *Finding Your Answers Within*, New York: Simon & Schuster, 1989

[2]Sutphen, Dick, *Earthly Purpose: The incredible true story of a group reincarnation*, New York: Pocket Books, 1990

[3]Sutphen, Dick & Lauren Taylor, *Past-Life Therapy in Action* (1983), Malibu: Valley of the Sun, 1987

[3]Talbot, Michael, *Your Past Lives: A Reincarnation Handbook*, New York: Harmony Books, 1987

Tatz, Mark & Jody Kent, *Rebirth: The Tibetan game of liberation*, New York: Anchor 1977

*TenDam, Hans, *Deep Healing: A practical outline of past-life therapy*, Amsterdam:

Tasso Publishing, 1996

[2]Thornton, Penny, *The Forces of Destiny*, London: Weidenfeld & Nicolson, 1990

[1]Tingley, Katherine, *Reincarnation* (1907), Albuquerque: Sun, 1981

[2]Toyne, Clarice, *Heirs to Eternity: A study of reincarnation with illustrations*, London: Neville Spearman, 1976

[4]Underwood, Peter & Leonard Wilder, *Lives to Remember: A casebook on reincarnation*, London: Robert Hale, 1975

[1]Van Auken, John, *Born Again and Again: How reincarnation occurs, why and what it means to you!*, Virginia Beach: Inner Vision, 1984a

[2]Van Auken, John, *Past Lives and Present Relationships* (1984b), Virginia Beach: Inner Vision, 1987

[1]Van Pelt, Gertrud, *Karma: The law of consequences*, Pasadena: Theosophical University Press, 1977

Van Pelt, G.W., *Doctrine of Karma: Chance or Justice*

[3]Van Waveren, Erlo, *Pilgrimage to the Rebirth*, New York: Weiser, 1978

Wachsmuth, Gunther, *Reincarnation as a Phenomenon of Metamorphosis* (1933), New York: Antroposophic Press, 1937

[3]Walker, Benjamin, *Masks of the Soul: The facts behind reincarnation*, Wellingborough: Aquarian, 1981

Walker, D.P., *The Decline of Hell*, London: Routledge & Kegan Paul, 1964

[3]Walker, E.D., *Reincarnation: A study of forgotten truth*, 1888, New York: University Books, 1965

Walli, Koshelya, *Theory of Karman in Indian Thought*, Varanasi Bharata: Manisha, 1977

[5]Wambach, Helen, *Reliving Past Lives: The evidence under hypnosis*, London: Hutchinson, 1978

[5]Wambach, Helen, *Life before Life*, New York: Bantam Book 1979

[4]Wambach, Helen, 'Past-life Therapy: the experiences of 26 therapists' in *Journal of Regression Therapy*, Volume I, No. 2, Autumn 1986

[2]Weatherhead, Leslie, *The Case for Reincarnation* (1958), Tadworth: Peto, 1971

[3]Webb, Richard, *These Came Back*, Grand Island, Florida: Religious Research, 1974

Weisman, A., *We Immortals: The Dick Sutphen past-life hypnotic regression seminars*, New York: Pocket Books, 1979

[3]Weiss, Brian, *Many Lives, Many Masters*, New York: Simon & Schuster, 1988

[4]Weiss, Brian L., *Through Time into Healing* (1992), New York: Fireside, 1993

[4]Whitton, Joel & Joe Fisher, *Life between Life: Scientific explorations into the void*

separating one incarnation from the next, Garden City: Doubleday, 1986

[4]Williston, Glenn & Judith Johnstone, *Soul Search: Spiritual growth through a knowledge of past lifetimes*, Wellingborough: Turnstone, 1983

[2]Wilson, Ernest, *Have We Lived Before?* (1936), 8th edn; Lee's Summit Unity School of Christianity, 1953

[3]Wilson, Ian, *Mind out of Time? Reincarnation claims investigated*, London: Gollancz, 1981

Wilson, Ian, *All in the Mind*, Garden City, NY: Doubleday, 1981; *Reincarnation?*, Penguin, 1982

[2]Wilson, Martin, *Rebirth and the Western Buddhist* (1984), 2nd ed; London: Wisdom Publications, 1987

Wood, Frederic, *Ancient Egypt Speaks*, London: Rider, 1937

Wood, Frederic, *After Thirty Centuries*, London: Rider, 1953

Wood, Frederic, *This Egyptian Miracle*, London: Watkins/Rider, 1955

[4]Woodward, Mary Ann, *Edgar Cayce's Story of Karma*, New York: Berkeley Publishing, 1972

[2]Woodward, Mary Ann, *Scars of the Soul: Holistic healing in the Edgar Cayce readings*, Columbus, Ohio: Brindabella, 1985

[5]Woolger, Roger J., *Other Lives, Other Selves: A Jungian psychotherapist discovers past lives*, New York: Doubleday, 1987

[1]Wright, Leoline, *Reincarnation: A love chord in modern thought*, California: Theosophical University Press, 1977

[1]Yott, D. H., *Astrology and Reincarnation: I. Retrograde Planets and Reincarnation; II, Intercepted Signs; III. Triangulation of Saturn, Jupiter, Mercury* (1977), York Beach: Weiser, 1989

Young, Robert, Loy Young & Lucia Cappacione, *Reincarnation Handbook: Techniques of past life regression*, Los Angeles: Reincarnation Research and Education Foundation, 1980)

WORKS IN DUTCH

[4]Beumers, Godfried & Pieter Wierenga, *Je hebt het allemaal in je: Verslag van een helende ontdekkingsreis onder hypnose*, Deventer: Ankh-Hermes, 1992

[4]Bontenbal, Rob, *Dat je verleden je zo in de weg kan zitten: Een brochure over reïncarnatietherapie* (1985), Amsterdam: SRN, 1993

[4]Brouwer, Els, *Mozaïek van vorige levens*, Deventer: Ankh-Hermes, 1978

[4]Cladder, Hans, *Drie jaar ervaringen met reïncarnatietherapie* (1983), Tijdschrift voor Psychotherapie, 1984

[4]Ginkel, H.J. van, *Leeft men meer dan éénmaal op aard? Een bijdrage tot toelichting van het reïncarnatieprobleem*, Amsterdam: Theos. Uitg. Mij., 1917

[2]Holthe tot Echten, R.O. van, *Reïncarnatie: Historische, ethische, wijsgerige en wetenschappelijke beschouwing*, Bussum: Van Dishoeck, 1921

[4]Kahnemann, Bert, *Ik leef mijn vorige leven*, Naarden: Strengholt, 1997

[4]Kamphoff, Matthijs, *Oude levens, nieuwe koersen: Reïncarnatie en de samenhang tussen opeenvolgende lvens.*, Amsterdam: Bres, 2000

[4]Kleyn, Jan A., *Je Gids naar een vorig leven: omdat een mens niet één, maar vele levens heeft*, Naarden: Strengholt, 1998

[4]Klink, Joanne, *Vroeger toen ik groot was: vèrgaande herinneringen van kleine kinderen*, Baarn: Ten Have, 1990

[3]Langedijk, Pieter, *Reïncarnatie, psychotherapie en opvoeding*, Deventer: Ankh-Hermes, 1980

[3]Langedijk, Pieter & Agnes van Enkhuizen, *Het oertrauma, of de schok van de incarnatie op aarde*, Deventer: Ankh-Hermes, 1987a

[3]Langedijk, Pieter & Agnes van Enkhuizen, *Leerproblemen en vorige levens*, Deventer: Ankh-Hermes, 1987a

[1]Licekens, Paul, *Reïncarnatie: Sleutel tot de zin van het leven*, Deventer: Ankh-Hermes, 1982

[5]Maesen, Ronald van der, *Cliënten over reïncarnatietherapie*, Amstelveen: NVRT/SVR, 1994

[5]Maesen, Ronald van der, *Reïncarnatietherapie voor stemmenhoorders*, Amstelveer: NVRT, 1999

[3]Penkala, Maria, *Reïncarnatie en preëxistentie* (1972), Deventer: Ankh-Hermes, 1973

*TenDan, Hans, *Reïncdarnatie, Denkbeelden en Ervaringsfeiten, Rondetafelgesprick*, Amsterdam: Bres 92 and 93, 1982

Van der Maesen, Ronald & Bontenbal, Rob, *Handboek Reïncarnatietherapie* Leusden: Tijdstroom, 2002

[4]Vidal de St Germain, Henri, *Spectrum van regressie en reïncarnatie*, Deventer: Ankh-Hermes, 1996

[4]Zuidinga, Petra, *De Noordzee-vrouw en andere herinneringen*, Amsterdam: Tasso Uitgeverij, 1997

WORKS IN GERMAN

[1]Archiati, P., *Erneuertes Christentum und Wiederverkörperung*, Stuttgart: Freies Geistesleben, 1996

Baer, Emil, *Das Geheimnis des Wiedererkennens*, Zürich, 1928

[3]Bock, Emil, *Wiederholte Erdenleben. Die Wiederverkörperungsidee in der deutschen Geistesgeschichte*, Stuttgart: Verlag der Christengemeinschaft, 1932

[2]Delacour, J.B., *Vom ewigen Leben*, Dusseldorf: Egon Verlag, 1974

Demetriades, Irmgard, *Reinkarnationsgespräche*, Gießen, 1983

[4]Dethlefsen, Thorwald, *Das Erlebnis der Wiedergeburt. Heilung durch Reinkarnation*, München: Bertelsmann, 1976

Ebertin, Baldur R., *Reinkarnation und neues Bewusstsein* (1986) 2ten Auflage; Freiburg i. Br.: Bauer 1989

Eckhart, K.A., *Irdische Unsterblichkeit. Germanischer Glaube an die Wiederverkrperung in der Sippe*, Weimar: Böhlau, 1937

Falke, R., *Gibt es eine Seelenwanderung?*, Strien, 1904

Hutten, Kurt, *Seelenwanderung*, Stuttgart: Kreuz, 1962

[2]Koch, Werner, *Reinkarnation: Heilung aus der Vergangenheit*, Aitrang: Windpferd, 1992

Neidhart, Georg, *Werden wir wiedergeboren?*, München, 1959

[5]Passian, Rudolf, *Wiedergeburt. Ein Leben oder viele?*, München: Knaur, 1985

[3]Rosenberg, A., *Die Seelenreise: Wiedergeburt, Seelenwanderung oder Aufstieg durch die Sphären*, Olten, der Schweiz: Otto Walter, 1952

Schmidt, K.O., *Wir leben nicht nur einmal*, Dettenbach: Buddingen, 1956

[4]Sigdell, Jan Erik, *Emotionale Befreiung durch Rückführung: Ein Handbuch für Reinkarnationstherapeuten und ihre Klienten*, Basel: Selbstverlag, 1993

Sigdell, Jan Erik, *Reinkarnation, Christentum und das kirchliche Dogma*, Wien: Ibera Verlag, 2001

[2]Steiner, Rudolf, *GA 009: Theosophie* (1904), pp. 61–90; Alle GA: Dornach: Rudolf Steiner Nachlassverwaltung

[2]Steiner, Rudolf, *GA 016: Ein Weg zur Selbsterkenntnis des Menschen* (1912: pp.78–85)

[1]Steiner, Rudolf, *GA 017: Die Schwelle der geistigen Welt*, (1913: pp.30–33)

[3]Steiner, Rudolf, *GA 026: Anthroposophische Leitsätze*, 1924–5: pp.34–40, 72–5, 177–96

[3]Steiner, Rudolf, *GA 034: Luzifer-Gnosis*, 1903-1908: pp.67–91, 361–363,

371–377, 381–383, 404–406)

²Steiner, Rudolf, *GA 053: Grundbegriffe der Theosophie*, 1904: pp.42–58

²Steiner, Rudolf, *GA 054: Welträtsel und Antroposophie*, 1906: pp.279, 306

¹Steiner, Rudolf, *GA 093a: Grundelemente des Esoterik*, 1905: Vorträge 8, 16, 21, 22, 29

²Steiner, Rudolf, *GA 095: Vor dem Tore der Theosophie*, 1906: Vorträge 6, 7, 8

²Steiner, Rudolf, *GA 097: Das christliche Mysterium*, Vortrag 14.6.1906

²Steiner, Rudolf, *GA 099: Die Theosophie des Rosenkreuzers*, 1907: Vorträge 6, 7

²Steiner, Rudolf, *GA 100: Menschheitsentwicklung und Christus-Erkenntnis*, 1907: Vorträge 7, 8 von '*Theosophie und Rosenkreuzertum*'

²Steiner, Rudolf, *GA 109/111: Das Prinzip der spirituellen Ökonomie in Zusammenhang mit Wiederverkörperungsfragen*, Vortrag 21.1.1909, Vortrag 7.3.1909, Vortrag 12.6.1909

²Steiner, Rudolf, *GA 114: Das Lukas-Evangelium*, 1910: Vortrag 10

²Steiner, Rudolf, *GA 120: Die Offenbarungen des Karma* (1910)

²Steiner, Rudolf, *GA 130: Das esoterische Christentum und die geistige Führung der Menschheit*, Vortrag 8.2.1912

¹Steiner, Rudolf, *GA 131: Wiederverkrperung und Karma* (1912)

¹Steiner, Rudolf, *GA 133: Der irdische und der kosmische Mensch* (1912): Vortrag 5

¹Steiner, Rudolf, *GA 134: Die Welt der Sinne und die Welt des Geistes* (1911): Vortrag I

¹Steiner, Rudolf, *GA 153: Inneres Wesen des Menschen und Leben zwischen Tot und Neue Geburt* (1914): Vortrag I)

¹Steiner, Rudolf, *GA 157: Menschenschicksale und Volkerschicksale* (1915): Vortrag 9

¹Steiner, Rudolf, *GA 181: Erdensterben und Weltenleben* (1918): Vorträge 5, 6

³Steiner, Rudolf, *GA 235: Esoterische Betrachtungen karmischer Zusammenhänge: Band I* (1924)

²Steiner, Rudolf, *GA 236: Esoterische Betrachtungen karmischer Zusammenhänge: Band II* (Vorträge 8 t/m 20)

²Steiner, Rudolf, *GA 237: Esoterische Betrachtungen karmischer Zusammenhänge: Band III* (Vortrag 2)

²Steiner, Rudolf, *GA 238: Esoterische Betrachtungen karmischer Zusammenhänge: Band IV* (Vorträge 2, 7, 8)

²Steiner, Rudolf, *GA 239: Esoterische Betrachtungen karmischer Zusammenhänge: Band V* (Vorträge 8, 16)

¹Steiner, Rudolf, *GA 240: Esoterische Betrachtungen karmischer Zusammenhänge: Band VI* (Vorträge 7, 8)

[1]Steiner, Rudolf, *Reinkarnation und Karma. Gesammelte Aufsätze* 1903–1923, Dornach: Rudolf Steiner Nachlassverwaltung, 1961

[1]Trautmann, Werner, *Naturwissenschäftler bestätigen Re-Inkarnation*. Olten: Walter, 1983

Vallières, Ingrid, *Praxis der Reinkarnationstherapie: Konsequenzen und Reichweite*, 5ten Auflage; Stuttgart: Stephanie Naglschmid, 1997

[3]Weden, W. & W. Spindler, *Ägyptische Einweihung: Erinnerung an ein Leben als ägyptischer Priester*, Frankfurt: Fischer 1978

WORKS IN FRENCH

Beaugitte, G & Pierre Neuville, *Marie-Lise*, 1958

Bertholet, Ed., *Petite iconographie de la réincarnation*, Paris: Delachaux et Nestlé

[5]Bertholet, Ed., *La Réincarnation*, Paris: Aryana, 1949

Celmar, M.L., *L'âme et ses réincarnations*, Paris, 1925

[3]David-Neel, Alexandra, *Immortalité et réincarnation. Doctrines et pratiques dans Chine, Tibet et Indie*, Paris: Plon, 1961

Delanne, Gabriel, *Documents pour servir à l'étude de la réincarnation*, Paris: Editions de la BPS, 1924

[4]des Georges, A., *La Réincarnation des Ames selon les Traditions Orientales et Occidentales*, Paris: Michel, 1966

Desjardins, Denise, *De naissance en naissance: Témoignage sur une vie anterieure*, Paris: La Table Ronde, 1977

Desjardins, Denise, *La mémoire des vies anterieures*, Paris: La Table Ronde, 1980

Drouot, P., *Nous sommes tous immortels*, Monaco: Le Rocher, 1987

[3]Dubuc, Pierre, *Vies passées heureuses: Outils thérapeutiques au present*, Saint-Zénon, Quebec: Louise Courteau, 1994

[3]Dubuc, Pierre, *Le cheminement de l'esprit vers la guérison de l'âme et du corps*, Quebec: Liberté Nouvelle, 1998

Koechlin de Bizemont, Dorothée, *L'astrologie karmique*, Paris: Laffont, 1983

Pascal, Theophile, *La Réincarnation* (1895). Paris, 1950; *Reincarnation: A Study in Human Evolution*, Theosophical Publishing Society, 1950

Pascal, Theophile, *Essai sur l'évolution humaine*, Paris, 1901

Pezzani, André, *La pluralité des existences de l'âme*, Paris: Didier, 1865

[3]Pisani, Isola, *Mourir n'est pas mourir*, Paris: Laffont, 1978

Pisani, Isola, *Preuve de survie. Croire ou savoir*, Paris: Laffont, 1980

[5]Rochas, Albert de, *Les vies successives* (1911), Paris: Chacornac, 1924

Saint-Savin, Charles, *La réincarnation universelle*, Paris: Dervy, 1947

Siémons, Jean-Louis, *Revivre nos vies antérieures: Temoignages et preuves de la réincarnation*, Paris: Albin Michel, 1984

Victor, Jean Louis, *Réincarnation et peintres mediums*, Edition du Nouveau Monde, 1980

Zahan, D., ed., *Reincarnation et vie mystique en Afrique Noire*, Paris: Presses Universitaires de France, 1965

WORKS IN ITALIAN, SPANISH OR PORTUGUESE

[3]Andrade, Hernani Guimarçes, *Um caso que sugere reencarnacão: Simone × Angelina*, São Paulo: I.B.P.P., 1979

[4]Andrade, Hernani Guimarçes, *Morte, Renascimento, Evoluição: Uma biologia transcendental*, São Paulo: Pensamento, 1983

Andrade, Hernani Guimarçes, *Reencarnação no Brasil: Oito casos que sugeram renascimento*, Matço: O Clarim, 1988

Arauco, S., *Tres Pontos Basicos sobre Reencarnação*, Lisboa: Fraternidade, 1982

Bezerra de Menezes, Adolpho, *A Loucura sob Novo Prisma*, Rio de Janeiro 1946

Brazzini, Pasquale, *Dopo la Morte si Rinasce?*, Milano, 1952

Calderine, Innocenzo, *La Reincarnazione*, Milano: Inchiesta Internazionale, 1913

Costa, Giuseppe, *Di la della Vita*, Turino: Lattes 1923

Domingo Soler, Amelia, *Hechos que Pruebam*, Ed. Argentina 18 de Abril

[3]Ferreira, Inácio, *A psiquiatria em face da reencarnação* (1955), São Paulo: FEESP, 1988

Lacerda, Nair, *A reencarnação atraves dos séculos*, São Paulo: Pensamento, 1978

Martins, Cesso, *Espiritismo e vidas successivas*, Rio de Janeiro: ELO, 1976

[4]Martins, Edison Flávio, *Abrindo as Janelas do Tempo: Pela Terapia de Regressão*, Campinas: Livro Pleno, 2001

Miranda, Hermínio, *Reencarnação e immortalidade*, Rio de Janeiro: FEB, 1975

Miranda, Hermínio, *A reencarnação na bíblia*, São Paulo: Pensamento, 1981

[3]Miranda, Hermínio, *Terapia de vida passada: uma abordagem profunda do inconsciente*, São Paulo: Summus, 1990

[2]Peres, Júlia P. Moraes Prieto, *Terapia Regressiva a Vivências Passadas (TRVP)*, São Paulo, 1994

Santesson, H.S., *Tudo sobre a reencarnação*, Rio de Janeiro: Record, 1969

QUOTED WORKS ON RELATED SUBJECTS:

Addison, James, *La vie après la mort dans les croyances de l'humanité*, Paris: Payot, 1936

Blavatsky, Helena, *Isis Unveiled: A master-key to the mysteries of ancient and modern science and theology*. 2 vols. (1877), Pasadena: Theosophical University Press, 1963

Blavatsky, Helena, *The Secret Doctrine: The synthesis of science, religion and philosophy*. 2 vols. (1888), Pasadena: Theosophical University Press, 1963

Boswell, Harriet, *Master Guide to Psychism*. 2 vols. West Nyack: Parker, 1969

Chapple, Christopher, *Karma and Creativity*, New York: State University of New York, 1986

Currie, Ian, *You Cannot Die*, New York: Methuen, 1978

Dean, Geoffrey and Arthur Mather, *Recent Advances in Natal Astrology: A critical review 1900–1976*, Cowes: Recent Advances, 1977

Dethlefsen, Thorwald, *Schicksal als Chance: Esoterische Psychologie, das Urwissen zur Volkommenheit des Menschen*, München: Bertelsmann, 1979

Edelstien, Gerald, Trauma, *Trance and Transformation: A clinical guide To hypnotherapy*, New York: Brunner/Mazel, 1981

Encyclopaedia Britannica, 'Second Council of Constantinople', Volume 6: 636, 1964

Fechner, Gustav, *Van het leven na de dood*, Den Haag: Servire, nd

Fielding, Hall, *The Soul of a People*, London: MacMillan, 1898

Fox, Oliver, *Astral Projection*, New York: University Books, 1962

Garland, Joanne, 'Walk-Ins: The original story', Paper presented at the International Conference on Paranormal Research, Colorado State University, Fort Colllins, 1988

Hampe, Johann, *Sterben ist doch ganz anders. Erfahrungen mit dem eigenen Tod*, Stuttgart: Kreuz-Verlag, 1975

Hanssen, P.J., *Hypnose in de praktijk*, Deventer: Ankh-Hermes, 1977

Hearn, Lafcadio, *Gleanings in Buddha Fields*, Tokyo: Tuttle, 1972

Hubbard, Ron, *Dianetics. De moderne wetenschap van mentale gezondheid* (1950), Kopenhagen: New Era, 1982

Keyes, Charles and Valentine Daniel, eds., *Karma: An anthropological inquiry*, Berkeley: University of California Press, 1983

Leadbeater, Charles, *Helderziendheid*, Amsterdam: Theosophische Uitgeversmij, 1904

Leadbeater, Charles, *Het Innerlijk Leven: Theosophische toespraken te Adyar*, Eerste en tweede serie, Weltevreden: Minerva, 1923

Le Cron, Leslie, *Hypnose*, Antwerpen: Ned. Boekhandel, 1976

Lefebvre, Francis, *Experiences Initiatiques*, vol. 3, Paris: 1959

Mehta, Rohit, *The Journey with Death*, Delhi: Motilal Banarsidass, 1977

Millard, Joseph, *Edgar Cayce. Profeet in trance*, Deventer: Ankh-Hermes, 1972

Monroe, Robert, *Experimenten buiten het lichaam*, Deventer: Ankh-Hermes, 1977

Nes, C. van, *Over dood en leven*, Den Haag: Van Stockum, 1958

Osborn, Arthur, *The Meaning of Personal Existence, in the Light of Paranormal Phenomena, Reincarnation and Mystical Experience* (1966), Wheaton: Theosophical Publishing House, 1967

Poortman, J.J., *Vehicles of Consciousness*, 4 vols., Adyar: Theosophical Publishing House, 1978

Powell, Arthur, *The Astral Body and other related astral phenomena* (m.n. hoofdstuk 24: *Rebirth*), London: Theosophical Publishing House, 1926

Powell, Arthur, *The Mental Body* (1927), London: Theosophical Publishing House, 1975

Powell, Arthur, *The Causal Body and the Ego* (1928), London: Theosophical Publishing House, 1978

Rato Khyongla Nawang Losang, *My Life and Lives: The story of a Tibetan incarnation*, New York: Dutton, 1977

Reichenbach, Karl von, *Researches on magnetism, electricity, heat, light, crystallization and chemical attractions in their relations to the vital force* (1849), Seacaucus: University Books, 1974

Roberts, Jane, *Seth spreekt: De eeuwige waarde van de ziel*, Deventer: Ankh-Hermes, 1979

Sagan, Carl, *The Dragons of Eden* (1977)

Schreiber, Flora, Sybil: *Het ware verhaal van een vrouw met 16 persoonlijkheden* (1973), Haarlem: Gottmer, 1974

Sinnett, A.P., *Esoteric Buddhism* (1883), Minneapolis: Wizards Bookshelf, 1973

Smith, Huston, *The Religions of Man*, New York: Harper & Row, 1958

Spiegel, Herbert and David, *Trance and Treatment*, New York: Basic Books, 1978

Stephenson, Gunther, *Leben und Tod in den Religionen: Symbol und Wirklichkeit*,

Darmstad: Wissenschaftliche Buchgesellschaft, 1980

Sugrue, Thomas, *There is a River*, New York: Henty Holt, 1942

Tepperwein, Kurt, *Handboek van de hypnose* (1977), Amsterdam: Meulenhoff, 1980

Ten-Haeff, W.H.C., *Ontmoetingen met paragnosten*, Utrecht: bijleveld, n.d.

Verney, Thomas with John Kelly, *The Secret Life of the Unborn Child* (1981), New York: Dell, 1986

Watkins, J. and H., *The Theory and Practice of Ego-State Therapy*.
In: Caryson, H. (ed.), *Short-term Approaches to Psychotherapy*, New York: National Institute for the Psychotherapies and Humans Sciences, 1979

Wheeler, Dave, *Journey to the Other Side* (1977)

Wickland, Carl A., *Thirty Years Among the Dead* (1924), North Hollywood, CA: Newcastle, 1974

GENERAL INDEX

abortion, 169–70, 221, 224–5
addiction, 140, 276, 285, 350, 357
Africa, 19, 20-1, 33, 325, 330, 341;
    identification, 164, 190, 339
age regression, 122, 123, 130, 134, 315
ahimsa, 28
akasha records, 68, 71, 171, 368
Alaska, 19, 20, 95, 101, 106, 205
alcohol, 144
alcoholics, 46–7, 276, 348
Alcyone, 49, 52
aliens, 252
alignment, 286
American Indians, 23
anatta doctrine, 10, 12, 22, 26, 43, 342,
    343, 368
angels, 24, 36, 37, 53, 54, 302, 307, 327
animal magnetism *see* magnetism
animals
    dreams, 257
    hypnosis of, 259–60
    identification with, 257–8, 263–6, 270,
      334
    reincarnation as, 11, 21, 22, 25, 27, 28,
      29, 31, 33, 35, 106, 265
    simultaneous incarnation with, 321
    as stage in evolution, 36, 44, 53, 80, 85,
      256–7, 260, 327
anthroposophy, 3, 42, 43, 52–60, 65, 110,
    261
    evolution of humankind, 53–4
    intermissions and change of gender,

    54–5, 330, 331
    and karma, 55–66
    and past-life recall 58–9, 340
Aquarian Age, 61, 66
archetypes, 170–1
art of living, 360–7, 368
artha, 25, 287, 288, 329
assimilation, delayed, 291–2
Association for Past-Life Research and
    Therapy (APRT), 161, 347
Association for Research and
    Enlightenment, 81
astral body, 45–6, 156, 227
astrology, 152, 159, 212–13, 330–1
Atlantis, 18, 83, 152, 156, 248, 249,
    252–3, 262, 269, 329
atma, 45, 47
atman, 24, 26
attachments *see* obsessions
Australian aboriginals, 23
Austria, 1
autism, 218, 240, 243, 314, 347, 352
automatic writing, 70, 76, 88, 150, 151,
    156
awareness/self-awareness, 310, 314, 322,
    328, 368–9

Babylon, 29
Bali, 20, 22
barriers, 124, 129, 142, 369
bio-energetic work, 345
birds, 25, 35, 257

birth
  experiences before and during, 123,
    197–225
  induced 212–13
  process of, 210–11
birthmarks *see* stigmata
blocks, 124–5, 127, 129, 133–4, 138, 369
  'shut-off commands', 143, 188
Bodhisattvas, 28, 274, 288, 369–70
Bogomiles, 35
Boras, 35
Brahminism, 12, 25–6
brain waves, 68, 131–2, 146–8, 153, 341
Brazil, 2, 4, 23, 180, 186
  child past-life recall, 95, 101
  spiritist hospitals, 79, 314, 323
Britain, 2, 124
buddhi, 45, 46, 47
Buddhism, 1, 3, 22, 26–8, 38, 40, 54, 274,
    342
  see also anatta doctrine
building elementals, 48
burial vs. cremation, 246
Burma, 19, 22, 26, 78, 95, 104, 105, 106,
    108, 222–3, 275–6, 325, 332

Cabbala, 32, 34, 36–7, 331–2, 337
Canada, 2, 23, 106
caste system, 25–6
Cathars, 34, 35, 181, 334
catharsis, 171, 179, 208, 336, 356, 370
Celts, 22, 28
channelling, xv, 14, 15, 61–2, 74–5, 90–1,
    151, 156, 157–60, 354
characteristics and tendencies, retention,
    276–8, 283
Chassidism, 32
child prodigies, 3, 94, 278
children
  cultural views on, 20
  early childhood, 218–19
  incarnation into, 203
  Inner Adults, 346

intermissions, 101, 106, 300, 320–1,
    339
and karma, 105, 271, 294, 300
spontaneous recall, 14, 15, 16, 18–19,
    21, 22, 93–108, 166–7, 171–2,
    181–2, 192, 196, 218–19, 219–20,
    231–2, 326, 339–40
past-life therapy, 346, 354
responsibility for death of, 292
wandering about after death, 237–9
Christian regressions, 171
Christian Science, 89, 154
Christianity, 2, 11, 20, 41, 54, 342
Christos experiment, 138, 142, 149, 153,
    267, 370
clairvoyance, xv, 51, 70, 72, 76, 141
as explanation of apparent memory,
    68–9, 112, 113, 180, 183, 193
collective memory, 112, 113
collective unconscious, 165, 170–1, 185,
    193
compensation, 50–1, 166, 186, 243, 292,
    370
competence, 286, 288
consciousness, 311–12
'elliptic', 139, 143, 312, 317–18
Council of Constantinople (553 AD),
    33–4, 160
creationism, 11, 12
cremation vs. burial, 246
culture, return to same 332–3

death, 226–47
  child's own decision, 219
  complete awakening, 241–2, 243, 246
  experiences of, 123, 128, 144–5,
    231–42
  fear of, 247, 363
  hanging about after, 235–7, 242, 243,
    246–7, 294, 299, 300
  haunting after, 240, 242, 243, 294, 299
  incomplete dying, 280, 299, 358
  passing away, 234–5, 242, 243

process of dying, 226–31
pseudo-existence, 240–1, 243–4, 246
responsibility for child's, 292
and sleep, 19, 38
traumatic, 101–3, 124, 142, 144, 168,
170, 204, 205, 206–7, 230, 246,
247, 264, 280–1, 318, 351
twilight existence, 239, 242, 243,
244–5, 246–7, 319
wandering about after, 237–9, 242, 243,
246–7, 294, 299, 300
deception, 165, 166, 176, 177, 178, 180,
181, 183, 191
déjà-vu, 111, 112, 113, 120, 165, 167, 178,
180, 181
demonic inspiration, 165, 171
Denmark, 76, 212
depersonalisation, 308, 309
derealisation, 308
descent, 201–10, 339, 370
deseparation, 308–9
determinism, 272, 273, 335, 371
devachan, 47, 51
devas, 255–6, 371
development
    disorders, 288–9
    personal, 313
    stages 287–8
    see also self-development
dharma, 25, 287, 288, 301, 303, 329, 335,
336, 356, 371
dianetics, 123, 140, 354–5
discarnates, identity, 309–11
    'psycho-plasticity', 327–8
    on reincarnation, 74–6
disease
    karmic influence, 51, 58, 76–7, 87, 338
    obsessive spirits and, 78–9
dissociation, 121, 371–2
do-it-yourself regression, 143–5, 149, 367
dreams 23, 69, 113, 115–17, 219, 230
    animals', 257
    announcing, 105–6, 221–3

lucid, 227, 240
recurrent, 117
waking, 138, 165, 169, 177, 185
drugs
    addiction continued through lives, 276,
    372
    inducing past-life memory, 140, 152,
    372
    regression, therapy and, 144, 181, 348,
    350, 372
Druse, 18, 19, 35, 50, 108, 276–7, 329,
330, 332

education, 275, 285, 289, 296, 297, 327
Ego-state Therapy, 306, 345
Egypt, 21, 28–9, 82, 158
    past lives in, 7, 70–1, 72, 73–4, 82–3,
    117, 152, 155–6
electro-encephalogram (EEG), 131
'elliptic' consciousness, 139, 143, 312,
317–18
E-meter (emotion meter), 131, 132, 140,
167, 176, 181, 355
England, 2, 4, 6, 100, 108, 332
engrams, 354, 355, 372
Enlightenment, 38, 54, 342, 342
Epicureans, 9, 30
Eskimos, 20, 23 see also Tlingits
esotericism, 3, 6, 35–7, 42–66, 140, 340,
341, 343
etheric body, 45–6, 48, 54, 156, 227–9,
230, 245, 302, 372
evolution
    as process of development, 284–5,
    287–8, 289, 297, 373
    of souls 36, 44, 53–4, 80, 85, 249–63,
    327, 372
evolutionary therapy, 258
extraterrestrials, 158, 250–3, 262, 259

false memory syndrome, 165, 169–70
families, return to same, 105–6, 332
famous past lives, 155–6, 166

and body relationship, 8–15, 19
body sitters, 202
'cohesion', 87
confronting/denying distress, 155
creation of, 82, 88, 327
'definite descent', 209
degradation, 303–4
and dreams, 19
encounters between arriving and
    departing, 10, 30, 174
entering foetus, 80–1, 201–2, 208–9,
    221
evolution of, 44, 53–4, 80, 85, 249–63,
    269, 327
group, 257, 259
jivas, 24
joyful leaving, 230
masculine and feminine halves, 84
as memory store, 141
and personality, 85–6
personalities of, 305–24
preparing for incarnation, 80–1
presumed wisdom, 152
'recycling', 87
split in one-egg twins, 168
twin, 85, 333–4
see also metempsychosis
    pre-existence
soul cake, 260–1
soul mates, 85, 333–4
Spain, 33, 123
spirit, 310
spiritism, 4–5, 76, 90–1, 239, 323
spiritist hospitals, 79, 314, 323
spirits, 253–6, 269
    earthbound, 14, 15, 326
    see also monads
'spiritual economy' 156
spiritualism, ix, xiv–xv, 6, 11, 12–13, 16,
    140–1, 165, 173–4
    and spiritism, 4–5
spontaneous recall, 7–8, 16, 168, 172
    of animal lives, 263

children *see* children
    under extraordinary circumstances,
        119–20
    of people, 113–15
    of places, 111–13
    rarity, 340
    triggered by books, 118–19
    triggered by objects, 117–18
    triggered by pictures, 117–18
    triggered by similar situations, 119
Sri Lanka, 19, 95, 97–9, 101, 103, 104,
    105, 106, 219–20
starters, 260–1
stigmata (birthmarks), 23, 105, 183,
    205–7, 280, 295, 339, 381–2
Stoics, 30
subconscious, 158, 306
Sufism, 10, 36
'suggestion', 95, 123, 181, 187
suicide, 291
super-ESP (super-extra-sensory
    perception), 123, 165, 171–3, 177,
    193, 382
Sweden, 1, 6

tanasukh, 36
telekinesis, 132
telepathic leave-taking, 229
telepathy, 107
    brain waves, 132, 147
    as explanation of apparent memory, 68,
        112, 113, 117, 127, 171, 173, 178,
        180, 181, 182, 183, 185, 343
    'light people', 256
    psychic body, 227
temple training, 382
Thailand, 19, 95, 100, 104, 106
Theosophical Association, 56
Theosophical Society, 174
theosophy, 3, 10, 42, 43–52, 64–5, 110,
    248, 325, 332
    and de Rochas, 5–6, 123
    and higher and lower self, 44–6, 325

INDEX OF

NAMES

Frieling, Rudolf, 65

Gabriel, Michael, 197, 204, 205, 225
Gallup, George, Jr., 2
Gardner, E. L., 65
Garland, Joanne, 203
Gauguin, Paul, 39
Georgewitz-Wietzer, Demeter (Surya), 73, 103
Gershom, David, 67, 179
Gershom, Yonassan, 32, 118–19, 199
Ghanem, Suzanne, 276
Glaskin, Gerald, 121, 138, 149, 153, 195, 267, 268, 367, 370
Goethe, W. G., 38, 155
Goldberg, Bruce, 62, 125, 127, 130, 182–3, 193, 209, 256, 262, 268, 270, 290, 292–3, 304, 316–17, 321
Gore, Al, 191
Gorkyi, Maxim, 263
Graham, David, 17, 22, 122, 152, 173, 175, 177, 180, 182, 183–5, 196, 303–4, 346, 363
Grant, Joan, xi, 7–8, 71, 89, 91, 118, 128, 141, 149, 155, 175, 197, 202, 208, 209, 217, 225, 239, 244, 247, 268–9, 276, 282, 293, 304, 323–4, 356, 357
Gregor, Norman, 66
Grof, Stanislav, 140, 356
Gruber, José, 258
Grundei, Hermann, 111, 119, 203, 320–1, 377
Guirdham, Arthur, 34, 74, 89, 91, 181, 195, 334
Gupta, I. D., 108, 196

Haich, Elisabeth, 155
Hall, Manly P., 65, 365
Hampton, Charles, 41, 65
Hanson, Virginia, 64, 304
Harrison, Peter and Mary, 100, 108
Hartley, Christine, 66, 152

Harun al Rashid, 66
Head, Joseph, I, 10, 39–40, 64–5, 94, 120, 361
Hearn, Lafcadio, 108
Heindel, Max, 42, 115
Herodotus, 28, 29
Hierokles, 29
Hodgkinson, Liz, 17
Hodgson, Joan, 214, 215
Hodson, Geoffrey, 65
Holthe tot Echten, R. O. van, 6
Holzer, Hans, 17, 103, 117, 120, 121, 164, 167, 193, 333
Hopkins, Jeffrey, 27, 40
Howard, Alan, 65
Howe, Quincey, 41
Howell, Olive Stevenson, 65
Hubbard, L. Ron, 104, 123–4, 140, 149, 161, 169–70, 203, 208, 236, 240, 245–6, 262, 263, 264–5, 270, 293, 354–6, 357, 366
Hughes, Thea Stanley, 365
Humphreys, Christmas, 65
Husemann, Friedrich, 65
Hussey, Helen Nethery, 91

Iarchas, 30
Inayat Khan, Hazrat 10, 65, 174
Ingalls, Arthur, 144, 157
Iranaeus, 36
Iverson, Jeffrey, 149, 195

Jalal-ud-din-Rumi, 36
James, 146
James, William, 154
Jamieson, Bryan, 143–5, 146, 149, 153, 367
Jarmon, Robert, 358
Jesus Christ, 8, 32, 33, 37–8, 53, 54, 59, 82, 85, 88, 109
Jinarajadasa, C., 65
John the Baptist, 33
Johnston, Charles, 65